Tom Trumble has worked in journalism recruitment. He graduated with honours in history, and has also studied music and journalism. He is the author of *Unholy Pilgrims* (2011), *Rescue at 2100 Hours* (2013) and *Tomorrow We Escape* (2014), all published by Penguin Random House. He lives in Melbourne with his partner, Gabrielle, and their two children, William and Ted.

Also by Tom Trumble

Unholy Pilgrims
Rescue at 2100 Hours
Tomorrow We Escape

SURVIVAL IN SINGAPORE

The triumph and tragedy of Australia's greatest commando operation

Elizabeth Choy, Operation Jaywick and the battle for truth in Changi

TOM TRUMBLE

PENGUIN BOOKS

UK | USA | Canada | Ireland | Australia
India | New Zealand | South Africa | China

Penguin Books is part of the Penguin Random House group of companies
whose addresses can be found at global.penguinrandomhouse.com

Penguin
Random House
Australia

First published by Penguin Books, 2025

Cover design by Luke Causby/Blue Cork © Penguin Random House Australia Pty Ltd
Front cover images: photo of Elizabeth Choy from *Elizabeth Choy: More than a War
Heroine*, Landmark Books, 2023; photo of the *Krait* from Australian War Memorial,
accession number 044211; photo of Robert Heatlie Scott courtesy the Scott family;
view of Singapore from the Cathay Building from Australian War Memorial,
accession number SUK14735.
Maps by Alicia Freile, Tango Media Pty Ltd, 2025
Typeset in 11/16 pt Sabon LT Std by Midland Typesetters, Australia

Every effort has been made to trace creators and copyright holders of quoted and
photographic material included in this book. The publisher welcomes hearing
from anyone not correctly acknowledged.

Printed and bound in Australia by Griffin Press, an accredited
ISO AS/NZ 14001 Environmental Management Systems printer.

NATIONAL
LIBRARY
OF AUSTRALIA

A catalogue record for this
book is available from the
National Library of Australia

MIX
Paper | Supporting
responsible forestry
FSC® C018684

ISBN 978 0 14377 805 9

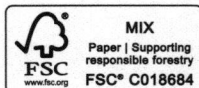

*We at Penguin Random House Australia acknowledge that Aboriginal and
Torres Strait Islander peoples are the first storytellers and Traditional Custodians of
the land on which we live and work. We honour Aboriginal and Torres Strait Islander
peoples' continuous connection to Country, waters, skies and communities. We celebrate
Aboriginal and Torres Strait Islander stories, traditions and living cultures; and we pay
our respects to Elders past and present.*

In loving memory of Angus Trumble, 1964–2022

观今宜鉴古 无古不成今
To see the present, one should learn from the past;
without the past, there can be no present.
Chinese saying

Singapore, municipal area 1942

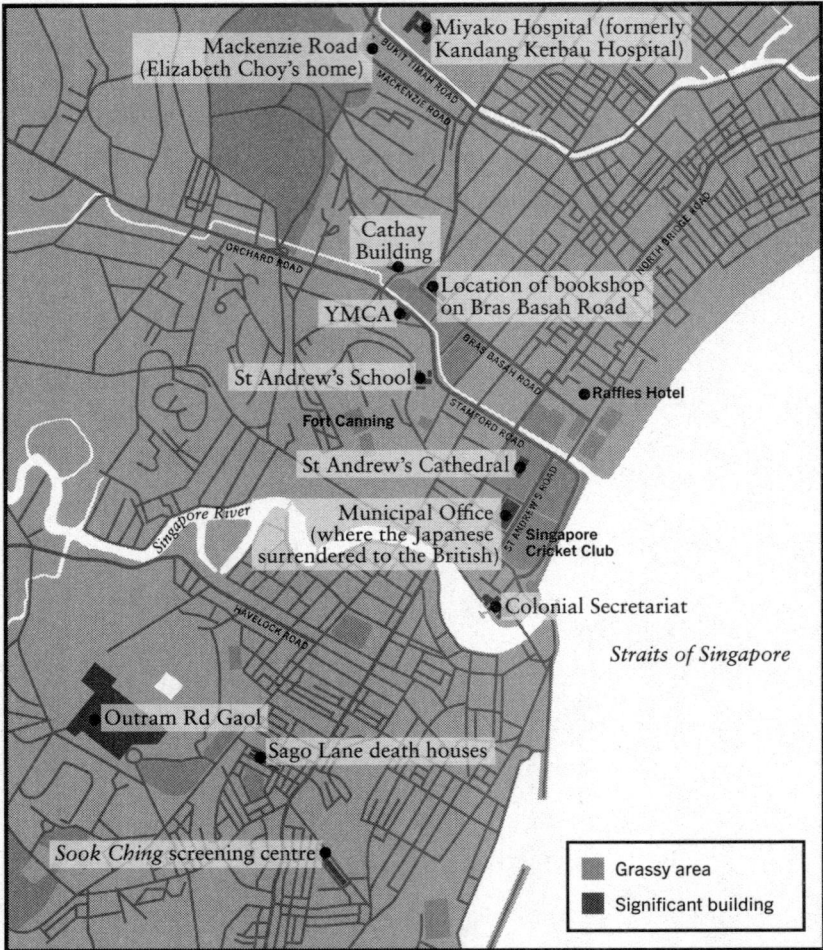

Miyako Hospital (formerly Kandang Kerbau Hospital)

Mackenzie Road (Elizabeth Choy's home)

BUKIT TIMAH ROAD

MACKENZIE ROAD

NORTH BRIDGE ROAD

ORCHARD ROAD

Cathay Building

Location of bookshop on Bras Basah Road

YMCA

BRAS BASAH ROAD

St Andrew's School

STAMFORD ROAD

Raffles Hotel

Fort Canning

Singapore River

St Andrew's Cathedral

ST ANDREW'S ROAD

Municipal Office (where the Japanese surrendered to the British)

Singapore Cricket Club

HAVELOCK ROAD

Colonial Secretariat

Straits of Singapore

Outram Rd Gaol

Sago Lane death houses

Sook Ching screening centre

Grassy area

Significant building

The *Giang Bee*'s final voyage and approximate route of the dinghy

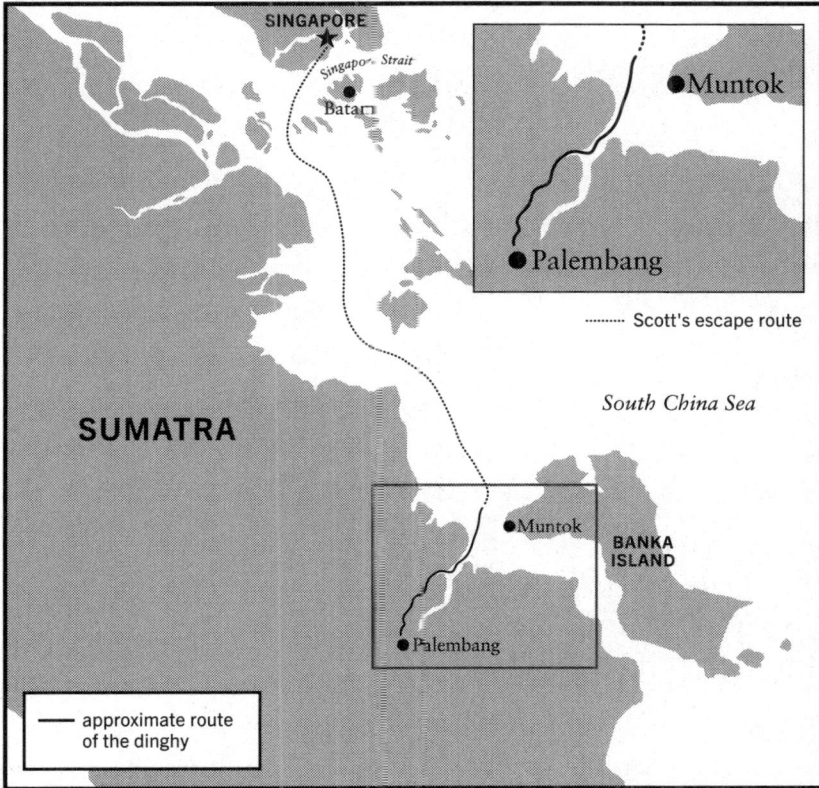

CONTENTS

Maps

A NOTE TO READERS

BY NO MEANS IS this book chiefly concerned with Operation Jaywick, the attack carried out on Japanese shipping in Singapore harbour that surely ranks as Australia's greatest commando operation. Nevertheless, the attack was the crucial moment around which this story pivots.

Rather than relate the story in a linear fashion, I deemed that a more impactful narrative telling played around with the timeline. To assist the reader, I have appended certain chapters with subtitles that identify where the story is up to on a timeline relative to when the attack occurred.

I hasten to add that nothing in this story is made up. Anything between quotation marks comes from an interview, journal, letter, memoir, classified file, official statement, court trial, affidavit, telegram or other historical document.

For consistency, I have used the imperial system – the preferred system of measurement in this period – other than when directly quoting a source that uses the metric system. All references made to dollar amounts are in the Singaporean currency of the period. And Japanese names appear in this book in the standard Japanese order of family name followed by given name.

Tom Trumble

Introduction
THE YMCA

Ten weeks after the attack

ELIZABETH CHOY COULD NOT say for how long she had been imprisoned before she was summoned from her cell to be executed. Keeping track of time was difficult in this place. The ceiling lights in the cells and corridors burnt day and night to prevent the prisoners from colluding in the darkness. For the guards, this had the added benefit of rendering sleep even more elusive, keeping the prisoners in a near constant state of exhausted unease – the perfect condition to tease out information and extract confessions. The constant light made time elastic. Minutes and hours stretched into one appallingly endless day punctuated with fitful sips of sleep, interrogation and occasional rations of rice that were less than half the size of a billiard ball. Some cells had a small open window high on the wall, designed more for ventilation than a view, which allowed Elizabeth to at least count the days by discerning the changing colour of the sky. But she could no longer rely on the count. The horror of her last interrogation had made her agony seem eternal.

Her interrogator, a devil with unsmiling eyes and an appetite for cruelty, had visited unimaginable suffering on Elizabeth. She withstood the torture and refused to confess. Enraged at her stubbornness, the interrogator had told her that the next time she was called from her cell, she would be driven to the beach in Johore and beheaded. 'Well, if you have to execute me for telling you the truth,' she had said to the guard through the tears and mucus that poured from her eyes, mouth and nose, 'I can't help it. Go ahead.'[1]

Years before, she had read, in the Gospel of John, that the truth would set you free. And maybe death was the only way of escaping this evil place and the extreme violence of the Japanese, the stench of the open commode in the cell corner, the cockroaches that crawled over her body, the sound of screaming prisoners being tortured, the sight of men dying in agony. Yes, she was ready to die; ready to face God's judgement.

The interrogator had sent her back to her cell after restating his promise: her end was imminent. Now he was coming good on his promise. The Japanese guard – one of the many young and nameless *Kempei Tai* auxiliaries who stood sentry in the bleak corridor that connected the cells of the YMCA building – called Elizabeth's name around a week later. The other prisoners – there were around fifteen in her cell at this time, all men – shuffled clear to make a path for her. They averted their gaze. Elizabeth did not blame them. The guard was watching. Offering a whispered word of encouragement or a comforting expression might establish, in the mind of the guard, a fatal association with Elizabeth, who was clearly a very dangerous prisoner. They had no wish to die in agony.

Elizabeth slithered under the narrow crawl space between the filthy, bug-ridden floor and the makeshift wooden cell bars. This crawl space was a cheap solution to providing a means of egress without fitting a cell door. It was also another *Kempei Tai* tactic aimed at debasing the prisoners before interrogation, reminding them of their lowly status as their bodies scraped the ground at the feet of their captors.

After sliding under the bars, Elizabeth stood up and fixed her dress, the same black frock she had been wearing since first entering the YMCA. She pushed her shoulders back and slightly tilted her head: poised and graceful to the bitter end. She followed the guard along the corridor where, only days earlier, she had seen a man die. He had been dragged unconscious into the corridor by guards and dumped directly outside Elizabeth's cell. Bloodied and bloated, the man drew painful, shuddering breaths over several hours. The intervals of his raspy breathing lengthened, then finally stopped. The guards left him in the corridor overnight; a warning to others of the wages of not giving the *Kempei Tai* what they wanted. By the time the guards returned the next day and tried to stuff his corpse into a gunny bag, rigor mortis had set in. They jumped on his outstretched arms and wrenched them backwards, laughing at the hideous crack as bones were snapped. With the dead man's arms jutting at grotesque angles, the guards were able to force the corpse into the bag. Even in death, the *Kempei Tai* found ways to degrade and humiliate.

Elizabeth walked on, following the guard. But instead of leading her outside, he guided her to the staircase. Elizabeth felt herself slipping into despair. Those stairs would take her back to the interrogation rooms on the upper levels. She had been tricked. Elizabeth was not going to be executed; at least, not today. She should have known the *Kempei Tai* were not finished with her.

Elizabeth searched for a way to escape, not from her physical reality but from the fear that threatened to overwhelm her. She turned inward, praying silently to God, asking for His guidance. This was not her only avenue out of despair. At other times, she would recall those sunnier days at St Andrew's School, helping the boys at maths and teaching them to become men. Despite all that she had been through, all that she had lost, those memories remained vivid. She could remember the names of all the boys she'd taught, the challenges they'd faced in their learning and at home, their pride when they'd solved a seemingly insuperable academic problem, their smiles when they'd seen her outside the school gates. What had become of those boys in this madness? Had they survived the Occupation?

Oftentimes, when her suffering became too much, she would shut her eyes and summon the sound of the boys singing 'The Bonnie Banks o' Loch Lomond', the headmaster's favourite song. She could hear their voices in her head, hear those lurid descriptions of shady glens, wildflowers, steep mountains, the gloaming before the moonshine and the sound of birdsong. Those lyrics painted in her mind an image of Eden: 'I think that [song] saved me, helped me keep my morale up.'[2]

The spirit of that song called to mind Elizabeth's home, the jungle village called Kudat that stood in the shadows of Mount Kinabalu in British North Borneo – the place the Dusuns and Kadazans called the Land Below the Wind. She would summon the memory of her grandfather, the old man seated on the platform each evening where the family dried their copra (coconut flesh), instructing the children to lie down while he pointed to the night sky: the blazing star that represented the heart of the Azure Dragon; the constellation of stars that comprised the White Tiger of the West; the cluster of stars the Europeans called the Seven Sisters. While Elizabeth and the other children gazed upwards, he would tell them ancient Chinese fables that invariably imparted the same moral: the wicked man was punished, the kind man rewarded. 'I think that is one of the loveliest memories I have – lying out on the huge platform on moonlit nights, looking at the stars, listening to the stories and then falling off to sleep knowing that we would be carried back into the house and put to bed.'[3]

As she climbed the stairs to the interrogation, Elizabeth passed a barred window, and caught sight of Orchard Road. A cyclist was making his way past a 'mee-man' – a hawker selling noodles – who was going about his business. He rapped his

clappers against his wooden cart – *tick tock tock tock tock*[4] –
calling hungry customers to him. There was something in this
familiar, quotidian detail of Singaporean life that made Elizabeth's
heart ache. Irrespective of the hardships of the Japanese occupation, life in Singapore rolled on. She was physically so close
to it, separated only by the bars across that window. Yet she
might have been in another world, trapped in this timeless hell,
forgotten by those outside.

The guard pushed open the door to the interrogation room,
where an officer was seated at a table. This was the room where
the devil had made her body pulse with fire. She would not forget
him. But the seated officer looking back at her was someone different. She had not encountered this man. He ordered her to sit
at the table. A translator walked around the table so that he was
directly opposite Elizabeth. As was custom, the officer marked the
beginning of the interrogation by levelling a set of accusations at
Elizabeth: she was a smuggler, a black marketeer, a fifth columnist, a spy, a saboteur. He then asked his first question. Elizabeth
had heard the question many times before; it was the question
they almost always asked first. 'How do you know Robert Heatlie
Scott?'[5]

PART I

1

HMS *GIANG BEE*

Nineteen months before the attack

THE ORDER TO EVACUATE the women and children was given at 7.30 p.m. Robert Heatlie Scott had been detailed to assist in lowering the lifeboats. He surveyed the darkening sea below. The gleam of the enemy searchlights trained on HMS *Giang Bee* caught the whitecaps of a growing swell. The motion of the ship was becoming more pronounced with each passing minute. What chance did women and children crammed aboard those wooden lifeboats have in such heavy seas?

The captain – a 53-year-old naval reserve officer named Lieutenant Harold Lancaster – had no choice. The Japanese destroyers *Fubuki* and *Asagiri* had their guns trained on the *Giang Bee*. These destroyers belonged to a flotilla of four vessels that included another destroyer and a four-funnelled Japanese light cruiser. The ships had appeared on the horizon several hours earlier, intercepting the *Giang Bee* on her run to Java. One of the ships fired two shots, each volley 'falling neatly and symmetrically on either side of [the *Giang Bee*]'.[1]

The anchor was lowered and the *Giang Bee*'s bow swung into the waves. They were 50 nautical miles from land at the mouth of the Banka Strait, a body of relatively shallow water between the east coast of Sumatra and Banka Island. Lancaster ordered the lowering of the white ensign that identified them as a British merchant vessel. He then raised a flag signal indicating that there were women aboard. Women were brought up from below and arranged along the deck to drum home the point. To demonstrate his willingness to surrender, Lancaster had his crew throw their weapons overboard in full view of the enemy ships.

Satisfied that the *Giang Bee* posed no threat, the cruiser and one of the destroyers turned north for Singapore. The two remaining destroyers turned their bows into the waves and lay alongside the *Giang Bee*. One of the destroyers started flashing signals by lamp. They were incomprehensible to Lancaster and his officers. In response, Lancaster hoisted a flag requesting the Japanese send a boarding party. A short time later, a Japanese motor launch was lowered into the sea. As the launch made its way over to the *Giang Bee*, a new sound emerged – the sound of an aircraft.

A muscular-looking aircraft with two propellors tipped her wing, revealing the red, white and blue roundel of the Royal Air Force emblazoned on her fuselage. A triumphant shout went up on the deck of the *Giang Bee* as the RAF Hudson – a medium bomber – circled the boats. The cheering was silenced by the roar of anti-aircraft batteries from the destroyers. The Hudson turned sharply to the south-west, heading back to land. Those on deck kept on cheering, assuming the Hudson was returning to Palembang in Sumatra to raise the alarm. Reinforcements would soon be coming.

Rob Scott was not cheering. The Japanese launch had returned to her destroyer the moment the Hudson appeared. Scott was a diplomat. He knew that this stand-off could only be resolved through dialogue. An opportunity to negotiate a non-violent surrender had just been lost. There might not be another chance to talk. Both ships exchanged lamp signals, neither side understanding what the other was saying. The situation for the passengers and crew aboard the *Giang Bee* had entered a perilous new phase. There was no fighting their way out of this one.

The *Giang Bee* was a Rotterdam cargo vessel of 1600 tons, bought by a Chinese trading firm to ply the waters between Malaya and the Dutch East Indies. Before the outbreak of war in the Pacific, she was requisitioned by the Admiralty. The Navy had fitted her out with a four-inch gun on her forecastle, an anti-aircraft gun atop her bridge and depth charges aft. 'She was,' as Scott observed, 'offensively and not merely defensively armed.'[2] She was now a ship of war, but utterly outmatched by a destroyer. Lancaster surely cursed. They had come so close.

The voyage from Singapore and Sumatra was dangerous. Through enemy-infested waters, under skies thick with enemy aircraft, the *Giang Bee* would not be allowed to pass unthreatened. Lancaster had initially refused to accept women, children and the elderly from Singapore precisely for this reason. He resolved to only take men of fighting age. But the naval authorities overruled him. The flotilla of evacuating ships numbered around forty-five and all had exceeded their capacity. What the *Giang Bee* lacked in deck space and passenger cabins she made up for in a large cargo hold suitable for the transportation of people. She was ordered to Singapore's inner harbour. Lancaster looked on helplessly as 200 passengers boarded his vessel. They probably stood a better chance of survival if they remained in Singapore.

Compounding Lancaster's frustration, the naval authorities ordered the Malay crew ashore to make space for British passengers. The *Giang Bee* was now 'without stokers, deckhands, stewards, signallers or wireless operators'.[3] They did not even have men to operate the ship's pitiful anti-aircraft defences, a World War I–era machine gun fitted with anti-aircraft sights. Officers were sent out to find able hands to help run the ship, among them Rob Scott, who knew much about the affairs of the

Far East and next to nothing about how to operate a ship, much less naval warfare. But he was fit, able and determined to help. An officer sent him below, where he stoked the boiler in the engine room from midnight to 4 a.m. Before his shift started, Scott sent his personal cook, Chu Yu-min, to the galley to prepare food for his party of twenty-five employees of the Malayan Broadcasting Corporation (MBC). Shortly after dawn and now in open water, enemy aircraft attacked the *Giang Bee*. The sea around the ship churned where the bombs detonated on the surface, spouts of water shooting skywards and spraying the deck. Near misses but no direct hits.

The attack woke Scott, who had been sleeping on the forward hatches, exhausted after his four hours at the boiler. An officer appeared, asking Scott to find another volunteer and head up to the anti-aircraft defences. The first man Scott encountered was William Beauchamp, one of his colleagues at the Ministry of Information. The two men made for their station atop the bridge, where sandbags stacked to chest height surrounded a Lewis machine gun. The task they had been set was beyond them. Scott was a reservist in the British Army with the rank of corporal. He was trained in the use of weapons. But his training did not include firing a thirty-year-old machine gun at an aerial target aboard a pitching and rolling vessel. Beauchamp had probably never even held a weapon before that moment. Even for an expert marksman, taking down a Japanese bomber or a fighter with a Lewis would be a matter of blindingly good luck rather than good management.

An officer gave brief instructions and then they were left on their own to defend the ship from an attack from above. For the remainder of the day, the *Giang Bee* was assailed from the air on five separate occasions. Scott and Beauchamp were probably more helpful as lookouts rather than gunners, shouting 'down to the captain on the bridge below [. . .] as each wave of Japanese aircraft came up from astern'.[4] The men took turns sending bursts of machine-gun fire skywards, failing to find a target.

A machine gun nesting amid sandbags atop the bridge may have served to disrupt the enemy bombers as they approached the target, forcing them to attack at a higher altitude to keep beyond the range of the gun, thus rendering their task more difficult. The Japanese bombers did indeed repeatedly miss the *Giang Bee*. But whether the machine gun had anything to do it with it is hard to prove. Dropping a bomb from an aircraft onto a moving vessel is exceptionally hard. Eventually, their luck ran out. Two bombs struck the ship just aft of the bridge, punching a hole through the upper deck. The bombs exploded in the lower deck where the passengers sheltered, killing two people instantly and wounding scores of others.

Scott and Beauchamp were unhurt despite the bombs coming perilously close to their station. They looked over the sandbags, down into the smoky cavity the bombs had made. The screams of the wounded could be heard above the ship's engines. Who lives and dies in war is always an arbitrary matter. Had the bomber released its payload a few split seconds later, both men would have been killed. But there was no time to ruminate on such things. Another attack was imminent. Scott and Beauchamp – who was 'coolness and courage'⁵ personified – got on with the job at hand, firing at another wave of bombers. Eventually, the skies cleared. The sun was low now. Lancaster called the men down. In the dying light, further air assaults were unlikely. Sunburnt, exhausted and utterly famished, having not eaten all day, the two men were climbing down the ladder to the deck when the four enemy ships appeared on the horizon.

A short time later, Scott was standing at the lifeboats, helping the young with their lifebelts, shepherding women and wailing children to their seats: 'It was a heartrending business.'⁶ The *Giang Bee* had four lifeboats, each capable of holding thirty-two grown men. As a coastal steamer, it rarely had need of more than 100 sailors to crew the boat. In an emergency, the lifeboats were sufficient in size and number to comfortably evacuate all hands.

The number of souls aboard the *Giang Bee* on the evening of
13 February 1942 far exceeded the total capacity of those four
lifeboats. Unreliable passenger manifests, hastily scribbled down
during the frantic evacuation of Singapore, listed 250 people.
Scott estimated the true number was closer to 300.

If the berthing capacity of each lifeboat was calculated according to the average weight of thirty-two grown men, Lancaster
figured he could squeeze an extra twenty souls onto each vessel.
There were, after all, women, children and infants on board, all
much lighter than the average male. But any more than that and
they risked capsizing the boats. That meant there was a spot on a
lifeboat for roughly 200 passengers. The thorny question of who
secured a berth on a lifeboat was complicated by the dispropor-
tionally high number of men on board. Back in Singapore, the
naval authorities had ordered that, where possible, men were to be
taken aboard vessels flying the White Ensign, such as the *Giang
Bee*, and women were to board vessels flying the Red Ensign.
(It was a strategy built on the presumption that the Japanese
would make a distinction between the two flags and only fire on
naval vessels. In the event, no such distinction was ever made.)
The policy meant that men outnumbered women three to two
aboard the *Giang Bee*.

There was thankfully enough room on the lifeboats for all
the women and children. That left an estimated eighty spots
for the remaining 180 men. Precedence, it seems, was given to
the elderly and to fathers whose children were on board. Seamen
were also prioritised to give the lifeboats a fighting chance of
making it through the night. Scott's wife and two children were
already safely evacuated to Australia, thank God. He was also
no seaman. He would be among the unlucky 100 who would
miss out. He knew, with absolute certainty, that he would never
see his family again. That could not be helped. In these last
moments of his life, Scott would endeavour to save as many
lives as possible.

Not that securing a berth in a lifeboat was an assurance of survival. The logistical challenge of lowering such an over-loaded boat in heavy seas was considerable. Even if safely placed upon the surface, the lifeboats faced the real possibility of being swamped in the rising swell. Those aboard would then have an arduous journey to make landfall through Japanese-controlled waters. And who knew what awaited them on land? They might fetch up on an island bereft of food and shelter, and abundant in malaria-carrying mosquitos and enemy troops. They nevertheless stood a better chance in the lifeboats than onboard.

Passengers made their way up from the hold. Anxious to keep their children together, mothers had to shout to be heard above the commotion of voices. A tongue of fire flashed from one of the destroyer's five-inch guns, followed by a concussive boom. The passengers fell silent. Had the attack begun? Everyone waited for the guns to roar once more after they were ranged. But no further report was heard. It was a warning shot. Attack was imminent. Time to leave.

Someone called, 'One hour to get off!'[7] A commotion of activity swept the deck as the passengers swarmed to the life-boats. Scott stood ready as final checks were made to the first lifeboat, ensuring the ropes attached to the davit's arms were secured to the lifeboat. The call went up to rotate the davits – the crane-like devices that lowered the lifeboats to the sea. Older women called out to Scott to delay, as friends and relatives were still coming up from below. A hysterical mother screamed that she was missing one of her children. But Scott knew that there was no time to wait. 'All we could do was to pack in as many as possible, lower the boat, and let it go, regardless of missing children and friends.'[8]

The first lifeboat to be lowered was located just aft of the bridge, not far from where the two bombs had exploded. Nobody voiced any concerns about the possible bomb damage to the davits or the lifeboat's rigging. Nothing could be done about it anyway.

The first two lifeboats to be lowered accounted for the majority of the *Giang Bee*'s complement of women and children. Aboard the lifeboat Scott was manning, mothers clung tightly to screaming babes. Other children buried their heads into their mothers' comforting embrace.

The arms of the davit rotated outward over the ship's side. The first lifeboat dangled precariously above the sea, swaying dramatically side-to-side. Two men on deck, each stationed at a winch fixed to the side of the davit, gripped the handle and turned. The lifeboat had barely started its descent when it jerked to a halt. The rope connecting the bow of the lifeboat was stuck fast. A baby's cry pierced the sea air. The crewman on the winch gripped the handle and tried to turn it with greater force. He managed a half-turn, causing the lifeboat to jerk again. The ropes groaned as they were brought to the limit of their tensile strength, when the winch handle went suddenly slack. The bow of the lifeboat collapsed. Scott looked on in horror. 'The lifeboat had tipped up, hanging by the stern, spilling her passengers into the darkness.'[9] A few desperate passengers clung to the seats, legs dangling beneath them, screaming out for help. The lifeboat made a final rotation in the stiffening breeze when the last rope snapped. The craft plunged nose-first into the sea. The lifeboat, half-submerged, surfaced before being swamped in the rolling swell, vanishing under the black surface.

No help could be given to those who had fallen into the sea. Scott and the other witnesses could only hope for a quick end to their suffering. In those tepid seas, aided by life vests, the torment of many of those in the water might have lasted many hours. Scott could not dwell on such things. He made his way aft to the next lifeboat, which was already filled with anxious passengers. Like the previous one, this vessel was located near where the bombs had exploded. The ashen faces of the women and skeleton crew of seamen aboard conveyed their inner thoughts: *Please, God, don't let the ropes snap.*

The davits rotated. The lifeboat swung over the water. The ropes were secure. The winches were turned and the ropes paid out slowly as the lifeboat was lowered onto the sea. The ropes that connected the lifeboat to the davits were cast off. Seconds passed, then panicked voices could be heard from below. One witness described the sound as heartrending: 'the sound of little children calling out for their mothers'.[10] Shrapnel from the bomb blast had holed the boat, which was now filling fast with water. Waves and tide had taken the lifeboat aft, but even after the boat slipped beyond view, the passengers on deck could still hear the appalling screams of the doomed as their lifeboat sank. They were mostly women's screams, begging for help as they struggled to keep their children alive.

By now the third lifeboat was fully loaded. Nearby, sitting forlornly on deck, was an injured man, delirious with pain. His legs had been broken in the bombing. He had been brought aboard with his wife and two blond-haired children, aged four and six. Surrounded by his young family, the man squirmed uncomfortably on the deck. There was room aboard this lifeboat for the wife and the children. A man approached the young wife.

'Hand me the children,' he said.

'No,' she said. She knew that there would be no berth for her husband aboard the lifeboat. His injuries were too severe. His chances of survival negligible. 'If my husband can't go, none of us will.'[11]

The woman slipped the lifebelts off her children and removed her own, handing them to the man, who looked on in mute horror. She helped prop up her husband and sat alongside him. She then gently placed 'her arm around her husband's shoulders, the other around her children'.[12] The mother and her children were among the few women and children who remained on the *Giang Bee*, the majority having drowned when the first two life-boats went down.

The last lifeboats were launched without incident. Aside from a few women from the Singapore and Malayan YWCAs and the Singapore Recreation Club, these boats held a higher proportion of men. They were comprised of Chinese labourers; Malayan planters and miners; professional jockeys and trainers of the Singapore Turf Club; lawyers, bureaucrats and an assortment of others drawn from an island once thought to be an impregnable fortress. Scott stood at the ready near the last boat as it was lowered. Once safely afloat, the lifeboat was freed from the davit's grasp. Scott looked on as 'a strong tide [swept] the lifeboat astern as soon as they cast off'.[13]

All eyes turned to the destroyers. Now that the lifeboats were clear, those enemy guns would surely begin an assault. There were now around 100 people left aboard the *Giang Bee*. All were convinced that there was no hope. Men went below decks in search of objects that might be used as rafts or flotation aids. They returned with mattresses and cabin doors. The lucky ones found lifebelts that had been secreted away in an obscure place within the ship.

Rob Scott found his former colleagues from the MBC. A few had managed to secure a spot on one of the final two lifeboats. The majority had remained on deck. These men were all engineering staff. Their employment preceded Scott's appointment as their manager and his dealings with them had been limited. Those that he found were preparing to abandon ship, 'with or without lifebelts'.[14] He bade them good luck and started to look for his colleagues at the Ministry of Information.

Scott felt a great affinity for these men. He was the Director of the Ministry's Far Eastern Bureau and had been responsible for hiring most of the staff. 'We had been working together, latterly very strenuously, and often under difficulties, as a team.'[15] Notwithstanding his staff's veneration of him, Scott saw them more than his subordinates. 'All were my friends.'[16] He shook each man's hand. It was the last time he saw any of them alive.

Finally, he farewelled Chu Yu-min. For nearly ten years, Chu had been Scott's ever-reliable servant. They had been together in Peking, Manchuria, Shanghai, Hong Kong, Canton, Chungking and Singapore. There was no task too difficult or too much trouble. He was Scott's cook, caterer, cleaner, shopper and errand runner. During the white-knuckle terror of air raids back in the Singapore office, Chu had displayed an enviable degree of equanimity. It was the sort of stiff-upper-lip fortitude and tremendous sangfroid, those quintessentially British traits, that Scott admired in a man. Neither saw the other as a friend or family. Chu had come from a culture in which rigid hierarchies of class were keenly observed. For Scott, it was nonetheless a painful goodbye. In fluent Mandarin, Scott wished Chu good fortune, effectively relieving him of his service. Scott looked on as Chu sought out something that would float, knowing that he would 'regret his loss equally with that of the others'.[17]

An uneasy quiet settled on the deck of the *Giang Bee*. Several passengers had already leapt over the side, clinging to hastily made flotation devices. Others delayed abandoning ship, figuring they stood a better chance the longer they remained on deck. After all, once the jump was made, survival depended on an untested float to cling onto and a favourable tide that would sweep them to Sumatra or some other friendly shore. Otherwise, they would need to chance upon a fishing boat or Allied vessel. They were under no illusions: it was highly unlikely any of them would live beyond that night. 'Most of those left on board – including myself – were convinced that there was no hope for us.'[18]

Scott was among those who delayed jumping. He could see the lamp flashing from the nearest destroyer. Presumably their guns would stay silent as long as both sides continued attempts to communicate. But there was no way to be sure. At any minute, the *Giang Bee* could be obliterated. Scott needed a raft. He ripped up fractured planks from the bomb-damaged deck, all the while keeping an eye on the destroyers, whose sinister outlines he could make out against the dark horizon. Once he had sourced enough wood he looked around for rope, cord, string or anything to bind them. Scott managed to find cord. It took him the next hour to assemble the raft, which did not exactly look seaworthy. But it would probably float.

Scott could see that the destroyer was still sending indecipherable lamp signals. Something stirred inside. He had formed a conclusion. By now, the stand-off had gone for four hours. Lancaster and his officers had assumed that the reason the Japanese had not attacked was to allow the lifeboats to be launched. But that had happened an hour ago. The destroyers' search lights clearly revealed that all the lifeboats were gone. Lancaster believed that the indecision of the Japanese captains aboard each destroyer was predicated on the shaky assumption that they truly cared about the preservation of civilian life. Scott found that highly unlikely. The Japanese wanted something else. But what?

It was at that point that Scott decided to jump overboard. The dictates of diplomacy held that empathy was the only path to resolving a dispute. To be empathetic was to imagine oneself in your opponent's position. Only then could you begin to understand the other person's perspective and motivation. Therein lay the key to finding a diplomatic solution to this impasse. But if the Japanese were not willing to send a boarding party and neither side's lamp signals could be understood, then this night was bound to end in disaster. It was time to go. 'I filled my water bottle, strapped it to my lifebelt, took off my shoes and stockings, and was on the point of jumping overboard when I heard my name called.'[19] A cry went out that Scott was to report to the bridge.

There was a final card that Lancaster wanted to play that might save the *Giang Bee*. It was a 13-foot dinghy resting upside down at the stern. Lancaster wanted Scott and several others to launch the dinghy and row it over to the destroyer to negotiate surrender terms. The captain's rationale for including Scott was obvious. He had more than a decade of diplomatic experience in the Far East, which included numerous visits and weeks-long stays in the British Embassy in Tokyo. Not only was Scott's Japanese proficient, he had greater familiarity with Japan's military adventures across East Asia than any man aboard – which was also why Lancaster's suggestion made him feel sick.

Scott had witnessed the Japanese warring from Manchuria to Shanghai. He was an eyewitness to the aftermath of various atrocities perpetrated against the civilian population throughout much of China. It was precisely for this reason that he resolved to send his wife and young children to Australia when war broke out in the Pacific. At that moment, his intuition was telling him that the opportunity for a diplomatic resolution to this deadlock had passed: 'To go straight into the arms of the Japanese like this was the last thing I wanted.'[20] He was also under no obligation to go. Scott was a civilian and not legally bound to follow an instruction. The temptation to grab his raft and leap overboard must have been great. He instead acquiesced to Lancaster's request, despite his misgivings. Though the chance of the plan working was remote, it was at least a chance.

The dinghy was turned right way up and attached to a derrick, which hoisted the small craft into the air. Including Scott, four men squeezed aboard the small vessel. Sub Lieutenant Ernest Langdon had command. Lancaster sent along Able Seaman S. Casey, a naval rating sent to shore by his other ship when he developed severe bronchitis before being evacuated aboard the *Giang Bee*, who had recently turned eighteen years old. Lancaster likely felt sorry for the boy and felt he stood a better chance if he surrendered to the Japanese. A Swiss diamond drilling engineer named Julius Planzer was also sent along. Why Planzer was included remains unclear. Lancaster probably believed that Planzer, as a citizen of neutral Switzerland, could act as an intermediary when brokering terms with the Japanese.

Beauchamp – Scott's former colleague and fellow anti-aircraft gunner – assisted in guiding the dinghy over the side of the boat with the aid of a sergeant who worked the derrick. Once successfully placed on the sea, the dinghy was almost swamped. 'The dinghy was built for harbour work in calm water and was in every way unsuitable for heavy seas at night.'[21] To maintain ballast, two men – sitting alongside each other along a seat in the centre of dinghy – took an oar, another manned the tiller and the fourth sat on a small seat in the bow.

Keeping the dinghy afloat was hard work. Not nearly as hard, however, as reaching one of the destroyers. The sheer size of the enemy ship had created the illusion that it was much closer to the *Giang Bee*. In fact, the destroyer was deceptively far off. The late hour complicated the matter. In the darkness, it was hard to get an exact fix on her location. A lightly weighted boat with limited ballast required all four men to constantly adjust their weight to match the motion of the waves. It took them nearly an hour to row across the expanse of water that separated the two ships.

As they approached the destroyer, the dinghy was suddenly flooded in light. One of the destroyers had trained its search-light on them. Scott estimated they were within 150 yards of reaching the destroyer when the ship inexplicably manoeuvred clear. For the next ninety minutes, the dinghy – closely watched under the relentless gaze of the searchlight – valiantly tried to reach either destroyer. But they kept drawing away. It was an absurd sight, a 13-foot wooden boat giving chase to a 390-foot destroyer. 'It was hopeless for a small, unseaworthy dinghy, at night, in a heavy sea, to catch a destroyer which did not want to be caught.'[22] Once again, they came within 150 yards before the destroyer moved clear.

The men of the boarding party never gave up as the destroyers drew farther away. Eventually, the beam of light was turned away from them and trained on the *Giang Bee*. The night air was rent with thunderous reports as the guns belched fire and smoke, sending 50-pound high-explosive shells into the *Giang*

Bee. Scott counted six rounds in total. He turned towards her: 'she glowed from stem to stern'.[23] He could see men leaping into the water to escape the inferno. The ship listed dramatically and went down within minutes.

Once she was gone, the destroyers dimmed their lights and surged away, making no effort to pick up survivors. Before long, the rumble of the destroyers' engines was lost in the sound of wind and waves. The dinghy bobbed in the swell, a blanket of low cloud now blocking out the light of the stars. All was dark.

2
THE BLOATED MAN

Ten weeks after the attack

THE INTERROGATION OF Elizabeth Choy lasted less than thirty minutes. After demanding details of her connection to certain British internees in Changi Prison, the *Kempei Tai* officer levelled the same accusations at Elizabeth as on previous interrogations – she was a spy; she was working with the British military; she had helped organise the attack; she was anti-Japanese. She denied everything. Unlike at previous interrogations, her denials were not answered with violence. The officer – who lacked the venom of the other interrogators – waited for her to finish and then half-heartedly asked a few follow-up questions. When it was over, Elizabeth was escorted back to her cell. The devil's promise – that the next time she was called from her cell, she would be driven to Johore and beheaded – proved yet another lie.

That did not mean she was out of danger. The *Kempei Tai* were unpredictable, capricious. She could be ordered back to the cell, taken to another interrogation room to be tortured again or summarily executed. Time would tell. For now, at least, God had spared her. She intended to repay His mercy by helping her cellmates. There were so many who needed help.

The stevedore Tan Yew Cheng suffered the misfortune of having worked a job whose location was in the vicinity of the explosions. Like any Chinese man of fighting age who worked at the harbour, Tan was a suspect. On the day of his arrest, he was taken to the YMCA building and led up to a dank room on the third floor. He was made to kneel before a *Kempei Tai* officer while he was flogged with an iron rod. 'I was questioned non-stop while this was going on and asked to confess whether I was an English spy or not.'[1]

Tan denied the accusation, and not simply because it was ludicrous. He was convinced that confessing to any crime – whether it be espionage, sabotage or any kind of anti-Japanese activity – would be akin to signing his own death warrant. Tan's denials ensured the beating continued for the rest of the day. He was struck on the back, legs and ankles with the rod until he fainted. Three days later, the Japanese took him back upstairs. He was tied to a table. A live electrical wire was pressed against his chest, stomach, thighs, tongue and teeth. The current caused one of Tan's gold teeth to crack. Writhing in agony, he was shown a list of names, many of which he recognised. These were men and women in his community, people he worked with at the docks. 'They promised that if I could pick out some of the names from the list they would release me.'[2] Tan said he knew none of them. The torture continued.

By the time Elizabeth Choy was brought to the prison, the bruises on Tan's face, back and torso had turned black. Elizabeth knew Tan, having taught his son back at St Andrew's. Not that the two risked talking in the cell. In those initial weeks after the first wave of arrests, the sentries watched all inmates closely. Talking was too dangerous. Three months would pass before they communicated to one another. By now, Elizabeth was expert in the prisoner sign language. She waited for the sentry to venture on his patrol of the corridor before she shuffled over to Tan, whose face was bruised and swollen; he had just returned from being beaten with a thick rope for thirty minutes.

Elizabeth quickly signed a question, asking if he was alright. Tan shook his head. He had been grappling with a dilemma. Throughout his ordeal, Tan had believed that confessing to the crimes to which he was being accused would not only mean that he would be killed, but would also risk his family's life. The interrogators had shaken that conviction when they threatened to kill his wife and children *unless* he confessed. If confessing meant saving his family, he would do it. But would it not be reasonable to conclude that if Tan was involved in anti-Japanese activity, his wife and perhaps his children were involved too? Surely confessing to these crimes would very likely result in the arrest of his wife? It was an impossible conundrum. Whether he confessed or not, his family was endangered. Tan gambled and decided not to confess. He was terrified it was the wrong decision.

'They are going to kill my wife and children,' he signed to Elizabeth. 'I think I'll go mad.'[3]

Tan looked at Elizabeth, hoping most likely for an assurance that he had done the right thing. He had no knowledge of the hell Elizabeth had suffered. When he looked at her he thought 'she was apparently in good health'.[4] She did not tell him about her own suffering at the hands of that devil interrogator. To do so would lend credence to the theory that Tan's wife was, in fact, in grave danger.

Elizabeth spent the next hours doing her best to lift Tan's spirits. She assured him that the Japanese were issuing empty threats to coax out a false confession. They would never dare harm his family. Of course, Elizabeth had no way of knowing if this was true. But it felt like the right message to convey. It also felt good to be able to help someone, to extend compassion and care to another to ease their burden. Not for the first time, Elizabeth was filled with gratitude that the prisoners had developed a way of communicating.

She was taught the sign language of the YMCA back in those frightening first weeks in the lead-up to her interrogations by a bald, middle-aged British man named John Dunlop. She had noticed him before. How could she not? He was a European who appeared to suffer alopecia, which resulted in total hair loss, including his eyebrows and whiskers. Elizabeth learned little more about this man, other than the fact that he was another Changi internee swept up in this horrible mess.

Dunlop started his lesson, pointing with his right index finger to the thumb of his left hand. Then, speaking in a voice that was barely above the sound of a breath, he whispered a word – the letter 'A'. He repeated the action and the sound until Elizabeth got it: the thumb represented A. He then pointed to his index finger and whispered the letter 'E'. He made his way around the fingers of his left hand, assigning a letter to each digit: the middle finger was 'I'; the ring finger was 'O'; the pinky finger was 'U'. Elizabeth nodded in understanding. The fingers of the left hand each represented a vowel.

The easy part was over. Dunlop then stepped her through the complexities of signing all the other letters of the alphabet. Each consonant had a unique mark. It might involve the left index finger drawing a line across the palm of the hand, or signing a cross or a zig or a zag – and so on. It was a slow, frustrating and time-consuming exercise. Not that Elizabeth minded. She welcomed the opportunity to occupy her mind. The fact that this newfound knowledge would take plenty of practice to master was perfectly fine. She was going nowhere.

Once Elizabeth became conversant in the sign language, Dunlop read her future. It turned out that he was an expert at the ancient form of divination known as palmistry. By analysing the lines, shapes and patterns of Elizabeth's palm, Dunlop claimed, he could interpret her character and read her future.

Elizabeth had encountered fortune tellers in Singapore before the war. Some would use Java sparrows, others joss sticks. Elizabeth, a devout Christian deeply sceptical of this kind of superstition, decided to indulge him. When Dunlop revealed his interpretation, Elizabeth knew it to be a whole lot of nonsense. He told her that she 'would be famous [and that] people would read about her in newspapers'.[5]

Dunlop's dubious claims at clairvoyance notwithstanding, Elizabeth marvelled at his ability to bring joy, relief and comfort into their miserable cell. He told her – through the sign language – that she would one day visit vast cities and strange exotic places, and see landscapes of indescribable beauty. Elizabeth found herself pleasantly distracted by the absurd idea of actually surviving this hell and touring the world. She would, if she ever had the chance, visit London, France and Switzerland, perhaps Lake Como in Italy. Most of all, she cherished the thought of gazing across the placid waters of Loch Lomond. When the hunger, discomfort and revulsion of her present circumstances threatened to overwhelm her, Elizabeth would return to such thoughts.

After her first session learning sign language with Dunlop, Elizabeth noticed numerous other detainees very discreetly touching their hands. For all of them, the sign language was liberating. The Japanese might have incarcerated them all in body, but they were not able to lock them into their own minds. It was also transgressive. Under the noses of the brutal guards whose job it was to violently dish out punishment for any person who spoke, the detainees were engaged in constant conversation, sharing and gathering information. In this way, Elizabeth came to learn about the reasons for her arrest and the peril that she was in. She learned that her fellow prisoners were accused of an array of criminal activity – from smuggling, theft or simply listening to foreign broadcasts on radio sets, to sabotage and espionage. The Japanese were intent on connecting individuals within the Chinese community to the British internees in Changi. It all related to some major attack down at the harbour. On first arriving at the YMCA, Elizabeth knew nothing of the attack. From Khoo Hock Choo, a registry clerk who had worked at Changi, arrested on the same charge as Tan, Elizabeth learned that some ships had been destroyed.

By now, having endured the worst of her interrogations, Elizabeth knew all about the attack. In the minds of the Japanese, she was a key figure in its planning and execution. Elizabeth and her husband, Choy Khun Heng, were on the list that Tan was shown during his interrogation. The names of several other men on that list – the ambulance driver John Long, the Bishop of Singapore, the businessman Wee Aik Tek – were all known to Elizabeth before she was jailed. Others she would meet in person as they were rotated through her cell; she would also hear their screams from above during their interrogations.

Days after she had spoken with Tan, while Elizabeth waited to be summoned by a sentry to be executed, a British man appeared in the corridor. He was grossly disfigured, a grotesquerie that only vaguely resembled a man: 'so bloated, like a fat caterpillar [. . .] like a big worm, poor thing'.[6] She remembered the sound of his breath, raspy and short, and the sight of his exposed torso, bruised and blackened. There were livid red sores across his arms and chest where he had been whipped with bamboo. Elizabeth regarded him with heartfelt pity. His appearance was only in part the work of the Japanese interrogators. This man was suffering beri-beri.

As the horribly bloated man shuffled slowly to his cell, he tripped and crumpled to the ground. The guards did nothing to help. Whether he stood or remained in the corridor and died seemed to make no difference to them. He managed to pull himself up to his knees. His eyes, narrow slits in his swollen face, locked with Elizabeth's. She recognised him now – here was the one whose story connected them all, the man the Japanese called *tatsujin supai*: the master spy.

Separated by only a few feet, the man looked through the wooden bars of the cell and directly at Elizabeth. Something in his bearing changed. A flash of recognition. The man quickly turned away, fearful perhaps that the guards shadowing his every move would see and accuse him of collusion or conspiracy. That would be deadly for them both. Through sheer will, he stood. Upright and balanced, he resumed his painful stagger down the corridor. Elizabeth lost sight of him as he walked around the bend in the corridor to his cell.

3

CASTAWAYS

Nineteen months before the attack

SUB LIEUTENANT ERNEST LANGDON, commander of the *Giang Bee*'s 13-foot harbour dinghy, which lurched in the rising swells somewhere in the Banka Strait, faced a dilemma. Before the *Giang Bee* went down, surely some aboard had managed to jump clear. But the dinghy – a vessel not the least bit suited to the open sea – had reached its capacity. Langdon could maybe accommodate one or two more passengers. With four fully grown men already on board, this would be the absolute limit before the boat became dangerously overloaded. If there were people alive in the water, the very act of returning the dinghy to the spot where the *Giang Bee* slipped beneath the waves was perilous. In their desperate effort to clamber aboard, the survivors might capsize the dinghy.

Langdon did not give the problem much thought. Searching for survivors was the humane thing to do. He swung the tiller around and ordered his oarsmen to row, the dinghy making its way to the place where the mothership went down. The dinghy's oarsmen – Rob Scott, the Director of the Ministry of Information's Far Eastern Bureau, and Julius Planzer, the Swiss diamond-drilling engineer – struggled to find a consistent cadence in the heavy swells. The oars either missed the water altogether or caught crabs, where an oar was driven into an oncoming wave with enough force to nearly vault the man at the other end of it out of the boat. Scott and Planzer kept their eyes on the sea, rowing while looking over their shoulders, timing their strokes accordingly. Sitting up front, peering into the darkness ahead, was the young naval rating, Casey. Wind-whipped and wave-soaked, Casey – who was barely yet a man – was battling severe bronchitis, his misery compounded by the near certainty that they would all die.

Judging distances across the sea is notoriously difficult without instruments, particularly in a heavy sea at night. Their best guess had them half a mile away from the *Giang Bee* when she sank. Fighting to stay afloat in that sea and moving at a slow pace, it took them nearly thirty minutes to get to the site of the tragedy. Too long. As they closed in, Scott and Planzer suspended their rowing and searched the roiling sea for survivors. All that remained of the outrage that had just occurred was some burning flotsam and scattered debris.

On board the *Giang Bee* before the attack, Rob Scott had been convinced that the destroyers would attack once it was clear that neither side could understand the other. The attack had nonetheless seemed wanton and cruel, particularly when no effort was made to collect survivors. Nevertheless, in Scott's view, this was unlikely to have been the outcome the enemy desired: 'I doubt whether the Japanese, when they first intercepted us, intended to sink us.'[1] The Japanese efforts to communicate by lamp clearly suggested they wanted the *Giang Bee* to do some-thing. But what? Other British merchant ships and vessels intercepted by the Japanese as they left Singapore were ordered to Muntok on Banka Island. The enemy gained a ship to be repurposed as a cargo or transport vessel for the Japanese Navy and there was no loss of life. None of this was known to Scott, of course. But he suspected that a message of this kind was what the Japanese were attempting to communicate: 'I think that if we had been able to understand the Japanese signals this is probably what they wanted us to do.'[2]

In Scott's mind, this only raised another question: why, having spent so many hours attempting to signal the *Giang Bee*, did the destroyers snub Lancaster's attempt to send a boarding party? Clearly it was not an issue of expending too much time. The destroyers evaded the dinghy for two hours, all the while continuing to signal the *Giang Bee*. The Japanese, moreover, were clearly not averse to negotiating in person. They had attempted to send their own boarding party earlier in the day before the RAF Hudson had aggressively circled overhead. Evidently, Lancaster's order to send a dinghy to the destroyers as a last-ditch attempt to negotiate was perplexing to the Japanese. After all, it went against convention: the surrendering captain did not send a boarding party; it was the other way around. Scott wondered if there was something else at play. A diplomat understands well that a harmless act in one cultural setting may be deeply threatening in another. Scott had spent eighteen months in Tokyo at the moment Japan was gearing up for a much wider conflict in the Pacific. Behind the familiar veneer of tradition, rigid formality and politeness was a culture that was utterly alien to him. This was a place where children were encouraged to play at executing suicide attacks, strapping wooden-shaped bombs to their backs and colliding into each other; where there was no greater glory than to give one's life to the emperor. Was it possible that, in the battle-ready minds of the Japanese officers aboard those destroyers, the dinghy was perceived as a lethal threat? Did they see, in the dinghy, an effort to transport explosives to damage or sink one of the destroyers? A definitive answer cannot be known. Both destroyers were sunk with the loss of all hands within a year.

A wave crashed over the side of the dinghy. Water was now lapping at their ankles. They bailed water out with their bare hands. Scott found a tobacco tin floating in the bilges and used it to scoop out the water. He stopped bailing when the sound of a plaintive cry carried to him on the sea wind. The others heard it too. They looked out to see two men drowning. The dinghy, dancing atop the waves, drew alongside the men. With great care, they hauled them aboard. They were Horace Kendall, a rubber planter from Ipoh, in north-western Malaya, and William Probyn Allen, a salesman from the Boots Pure Drug Company.

Kendall and Allen collapsed at the bottom of the boat, gasping for air. The two men had jumped clear of the sinking ship without having been obliterated, burned or wounded by the torrent of firepower hurled at the *Giang Bee*. They had managed to avoid the dreaded drag that threatened to pull them to the depths when the ship went down, before treading water for half an hour. They were utterly exhausted, barely capable of speech.

Kendall and Allen were, in Scott's opinion, 'colossal',[3] weighing 230 pounds (104 kg) and 250 pounds (113 kg) respectively. The dinghy was now dangerously low in the water. 'Even when we all kept as still as possible we had only an inch or two of freeboard.'[4] Allen lay flat on his back so that his body went under the seat across the middle of the dinghy, his head towards the bow. Casey, enfeebled with illness and desperately needing to remain dry, huddled in the bow. Planzer, whose lack of experience on boats was showing, remained on the oars. Scott – who had learned to row while on a family trip to Trinidad in his mid-teens – and Langdon took turns on the tiller: 'Altogether, about as sorry an outfit as ever disgraced the high seas.'[5]

While manning the tiller, Scott took stock of his situation. He was dressed in a sports shirt, a pair of khaki shorts and a lifebelt. His wallet – with $37 of Singaporean currency – was in his back pocket, along with a letter from his daughter, Susan, and a letter from his son, Douglas, written when they had arrived in Sydney.

Another pocket was stuffed with four handkerchiefs, and a full water bottle was lashed to his belt. Scott's water bottle was the extent of the castaways' provisions.

The wind strengthened; the seas grew more unruly. They were two degrees below the equator, but Scott was starting to feel the cold, the sea wind whipping his sodden skin. He looked up and then scanned the horizon. 'A stormy night, heavy seas, stiff wind from the north, fairly clear starry sky with scudding clouds.'[6] But where were they? The key to survival was getting to land. Landon, who had been on the bridge when the four enemy ships intercepted the *Giang Bee*, believed that they were at the northern end of the mouth of the Banka Strait, somewhere between Sumatra and Banka Island. But he had no idea which landmass was closer. They were also without a compass to guide them. Langdon and Scott had a heated disagreement over directions: 'We got confused between the true and the false Southern Crosses, and argued which was which.'[7]

As the sea became ever more turbulent, the direction in which they were headed mattered less than remaining afloat. Keeping the bow pointed directly at the incoming waves – the best method to negotiate heavy seas in a vessel of any size – was no longer viable. The dinghy was too low in the water. With reduced buoyancy, it was driving into the waves rather than riding over them, scooping up gallons of water each time. Langdon settled on a new approach: 'We found that we could stay afloat only by putting the stern square into the wind, in front of the waves.'[8] In effect, they turned the dinghy into a surfboard.

The method required 'the steersman [. . .] to twist round and watch every single wave as it came up, the bows veering this way and that'.[9] It was exacting work for the man on the tiller. The high and rounded shape of the bow and the absence of a keel meant the dinghy – 'possessed of an imp of mischief'[10] – threatened at any moment to turn broadside to the waves. The oarsmen provided some assistance in maintaining the dinghy's direction.

Of course, bringing the oars into play in such a scenario was risky. An oar dug deep into the face of a wave could act as a sea anchor, causing the dinghy to pitch, rotate and turn turtle.

But the greatest threat came from fatigue. Scott, who had slept only a few short hours on the forward hatches of the *Giang Bee* after stoking through the previous night, fell asleep at the tiller. The dinghy 'promptly swung round broadside on to the next wave, and the water tumbled over the side, drenching everyone, nearly swamping us, and soaking the unfortunate Allen',[11] who had remained prostrate on his back throughout the harrowing ordeal. Langdon relieved Scott at the tiller for a lengthy stretch. Eventually, exhaustion caused him to make errors too. Scott was not the least bit refreshed when he resumed his position at the tiller. It was not long before the dinghy took another dangerous turn, drenching the men. While all hands frantically bailed, Scott apologised to Allen, who again bore the brunt of it.

'Never mind,' said the good-natured Allen. 'I'm only sorry I can't help.'

'Yes, you can,' said Scott. 'Keep me awake. Talk to me. Pinch me. Kick me. Anything. But keep me awake, or we are going to sink.'

'All right,' said Allen, before instantly falling asleep. Scott drifted off not long after. He awoke to the sound of the men shouting. Scott had let the dinghy drift sideways, and wave after wave was pouring into the dinghy. With barely a fingernail of freeboard above the waterline, the men frantically bailed. 'After that I had to give it up as a bad job, and Langdon got no more sleep.'[12] Near misses notwithstanding, they survived the night. It was an impressive demonstration of small-boat seamanship given the inexperience of the dinghy crew.

Dawn revealed no wreckage, no ships and no land. The wind died, diminishing the size and ferocity of the swells and allowing the use of the oars. With the sun as a compass, they decided to turn south-west for Sumatra. If Langdon was correct about the position of the *Giang Bee* when she foundered, then Palembang was their best option. The large Dutch town, enriched by oil, was situated some distance inland on the River Musi. The RAF operated an aerodrome at Palembang. Their hope was to board a plane destined for Java and thence catch a connecting flight to Australia, where Scott would be reunited with his family. But first they needed to make it to Palembang and that meant making landfall and chancing upon a local fisherman or villager along the Sumatran coast who might help.

By now the sea was in a tranquil mood. The lack of wind made the temperature soar. Langdon was the only one among them who had protection from the sun – a naval peaked hat that in fact provided little cover. Thirst began to tighten its grip on them all. Scott was the sole man on board with a water bottle. They agreed to delay opening the bottle for a day or until their thirst became intolerable. By the time the sun was directly overhead, exposure and dehydration set in. The men grew lethargic. The deadening beat of the oarsmen pulling hard lulled Scott into a nightmarish slumber: 'I passed to dreams of banquets, then of sideboards laden with great jugs of iced fruit squashes, then of glasses of iced water then [. . .] blissful visions of scooping dirty water out of the gutter.'[13] Dreams, which he had studied at Oxford as part of his psychology minor, were a source of fascination to Scott. He found it interesting that the body's needs progressively distilled the subject of the dream into what he truly needed. He did not need luxurious banquets or flavoured drinks. He needed water. 'I never once dreamt of anything alcoholic, even beer.'[14]

Aircraft passed overhead in both directions. The men leapt to their feet, very nearly capsizing the boat. They waved their arms but the pilots either did not see or ignored them. Likely for the best, at least in Scott's view: 'They were probably enemy, so we were just as well off without an answer.'[15] The aircraft were headed in the direction of smoke trails snaking across the horizon. It was a sight met with mixed emotions. On the one hand, the smoke was the clearest indication that they were approaching land. On the other, it was also evidence of a fierce battle being waged. Assuming they made it to Palembang, what would they find there?

The afternoon passed into a clear evening. The relief of being liberated from the blazing intensity of the sun's rays was tempered by the prospect of rowing blindly through another night. As the day ended, during that brief moment where the gloaming merges imperceptibly into black night, Langdon and Scott took note of the position of the stars in relation to the sun's dying light. At the helm, Langdon pointed the bow at a constellation of stars in the south-western sky. The sea was now becalmed. The men took turns to row, their bodies yearning for water and food.

In the small hours of the morning, the wind changed, bringing with it 'the sweet odour of land'.[16] Scott was at the helm. 'I had never noticed it before – I mean the smell of land from the sea.'[17] It was pungent and thick, the glorious stench of rotting seaweed and decaying plant matter. The rising sun breached the edge of the sea and revealed a low mangrove swamp with clumps of coconut palms. Sumatra.

They rowed south, searching for a beach to land the dinghy. The wind that had carried the scent of land to them had freshened into a stiff northerly and gained strength through the morning. By noon, it was at gale force, sweeping them down the coast. They needed to make landfall. The dinghy passed the very narrow mouth of a creek that appeared to widen into a river. Beyond overhanging mangroves, they could see a single-masted *prau*. The long and slender boat popular among Malay fishermen was moored to an overhanging branch. There were two men aboard.

The castaways turned the dinghy into the creek and headed for the *prau*, fighting the ebbing tide as the water surged from the creek and into the open sea. As they entered the narrow mouth of the creek, the dinghy came to a standstill. The oarsmen pulled furiously against the rushing water, but the tide overwhelmed their sleep-deprived and dehydrated bodies. The two Malay fishermen watched curiously from the deck of their craft as the dinghy started to swept backwards.

Kendall arrived at a solution. He could see the sandy creek bed a few feet below the rushing surface. He figured he could wade to the *prau* on his own. With one less body on board, he would also lighten the burden on the oarsmen. Maybe he could help push the dinghy as he went. He had underestimated the extent of his fatigue and the power of the tide, however. The moment Kendall leapt out, 'he was whisked astern in waist high water and nearly drowned'.[18] He caught a rope thrown from the dinghy and thrashed about, desperately trying to keep his head above the surface. But he was unable to stand up against the rushing tide. Scott heard someone shouting from the *prau*. The fishermen were pointing at a rope they drifted down to the dinghy. Scott reached over and grasped it. 'Instead of Kendall pushing us along, we were hauled up by the Malay, and in turn we hauled Kendall along in the water like an obstinate pig going to market.'[19]

The dinghy was tied off to the *prau*. Kendall was hauled aboard first. Half-drowned and retching water, he collapsed on the deck. The two fishermen then helped the others aboard. They were extremely fit men, one in early middle age – the leader of the duo – his subordinate maybe ten years younger. Both Kendall and Langdon were fluent in Malay. The two men on the *prau* spoke a Sumatran dialect which seemed a variant of Malay, so they could understand each other well enough.

The elder man said that they were from a village at the mouth of the River Musi, not far from Palembang. They plied these waters with their stores of rice and sugar, which they would exchange for dried fish in the coastal villages to the north, hauling in a catch of fish as they went. On a return run from their journey north, they had decided to take shelter in the creek when the weather turned; they had planned to wait there 'till the wind subsided'.[20]

Scott's bottle containing the only water on the dinghy remained unopened. The fishermen overwhelmed the men with generosity. 'They were extremely kind to us, giving us rice and fish and coffee, drying out clothes, and offering to put us up for the night.'[21] The castaways accepted the offer. The sun was low on the horizon. In their exhaustion, they turned in early. Replenished after their feast on the *prau*, Scott shut his eyes. In the split second before giving in to exhaustion, Scott calculated that, save for two miserable hours on the forward hatches of the *Giang Bee*, it was his first sleep since he left Singapore on Wednesday, 11 February. It was now Sunday evening, 15 February 1942. He fell into a profound sleep.

Hours earlier, Singapore – the island that had served as a British trading post for 146 years and became the British Empire's jewel in the Far East – had capitulated to the Japanese.

4

SOOK CHING

Nineteen months before the attack

THREE DAYS AFTER THE Fall of Singapore, Japanese soldiers walked the streets of Chinatown, bellowing into handheld megaphones. All Chinese men aged between eighteen and fifty years of age were to report to the nearest screening centre. The order – referred to by the Japanese as *dai kensho* or 'great inspection' – was not a surprise. Posters listing the screening centres and instructions on the time men were to show up had been plastered throughout Chinatown not long after the British capitulation. Not everyone saw the posters. Venturing outside was dangerous. Those who did not see the posters learned about the directive from friends and family. When word of the order reached Elizabeth Choy, the message had become muddled, key details omitted or changed. She was told that all Chinese people, irrespective of sex and age, were required to turn up to a screening centre.

When she heard the urgent amplified voices of the soldiers on their megaphones, Elizabeth led her entire family onto the bomb-damaged street. Among those who followed Elizabeth were her husband, Choy Khun Heng, her father, Yong Than Yin, and her stepmother, three sisters, sister-in-law, who was heavy with child, and an adolescent niece and nephew. Elizabeth's family had been sheltering together at her cousin's house after a bomb had destroyed the kitchen and much of the living area in the family's two-storey Mackenzie Road home. The nearest screening centre was adjacent to the police station in Tanjong Pagar. They walked in silence, the children uncharacteristically quiet, sensing perhaps their elders' fear.

Black smoke from an oil tank down at a naval base set afire by the retreating British blotted out the mid-morning February sun. Thousands of people walked the streets. Japanese infantrymen were going into homes and forcing people to report to a screening centre. For the first time in seventy days, the constant sound of shelling, the dread whistle of bombs plummeting down from high altitude, the cacophonous boom of targets being obliterated, fighter aircraft strafing targets and machine-gun fire was gone.

During the Battle of Singapore, back when she had been working in a casualty centre as a volunteer nurse, Elizabeth had prayed for the fighting to end. The screams of the innocent being carried to beds, their limbs ripped off, or the horrifying gurgle of people drawing their last breath, eyes widened in a mixture of fear and agony, clasping intestines that were spilling from open wounds in their stomach, had been almost too much for her. But the sounds of children crying in the commotion and Japanese soldiers shouting instructions was no less sinister. The Japanese made no effort to conceal their jubilation. And why shouldn't they be jubilant? They had achieved the impossible: the Japanese had defeated a force twice as large and taken Britain's so-called impregnable fortress.

Elizabeth cast an eye over her family. Kon Vui, her eldest brother, was the only one missing. He was a dentist attached to a British unit, and she had no idea of his current whereabouts. Walking close to Elizabeth was her ten-year-old sister,

Marie Su-Tshin. She was three days old when their mother died in the family village of Kudat, in British North Borneo. Even now, in this fearful moment, Elizabeth could feel her mother's presence. 'I do not know how many people believe in the presence of the dead [. . .] I can feel her person always with me, and in our spiritual manner I talk to her and feel her very near.'[1] Elizabeth was twenty when her mother died in 1931. She had been sent to Singapore to receive a level of education beyond what could be offered in the mission schools of Kudat. She had not even known her mother was ill. After falling to her knees and praying to God – *have mercy upon her soul, shed light upon her soul* – Elizabeth made a promise to her mother: 'I promised her that I would look after her children for her.'[2] Little Marie was raised by their grandmother in Borneo before being sent to Singapore not long after her first birthday. Elizabeth's younger brother, Chau Vui, a boy of five at the time of his mother's death, was sent along with Marie. Chau Vui was his father's pride and joy. He was now putting on a show of courage: shoulders back, chin up.

They passed dead bodies that lay crumpled at the side of the road. After two months tending to the sick and wounded as a nurse, Elizabeth was familiar with corpses. She knew the length of time for the smell of dead flesh to become intolerable. These bodies had passed that time. Even the smoke from the house fires that had burnt incessantly for days could not diminish the stench. They had probably been rotting in the scorching heat and humidity for at least three days.

Leaflets dropped from Japanese aircraft in the lead-up to invasion fluttered amid the debris and the dead. They featured caricatures of the British – gluttonous, corpulent, idle – sun-baking on plantations while Asian slaves worked the fields. Others depicted an obese British colonial master dining on steak and chips while starving Indian troops looked on with desperate eyes and drooling mouths. Some had been sent for the benefit of the British (a crude depiction of a young European woman in the arms of a Japanese soldier with the caption 'Nightmare of your neglected wife: "Oh Tommy! I am going crazy!"'), while others were for the Malay and Indian population ('Pack up your troubles in your old kit bag and co-operate with the Nippon Army').[3] But there were no pamphlets for the Chinese. The Japanese had no intention of including the old enemy as equals or even subservient partners in their vision of an Asia ruled from the Chrysanthemum Throne. The Japanese had other plans for the Chinese.

Elizabeth and her family arrived at the Tanjong Pagar screening centre, where ropes and barbed wire cordoned off a large section of the road. Sentries were posted along wooden barricades in the lanes and roads that marked entrance points. This was one of five major screening centres. There were at least eight smaller centres dispersed throughout Chinatown. The sentries and administrative staff who manned these temporary facilities were ill-equipped to manage the exacting task before them. The municipal region of Singapore had a population of more than 850,000 people, at least 650,000 of whom were Chinese. That meant around 325,000 Chinese men were expected to be processed in these centres within a few days.

The Japanese, however, were not completely unprepared. The *Kempei Tai* – the military police unit attached to the Japanese army – had mobilised 1000 auxiliary personnel in preparation for the inspection. Spies operating throughout Singapore before the capitulation had compiled lists of undesirables – names and photos of men involved in Japanese trade boycotts and the China Relief Fund, an organisation set up in 1931 to send money to support efforts to fight the invading Japanese in the homeland. There were also lists of names of men who had enlisted in the Chinese Contingent of the Straits Settlements Volunteer Force. Additionally, the Japanese were also on the lookout for communists, looters, men with arms: anyone, in short, who might pose a threat to the new order. The great inspection was, in fact, a mopping-up operation for which the Chinese in Singapore provided a more fitting name: *Sook Ching*, literally 'purge through cleansing'. Beyond the important function of removing undesirables, *Sook Ching* was a deliberate ploy to assert control through intimidation and fear.[4]

The centre at Tanjong Pagar was a mass of confusion. As one man observed: 'Thousands were lining up to get clearance. And we got to squat along the centre row. They had a long table there, high ranking Japanese officer and a few other junior officers and maybe one or two Chinese or Malays who were either informers or in the police force.'[5] There were not only men of fighting age in the line, but women, children, the elderly and the infirm. Elizabeth and her relatives were not the only family to have received the wrong message. A Japanese sentry directed Elizabeth's family towards the line. They spent the night on the pavement. Another family shared some of their food, the majority of which was given to the children. The next morning, Elizabeth, the women and the younger children were told to go. They were each 'chopped' – stamped on the arm, certifying that they had been examined – and ordered to return home and stay off the streets. Choy Khun Heng, Chau Vui and Yong Than Yin were all ordered to remain.

Now that the air raids were over, Elizabeth elected to take the family back to the house on Mackenzie Road. The shell that had ripped off the side of the house had landed in an alley that was a popular thoroughfare running along the rear of the property. The bomb was likely intended for a platoon of British soldiers who had retreated to the position directly outside the house. Elizabeth had felt immense pity for them. 'I saw the British soldiers looking so desperate, and they were tired and thirsty and they came and asked for tea. And I remember my neighbours and myself boiled water and tea for them, and they were grateful for the drink.'[6] The next day, the fighters and medium bombers paid them a visit. 'The shelling was an awful experience – a shell would drop near, then another time would whizz just above our heads [. . .]

I remember the enemy planes coming so low with machine guns firing at the soldiers.'[7] God knew what happened to them.

While Elizabeth and her family sheltered at her cousin's home, the house on Mackenzie Road was ransacked. An enormous number of items – many of them precious gifts given to Elizabeth and her husband on their wedding day three months earlier – were taken. Elizabeth's sisters were distressed at the loss of family heirlooms and possessions. What did it matter now? 'That was immaterial,' Elizabeth said, and went about cleaning the house, when three drunk Japanese soldiers entered through the gaping hole left by the shell.[8] Elizabeth motioned for the women and children to stand behind her. She stood to her full height and held the gaze of the soldiers, whose smiles were crooked and voices too loud. They barely acknowledged the occupants, aimlessly picking their way through the house, taking the remaining few items that had not yet been looted.

A scream ripped through the living room. It was Kon Vui's wife, Maureen. Another soldier had slipped into the house unseen and gone upstairs to where Elizabeth's six-months-pregnant sister-in-law had been resting. The women looked at Elizabeth, horrified. The screaming from upstairs intensified. Elizabeth looked around the room, her eyes resting on a mattress. What on earth could she do with a mattress? She beckoned to the other women to help. With her sisters holding one end of the mattress and Elizabeth holding the other, they headed upstairs, the children following closely. The mattress, she hoped, offered a vague pretence to go upstairs and interrupt whatever horror was taking place. The Japanese soldiers cared little about the Chinese women lugging the mattress up the stairs and even less about a woman being raped in the room above.

Elizabeth banged on the door with her fist. 'Open, open, open!' she screamed.[9] The wailing inside abruptly stopped. A second later, the Japanese soldier – inebriated and perplexed – opened the door, his belt undone. Maureen was cowering in the corner of the room, tears streaking down her face. Without invitation, Elizabeth and her sisters made their way inside with the mattress. They placed it on the floor. Someone produced sheets and they set about making the bed, as if it was the most natural thing in the world. The soldier walked out. Elizabeth went over to her distressed sister-in-law and hugged her. The mattress proved a useful prop, a flimsy justification for entering that room. *Mentsu wo tamotsu* or 'saving face' – the principle of personal dignity and honour – is deeply ingrained in Japanese culture. The soldier beat a hasty retreat because of the shame of being looked upon by that small group of women and children. He could not tolerate the loss of face.

A day later, Elizabeth's father and husband arrived at Mackenzie Road. Her brother, Chau Vui, had been taken. Choy explained that he had been separated from his father-in-law at some point. After a long night of waiting, he was chopped on the arm and told to go. Worry lines were etched across Yong's face. He recounted that after the women, children, elderly and infirm were sent home, the work of the inspectors at the screening centres took on a new level of intensity. Order was maintained through the threat of violence. On occasion, a Japanese sentry would walk up to a man and punch or slap him in the face, usually without provocation. The few who dared retaliate were led away at gunpoint. Among the uniformed soldiers were Japanese men in civilian clothes. They wore crisp white shirts and tan-coloured sharkskin suits and their hair was neatly combed. These were *Kempei Tai* officers. They were looking for Tan Kah Kee, the leader of the China Relief Fund. Tan was gone, having managed to escape to Sumatra. In addition to searching for Tan, the *Kempei Tai* officers pointed out men in the line, accusing them of being communists or criminals, or of being involved in various anti-Japanese activities.

Chinese informants with hoods covering their faces to conceal their identity roamed the lines, pointing out men who were quickly arrested. Some hooded informants had taken the opportunity to settle scores, fingering men with whom they had a personal or professional feud. But most of these informants had been black-mailed or bribed. The Japanese also duped Chinese officers in the volunteer forces into identifying enlisted men. Captain Yap Pheng Geck pointed out men in his unit, having been assured by the Japanese that they would be safely imprisoned as prisoners of war.

The Japanese planners of *Sook Ching* had identified educated Chinese as a particularly dangerous group, since intellectuals could organise resistance and rebellion. Given the chance, they could transform the humble labourer into a deadly saboteur, the impressionable youth into a fifth columnist, the coolie into a spy. Intellectuals were deemed to be easy to spot. If a man had soft hands, for instance, he was probably sufficiently educated to have secured a job that did not require hard labour. Such reductive thinking was applied to men who wore glasses. What use did a labourer have for glasses? Even if he was a little short-sighted, glasses would only get in his way. As such, bespectacled men were pulled from the line and loaded into lorries along with countless others.

As the second day passed to night, Yong and his son sat quietly on the pavement with their heads down, knees folded up to their chests. By sunrise, the selection process appeared to have come to an end. An inspector approached Yong and demanded his name, which was duly given. Yong was chopped on the arm and told to go. The Japanese soldier regarded Chau Vui. He reached down and hauled the teenage boy to his feet and roughly pulled him away. Yong stood up and reached out for his son. Another soldier who had been silently observing approached and shoved Yong backwards. The old man nearly toppled over. When he regained his balance, the soldier raised his rifle and pointed the barrel at Yong's chest. Chau Vui was marched away. He turned to his father, his face a mask of terror. 'Daddy, what's going to happen me?' Chau Vui called out. 'Why can't I come with you?'[10]

With his father demanding that his son be released, Chau Vui was led away.

Three days passed and there was no sign of Chau Vui. Yong approached his eldest daughter and asked her to search for him. A man walking the streets of Chinatown was asking for trouble, regardless of whether he had been chopped or not. It was presumed to be marginally safer for a woman. Elizabeth left the house without hesitation. 'Of course, it was very dangerous to go about in those days, but seeing his misery and sorrow, I went out and tried to find out what had happened.'[11]

No serious effort had been made to tidy up the streets. The dead still lay amid the charred ruins. On returning to the Tanjong Pagar screening centre, Elizabeth found soldiers packing up the ropes, barbed wire and barricades. She approached a soldier and asked where the men loaded onto lorries had been taken. He told her to go home. She walked to the other screening centres in Neil Road, Tiong Bahru, Jalan Besar and elsewhere. The soldiers at those centres ignored her questions, perhaps not understanding her English. One even slapped her across the face. Desperate for any answers, Elizabeth approached the scores of other anxious wives, sisters and mothers who roamed the streets searching for their men. Most were nearly hysterical with worry. Elizabeth began to hear distressing rumours of mass killings. The situation was far worse than she could possibly have imagined.

The *Sook Ching* atrocities took two weeks to conclude. The men identified as undesirable were driven to Changi Beach, Punggol Beach, Bedok and various other sites. Some were machine-gunned to death after digging their own graves. Others were tied to trees and used as bayonet practice. Bodies were piled into mass graves or laid along the beaches, the ebb tide taking the corpses out to sea. The more diligent units tasked with carrying out the massacres walked the killing fields and bayoneted those who survived the machine-gun bursts. To expedite the process, some units simply poured drums of petrol over the bodies and set them alight, the dying writhing in agony as they were burnt to death beneath the bodies of their friends and family.

A European who lived not far from the beach at Bedok witnessed unimaginable horror:

> I looked through [. . .] our kitchen window and we saw lorry-loads of Chinese with hands tied behind their backs. And they were brought to somewhere near my place. A little further up there, there's a hill. And they went up the hill and they were told to run down. As they were going, they were machine-gunned. I heard that machine-gun like cracker firing. And we had tears in our eyes and we knew what was happening then. [An Indian friend went down there] and had to go and pour some oil because the bodies were not properly buried. He dug a hole and put the bodies properly in the hole and covered them because the bodies were getting rotten and the stench also.[12]

On 24 February, an article appeared in the *Syonan Times*, the daily newspaper that had replaced the *Straits Times*. Under the headline 'Nippon Army aims to bring happiness and peace to Syonan', the Japanese made reference to the massacre and the shallow justification for it: 'In order to eradicate the past misfortunes of the Syonan population[,] the Syonan Defence Troops have meted out severe punishment to trouble-brewing Socialists and [a] number of other Anti-Nipponese Organisations [. . .] These are abnormal times and rough and ready justice shall be meted out in the shortest possible time.'[13] When it was over, thousands had been murdered. The death toll remains a controversial matter. Official Japanese records put the number killed at 5000. Survivors claim this number is grossly underestimated. Most believe the death toll was at least 25,000, but probably closer to 50,000.

Elizabeth spent several hours scouring the streets for her brother and gathering information. She returned home heartbroken.

She knew Chau Vui was dead. Rather than tell her father that his favourite child was murdered, Elizabeth told Yong Than Yin that she could not find his son. Yong ventured outside, risking his life to search for his son. He spent days aimlessly wandering the streets, calling out for Chau Vui. His son never answered.

5

SUMATRA

Eighteen months before the attack

THE OLDER OF THE two Malay fishermen agreed to take the hapless European castaways and their dinghy to a village at the mouth of the river Musi. The northerly winds had grown stronger through the night. He was not interested in beating against the wind to sell fish to the coastal villages to the north. 'He said he could make no progress northwards till the wind went down, so might as well take us south.'[1]

The dingy was tied to the stern of the *prau*. After untethering the bowline from a mangrove branch, the *prau* was instantly seized by the tide. The younger fishermen unfurled the triangular sail, the *prau* listing gently as the canvas filled. Perched high at the end of a raised plank above the stern – 'rather like sitting on the high end of a sea saw'[2] – the elder fisherman was in constant motion. With his feet he worked the pedals that controlled the vessel's two rudders, reaching down and using his hands when sharper manoeuvring was required. His eyes darted this way and that, seeing everything – the rushing water, the sail holding the wind, the swamps, mangroves, trees and snags that threatened to capsize the *prau*, and the empty dinghy in tow, dancing 'like a walnut shell in a trout stream'.[3] Scott noticed, with alarm, that the banks of the creek tapered towards the entrance. 'I could not see how [the fisherman] was going to get out of a narrow creek 12 feet wide, winding round mangrove trees and through the swamp, against the tide and wind.'[4]

The dinghy – 'still cursed by its private and malicious devil'[5] – only complicated the matter. It was determined to be a nuisance: it 'tried to go to the left of trees when we had to go to the right, and stuck its head into every bush it saw'.[6] The younger fisherman had to leap off the *prau* when the dinghy was caught in a tree or a shrub, while the elder man adjusted the sail. They finally made it through the narrow headway and back out to sea, which had been whipped into a lively mood. Scott and others were in awe of the helmsman. 'It was the finest demonstration of seamanship I had ever seen.'[7]

There was still work to be done. Wind and tide threatened to drive the *prau* into the muddy banks and mangrove outcrops that lined the jagged shoreline. To make it safely out to sea, they would need to make a series of sharp tacks and jibes. To turn about in a hurry on the *prau* required three men, 'one steering and two on the sails'.[8] Above the sound of the wind and waves, the fishermen shouted to Langdon that he needed one of the castaways to steer. Scott volunteered. While he worked the rudders with the pedals – Langdon shouting translations of the elder's instructions – the two fishermen 'set about undoing ropes [to] swing the boom across, untying bits of string and wire, loosening here and tightening there'.[9]

Once safely clear of the shoreline, the mainsheet was paid out. The bow swung around to the south. Wind astern, the *prau* bowled along at a good pace. Perched high on his throne, Scott surely felt like a master of the seas as he harnessed the power of the wind and waves that he could feel through his feet. The others were in less exuberant spirits. Young Casey was yet to recover from bronchitis, Kendall was low with the fever and Allen had not fully recovered from nearly drowning the day before. Planzer was eager to find a ship. Whether it was Japanese or British seemed not to matter to the Swiss engineer. If they were captured by the Japanese, he was certain that 'they would somehow let him go on to the nearest Swiss Consul, so that he could find his way back [. . .] through some neutral country'.[10]

Scott thought Planzer was being too cavalier. With its airfield and oil refineries, Palembang – their destination – was surely a target of the Japanese. What obstacles might stand between them and the town? How could they even be sure that Palembang was still Dutch?

While keeping a weather eye on the horizon, Langdon noticed something in the mangroves off the starboard quarter reflect the sunlight. He called out to the others, pointing out the shining object. All hands turned shoreward. Waves gently lapped against the wing and fractured tail assembly of a Hudson aircraft that breached the surface of the water. The machine was 'entangled in shallow water in the mangrove swamp'.[11] Scott, who was relieved of his duties at the helm, wondered if this was the same aircraft that had circled the *Giang Bee* and the enemy destroyers three days earlier. Perhaps the destroyer's anti-aircraft gunners had put a hole in the petrol tanks or inflicted catastrophic damage? Or perhaps the Hudson had encountered a Japanese Zero on its return to Palembang. The cockpit was submerged in water. There were no signs of life. The *prau* sailed on, the men silent as the wreck fell from view.

By the afternoon, the *prau* was enveloped in the shadows of the palm-covered hills that loomed up in the hinterland. As they approached the estuary that marked the mouth of the Musi, large grey shapes appeared on the horizon: ships of war. Scott could see 'a chain of small boats [. . .] plying to and fro, linking [the ships] to the shore'.[12] They looked to be Allied transports lying off the estuary, depositing personnel and supplies. The men hooted for joy. Langdon remained silent, peering intently at the ships. Something was amiss.

Once in the mouth of the estuary, the *prau* no longer enjoyed the protective shadows of the hills. They were in full view of the ships. When within half a mile of the nearest transport, Langdon hissed an instruction to the fishermen. The two Malayans looked at him, confused. Langdon spoke again, calm but firm. This time, they snapped to action, preparing to bring the boat around. Looking closely at the nearest ship, Scott could make out a flag flying at the stern. They were close enough to see the blood-red disc and banded rays on a white field.

Langdon called out to Scott to get back at the helm. To turn the boat around quickly required the two fishermen on the sails. But they were close enough for the Japanese to see the men on the native vessel. Sitting a European atop that high perch would be inviting a disaster. A Malay hat was slapped on his head and he was handed a *baju* – a long-sleeved shirt with a rounded collar and a short slit opening down the front: the attire of Sumatran fisherman. Scott was helped up onto the raised seat to steer while the others lay flat on the deck. The fishermen pulled hessian sacks over them. Scott worked the rudders while the fishermen pushed the boom across and adjusted the ropes. The *prau* came about, the sails spilling the wind before being hauled in, the mast and rigging bracing as Scott brought her close up against the northerly. He set course for a bank of mangroves, bracing for a volley of enemy fire: 'I felt horribly conspicuous, stuck up there on the stern above the deck, with my back to the Japanese, expecting a stream of machine gun bullets through the small of my back at any moment.'[13]

But no bullets were fired. The *prau* was of little interest to the Japanese. They were evidently too immersed in landing personnel and supplies to concern themselves with local fishermen. Scott guided the *prau* into the estuary. He lost sight of the ships behind mangroves as the estuary split into rivers and creeks. With the Japanese landing in force, the Musi – with a channel deep enough to accommodate ships of war – was now too dangerous for them to sail. They would take a circuitous route to Palembang.

The elder fishermen took the helm and steered them a mile up the river to a seemingly 'deserted village [comprising] huts with attap (palm leaf) reefs built out on piles over the sea'.[14] As they approached the huts, the elder fisherman called out. A few villagers cautiously emerged. The *prau* was moored to one of the huts. The elder fisherman disembarked and engaged in a whispered conversation with the villagers. He returned looking 'very perturbed'[15] and cast off.

Once they had sailed beyond sight of the village, the fishermen brought the *prau* to the bank. After tying her to a mangrove tree, the elder fisherman turned to Langdon. He could no longer take them to Palembang. The villagers had said something, but he did not reveal what exactly. He simply implied that the six men on his *prau* were 'dangerous cargo'.[16] Clearly the Japanese had threatened to kill anyone who aided displaced Allied servicemen and civilians. Perhaps some local people had already fallen foul of the Japanese and had been tortured or executed as a warning to others. Whatever was said at the village, the fishermen were quite firm: come the morning, the six men would be returned to the dinghy and they would go their separate ways.

Langdon offered them extra money to take them to Palembang. But Palembang seemed to be the very last place the two men wanted to go. Besides, they said, 'their *prau* was a seagoing craft, [the] dinghy was now more suitable for the shallow creeks'[17] that wended their way up to Palembang. If the *prau* could handle the open seas, why not take them to Batavia, the capital of Java? Langdon even invited the fishermen to name their price. Langdon would give them $37 Singaporean as downpayment. The balance would be paid on arrival at their destination.

The fishermen declined. No amount of money was worth taking such risks. The fishermen would offer directions through the labyrinth of creeks, rivers and canals that offered a backway into Palembang. Beyond that, the Europeans were on their own.

Langdon gathered the men for a conference. They had two options: they could commandeer the *prau* by force and make for Batavia or attempt to row the dinghy to Palembang. Hurling the fishermen overboard seemed particularly ungracious – 'a mean return for their kindness'.[18] Besides, how would they sail such a complex craft? Scott slept uneasily that night. He knew that in short time they would very likely be captured. The next morning, he thanked the fishermen in Malayan and handed the elder of the two his precious watch. It was a gift from his wife. 'I hated parting from it but preferred to see it used by someone who had befriended me than taken from me by a Japanese.'[19] Much later, Scott felt vindicated when he saw Japanese guards wearing watches taken from prisoners. At least his watch would keep time for a friend.

The six men farewelled the fishermen and boarded the dinghy. They pushed off and rowed south. The river cut through mangroves and swamps. Creeks and channels branched off like the veins from an artery, drawing intricate patterns through the surrounding floodplains. The river narrowed into a placid backwater hemmed in by cultivated coconut and banana trees. There were rice paddies and exotic vegetable gardens too. Occasionally they would pass small villages comprising open huts. They called in on the villages and were given fresh fruit and drink. But the further north they rowed, the reception became less hospitable: 'one village headman shoo'ed us away at once, giving us some cold rice only'.[20] He told them a Japanese patrol had paid his village a visit in launches. The headman was terrified.

As the sun set, they moored the dinghy to a branch and rested for a few hours. The following morning, they rowed to the village of Kenten, 6 miles north of Palembang. The fishermen had told them that this was as far as the backwaters would take them. If they chose to remain in the dinghy, the only way to Palembang was by the Musi. Otherwise, they would have to abandon the dinghy and walk the rest of the way. As they approached, half-naked men and women stopped and stared at the curious sight of six large Europeans crammed into the small wooden boat, slowly making their way down the river. They needed to rest. Allen, Kendall and Casey were still in poor health. They beached the dinghy and were met with the warmest reception they had experienced since parting ways with the Malayan fisherman.

A village elder assigned the six Europeans to a Chinese father and his English-speaking son, who were instructed to tend to the needs of the white men. They were given the run of a small two-room house. Food, coffee and cigarettes were brought in. The generosity of the Chinese boy knew no limits. Nothing was too much trouble. When he discovered that Scott was a pipe smoker, he fetched a pipe and tobacco. When one of the men requested sugar to sweeten his freshly brewed tea, the boy sourced boiled sweets and ground them to a fine grain, apologising for the substitute sweetener.

Scott could have been back in Singapore before the war, smoking his pipe and enjoying refreshment after a long day of work. The relaxed atmosphere was broken when the boy told them Palembang had been captured by the Japanese three days previously. 'Palembang had been the goal of all our sweat and efforts for five days. We were dead beat.'[21] Planzer held firmly to his conviction that the Japanese would arrange for his immediate transportation to the nearest Swiss consulate. Scott was not convinced. Planzer's identifying documentation was at the bottom of the Banka Strait with the *Giang Bee*. Even if the Japanese believed him, why would they go to the trouble of helping an individual from a neutral country? But Planzer would not be dissuaded. The next day, he would march into Palembang and surrender to the Japanese.

For Allen, Kendall and Casey, meanwhile, the news out of Palembang sapped their last energy reserves. They would stay in Kenten and take their chances with the villagers. That left Langdon and Scott. The officer and the diplomat retreated to the other room and discussed their options.

If the goal was to avoid capture at all costs, then they would have to row back to the coast and find a seagoing vessel and sail it to Java. It was an option beset with variables and unknowns. For starters, they would need food and water to make the 300-nautical-mile journey to Java. Finding villages willing to help would be tough. 'The Japanese were punishing individual Malays and whole villages for helping Europeans, especially British and Dutch soldiers.'[22] Then there was the matter of getting hold of a seagoing vessel. The likelihood of finding a Malay willing to trade a boat they could actually sail for a measly $37 was remote. That meant taking a vessel by force. But even if they managed to row the 70 miles back to the coast without being captured, secured enough food and water for a lengthy sea voyage and even commandeered, without weapons, a vessel that could sail 300 miles without maps or compass – 'going down a strange coast, patrolled by Japanese warships'[23] – what would they find in Java? Now that the Japanese had Malaya and almost certainly Singapore, Java was the next great jewel to claim. If Java fought on, then it would be besieged or subject to attack.

And then there was the thought of Allen, Kendall and young Casey. These men had no interest in surrender and no means of escape. Langdon felt especially concerned for Casey, who, as a naval rating, was his subordinate and responsibility. Scott felt a similar kinship to the rest of the men: 'we did not want to leave the others'.[24] But the prospect of capture was almost worse than death.

They held off making a final decision. They would wait until next morning. Better to make a call with the clarity that comes from sleep. The sick men turned in early. Langdon, Planzer and

Scott, meanwhile, feasted on more fresh food and sweetened tea. Scott packed the bowl of the pipe the boy had handed him with fresh tobacco. Tamped down evenly with his thumb, it was soon burning clean and even. It was Wednesday, 18 February. Six days had passed since they had left Singapore. They had survived aerial bombardment, sinking, and two days and nights aboard a dinghy in stormy seas, they had come within half a mile of a large enemy invasion force and they'd managed to row a great distance to within walking distance of Palembang. That they were even alive was a miracle. They were enjoying each other's company, glad to have overcome such adversity and grateful for the food in their bellies.

Neither of them saw anything abnormal about the luxuries showered on them. That it was totally inconsistent with the hostile reception they had received at other villages did not seem the least bit suspicious, even though they were much closer to Japanese-controlled Palembang. Neither stood sentry outside the hut or kept watch on the goings-on in the village. It was a fatal misjudgement. The headman's chief concern was the welfare of his people. The Japanese had warned him of the consequences of harbouring enemy soldiers or European civilians. While the white men rested, the headman slipped out of the village, setting off for Palembang to report that there were fugitives taking refuge in his village.

6

MACKENZIE ROAD

Seventeen months before the attack

TOKYO'S GEOPOLITICAL VISION FOR the whole of Asia was called *Dai Tōa Kyōeiken*, or the Greater East Asia Co-Prosperity Sphere. Promoted as a Japanese-led coalition of Asian nations underpinned by the alluring appeal of self-government to create an Asia for Asians, it was in fact a facade for Japanese imperialism. Rather than casting off the yoke of colonial rule, an old system of European control and exploitation was replaced by an even more oppressive Japanese version. Throughout South-East Asia, conquered nations became vassal states, overlorded by an oppressive Japanese administration. Japan's occupation and management of Singapore was perhaps even more paternalistic, controlling and violent than in many other occupied territories. And for good reason: Singapore was a rare jewel in the Emperor's crown.

Situated at the crossroads of the Malay Peninsula and the Malay Archipelago, and with a deep-water harbour and a large aerodrome, Singapore had obvious strategic military value. But it was so much more. This island had been a symbol of British strength and prestige for well over a century. Capturing Singapore was a moment of immense historical significance – a world-changing event and a monumental achievement in the history of Imperial Japan. As if to confirm its coveted status, Singapore would be the headquarters for Japan's Southern Expeditionary Army Group, whose commanding officer, Field Marshal Count Terauchi Hisaichi, selected the Cathay Building on Orchard Road, the tallest structure in South-East Asia, for his office. Much of Japan's campaign strategy in South-East Asia and the South-West Pacific and the movements of over one million personnel was masterminded, organised and ordered from within this skyscraper.

But as with other conquered territories, winning this great prize in battle would prove far easier than maintaining control over the population. Singaporeans were generationally indoctrinated to believe in the superiority of the British. They needed to understand that this island belonged to Emperor Hirohito now; the British were gone forever. The Japanese started with a name change. Singapore became Syonan-to*, which meant variously 'Brilliant South Island' or 'Light of the South Island'. The use of 'Syo' – meaning 'brilliant' or 'bright' – was a nod to Emperor Hirohito's title of Syowa Emperor, a word composed of two kanji characters meaning 'shining' and 'peace'. The clock was brought forward one hour to match Tokyo time. Japanese language and customs were taught in schools. In some classrooms, the children paid homage to Hirohito, facing Tokyo and bowing each morning. Japan's public holidays became Syonan's holidays. And at the cinemas, a steady schedule of Japanese movies and propaganda were screened.[1]

While engaging in these less-than-subtle attempts to indoctrinate the people into accepting Japan's divine right to rule, the occupying force attempted to simultaneously portray life in

---

* 'Syonan-to' referred to the whole of Singapore Island. The shortened 'Syonan' generally referred to the municipal area.

Syonan as no different to life in Singapore. In truth, Syonan was a paranoid Japanese colony that would morph into a place of vice and corruption, bringing financial advantage to the Japanese. The new administration tapped the island's gambling fever, running lotteries under the guise of funding health and social programs for the needy while lining their own pockets. Gambling dens were opened in adult amusement parks adjacent to newly established comfort houses, where young women and girls predominantly of Korean, Malay or Indonesian descent were forced into sex with Japanese officers and soldiers. Syonan's 'comfort houses' were, as one historian notes, 'a system of legalised military rape on a never-before-known scale and the number who were taken into sexual servitude will never be known'.[2] Japanese soldiers profited from the black markets, which increased in direct proportion to the scarcity of essentials along with hyperinflation. The people endured great misery that worsened as the war raged on. Every ethnic group – whether they be Malays, Thais, Formosans, Koreans or Indians – suffered. But no community suffered as much as the Chinese.

The Chinese of Syonan were a diverse community comprising five different ethnicities – Hokkien, Cantonese, Teochew, Hakka and Hainanese.[3] These groups spoke different dialects, celebrated different traditions and observed unique customs. They were, however, united in their fear and loathing of the Japanese. As many as 250,000 Chinese migrated to Singapore in the decade preceding Britain's capitulation, taking the Chinese population to more than 670,000. Most of the newly arrived Chinese had fled their wartorn homeland, narrowly escaping the atrocities that trailed in the wake of Japan's brutal conquest of China. Should the fires of rebellion burn across Syonan, the Japanese believed, the flame would be lit by the Chinese. To this end, the *Sook Ching* massacres were deemed necessary in nipping insurgency in the bud. In murdering tens of thousands of men of fighting age, the leaders and footsoldiers of a rebellion were being removed. As for those who survived the atrocity, *Sook Ching* served as a warning to anyone who would violently act on their anti-Japanese sentiments. If there were voices advocating a widening of the killing to a genocidal scale, something of which the Japanese had proven themselves capable in Nanking and elsewhere, then they were tempered by one simple fact – the Japanese in Syonan needed the Chinese.*

The Chinese were the farmers, blacksmiths, mechanics, electrical machinery workers, tailors, shoemakers and carpenters. They were the painters, automobile drivers, street vendors, rickshaw pullers, traders and shopkeepers and assistants. They were the doctors, teachers, coolies, domestic servants and clerical workers. They were, in short, the white- and blue-collar labour that drove the island's economy, staffed the schools and hospitals, kept the public amenities and services running. In character and culture, Syonan-to, just like Singapore before it, was Chinese.

Rather than carry out a genocide of the Chinese, the Japanese implemented a policy of restriction, intimidation and control. Prosperous Chinese businesses were co-opted and run by the Japanese and, in some cases, Chinese property was confiscated. Money was used to entice Chinese informants – many of whom had lost their jobs and needed to feed their families – to rat on neighbours and friends. Japanese patrols were beefed up around Jalan Besar, Tanjong Pagar, Paya Lebar, Chinatown and all the other densely packed Chinese suburbs. Soldiers barged into Chinese homes, demanding to see registration papers or chops on arms while looting and pilfering anything not bolted down. It was a manufactured climate of fear intended to dissuade anyone from embarking on a career as a fifth columnist.

---

* The Japanese army was not beyond committing such an atrocity. From December 1937, an estimated 200,000 to 300,000 Chinese civilians and disarmed soldiers were murdered, and tens of thousands of women were raped in the Chinese city of Nanjing (Nanking) over six weeks. The Rape of Nanking is generally considered one of the worst atrocities in history.

The Japanese need not have worried about Elizabeth Choy. The prospect of being an insurgent or engaging in any sort of anti-Japanese activity never entered her mind. She was pre-occupied with keeping her family safe. Living in a house with a blasted wall that opened out onto a busy alley was untenable. The soldier's attempted rape of Elizabeth's sister-in-law made that fact painfully obvious. Elizabeth needed to find an alternative living arrangement for her family. The neighbour's garage offered a solution. It was an airless room that smelt of engine oil, with a hard floor and wooden walls lousy with insects. But the garage door could be locked from the inside and that was something. To provide some fresh air, the door could be kept open during the day and shut at night when drunk soldiers were more likely to invite themselves in. The garage provided a sanctuary. Not only was it inconspicuous and unprepossessing – the last sort of place you would expect to find people sleeping – it was secure. The neighbours gave Elizabeth and her family permission to move in. The garage was swept, the walls washed clean of bugs and the mattresses transferred from the house.

The first weeks in the garage were hard. The dreadful sleeping arrangements, the continued looting of practically everything in Mackenzie Road, the fear of Japanese violence and the tragedy of Chau Vui's disappearance weighed heavily on them all. None more so than Elizabeth's father, who became increasingly despondent over the murder of his youngest son. In this period of gloom, the safe return of Elizabeth's eldest brother, Kon Vui, provided a des-perately needed morale boost. Kon Vui was spared by the Japanese because of his qualification and professional experience. Syonan needed dentists. Maureen, Elizabeth's sister-in-law, was beyond relieved. The prospect of raising a child in an occupied territory without her husband was unimaginable. Maureen surely melted in her husband's arms when, unannounced and unbidden, he returned.

It was decided that Maureen would give birth in the Mackenzie Road house, the garage being deemed unsanitary. A mattress was brought back from the garage and taken upstairs to the family home and placed in the very room where Maureen was nearly raped. She at least had one thing in her favour: she had married into the Yong family and most of the Yong women were nurses. Two of Elizabeth's sisters, Annie Su-Ni and Dori Su-Yung, had followed numerous aunts and cousins into the profession. Although untrained, Elizabeth had been a volunteer nurse in the medical auxiliary unit, treating wounded soldiers and civilians in those harrowing first two months of the Pacific War. Sister Annie – temperate, kind and warm, she would become known as the 'the ray of sunshine' by internees she nursed during the war – would serve as midwife. Several other women in the family would drop in throughout the labour to assist. Kon Vui was instructed to remain downstairs, where he paced the living room for twenty-four hours. A howling cry signalled the end of Maureen's labour. She gave birth to a boy who had a set of lungs on him that could be heard across the neighbourhood. They named him Victor.

Elizabeth's unbridled joy at the arrival of little Victor was tempered by the reality that the family needed money. Choy Khun Heng's bookkeeping job at the Dutch-owned Borneo Company ceased to exist when the company folded in the face of the Japanese invasion. Elizabeth's two sisters were working as nurses but earning a pittance. That meant they were heavily reliant on Kon Vui, who had taken out a lease on a dental room recently vacated by its previous occupant, who had evacuated before the capitulation.[4] But Kon Vui's salary was not enough to put food on the table for the entire family. Elizabeth needed a job, yet her chosen profession was out of the question.

Elizabeth had been teaching – 'the noblest, most difficult but most satisfying profession', as she would describe it[5] – for a decade. She was exceptional at it. After a two-year stint at Church of England Zenana Mission School (CEZMS) – the oldest girls' school in Singapore, which subsequently became St Margaret's – Elizabeth was headhunted by Canon Reginald

Sorby Adams, principal of St Andrew's. Adams would write of his star recruit:

> From the first, even before she received her training in teaching, [Elizabeth] showed a love and leadership among small children that gave them so much more than material knowledge. Her warm sympathy with them enabled her from the outset to build up in them values that I have seen come to fruition in her pupils as they grew up. It was always a joy to watch [her] at work with her 'family', which her class inevitably became.[6]

Teaching was more than a job for Elizabeth. It was her vocation. During the Battle of Singapore, Elizabeth remained at St Andrew's as a volunteer nurse after the school was converted into a casualty centre to manage the influx of civilians wounded in Japanese bombing raids. Some of the very classrooms where Elizabeth had taught – rooms that had days earlier echoed with children's laughter – were transformed into a hellscape of maimed, burnt and grievously injured people of all ages. The wounded were stretchered into the school clutching their stomachs with blood-drenched hands where shrapnel had ripped deep gashes. Some were missing limbs, others scorched beyond recognition. The floor under each bed was befouled with blood and dirt. The stench of sweat and flesh hung in the stifling air of every classroom. The trauma of that experience and the long, stressful hours of work very likely contributed to Elizabeth's miscarriage in the weeks before the capitulation. Although she would never ascribe the loss of her pregnancy directly to her harrowing nursing experience, Elizabeth developed an abiding conviction that this was not the work God had intended her to do.

But what *could* she do? The Japanese would never permit a Chinese teacher employed in schools styled in the British fashion in Syonan's education system, nor would she want to participate in the indoctrination of children. In the end, she would find work in a hospital, but not as a nurse. Sister Annie – who was now working at Miyako Byōin, formerly a mental facility renamed and repurposed to treat Japanese military personnel and civilians – had an idea.* Miyako was up in Yio Chu Kang, a long way from the municipal area and with next to no transport. Elizabeth remembered, 'It was a very out-of-the-way place [. . .] no shops around and very hard to get food or if you [wanted] anything to eat [you] just couldn't.'[7] There was a dire need for a canteen on site to feed the medical and administrative staff. Annie spoke with a leading doctor about Elizabeth and her husband's situation and relayed a message.

'Why don't you come to our hospital and start a tuckshop, a canteen?' the doctor asked. 'Our nurses have nowhere to go. You will have a canteen there, it will be a great help to them.'[8]

The Choys agreed. A room was made available for the canteen. Before long, it became a repository of medicine and food dropped off from the families of the patients. Food, messages and lucky charms from Indian, Chinese, Eurasian and Malayan families would be left with Elizabeth to be delivered to loved ones in the hospital.

The reputation of the Choys grew. Soon, Chinese men of influence, successful businessmen who had accumulated great wealth before the war, would drop off at the canteen boxes of supplies and medicine, possibly sourced from the black market. While busily at work sorting food and supplies, Elizabeth was approached by a priest who had been ministering to the faithful in the hospital and, on occasion, delivering last rites. He greeted Elizabeth warmly. The two were known to each other, having met at St Andrew's. He was a close friend of Canon Adams and no ordinary priest. His name was Reverend John Leonard Wilson, the Bishop of Singapore. And he had a favour to ask of Elizabeth.

---

*   Some patients were simply evicted from the hospital and told to go home. Around 500 were sent to St John's Island, a sparsely populated place ill-equipped to cope with an influx of mentally ill patients; many would die of starvation.

7

THE SURVIVOR OF RADJI BEACH

Sixteen months before the attack

THE JAPANESE AMPHIBIOUS AND airborne infantry forces were twice the strength of the British, Australian and Dutch infantry units tasked with defending the southern Sumatran city of Palembang. The Japanese were determined to take the city. The nearby oil refineries in Plaju were deemed crucial in feeding Japan's insatiable war machine. The airfield, moreover, was large enough to accommodate several squadrons. The battle was over in two days, though establishing an occupying force would take longer, as the units that spearheaded the invasion were already being deployed to other theatres. Logistical and administrative support was desperately needed. In the intervening period, the Dutch municipal authorities functioned as a proxy to fill the shortfall in people.

As such, when the village headman of Kenten reported that six Europeans were taking refuge in his village, it was not a Japanese soldier to whom he reported but a Dutch official. The Dutchman – deeply fearful of being caught aiding displaced

European civilians – instructed the headman to feed and shelter the six men, but to not let them leave. He then alerted the Japanese. The following morning, Robert Heatlie Scott and his five fellow travellers awoke to a small unit of Japanese soldiers waving rifles in their faces. The men looked on forlornly as the 'precious dinghy [was] taken away'.[1]

Scott and the others were effectively under house arrest. The Chinese boy continued to wait on them, providing food and drink and even tobacco for Scott. Relative to the abject misery and rough treatment the men expected, this experience was akin to being held in a gilded cage. Two weeks later, they were marched, barefoot, to the newly established Japanese headquarters in Palembang and then taken to a nearby prisoner-of-war (POW) camp that held 150 enlisted men and around a dozen officers. The camp's internees comprised mostly airmen and ground personnel captured at the fall of Palembang. Along with Scott, Allen, Kendall and Planzer, there was a smattering of other civilians in the camp: 'G.W. Tarry, a Malaya Broadcasting engineer, who had got ashore from the *Giang Bee* by lifeboat; Rasmussen, an amusing little Danish merchant skipper, remarkably like Hitler, whose ship had been set on fire and sunk by the Japanese; and a New Zealand engineer named Gordon Burt.'[2]

The civilians were essentially made subservient to the officers, a situation Scott found galling by dint of the idiocy of the Royal Air Force commodore who was the ranking officer: 'a nitwit who seriously believed that the Japanese could be persuaded to send a plane to drop a list of [their] names on Allied Headquarters in Java or in Darwin.'[3] Scott reluctantly participated in making the list, knowing all along that it would amount to nothing. Why would the Japanese risk flying over an Allied military base simply to drop a piece of paper out of a plane that listed the names of enemy personnel? It called to mind the delusional beliefs of Planzer, who clung to the notion that the Japanese would recognise his neutrality and arrange passage for him back to

Switzerland. This sort of utter detachment from reality, coupled with high-minded statements about gentlemanly conduct in war, riled Scott, particularly when he witnessed officers speculating on the war's end.

'It will be over by the northern autumn of 1942,' one asserted.[4] Allowing for the land and sea the Japanese already controlled after three months of fighting, such predictions seemed ludicrously optimistic. Scott could no longer bite his tongue: 'I won no friends when stating that, in my opinion, the war had another three years to run.'[5] His opinion was dismissed as the ill-informed musings of a non-military man. He did not deign to inform these men that he knew a good deal more about what the Allies were up against than any of them. The officers may know his name, but they knew little of his background. The less they knew, he reasoned, the better.

While under house arrest in Kenten, Scott had agonised over whether to give his name to the Japanese guards. This senior figure in the government of Singapore and a diplomat with extensive knowledge of China and Japan would be of great interest to the Japanese. But if he concealed his true identity and the Japanese ever found out, they might conclude that he had something to hide. He elected to tell the Japanese his name and gave his occupation as a civil servant. It was a catastrophic mistake.

At the end of March 1942, Scott and the other civilians in the POW camp were relocated. Scott was glad to be rid of the commodore, who was at once intolerable and incompetent, even asking Scott to 'report on the sewage system [only to find] he had already asked two others to do the same job'.[6] The civilians were taken to the western edge of Palembang, where an abandoned school had been repurposed as a civilian internment camp. An assortment of around twenty Dutch houses and bungalows, whose former residents either fled before the invasion of Sumatra or were forcibly removed, were now accommodating internees.

There were around 120 British and Eurasian women and children in the camp, including thirty-two nurses from the 2/13th Australian General Hospital. These nurses were the surviving members of a party of sixty-five who were evacuated from Singapore aboard the *Vyner Brooke* – a cargo vessel requisitioned by the British Navy as an armed trader – with 188 women and children on board. The *Vyner Brooke* was bombed off the coast of Banka Island and sank bow first within thirty minutes. Around 150 survivors took to the lifeboats or leapt straight into the water. Most of the women Scott encountered had been in the water for twenty-four hours. Aided with lifebelts, they washed up on the shores of Banka Island, having swum through waters infested with crocodiles and highly venomous sea snakes. Eventually, they made it to the Japanese-occupied town of Muntok. They were taken prisoner and held captive in the Muntok cinema before being transported across the Banka Strait to Palembang. But one of the nurses among the group had an altogether different tale to tell. Scott never learned which one. The others concealed her identity. Should the Japanese discover her devastating secret, they would all be executed. Her name was Vivian Bullwinkel.

Vivian was among twenty-one nurses who managed to find a berth on one of the lifeboats that was launched before the *Vyner Brooke* went down. Over the course of the next three days, the boats all made it to Banka Island. In addition to the steady trickle of survivors from the *Vyner Brooke*, they were joined by service-men, civilians and merchant sailors, all of whom had been on vessels sunk *en route* to Palembang. While encamped on Radji Beach, a sandy beach around 5 miles north-west of Muntok, the decision was made to surrender to the Japanese following failed attempts to source food and fresh water from local villagers.

On the morning of 16 February, a Scottish merchant officer, Lieutenant William Sedgeman, who had assumed command of the group, went to Muntok to alert the Japanese authorities of their whereabouts. While he was gone, Matron Irene Drummond – the ranking nurse – decided the civilian women and children, highly agitated from hunger, fear and exhaustion, should make a start for Muntok. A walk of several miles through rough jungle scrub would be arduous for all of them. Better to get it over with. Matron Drummond decided to remain on the beach and tend to the sick and wounded men.

Not long after leaving Radji Beach, the group of women and children sent off by Drummond encountered Sedgeman leading a unit of Japanese soldiers bearing rifles with bayonets fixed. One soldier lugged a heavy machine gun. The Japanese instructed the women and children to wait while they continued on to Radji Beach. The women ignored the order and made for Muntok. It was a decision that almost certainly saved all their lives. The Japanese unit they had just encountered belonged to the 229th Infantry Battalion of the Japanese Army's 38th Division.*

After leaving the women and children at the side of the track, the soldiers marched on, arriving at Radji Beach mid-morning. Vivian Bullwinkel counted twenty-five soldiers, noting their uniforms and weaponry: 'They all had khaki shirts and trousers after the style of jodhpurs and little caps with a star in front of them and they all carried rifles with bayonets on them [. . .] The one in charge was only a small fellow and was dressed very nattily and much tidier than the others. The suit he had on seemed to have been tailored.'

The Japanese marched around half of the men off behind a headland. Then they returned to gather the next group. A couple of soldiers remained to keep an eye on the women. There came the sudden report of a succession of quick shots, slightly muffled by wind and waves. The Japanese came back and sat down in front

---

* On Christmas Eve during the Battle of Hong Kong, members of the Japanese Army's 38th Battalion had stormed St Stephen's College, which was being used as a hospital. Wounded British, Canadian and Indian soldiers were bayoneted in their hospital beds. Three nurses were dragged off and gang-raped. Their mutilated bodies were found on Christmas Day.

of the nurses. They cleaned their bayonets with rags. Nobody spoke. The officer in the tailored suit, sword hitched to his belt, stood up and told the nurses to walk down to the shoreline. They all knew what was about to happen, but they had no choice but to follow the order. Before entering the sea, Vivian turned to see the machine gunner had set up under a canopy of trees 25 yards back from the beach. As they stepped into the waves, Matron Drummond's voice rose above the sound of the sea. 'Chin up, girls,' she said. 'I'm proud of you and love you all.'[8]

Vivian Bullwinkel recalled, '[W]hen we got up to our waists [in water] they started firing up and down the line with a machine gun.'[9] Matron Drummond was among the first shot. She fell to her knees, her glasses falling from her face. While she groped helplessly for her glasses, the machine gunner sent another burst into her back. Vivian continued to march out to sea, awaiting her death. She could hear the other nurses reciting prayers. Some spoke the names of loved ones. 'The conduct of all the girls was most courageous. They all knew what was going to happen to them but no one panicked. They just marched ahead. We knew we would certainly be killed. We just mutely waited. There were no cries for mercy. We knew no appeal would touch the Japs' heart.'[10] The machine gunner swept his weapon along the length of the line, the nurses crumpling into the water, the waves turning red. Vivian felt a sharp pinch in her lower back. She fell forward. 'Being young and naive, I always thought that if you were shot by a bullet you'd had it. With the force of the bullet I overturned and lay there. As time went by, to my amazement, I was still alive.'[11]

The force of the bullet had turned her body around so that she was floating face-up. She did her best to keep still as the waves washed water into her mouth. Fighting the urge to vomit, Vivian allowed the waves to take her to shore. 'I haven't any idea of time but when I found the courage to sit up and look around, there was nothing – none of the girls anywhere, none of the stretcher patients and the Japanese had gone too.'[12] The wind on her wet skin caused Vivian to shiver. She scurried up the beach and hid in the jungle. Under the canopy of a palm tree, she took stock of her wound. The bullet had struck her above the left hip, miraculously missing organs. She was alive, but utterly exhausted. She lay down and fell into a deep sleep, waking an indeterminate period of time later to the sound of soldiers chattering. A short distance away, the murderers were making their way along the beach. Vivian was poorly concealed. She kept still, praying that none would turn her way. They continued on. Vivian did not move for several hours. Desperate for a drink to slake her thirst, she crept towards a nearby spring. On arrival, she knelt down to take her first sip when the sound of faint voices gave her a start: 'Where have you been, nurse?'[13]

The voice belonged to Private Cecil Kingsley, an English soldier. Kingsley's bloodstained hands clutched his abdomen, where the Japanese had run him through with bayonets. He had already lost part of his arm in the bombing attack on the *Vyner Brooke*. Were it not for Vivian's care, Kingsley would likely have died that day. For nearly two weeks, they hid in the jungle, sourcing food from local women who – against the instructions of their understandably terrified chief – provided cooked fish, rice and chopped pineapple. But the pair would not be able to live in this fashion for long. If they wanted to survive, they would have to take their chances and hand themselves over to the enemy.

They walked the track to Muntok and were eventually stopped by a Japanese vehicle, a naval officer in the back seat. Fearful of summary execution, Vivian and Kingsley were ordered into the car, fed biscuits and given tea before being driven to the cinema at Muntok.

The gamble to turn themselves in paid off. The Japanese guarding the POWs and internees in the cinema did not belong to the notorious unit responsible for the atrocity at Radji Beach. Vivian was reunited with the surviving nurses who had been taken prisoner weeks earlier. Private Kingsley, meanwhile, was taken directly to a medical ward the prisoners had established. The following day, Vivian was summoned to his bed after he had repeatedly asked for her. He thanked her for keeping him alive and then suggested that it was best for her to leave. 'I will stay with you a little longer, Kingsley,' she said, taking hold of his hand.[14] Kingsley closed his eyes and died minutes later.

The other nurses bombarded Vivian with questions. Where had she been? How had she survived? And what was the cause of the small burnt patch at the back of Vivian's uniform? Vivian revealed that the uniform was ripped and burnt by a bullet that had passed through her body. Shocked, the nurses insisted on a medical examination. The wound where the bullet entered her back left loin appeared to be healing. But the wound where the bullet had exited through her abdomen below her ribs was pus-filled and infected. She was not in danger. But how had she suffered such an injury? Vivian batted away their questions. Were the Japanese to discover that she had survived the massacre, they would undoubtedly execute her. What better way to wipe all evidence of an atrocity than killing the sole survivor? She also worried that telling the other nurses would only endanger their lives. But the persistent questioning wore her down.

> The girls kept asking after the others. I tried to deny that I knew anything but finally I broke down and told them. Our senior Sister went to speak to some Englishmen and told them the story. They told her I should forget about it, deny everything and admit to nothing because not only would I be taken out and shot, but everyone else [would be] as well.[15]

The nurses followed the advice. Eventually, they were shipped across the Banka Strait aboard a rundown freighter and transported to the POW camp at Palembang, where they were met by the ranking officer – the air commodore who had so irked Rob Scott. The commodore immediately made representations to the

Japanese guards, seeking to keep the nurses in the camp. These women, he argued, belonged to a unit in the Australian Army. As such, they should be treated as military personnel. The commodore figured that the nurses would enjoy greater protection in the POW camp than elsewhere. The Japanese ignored his demands, transferring the nurses to the civilian camp.

Before leaving, Vivian met the commodore in private. She revealed the horrifying atrocity on Radji Beach. It is impossible to say whether he was responsible for discussing what Vivian told him with others. But by the time Scott and the other members of the dinghy party arrived at the civilian camp, they already knew the tale. 'I realised who they were as soon as I met them,' Scott would observe. 'But they would not tell me which was the one who had survived the slaughter: they were anxious to keep it quiet till after the war, for fear of being all disposed of to suppress the evidence.'[16]

The massacre of the nurses dominated the whispered conversation among internees. There was, however, another gruesome murder that for Scott was particularly chilling. In Muntok, an Australian gentleman – white-haired and elderly – was beaten by the Japanese and forced to dig his own grave, before he was stood at its edge and shot. Prior to his execution, the man had remonstrated with the Japanese for taking his personal possessions. He was also seen making entreaties to an officer in Japanese. His name was Vivian Gordon Bowden, the Australian Government Commissioner in Singapore.

Scott first met Bowden in Shanghai in 1933 and had recently sat with him on the Governor's War Council in Singapore. Prior to his execution, Bowden had attempted to use his diplomatic status as a protective cover His effort backfired. To date, no Japanese soldier or officer had quizzed Scott on his background. The very fact that Scott knew the story of the nurses demonstrated that people were too cavalier with information. It also revealed to him 'how news gets round between camps and even in prison, between cells'.[17] Eventually, the Japanese would discover his identity. It was just a question of time.

The nurses were relieved that Scott and the men had arrived. The commodore's concerns for their wellbeing were valid. A middle-aged English rubber broker from Singapore – one of the very few men in the camp – was appointed leader of the civilian internees. In effect, he became responsible for all the prisoners, which included a high proportion of young women, among whom were a number of Eurasian ladies who had 'boldly described their profession as either "cabaret" or "dancing"'[18] upon entering the camp. The arrival of these women prompted the immaculately attired and deeply vain officer in command of the camp, Captain Miachi, to convert one of the bungalows into a club. The plan was to 'stock [the bungalow] with drinks, put a couple of women in charge, and get younger women to attend for [the Japanese officers'] entertainment'.[19] Four other bungalows either adjacent to or near the 'club' were prepared with beds reserved for the Japanese and their companions.

The rubber broker – presumably operating under the assumption that refusal on his part would result in his execution – raised no objections. He even helped get things set up, assigning 'the bibulous wife of an army sergeant'[20] – who was taken prisoner in Singapore – as club manager. Miachi, who spoke reasonable English, indicated that the white women would be rotated through the club to serve drinks and provide entertainment. Nobody was under any illusions as to what the Japanese truly wanted.

The nurses would suffer anything – even death – rather than submit to being sexually enslaved by Miachi. They flatly refused to cooperate and were threatened with execution. Given what they had already endured, the nurses had every reason to believe the Japanese would come good on their threat. Miachi need not execute the nurses. He had a far more effective lever to pull. He cut rations. Scott knew that 'this put the [nurses] in a very awkward hole: there were a lot of children, and their mothers blamed the nurses for starving the children'.[21] Being responsible for denying food to hungry children and the sick and enfeebled was intolerable for the nurses. When the Japanese announced that twelve nurses were expected at the club's opening night, they had no choice but to relent. They would not, however, meekly surrender to Miachi's depraved whims without staging some form of resistance.

Excluding the sick and those wounded from the bombing raid on the *Vyner Brooke*, every nurse would go. They were enacting the safety-in-numbers principle. In an effort to make themselves unattractive, the nurses wore either tattered uniforms or filthy frocks. They rubbed ash and dirt in their hair and wore shoes with no socks. One nurse wore no shoes at all. They looked like vagrants and it paid off. After several hours of stilted conversation, the Japanese sent them off with strict instructions to dress properly or suffer the consequences.

For several weeks, the nurses continued their policy of non-cooperation, refusing to submit to the Japanese. One nurse even slapped an officer in the face when he tried to kiss her, knocking him to the ground. Astonishingly, her brave act went unpunished, probably because there were no witnesses. The officer did not want to lose face by admitting he had been physically bested by a woman. But these were Pyrrhic victories. Miachi was losing patience. He decided on punitive measures. For refusing to sexually enslave themselves to the Japanese, the nurses, along with all the internees, would endure severe rationing. Women and children were now forced to survive on the tapioca roots they dug up. By now, 'practically the whole camp was ranged against them'.[22]

Accounts differ as to how it ended. One nurse told Scott it all came to a head one night when she and three others were summoned to the club. At all times, they would remain together, even if it meant following a nurse into the bathroom. The nurse had a knife concealed in her frock. Were one of the Japanese soldiers to take her to one of the bungalows and force himself on her, she would attempt to kill him. The only question was whether to 'knife him on the road [to the bungalow], or to wait till they got inside'.[23] The Japanese were well into their cups when they insisted the girls go with them outside. The nurses refused. Fed up with their recalcitrance, the officers got physical. The nurses made for 'the bathroom [then] through the back door, and across the fence down to the house of the doctor'. The doctor was Jean McDowell, a Scot and their 'one friend in the camp'.[24]

McDowell was appalled at this latest outrage. She was on good terms with a Dutch doctor whose practice was the medical clinic of choice for senior Japanese officers. Perhaps he could exert some influence on the behaviour of Miachi and his men? After hearing the four nurses recount their terrifying ordeal, McDowell 'left the camp, slipped past the guard, and went to [the] Dutch doctor'.[25] Disgusted, she reported the goings-on in the club to the Japanese general commanding the area, who in turn summoned Miachi and his officers, where 'a first-class row'[26] ensued. The club was closed down.

Scott and the others arrived shortly thereafter. The nurses were relieved to see them. Although there had been two brave civilian men who had insisted on accompanying the women to the club, they could not expect to provide around-the-clock protection to the nurses. These new arrivals bolstered the number of body-guards and might even act as a deterrent. Scott and the others all 'valiantly promised to see them through any more trouble and told them to come to our bungalow at once for protection if they got in a jam'.[27] Privately, Scott was worried: 'what, after all, could we do if a party of Japanese officers turned up drunk one night and went into the nurses' quarters?'[28] If they came to their aid, they would very likely all end up dead. Scott need not have worried. The necessity to play the hero never eventuated. Within a week they would be transferred from the women's camp to a prison in Palembang. Scott's misery would soon begin to compound.

8

THE BISHOP

Three months after the attack

ELIZABETH CHOY WONDERED HOW long it would be before the newly arrived and incessantly talkative prisoner would be dragged from the cell and beaten. He at least had the sense to speak in a hushed voice. It was, however, merely a matter of time before he'd be caught. The severity of his beating would depend on who caught him. A less vigilant sentry might knock the wind out of him or send him back to his cell with a black eye. Other sentries, the men who relished violence, might inflict a life-long scar or break a bone; he might even lose sight in an eye. The new prisoner was oblivious to the danger. He had not come to terms with the reality of his circumstances. He was convinced of his invincibility, deaf to the whispered warnings of the more experienced cellmates. His bravado – his fearlessness – was all the more incredible because he could hear prisoners being tortured on the upper floors. That the same fate awaited him did not enter his thinking.

Each prisoner's experience in this foul place was different. Nevertheless, Elizabeth had come to believe that every prisoner of the Japanese went through predictable emotional stages during their incarceration. This man, only recently incarcerated, had moved past the initial shock of his circumstances. He was growing accustomed to the constant buzz of the electrical lights that burned night and day; the wretched stench of the open concrete commode in the corner of the cell; the shrieks of agony and torment of those being interrogated; the sight and sound of the cockroaches and other bugs that scurried across the floor and up the walls. Having survived this unpleasant baptism, he now passed into the next phase – a steadfast belief in how to attain utopia. 'When one was fresh in the cell,' Elizabeth recalled, 'one could think about what an ideal world would be, and how to have peace in the world.'[1] He was also in his most generous frame of mind.

The other prisoners hemmed in closely around him, waiting to pounce when their new cellmate was issued his ration of rice. 'The food was given to us three times a day, morning, noon and evening – a tiny ball of rice with some vegetables or some tiny pieces of fish or meat, and nothing else.'[2] The others in the cell had seen this behaviour in the new arrivals, knew that this was the brief moment where he might share his food. He had not been living on starvation rations for long enough to truly understand what it meant to be hungry. Convinced of the righteousness of his mission, he would back up his high-toned moralising by forgoing his own precious food to bolster the meagre offerings of his ravenous cellmates. Torture might well attend his transition out of this delusional stage. More likely the talk of world peace would abruptly stop 'when hunger pangs demanded satisfaction. By then it would be nigh impossible to think constructively.'[3] At that point, thoughts of utopia would become a distant memory. Like the other prisoners, he would now jealously guard every precious morsel, ever watchful of his cellmates pinching the pitiful scraps of protein mixed into his portion of rice as his bowl was passed back through the cell.

The final phase, when he came to realise the naivety of his utopian convictions, would occur during his first interrogation. The instruments of torture – the iron rod, the knotted rope, the bucket of water, the sharpened wooden slat, the battery – would take him to scarcely imaginable levels of pain and torment. If he survived interrogation, and many men did not, then his only hope to keep his sanity was to look inward. If he could find in that solitude a happy memory or stillness or faith in God, then he might ward off madness. Elizabeth could not really help him with that. But she could help in other ways.

Despite the agonies and humiliations of her ordeal, Elizabeth's faith in God was resolute. God was good. God was sovereign. God spared her life and He had done it for a reason: to help others. When Elizabeth looked around her, she saw others wallowing in despair. 'The people were so depressed. They didn't know what to do.'[4] After her most recent interrogation, Elizabeth had committed to improve the appalling circumstances of life in prison for her cellmates. She started by cleaning up the cell.

Excluding the terrifying prospect of being tortured, few elements of incarceration dispirited the prisoners more than the filthy commode in the corner of each cell. The tap above the commode was the cell's only water source. This meant the prisoners had no choice but to use the tap to wash and hydrate while inhaling the vile stench issuing from the latrine's filthy, moss-covered raised concrete platform. To wash in such a manner was humiliating and degrading, particularly for the women who passed through Elizabeth's cell. She felt that her background equipped her better than most for the unpleasant experience. 'It's not so bad for me because back in North Borneo we were used to it; we didn't have proper facilities there anyway. Even for some households in Singapore in those days, there were no proper toilets. But for the [others] it must have been really bad for them, to exist like that in the cell.'[5]

There was nothing in the cell that could be used to clean the commode. She needed cleaning equipment. The only solution was to ask the Japanese sentry outside the cell, which meant breaking the cardinal rule – no talking in the cells. Elizabeth reasoned that it was worth the risk. Besides, what could this sentry do to Elizabeth that had not already been done to her? She cleared her throat and told the sentry outside the cell that she needed a scrubbing brush to clean the commode. The sentry looked at his feet, bent down and picked up a stone that was half the size of fist, and passed it through to Elizabeth.

The *Kempei Tai* attained information by exposing individuals to unrelenting discomfort, pressure, fear and, of course, violence. They also used humiliation. It would be reasonable to conclude that the sentry saw in Elizabeth's request an opportunity to degrade her. Cleaning a filthy commode with a stone – an object ill-suited to such an endeavour – would make the job more arduous, adding to the demeaning and undignified nature of the exercise. Elizabeth did not see it that way. She saw the stone as a gift and the sentry's decision to give it to her as an act of charity. She scorched the surface of the commode with ferocious intent. Periodically, she would turn on the tap, washing the loosened pieces of excrement and fungus down the hole. Gradually, the green and brown skin of the commode returned to its original grey. The sharp stench was reduced too. In the act of her scrubbing, Elizabeth discovered some holes at the base of the commode that were the source of the fetid water that had leaked around its perimeter. She tore strips off her cherished blanket – the one possession she was permitted to keep – to plug the holes.

The improvement in the horrific living circumstances of the detainees could only have been marginal. Elizabeth was just grateful to be able to do something that helped. A job of work – no matter how disgusting – was considerably better than the 'truly unbearable'[6] nature of sitting for hours on end doing nothing; where, as the ancient proverb foretells, idle hands are the devil's workshop. Elizabeth went looking for something else to do. Sometime later, when a senior Japanese officer toured the prison and expressed outrage at the filthiness outside the cells, Elizabeth was only too happy to volunteer to clean it up. In a unit obsessed with power dynamics, class and face, a sentry cleaning the corridors in full view of the prisoners was an intolerable situation: a self-wounding humiliation that would pierce the aura of invincibility that induced such fear in the prisoners. The sentries were only too happy to acquiesce to Elizabeth's offer.

Scrubbing brushes and buckets of water were sourced. Elizabeth slithered out of the cell and set about washing the corridor, furtively taking glances into other cells. They were all crowded with sick, tortured and desperate people. Elizabeth observed with satisfaction that many prisoners were conversing in the sign language she had learnt. In all probability, prisoners proficient in this discreet form of communication were returned to different cells following interrogation and so were able to teach their new cellmates.

When the sentry was not looking, Elizabeth signed a greeting to several prisoners, who responded in kind. She would have recognised some of the men – Wee Aik Tek, the businessman who had raised money (much of it from his own pocket) for the internees in Changi; John Long, the British internee who had been the courier, collecting the money, supplies, radio parts and messages that Elizabeth and Choy had kept in the canteen to be smuggled back into Changi. But there was one man in particular she wanted to see. As she made her way further up the corridor, Elizabeth saw him. He smiled at her through a bruised and bloodied face. That the Bishop of Singapore could even maintain a smile was a miracle. But inside he was heartbroken to see Elizabeth. Somebody must have talked.

Reverend John Leonard Wilson was a man of medium build, with a receding hairline, a trusting expression and a round, cherubic face. He was consecrated Bishop of Singapore in July 1941, having served as Archdeacon of Hong Kong and the Dean of St John's Cathedral for three years, and if there were any lingering questions as to the plan God intended for Wilson in Singapore, they were swiftly answered when war broke out in the Pacific three months after he took charge of the bishopric. In the maelstrom of battle, the civilians and soldiers of the Singapore Diocese needed more than the Eucharist; they needed food, shelter and medical care. With the hospitals overrun with wounded, the bishop cleared the pews from the cathedral and repurposed the nave as a casualty clearing station. But not even God's house was safe from the incessant bombing and shelling. On the last day of the battle, a shell punched through the cathedral roof and exploded in the aisles, killing sixteen men.

Hours before the British capitulation, the bishop administered communion to Lieutenant General Arthur Ernest Percival, General Officer Commanding Malaya, before he was driven to the Ford Motor Factory to negotiate terms of surrender with the Japanese. Later that day, the bishop held evensong. Outside, the guns were silent; the furious din of exploding bombs was mercifully at an end. The wounded lay in the bloodstained nave before him, nurses tending to those on the brink of death. The stink of open wounds and rotting flesh mingled with the charred ruins of the bomb damage sustained the previous day. Otherwise, all was silent, 'the stillness broken only by the tread of boots on the stone paving and the low murmur of voices'.[7] A shaft of late-afternoon light slanting through the shattered windows struck the bronze crucifix above the altar from where the bishop looked out to his desperate congregation.

He saw the wounded forlornly return his gaze. In the darkening haze 'studded with the glow of many cigarettes, and the occasional flare of a match',[8] the bishop instructed the faithful to join him in singing the hymn 'Praise, My Soul, the King of Heaven'. He was later asked how he could reconcile the agony of the battle that had just been lost along with the tragedy of the occupation to come with some of the words of the hymn – 'Father-like he tends and spares us [. . .] in his hand he gently bears us': how could a sentiment like this be felt amid such horror? Wilson pondered the question. He would later write, 'This is not an easy faith to keep when so many demands are made upon us but the love of Christ constraineth us and casteth out all fear.'[9] The bishop knew that these people needed comfort and assurance to prepare them for what was to come. 'It means that God cares for us whatever our situation we may be in,' he responded. 'His inward peace [. . .] courage [. . .] this is what we prayed for. That we will come through with honour.'[10]

When the Imperial Japanese Armed Forces took control of Singapore, Bishop Wilson along with the Assistant Chaplain of the Cathedral, Reverend John Hayter, and Canon Reginald Sorby Adams, Principal of St Andrew's School, were spared internment. God, the bishop reasoned, had sent him an ally in the form of a Japanese officer named Lieutenant Andrew Tokuji Ogawa. A member of the *Nippon Sei Ko Kai*, the Anglican Church in Japan, Ogawa – who 'served for a few days on the staff of Changi Internment Camp and was then made Director of Education and Officer in Charge of Religious Affairs'[11] – was educated in an American Episcopal university. He was devoutly Anglican at a time when Anglicans in Japan numbered in the low thousands. Ogawa was responsible for keeping the churchmen out of Changi. He had argued to the Japanese authorities that the bishop and his two most trusted aides would assist in maintaining civil order and smooth the transition into the occupation.

'Ogawa was extremely useful in seeing that there was religious liberty,' the bishop wrote. 'His task was not always easy, because the military police were suspicious of his Christian interests, and he took a courageous stand on this point.'[12] Ogawa became the bishop's trusted friend. On Whitsunday, three months after the occupation began, the bishop preached a sermon at the cathedral and Ogawa read the lessons in English.

With Ogawa's influence, the bishop, Reverend Hayter and Canon Adams were permitted to live in Bishopsbourne, the bishop's stately two-storey residence. Ogawa was a regular guest. They spoke of the need to spread the word of God to all those suffering. He continued to prove that he had clout, securing the release of Canon Adams from *Kempei Tai* custody after his arrest for 'throwing a packet of cigarettes over a fence to Australian POWs'.[13] Ogawa also arranged for the three men to visit Singapore's POW and internment camps, to tend to the spiritual needs of those held captive, frustrating the *Kempei Tai*, who were anxious to sever all contact between the British and the Asian populations of Singapore and itching to have Bishop Wilson interned.

While visiting Changi, Wilson was approached by a member of Changi's Central Committee. The committee, which comprised several internees who held senior positions in government and business before the capitulation, effectively acted like an elected body representing and advocating for the internees. An office was even set aside near the guardroom at the entrance to the prison for the committee's use. The Japanese, the committee member explained to Wilson, were not doing enough to keep the internees fit, healthy and alive. Rations were inadequate both in substance and nutritional value. The meat or fish that was provided to the internees around twice a week was of 'a very uncertain factor'[14] and oftentimes rotten. There were, moreover, no green vegetables, nor any medicine.

Despite the committee's repeated entreaties, the Japanese blankly refused to supply medicine and additional food to the internees, including children, the elderly and the sick. They were not averse, however, to 'making purchases on behalf of the Committee'[15] for the camp, naturally taking a commission for making whatever purchases were required. The committee borrowed money from internees – some of whom had brought tens of thousands of dollars into the camp – who were given

'IOUs backed by the bank and government representatives'.[16] This money was dished out to the guards for the purchase of essential supplies.

But the well was drying up. Another source of finance was needed, and quickly. In addition to buying essentials to keep the internees alive, the committee also wanted to have enough money to provide an allowance for the internees. The bedrock of any functioning society, no matter its size, is a financial system. If the internees had money to spend, they would be motivated to earn more by selling their own produce or offering services. It would all depend on cash, and quite a lot of it. The bishopric was not exactly awash with dollars. What little money remained in those first few months of the war was needed for the ever-growing numbers of desperate and destitute. But Wilson promised to do what he could. He visited the parishes of St Matthew's, Holy Trinity, True Light, St John's and Pasir Panjang, where Anglican services in Cantonese, Foochow, Teochew, Hokkien and Hinghwa continued. He moved among each congregation, asking for donations for the interned and imprisoned. But there was never going to be enough. The use of his influence to prise money from those who could not afford to lose it sat uneasily with him. Besides, he had a better idea.

The bishop was not only a well-connected man; he also proved to be a resourceful one. In a meeting whose location has been lost to history, he secured an initial loan of $200,000 from a man he described as 'a neutral',[17] to be paid in instalments of $10,000. The loan – an enormous sum of money at that stage of the occupation – was advanced to the Church 'to be repaid after the war with six per cent interest'.[18] The bishop would never share the identity of the neutral with anyone, not even John Hayter or Sorby Adams; nor did he tell them the negotiated interest rate. The less they knew, the better for their own safety and the safety of the neutral, who would not be looked upon kindly by the Japanese if the arrangement ever leaked.

The neutral's name was Hans Schweizer-Iten, President of the Swiss Club in Singapore and Managing Director of Diethelm & Co., a successful Swiss trading company that established a presence in Singapore in the late nineteenth century exporting and importing textiles, machinery, chemicals and consumer goods. It was Schweizer-Iten whom the bishop first approached to request a loan from the Swiss business community. The businessman was only too happy to assist.

In those first few months of the occupation, no greater problem bedevilled the Swiss in Singapore than finding a means to remit money to Switzerland at a time when there was no way of getting their cash and investments out of Japanese-controlled areas. Nothing devastates an economy quite like war and occupation. Anyone could see that food scarcity, unemployment and hyperinflation would be economically ruinous. The bishop was offering the Swiss a solution. They could withdraw their money from the banks in Singapore or sell stocks in Singaporean business interests and investments, hand the cash over to Schweizer-Iten, who would in turn loan the money to the Anglican Church – a centuries-old institution with probably the best credit rating attainable in Singapore – and then turn a profit on the repayments when the debt was due at the end of the war.

Although highly profitable, the arrangement was not without considerable risk for Schweizer-Iten. Since the beginning of the occupation, he'd been on the *Kempei Tai*'s watchlist as someone with deep connections with the former British administrators of Singapore. Begrudgingly, Schweizer-Iten's neutrality was acknowledged, but senior voices inside the *Kempei Tai* who remained convinced that the Swiss businessman was in league with the enemy needed to be assuaged. A compromise was reached: Japanese officers would regularly pay visits to Schweizer-Iten's home and a solider would escort him whenever he ventured outside.

To prevent the Japanese from discovering the financial agreement struck up between the Church and the Swiss business community, Schweizer-Iten and the bishop devised a plan for when and where the exchange of money took place. The plan – communicated by way of intermediaries that included a Japanese army sergeant named Fujibayashi, who was on Schweizer-Iten's personal payroll and who helped keep Schweizer-Iten out of trouble – was straight out of the pages of an Eric Ambler or Graham Greene spy novel. 'We used to go to the same second-hand bookshop in Bras Basah Road, where I used to deposit in a book the money I advanced to him as a loan to the Anglican Church,' Schweizer-Iten later wrote. '[The bishop] usually entered immediately after I left and got hold of the sums of money placed there for him. We thereby avoided visible contact, as we both were mostly supervised.'[19]

For the bishop, receiving the cash instalments from Schweizer-Iten was a relative cinch compared to smuggling the money into Changi. Taking the money into the camp himself was out of the question, since every time he visited an internment or POW camp, he was searched for contraband. Not only would the money be confiscated, the bishop would likely end up in a cell. The guards might be willing to turn a blind eye to the discovery of small sums of money, and probably help themselves to a slice of the pie on its way in. But such a huge amount of money entering the camp could not be ignored. It could be used for nefarious means, such as purchasing arms to aid a rebellion. The bishop needed a smuggler.

He shared the problem of a how to get the cash into Changi with Sorby Adams and John Hayter. Adams knew someone who might be able to help: a woman who ran the canteen with her husband at Miyako and who had once been his star teacher at St Andrew's. The devout teacher was a congregant at St Andrew's with her family. Wilson paid her a visit at Miyako and explained what he needed. She agreed without hesitation, despite the bishop warning her of the considerable risks involved.

With Elizabeth Choy on board, the bishop arranged for his secretary – an Indian named K.T. Alexander – to regularly drop in to the canteen with consignments of up to $10,000. Keeping himself at arm's length was a clever move; involving Alexander in the operation was ingenious. Like most in the Indian community, Alexander enjoyed a far greater degree of liberty than European, Eurasian, Malay and Chinese civilians. Anxious to win the Indian people to their side, the Japanese largely left them alone. He could enter the hospital without harassment or, it seemed, suspicion.

For a year, Elizabeth and her husband would receive bundles of cash concealed in parcels and stuff the money into cigarette cartons, small pipes or other receptacles before handing it all over to a courier, an internee named John Long. Once a week at least, Long would drive sick internees to Miyako from Changi in his ambulance with a Japanese sentry – usually someone different each trip – who had been assigned to accompany him. Some of those sentries were unaware of the operation. They believed that Long visited the canteen to fetch food supplies for the camp. For those sentries who knew what was going on, Long bought their silence with a bribe.[20]

Elizabeth would hand over the goods to Long, inside of which would be secreted thousands of dollars. Long drove the money back to Changi, smuggled it through the gate by concealing it within his vehicle and then delivered it to the camp treasurer, a banker named Walter Thomas Yoxall. Like any good banker, Yoxall carefully accounted every cent brought into the camp and jotted it down in a book. Portions of the money were used to pay for food and medicine. Every internee received an allowance of $5 a month. The rest was hidden in Yoxall's cell for safekeeping.

The *Kempei Tai* were oblivious to the money being smuggled into Changi. But they harboured deep suspicions about the bishop. A year into the occupation, Ogawa – who had been promoted to captain – was warned that he had grown too close to the bishop and that he was probably being used by the Church. They all but instructed him to sever all contact. On his last visit to

Bishopsbourne, Ogawa warned Wilson that he could no longer protect him. In anticipation of his arrest, he made arrangements for Alexander to continue collecting the cash advances Schweizer-Iten left at the bookshop and deliver the money to the Choys. Weeks later, in March 1943, the bishop, Hayter and Adams were interned in Changi. Ogawa had been closely monitored by the *Kempei Tai*. He lost his post as Director of Religion and Education – which had necessarily put him in the orbit of European Christian leaders – and was sent to Sumatra in May. Without his protector, Wilson would inevitably be at the mercy of the *Kempei Tai*. They had their man in Changi; but for months they lacked a pretext to interrogate him.

The opportunity came in the form of an attack down at the harbour that set Singapore's night sky ablaze. The bishop was bundled into a car and driven to the YMCA. He was accused of being a spy and a central figure in the attack. The *Kempei Tai* had long suspected Wilson of being up to no good, and set upon him with malignant, vicious force:

> I was made to kneel with a sharp-edged piece of metal behind my knees. My hands were tied behind my back and I was roped under the knee-hole of a desk in a very painful position. Japanese soldiers tamped upon my thighs and twisted the metal behind my knees so that it cut into the flesh. I remained in this position for nine to ten hours, sometimes being interrogated, other times being left under two Japanese guards who kicked me back into position whenever I moved to try and get release.[21]

This was the first day of his ordeal. On the second day, he was hauled back from his cell to face his confessors and tied onto a table face-up then flogged with ropes. At a certain point, the interrogator asked Wilson if he still believed in God. 'I do,' was the bishop's response.

'Then why does God not save you?' asked the interrogator, resuming the torture.

'He does,' responded the bishop, through gritted teeth, 'but not from the pain. He saves me by giving me the spirit to bear it.'[22]

Six guards proceeded to flog Wilson 200 times with a thick rope. He muttered 'forgive them'[23] between each punishing stroke before he fell unconscious. Nevertheless, he looked upon his torturers with pity and forgiveness: 'By the grace of God, I saw those men not as they were, but as they had been. Once they were little children [. . .] and it's hard to hate little children.'[24]

It was clear to the bishop's interrogators that there would be no hope of extracting a confession through physical torture. After regaining consciousness, they told him that he would be taken to a dungeon and denied food and water until he confessed to all charges. If he continued his denials, Wilson was told, he would be left to die. He was carried back to his cell. There was no skin on his legs from the thighs to the ankles. It took three weeks before he could walk again. Each morning, he waited for the Japanese guards to come good on their promise. To keep himself from falling into despair, the bishop found solace in the pitiful view offered through the tiny window high up at the back of the cell. 'I could see the glorious red of the flame of the forest tree. Behind the flame tree I glimpsed the top of Wesley's church.'[25] To the song of the golden oriole, the bishop would mouth the words of Wesley's hymns. Through this practice, he 'felt the presence of God and received from Him the strength and peace which were enough to live day by day'.[26]

It was an experience that strengthened his resolve to never incriminate anyone else, even if they did put him in a dungeon. He was no spy, but he knew every detail of the smuggling operation that he had devised and all the individuals involved. Although it was a humanitarian effort, the clandestine nature of the operation could easily be misinterpreted as something nefarious. Were he to share what he knew with the guards, Wilson would bring pain, misery and possibly death to many people. He would hold his tongue.

Clearly somebody else was sharing the secrets of the operation with the Japanese. How else could Elizabeth be here? She would rightly feel aggrieved at this betrayal. But instead of resentment staring back at him, the bishop saw in Elizabeth's expression a look of hope. She appeared elated to be so close to him. The mere knowledge of his presence within the YMCA had, in fact, been a source of great comfort to her: 'I felt much better because until then I thought I had been taken in for some terrible reasons, but when I heard the bishop was there, I knew it must be connected with our sending supplies to those interned.'[27] Now that she was close enough to reach into his cell, Elizabeth felt something like jubilation.

An idea came to her. She waited for the sentry guarding the corridor to turn his back before signing a greeting to the bishop. She then requested communion. The bishop gestured to the man next to him. There was a flurry of movement as prisoners signed a message back to the man sitting closest to the commode. A cup of water drawn from the tap above the commode was passed to the bishop. He consecrated the cup of water as a substitute for wine and a tiny portion of rice as a substitute for bread.

From the corner of her eye, Elizabeth could see that the sentry had turned away. She crept towards the bishop, who passed the 'bread' through the bars of the cell. The Body of Christ. Elizabeth placed it in her mouth. Wilson then quickly passed her the cup of water. The Blood of Christ. She took a small sip and smiled, spiritually nourished. She knew in that moment that she could bear anything. Elizabeth smiled and returned to her scrubbing.

9
THE DIPLOMAT

Sixteen months before the attack

ROB SCOTT WAS DESTINED to become a diplomat. Born in Petershead, Aberdeenshire in 1905, he was the second of four children. His mother was a schoolteacher and his father a civil engineer whose career required travel. In 1915, Scott's father was appointed city engineer in Port of Spain, and the family relocated to Trinidad. The peripatetic nature of Scott's upbringing required him to be nimble, to adjust to completely new environments and novel situations. He became expert at ingratiating himself into different social hierarchies, a skill that would be extremely useful in his professional life. He was, in short, exceptional at befriending people. He spoke with a received British pronunciation, an accent picked up from his primary years of education at Inverness Academy and distinct for its clarity, precision and formality, certainly nothing like the heavy inflections and intonations of the Scottish brogue of his birthplace. His voice was, in a sense, hard to place among the myriad accents of the British Isles but could be said to have had associations with the upper classes.

Not that Scott was a snob. He exemplified Kipling's advice, to 'talk with crowds and keep your virtue, or walk with Kings – nor lose the common touch'. A former colleague described him thus:

> He was the most accessible person in the world. A constant stream of people came to see him. He brought to his work a tireless energy, an accurate and shrewd mind that was brimfull of ideas, great tact in dealing with people, so that all those that met him liked and respected him.[1]

Indisputably, Scott was a fierce intellect. He completed his schooling in Port of Spain at the age of fifteen and was awarded an island scholarship to New College, Oxford. The college declined his admission on account of his age but were prepared to take him two years later. While he waited, Scott returned to Inverness Academy, his alma mater employing him as a teacher. Once admitted into Oxford, Scott attended various cultural activities – plays and concerts – participated in literary societies and sporting clubs, all the while keeping a rigorous social life. This was the early 1920s, a period of changing cultural and social dynamics within the university. The Great War had altered Oxford in ways that went beyond the addition of numerous memorials for the fallen that had been raised across the campus. A changing intellectual climate was reflected in the Oxford curriculum, where there was a growing emphasis on economics, global politics and the social sciences.

But it was in the Oxford Union – where a new tradition was being forged of debating transgressive and subversive topics like socialism, communism, pacificism and women's rights – that the lens of Scott's worldview was widened. During his time as the union's secretary, the society played host to Winston Churchill, H.G. Wells, Harold Macmillan and numerous other public figures, authors and radical thinkers. Scott would also be a member of the committee of the National Union of Students and a regular British delegate to student conferences in France, Switzerland, Denmark and elsewhere. An avid supporter of the League of Nations, he served as the inaugural president of the British Universities League of Nations Society, whose members were described as 'youthful hot gospellers for the League'.[2]

After graduating, Scott, who had transferred to law, was called to the bar at Gray's Inn in 1927. But a career as a barrister was not in Scott's future. He craved something more adventurous, something more exotic: to be, as it were, a witness and participant in the changing world order. He would realise this future in the consular service. Scott sat his civil service examinations, a comprehensive and demanding process that tested applicants on their intellect, communication skills, adaptability, integrity and interpersonal prowess. Of all applicants, Scott was awarded third place across all the tested domains, and so essentially had his pick to work in any of the vast array of consulates in the largest empire in human history. He chose a geopolitical zone he found endlessly fascinating, and that was rightly perceived to be on the cusp of immense upheaval – the Far East.

In 1928, Scott was sent to Peking as a graduate, where he spent three years learning Mandarin. His quick mastery of the language led to his appointment as the junior interpreter in the Chinese Secretariat as ancient enmities between Japan and China were escalating. In 1931, he was dispatched to Manchuria to observe the Japanese military build-up in the northern Chinese province, where he visited the Japanese encampments as troops amassed ahead of an imminent invasion. After the Japanese attacked, Scott was embedded with the Chinese officers – again as an independent observer – witnessing the futile efforts of the Chinese National Revolutionary Army to resist the Japanese in the famous battle of Nonni River Bridge, one of Japan's first and most violent incursions in the Manchurian conflict. Scott's timely and accurate accounts of the battle and the subsequent fighting along the Siberian border caught the attention of Sir Miles Lampson, the British Ambassador to China. Sir Miles appointed Scott his private secretary.

Scott's meteoric rise in the consular service was built on intellectual rigor and exceptional judgement. But these qualities only partly explain his success. He was at once charming and discreet, exceedingly useful characteristics for a diplomat. Above all, he was liked. A handsome man with a broad, open face, a stylish moustache and dark hair that became progressively flecked with grey as the 1930s rolled on, Scott was completely at ease at social gatherings, asking questions of others – often in different languages – and keenly listening rather than babbling into silence or dominating conversation with his own opinions and views. Scott was seen to be a leader and an organiser, a man you could trust.

The subsequent two months with Sir Miles were tumultuous. He arrived in Shanghai at the beginning of 1932, shortly before the January 28 Incident. Several powers, including Japan, had extraterritorial rights in Shanghai. Japan would use this as a pretext to extend its influence beyond Manchuria, sending several ultranationalist Buddhist monks with instructions to provoke a fight with the locals, a mission the monks accomplished by shouting anti-Chinese slogans to a group of worked-up civilians. In the ensuing scuffle, a monk was killed, a factory burnt down, a mass anti-Japanese protest staged and a Japanese military assault authorised. Thirty thousand Japanese troops were sent to Shanghai, supported by a significant naval presence. The fighting started on 28 January 1932 and in the month-long battle that followed, 17,000 were killed, most of them civilians. Nobody, least of all Scott, seriously believed that the intervention of the League of Nations and the subsequent ceasefire would curtail Japan's expansionist ambitions in China.

Scott remained with Sir Miles for two years, looking on as China was ripped apart by communists, nationalists and an increasingly belligerent Japan. On Sir Miles' recommendation, Scott was made vice-consul and then acting consul in Canton in 1935.³ He held several titles over the following two years, including British Trade Commissioner in Hong Kong, Commercial Attaché in Shanghai – during intense fighting with the Japanese – and finally Assistant Financial Adviser to the British Embassies in Japan and China. Now fluent in Mandarin and – after intense study – proficient in Japanese, Scott toggled between Tokyo and Shanghai as the two countries waged all-out war.

Scott took leave in 1939, returning to England at the very outbreak of war in Europe and was seconded to the Ministry of Information, where he was duly appointed Director of the Ministry's Far Eastern Bureau. His blended knowledge of the region's fraught political dynamics, diverse cultures, military capabilities and social constructs was probably without equal in the Foreign Service. Scott's appointment required him, among other things, to organise British propaganda throughout Asia from scratch. He quickly set up offices in Tokyo, Shanghai, Chungking, Hong Kong, Bangkok and Batavia, and peopled them with British press attachés. There was, at least in 1939, misplaced hope that through diplomacy and propaganda, Britain might be able to sway Japan to remain neutral in the affairs of Europe while constraining their ambitions through Asia, thus averting a catastrophe in the Pacific. In a memorandum to the Secretary of State for the Colonies, Scott wrote:

> We cannot hope that official propaganda directed towards Japan will have any immediate affect on opinion in Japan but there would be a long run advantage if it could be designed to encourage those elements in Japan who are at present powerless but whom we must hope to influence ultimately.⁴

He drafted messages that avoided criticism of Emperor Hirohito, but instead targeted the hardline politicians who, he contended, were corrupting the Japanese military. It was all aimed at driving a wedge into the political ruling class, to try to galvanise more moderate voices, to convince reasonable and rational individuals in the government that warring with the European powers would only bring ruin to Japan.

But the British were hopelessly late to the game. Japan's army propagandists had been agitating for militarism and war since the 1920s. The rapacious appetite of the Japanese press for stories of victorious battles had created a groundswell of enthusiasm in favour of the invasion of Manchuria and the establishment of the puppet state of Manchukuo. When public support for Hirohito's ever-widening sphere of occupation in China began to wane as sons, brothers and fathers returned to Japan maimed or traumatised – if they came home at all – the army ramped up the propaganda. Stories of glorious sacrifice and victory were fed to the press and slickly produced films were released to the theatres, none more influential than *Japan in Time of Emergency*.

'In this film,' as one historian notes, 'the armed forces used Hirohito's spiritual authority to endow the empire – and themselves – with a moral mission to expand.'[5] The film lambasted Western decadence while celebrating the virtues of soldiering and war. There were montages of patriotic businessmen donating aircraft, rapid industrialisation and women soldiers in training. Most affecting of all, though, was a tribute to the 'three human bullets' (*bakudan sanyūshi*, three soldiers who blew themselves up along with a Chinese barbed-wire encampment during the January 28 Incident in Shanghai. Finally, the film's narrator issued a dramatic call to arms:

Ninety million people must become one and join the emperor in spreading the imperial virtue. For this we must unite and advance until the very last minute [of battle]. In this way, we will secure the glory of final victory.[6]

The British were not merely dealing with Japan's highly advanced propaganda strategy. As a colleague of Scott's in the

Ministry noted: 'Tokyo was stiff with German propagandists and Nazi agents of all kinds. We had to try to counteract their malign influence which was concentrated on luring Japan in the fray on Germany's side.'[7] Some within the Far Eastern Bureau claimed that their work was highly effective, 'more than once it helped delay Japan's entry into the war'[8] – an exceptionally bold claim that remains impossible to prove.

Scott returned to England to report the Ministry's progress in Japan. On the flight home, his plane landed in Marseille to refuel at the very moment the port city suffered its first German air raid of the war. The press reported that 'a message about the raid had been sent to the plane in which he was flying but it was not received. The aircraft landed during the raid, and the passengers dashed for shelters where they remained for two hours.'[9] The incident possibly influenced Scott to relocate his headquarters from Hong Kong to the Cathay Building in Singapore. Perhaps the falling bombs, even though in a different theatre, crystalised his belief that the world would soon be enveloped in a wider conflagration that would absorb the Far East.

Whatever the reasoning behind the decision, there were advantages to setting up in Singapore. When the war with Japan started, Scott's office would be in the same building as the men who would be charged with the defence of Britain's possessions in the Far East. He could better influence their thinking when in such close proximity.

The relocation of the Ministry of Information to Singapore was reported in *The Sunday Times*. The article carried a cartoon of Scott and the two other bureaucrats, who together comprised a triumvirate popularly referred to as the 'Malayan Information Chiefs'. In the cartoon, the three men are arranged behind a fictitious 'inquiries' desk. The local press – represented as a muzzled dog – barks incessantly, demanding answers. Dr Victor Purcell, Director General of the Malayan Department of Information and Publicity, uses his fingers to plug his ears (hear no evil);

the former journalist and newly appointed Director of Information, George L. Peet, presses his finger against his pursed lips (speak no evil); and Rob Scott, the most senior of the men, leans back in a chair, smoking his pipe, eyes blissfully shut (see no evil). The article elevated Scott's social status. He and his wife, Rosamond, were sent a torrent of dinner invitations from those eager to acquaint themselves with this newly arrived and very good-looking couple.

Scott's standing in Singapore society was propelled to even greater heights when his voice was heard on the airwaves providing updates to the public from the MBC's Singapore Station in the Cathay Building. In those broadcasts, Scott acted as news teller, political analyst and morale booster. He discussed everything, including Japan's self-wounding policy of aggression and the attendant hardships of life in militarised Japan ('the quality of everything has gone down'); Britain's solidarity with China ('they feel as if their war is our war; they are fighting for us, and for all the victims of aggression'); the fact that the fight for Europe was the same fight that would be waged in the Pacific ('make no mistake – the Germans are fighting in the Far East'); and a dramatic call to arms ('it is the Battle for Britain: yes: but it is also the battle for Singapore, for you, for your family, for your home, for all who want to escape the clutches of Nazi tyranny').[10]

But if there was a moment when Scott could be said to have attained celebrity status, it occurred when Sir George Sansom – the Japanophile and diplomat who had spent more than three decades in the British Embassy in Tokyo, lately appointed adviser to the military and administrative leadership in Singapore on economic warfare – was seconded to General Sir Archibald Wavell's staff in Batavia and resigned his seat on the Governor's War Council. Scott was named as Sir George's replacement. After lengthy stints in Tokyo, there was no person in Singapore with greater insight into modern Japanese culture and politics than Scott. His appointment to the council, at the age of thirty-five, marked a high point in an already stellar and unblemished career.

Scott would now meet daily with the Governor of the Straits Settlement and High Commissioner of the Malay States, Sir Shenton Thomas, the General Officer Commanding Malaya, Lieutenant General Arthur Ernest Percival, the Air Officer Commanding, Air Vice Marshal Conway Pulford, the Senior Naval Officer, Rear Admiral Ernest Spooner, and the Australian Government Commissioner, Vivian Gordon Bowden, who were the current members of the war council. The council had, in fact, been set up earlier by Duff Cooper, a member of Churchill's clique who had been Scott's boss as Minister of Information before his appointment as Minister Resident in Singapore. Prior to his official seat on the war council, Scott had witnessed the first council with Cooper in the chair.

It was a stormy meeting. [Commander-in-Chief Far East Command] Brooke-Popham pointed out that he took his instructions from the Chiefs of Staff, [Governor] Thomas that he took his from the Colonial Secretary, the Admiral (Sir Geoffrey Layton) that his were from the Admiralty. My master being the Minister of Information, my addition to the War Council in the last stages of the campaign meant yet another if minor strand in the tangled skein of responsibilities.[11]

By the time Scott was given his seat on the council, Duff Cooper – who 'understood publicity and propaganda'[12] and had advocated for Scott – and Brooke-Popham were gone. But the council's dysfunction endured. In Cooper's absence, the council's general derision of Scott's work was palpable. He was at pains to remind the members of the need to step up the anti-Japanese rhetoric, to begin a campaign of fearmongering among other Asian nations about the Japanese – essentially to carpet-bomb South-East Asia with anti-Japanese radio broadcasts. Scott would acknowledge, with a kind of grudging respect, that 'the Japanese propaganda campaign has clearly had some success in convincing Asiatics that Japan is freeing Asia from imperialist domination, or, at least, they would find themselves better off under Japanese rule'.[13] The work of the Ministry was to respond to that campaign, to inflame negative attitudes towards the Japanese among Asian peoples while fighting back against Hirohito's hollow promises of freedom and self-determination. It was a hard case to make. As Scott wrote in a memorandum on strategies in response to the Co-Prosperity movement:

> It must be admitted that we are in an embarrassing position for propaganda, because propaganda needs to be in terms of black and white. Most of the specific accusations to be brought against Japanese imperialism have also been brought against the British Empire, and we must expect our listeners to be well aware of this. And it is not much use enlarging on the bad conditions inside Japan itself, when our listeners can argue that their conditions at home are comparable [under the Europeans].[14]

Scott argued vociferously in favour of repeated broadcasts on the MBC that dwelled on Japan's track record of invading countries and uprooting national cultures, the cruelty and inhumanity of their treatment of non-Japanese people and their profoundly oppressive occupations. His seat on the council – which controlled the censorship channels, publicity and the powerful MBC – was his best opportunity to guide the higher-ups to his way of thinking.

Yet at every turn, Scott was met with doubt and denial. The council saw him as a replacement for Sir George, whose function was to advise on matters that related to Japanese culture and modern politics, to offer insight into Japanese thinking. His work with the Ministry was barely raised. Scott continually sought the council's approval to advance his anti-Japanese propaganda strategy through Malaya and beyond. His efforts were all to no avail. Scott would conclude that the war council was 'an ineffectual committee debating issues sometimes difficult but relatively secondary. Should the Singapore police be authorised to shoot soldiers looting liquor shops? Should the floating dock at the Naval Base be scuttled, lightly damaged, so that it could be brought back into use?'[15] It was infuriating. A colleague who would serve as Scott's assistant in the last two months before the capitulation had this to say of him:

> Rob was a man who could have handled the Singapore situation, or any situation, with complete competence, could have cut through the red tape, and told people where they got off, and given strength and confidence to the people round him. But he was still in his thirties. It was only by threatening to resign from the War Council that he secured, ten days before Singapore fell, the full control over Press and publicity and censorship channels for which he had long been asking.[16]

The decision to threaten resignation was another arrow in Scott's diplomatic quiver. His customary method of overcoming resistance was through a technique of negotiation by stealth, to guide those who stood in opposition to his position by making gentle nudges, the strategic use of silence and useful observations;

to have his opponent arrive at Scott's viewpoint as if of his own volition. But there were times when he had to be more forceful. These exceptional skills in negotiation are what made him such an effective diplomat. He understood people, knew when to accommodate someone's wishes, knew what drove them, knew when to pick a fight. They were, in part, the function of his dilettante's interest in the mysteries of the human mind, forged in his wandering upbringing, crystallised in university where he took psychology as a minor, mastered in the embassies of Asia.

Scott would discover that Japanese internment was yet another arena offering him fascinating character studies in human psychology. The extremes of incarceration – with the attendant hardships of limited food, disease and the ubiquity of death – was not so much character-building as it was character-revealing, and what was revealed was often unexpected and surprising. The military man – with his senior rank, decorations and lifetime of service – popularly imagined as the epitome of stiff-upper-lip resilience, fortitude and courage, was so often utterly useless in camp. Scott observed:

> You might have expected that the officers would have set a good example to the men, in the [. . .] camps. By and large I don't think they did [. . .] Even in my short time in the [POW] Camp in Palembang [. . .], I noticed that the officers – with whom I lived – took more than their fair share of the miserable rations of pork or other delicacies that occasionally came our way. I was shocked at this, but apparently both men and officers accepted it as an unalterable law of nature.[17]

By contrast, the young woman – outwardly the very essence of vulnerability, timidity and dependence – would often prove to be made of iron, capable of surviving horrors unimaginable in civilised society, like Vivian Bullwinkel and the nurses of the *Vyner Brooke*. Stereotypes were no guide. Sex, occupation, personal circumstances and – to a point – age had nothing to do with it. But there was one type of individual about whom Scott had formed an intractable view. The storyteller, in Scott's estimation, stood a better chance of surviving incarceration than many others. The quality of telling a good story, Scott observed, 'seems to go with such a vivid imagination that people like that are often outright liars'.[18] Liars not only stood a better chance of surviving jail. They thrived.

There seemed no better example than Gordon Burt. An engineer from New Zealand employed by the Shell Company in Malaya, Burt escaped Singapore aboard the *Siang Wo*, where he acted as Chief Engineer. After disembarking the *Siang Wo* at the mouth of the River Musi on the east coast of Sumatra, Burt talked his way aboard a launch headed to Palembang with RAF personnel. The airmen crewing the launch were in need of a mechanic. Burt jabbered on about his engineering skills and secured a berth. The launch made its way up the Musi, headed for Palembang. En route to their destination, a Japanese gunboat appeared coming the other way and attacked. Several airmen were killed in the exchange of gunfire, and the launch's engines were damaged. Burt panicked, leaping overboard and abandoning the passengers and crew at the very moment they needed a mechanic to fix the engines.

Despite a valiant effort to defend the launch against the gunboat's superior firepower, it was eventually sunk. Several survivors made it to the bank of the Musi. Burt was nowhere to be seen and was presumed to have drowned. The survivors, meanwhile, managed to evade capture by hiding in the jungle. Once the gunboat had moved off, the survivors set about making rafts from branches, reeds and bark. The rafts were launched the following morning. Given the gunboat had come from the direction of their destination, the survivors rightly concluded that Palembang had fallen. The situation called for them to head back to the mouth of the Musi in the hope of rendezvousing with an Allied ship.

They barely made it a day on the river in their makeshift rafts before being captured.

The survivors – now prisoners – were transported to the military POW camp in Palembang, where they were unhappily reunited with Burt, who had managed to survive. Burt had been peddling the tale that he was the sole survivor of the Japanese attack on the launch. In his telling, the gunboat sent a shell into the launch's fuel tank, causing the vessel to explode. By some miracle, Burt survived the explosion and was catapulted into the river. He made it to the riverbank before being captured. He wove into his tale a gallant scene of defiance against his captors, where he narrowly averted execution – a point impossible to verify, but almost certainly made up – before being dragged off to the POW camp.

Infuriated, the surviving airmen set the record straight. By the time Scott and the others turned up, 'Burt's stock was definitely low'.[19] The airmen 'rejoiced that [Burt] was a civilian, as this meant he could be pushed out to a civilian camp'.[20] Before he was transported from the POW camp to the women's camp with Burt, Scott was warned by the airmen: keep a close eye on the shifty engineer. Clearly Burt had taken liberties with the truth. But that, in Scott's view, did not necessarily mean he was a reprobate or even unreliable. Scott would keep an open mind before forming a judgement on Burt's character. It would not take long. The Japanese assigned the six new arrivals to an empty house inside the boundary of the women's camp. Within a day of living together, Scott's verdict on Burt's character was in; Burt was 'a nasty bit of work'.[21]

It was not so much the fact that the man was an inveterate liar. It was his selfish conduct that riled Scott the most: 'if the rest of us were out of the cell when food came round [sic] we could not trust him to play fair.'[22] Scott's serious misgivings about Burt notwithstanding, there were undeniable advantages to sharing lodgings with him. The house was furnished 'with two beds and two chairs and one table'[23] and nothing else. This posed a particular problem in the preparation of food, rations being delivered uncooked. Burt saw an opportunity. Japanese security in the camp was lax. They could loot several vacant Dutch homes nearby for crockery, cutlery, pots, pans and anything else of use. From places unknown, Burt sourced some electrical cord and hooked up the house – which was wired for electricity – to the mains. But they still had no means of cooking the food. A solution materialised in the form of Mrs Harding, a well-heeled Englishwoman and former resident of Singapore who called on the men for a favour. After professing concern at the fate of her horses back in Singapore and her half-dozen pairs of riding boots – 'for some reason she seemed to regret not having them with her'[24] – Mrs Harding produced a broken-down electric hotplate. She had heard that there was an engineer in the house. Could he mend it?

'Certainly,' said Burt. He told her he would need a day. The hotplate took about ten minutes to fix: 'it was just a matter of a broken wire.'[25] The hotplate was used to cook up the daily ration of rice. The next day, while Scott was preparing lunch on the hotplate, Burt spotted Mrs Harding approaching the house. He hurried outside and intercepted her before she could come in. Scott heard the conversation from the pantry.

'Was the hotplate mended?' Mrs Harding enquired.

'Oh no,' said Burt, 'it will be a big job – not sure if I can manage it.'[26]

Burt saw no need in returning it. The others, though, were uneasy about the deception: 'We kept the plate for about three days, when we felt too ashamed to keep it any longer [we] returned it.' It was unseemly, but Scott had to concede that Burt 'had his uses, being quite unscrupulous'.[27]

Oblivious to having been duped, Mrs Harding invited the men for tea. Beyond her stated gratitude for Burt's mechanical skills, she was all praise for Scott, who had organised a regular church service. 'We could not raise a Prayer Book or Hymnal. So Allen [William Probyn Allen, one of the dinghy passengers] – who had a prodigious memory – wrote out the words of some hymns, and I read a bit from the Bible, and we got through it somehow.'[28] The service drew a healthy congregation that included the Scottish doctor, Jean McDowell, who worked miracles with the sick 'with practically no supplies, drugs, or equipment'.[29] There were some basic materials sent from the Dutch doctors in town. Some medical supplies managed to get to McDowell, despite the Japanese stealing 'what they wanted for themselves [. . .] to sell in the black market'.[30] Drugs, especially morphine, would fetch high prices as the war progressed. McDowell used the little that remained to treat sores and other ailments. More than her ability to prescribe helpful remedies and her medical treatment, McDowell's willingness to ease the suffering of the sick won her many admirers. Along with that of the Australian nurses, McDowell's absence was sorely missed when the Japanese broke up the camp.

It happened without warning. Six days after Scott's arrival, the men were loaded into trucks and transported to 'an uncomfortable row of Chinese shop-houses in the town, surrounded by barbed wire'.[31] No explanation was provided. Scott believed the decision was tied to the ill-discipline of Miachi's men and 'the scandal of the abortive club affair in the British women's camp' and subsequent 'loss of face'.[32] More likely it was owing to lax security at the women's camp and an influx of internees. Overnight, the Dutch civilians and municipal workers who had been used as transitional labour and security while the Japanese occupation of Sumatra was organised lost their liberty. They were herded into the Palembang prison. Scott and the other civilian men soon followed.

The prison comprised four concrete double-storey blocks built around a central exercise yard. Scott shared a one-man cell with Burt, Kendall and another man. Three would sleep on a concrete platform – 'we had 22 inches by six feet each'[33] – and one man slept on the floor. Their pillows were made of stone. The prison probably had enough space to house fifty or so convicts and was now accommodating 150 civilian internees. 'Later another 80 or so British civilians turned up, which made things worse.'[34] (Before the war's end, the number of internees in the jail ballooned to 480.) Sanitation was poor and the water supply 'quite inadequate'.[35] Two dirty oil drums and a metal dustbin were repurposed to boil rice and vegetables in bulk. Scott was kept busy preparing vegetables for the entire camp, observing, 'It takes an awful lot of de-stringing to get the string out of string beans for 150.'[36] When he wasn't on cooking duty, Scott was giving English lessons to the Dutch, who, in turn, taught him their native tongue. In this fashion, he kept his mind active and avoided entering the listless spiral of ennui that afflicted so many internees and invariably led to helplessness and despair.

The class was a source of great interest and entertainment to the internees. The Dutch willingly turned up to learn, while the English speakers volunteered to help the students. The attendees were a fascinating array of characters. There was an Australian named John Quinn, a fellow diplomat Scott had met in Singapore who acted as Scott's teaching assistant ('it was a little comical for an Australian and a Scotsman to be laying the down the law about the proper English accent'[37]). There was Allen with his photographic memory, who kept himself busy speaking ancient Greek to a Dutch priest, teaching Burt Spanish and other internees French, and who declaimed Milton to Scott's class in his 'beautiful speaking voice'.[38] There was the Dutchman H. Jan Hilling – Manager of the Shell Company, who was fluent in English and very able at helping the students with pronunciation – with whom Scott discussed world affairs, occasionally in Dutch, and who lent 50 guilders to the moneyless Scott ('the way he put it [. . .] he had too much money and was afraid the Japanese would take it away'[39]).

In a cell not far from Scott's was Norman Wooten, Australian Assistant Trade Commissioner, who had first met Scott in Shanghai. There was the American journalist William Henry McDougall, one of Scott's teaching aides, who had been reporting on the Japanese in their homeland in the years before the war, followed their military adventures in China, evaded capture in Shanghai after the attack on Pearl Harbor only to be captured in Sumatra. (McDougall 'read news bulletins in the style of American broadcasters, using all the slang he could think of, much to the bewilderment of the class'.[40]) And finally, there was the charming Andrew Carruthers: amateur thespian, businessman with Boustead & Co. – the immensely profitable trading company founded in Singapore over a century earlier – and professional broadcaster with the MBC, who taught the internees elocution. ('Carruthers read news bulletins in faultless BBC English, early brand'[41] – the so-called 'Oxford accent' once preferred by the BBC.)

For both students and teachers, the class served the dual function of activating minds in need of stimulation and building a sense of camaraderie among the internees. But few benefited more than Scott himself. Teaching those Dutchmen brought a sense of accomplishment and purpose. He rejoiced in being in the company of similarly erudite men who shared a deep curiosity about the world.

But these sunnier moments were overshadowed by the spectre of death. For Scott, nothing was more devastating than when it was his turn to tend as orderly in the so-called hospital, an ironic name used to describe the 'shocking little hut in which we could put only seven or eight of our most serious cases, mostly dysenteries'.[42] These sick men would pass as much as a litre of fluid an hour. They were racked with fever and delirious through dehydration. The water they craved was befouled and very likely made them sicker. 'It was horrible work,' Scott wrote, 'attending these dying men in the still dark hours of the early morning, by the dim glimmer of a blacked-out lamp – the only light the

Japanese would permit.'[43] The hut was equipped with mattresses but no bedding. Those attending to the sick managed to elevate the beds off the concrete floor. But the frequency and volume of bloody diarrhoea overwhelmed the ill-suited kerosene tins that served as bedpans: 'they were soon filthied [sic] by blood and mucous and could not be cleaned.'[44]

The Japanese indifference to illness and death appalled Scott. In time, he would acknowledge that they appeared similarly unconcerned about the treatment of their own sick and wounded. Nothing, it seemed to Scott, frustrated the Japanese more than 'the paraphernalia of ambulances, and doctors, and stretchers, and stretcher bearers and all the rest of it, when they were engaged in operations'.[45] Later, an English-speaking Japanese guard would offer an explanation: 'If a wounded man dies without attention within 48 hours or so, he was probably a serious case, and would have been a liability to Japan perhaps for life. If he can survive 48 hours without treatment, he is likely to recover and will make a good soldier again.'[46] The Japanese nonetheless respected the savage toll that disease wrought on an army or an occupying force. As such, an uptick in quality rations generally followed prisoner deaths in the hope of preventing an epidemic. Before long, however, the food diminished in quality and quantity and the soiled mattresses were occupied once more and the grim cycle continued.

This callous disregard for the sick and dying was devastating to their family and friends. The profound suffering inflicted upon the white-haired William Roberts, a sixty-year-old jack-of-all-trades and a British beachcomber, stuck in Scott's mind. Roberts was interned with his wife, Freda, son, George, and teenage daughter, Joyce. Unbeknown to Roberts, Freda was hit with a particularly virulent strain of dysentery while in the women's camp. She was taken to a hospital run by nuns where serious cases in both the civilian camps were sent. One day, a Japanese guard summoned Roberts and drove him to the hospital because his wife's condition had deteriorated. She was already dead when he arrived.

When Roberts had been separated from his wife several weeks earlier, she was in good health. She told him she would take care of their daughter. After viewing the corpse of his wife, he begged the Japanese to let him see Joyce. They denied the request. He returned to the prison camp. He would subsequently die of dysentery four months later. His son, George, an architect at a prominent Malayan firm, succumbed to beri-beri two years later. Joyce, seventeen years of age when her mother died, endured unimaginable fear, loneliness and illness. She survived the war.

Scott would never forget a conversation he had with Roberts the day after he was permitted to see his dead wife. Roberts came to see him. He was shaking. He leant against the wall of Scott's cell, staring into the middle distance, seeing nothing. In a trembling voice, he repeated the same sentence throughout the night: 'And, Mr Scott, think of it – think of it – the ants were at her already – the ants were at her already.'[47]

10

CELL LEADER

Four months after the attack

THE DECISION TO ARRANGE an exercise regime for the prisoners in the YMCA was in response to the high incidence of constipation across the prison population. Little wonder the prisoners were backed up. Not only was food scarce, the little they were rationed was totally lacking in fibre – not that the Japanese saw the issue as stemming from diet. They believed it came down to a lack of physical exercise. To ensure a more organised workout, the guards allowed the prisoners to appoint one of their cellmates to lead each cell. Elizabeth was unanimously appointed leader of her cell.

The guards had instructed that each cell leader had to call out the numbers within each set of exercises in Japanese: '*Ichi, ni, san, shi* . . .' and so on. Bishop Wilson, who was the leader of his cell, would instead call out words of encouragement so that they could be heard throughout the whole cell: 'Be of good cheer! Lift up your hearts!'[1] The Japanese did not intervene. They may not have understood.

For Elizabeth, the opportunity to move after months spent sitting or lying on that revolting cell floor was a great relief. She intended to make the most of it, leading her cellmates in a vigorous routine of exercises that involved jumps and squats. The *Kempei Tai* guards – who never intended for the exercise sessions to be enjoyable – would interrupt the sessions, ordering the prisoners to run around the cell in circles for up to an hour. It was exhausting, but only the most weakened detainees resented the order. Running was infinitely better than sitting idle for hours on end.

The workouts had the added advantage of allowing the prisoners to properly sweep the bugs off their bodies. The bug infestation in the prison had reached plague proportions. They clung to sweaty bodies, nested in hair, crawled between toes. Exhausted and despairing, the prisoners had given up trying to swot them away. For Elizabeth, the insects called to mind the mosquitoes, scorpions, centipedes and blood-sucking leeches of Borneo, the one abiding hatred of her otherwise idyllic childhood. In the YMCA, they were a source of great discomfort, keeping her awake at night. While jogging around that small cell with the others, Elizabeth swept them off her body and killed the colonies of bugs that clung to the walls of the cell.

In these moments, Elizabeth reflected on the reason her cellmates had selected her as leader. It was obvious: 'because everyone knew I was a schoolteacher.'[2] There was, after all, no better person than a teacher to lead a small group of people – irrespective of whether they were children or adults – in a confined space. And there were no better teachers in Singapore than Elizabeth.

Without realising it, she had been training for the profession since she was a child. Growing up as the eldest of six siblings and numerous other cousins and friends where she was relied upon to look after the young ones, she had learned what motivated young people, how to keep them in check and how to get the best out of them. This instinct for guiding young minds was honed while she raised her brothers and sisters in Singapore following the death of their mother, and burnished while volunteering at the convent where she finished her schooling to look after the orphans and children left on the doorstep by the poor and destitute. She saw in teaching something more than a profession. It was her vocation, a calling from on high, the work God had put her on Earth to do.

But her path into the profession was not an easy one. In her final year of school, Elizabeth sat the Senior Cambridge examination, the requisite test to gain admission to university. She was dux of her class and was offered a scholarship to Raffles College. And then came the Great Depression. With global production grinding to a halt, demand for rubber and tin – the two precious Malayan commodities that sustained the Singaporean economy – dramatically diminished. In response to the inevitable economic decline that ensued, the British administrators clamped down on migration and raised tariffs on local imports and exports. Free trade and free immigration, the policies that had served as the lifeblood of the British Empire's possessions in the Far East, were curtailed. For the first time since the colony kept migration records, more people left Singapore than migrated to the island.

The Chinese community was hit hard. The once robust trade along High Street, South Bridge Road and North Bridge Road was dying. Those rows of busy thoroughfares where shopkeepers hawked their wares were now lined with empty stores, every other place locked up with a 'To Let' sign hanging from the front door. It was not only private enterprise that was hit. Civil servants were retrenched in high numbers. Those that were kept on were forced to accept pay cuts as the government embarked on a policy of austerity. Amenities and services deemed unessential were scrapped, which included the government-funded scholarships to Raffles College.

The termination of the scholarships put an end to Elizabeth's hopes of further study. Her only hope was her family. Notwithstanding their precarious financial situation, the Yongs would probably have found the money to send Elizabeth to Raffles College, but Elizabeth never asked her father. She knew he needed her help to feed her five siblings while they finished their schooling. Being denied the chance to study at university would often give Elizabeth pause. 'It is my one regret that I could not continue my education after my Senior Cambridge: if I had been able to do this, I think my contribution to society would have been greater.'[3] Elizabeth's academic performance and, more importantly, her empathetic and unimpeachable character ensured that she secured work as a teacher at the Church of England Zenana Mission School (CEZMS). She shone in the role, instantly commanding the students' respect, turning around the results of those who had been lagging and pushing the academically advanced to even greater heights.

When it came to teaching, Elizabeth's guiding principle was to focus on the good that she believed was inside all children. 'Fundamentally all children want to be good and they try to be good.'[4] She would actively listen to them and then respond, rather than lecture and berate. She would never hold back words of praise. 'Very often we take it for granted and are so sparing in our words of encouragement or appreciation. We forget that a good word in the right place will go a very long way.'[5] She was firm but never used violence, threats or intimidation in the classroom. Using the disciplinary levers of guilt, shame, humiliation and most of all corporal punishment were counterproductive. 'For children to be getting kicks all the time is not good for them. That is the wrong way to bring out the best in them.'[6] In an era of strict disciplinarians, Elizabeth's approach was unconventional.

But her results, particularly with the behaviourally challenged kids, were impressive. The other teachers would send 'the children who would give trouble to the teachers' to Elizabeth, who would turn them into attentive, well-behaved and respectful students. The supervisor assigned to Elizabeth to monitor her first year at the school could not believe what he witnessed. 'Miss Yong*,' he asked, 'did you ever take up psychology?'[7] Elizabeth explained to him her methodology: 'The way to get the best out of any child is to find the little bit of good in him, and then encourage that, make him understand that he is capable of doing good, and help him on. Instead of looking at the bad side try to look for the good, and guide and encourage him that way.'[8]

Educationalists, principals and other teachers throughout Singapore began to hear about this teacher working miracles at CEZMS. She was offered a position at St Andrew's, the boys' school led by Canon Reginald Sorby Adams. Unlike St Margaret's, every staff member at St Andrew's had received formal teacher training. Elizabeth demurred. She was not ready for such a school. But Canon Adams, a liberal missionary who delighted in unconventional approaches, set her mind at ease. Elizabeth's upbringing and life experience had prepared her in ways that no college or university degree could match. She accepted the position and set out to vindicate the faith that Canon Adams had in her teaching abilities, even if she could not fully see it in herself. She brought her signature approach of kindness, empathy and patience to teaching the boys at St Andrew's.

Just like at St Margaret's, the academic performance and general wellbeing of Elizabeth's students shone. She dedicated herself to getting to know the children in her class. In some cases, that meant visiting their homes, particularly the homes of those kids prone to raising hell in the classroom or those who were falling well behind. Invariably, these pupils were from broken or impoverished homes. Elizabeth would sit with the parents and discuss their child's difficulties. By and large, the parents were receptive to her feedback, taking on her suggestions around strategies at home that could be used to improve the child's performance. Not only would she make this extra investment in time,

---

* Yong was Elizabeth's maiden name.

often she would dive into her own meagre savings and provide some small material support if she thought it would help. Even in those circumstances where she met a frostier reception, Elizabeth would see an improvement in the child. She would later write: 'When the best is given, the children know it and they and their parents will be grateful to you. A teacher's caring and unselfish attitude endears her or him to the children.'[9]

Raised in the Presbyterian missions of North Borneo, schooled in a Catholic convent in Singapore and employed in Anglican schools, Elizabeth's philosophy was a fusion of Christian denominations blended with the Confucian teachings of her father. She regarded Christ and Confucius as 'two great leaders of mankind'[10] whose doctrine overlapped in numerous ways, most clearly in Christianity's Golden Rule – 'Do unto others as you would have them do unto you' – and the Confucian teaching 'What you do not want done to yourself, do not do to others'.[11] She dedicated herself to this principle, demonstrating it through leading the classroom just as she did when leading her cell while imprisoned. She was steadfast in her belief that a person needed to have faith in a higher being, and recognised that adherents of Buddhism, Hinduism and Islam 'get strength and comfort from their religion',[12] just as she drew strength and comfort from the Christian God. There was no greater source of bewilderment to Elizabeth than atheists. 'I wonder where those who do not believe in God get comfort and strength from, when they are in despair or distress.'[13]

Elizabeth's time as a prisoner of the Japanese had imbued in her a philosophy that echoed the virtues of the ancient Stoics. One subsequent insight – 'Nothing can do me any harm, except myself [. . .] nobody can make me angry [except when] I get angry with myself [. . .] if others do something to hurt me [. . .] I can't control other people's actions [. . .] I just pray'[14] – might have come from Epictetus, Cato or Marcus Aurelius. Like the great Stoics, Elizabeth understood that there were great global forces outside of her control that she was powerless to stop. But her insistence to others that you must focus on the positive – 'get away from these morbid things'[15] – was a demonstration of her belief that, even when physically incarcerated, freedom can be found in one's thoughts. Again, just like the Stoics, Elizabeth also believed in justice: 'That's what I told [other prisoners], I said . . . "If you have not done wrong you will be all right. You must believe in that." Justice will triumph, don't worry.'[16] Elizabeth was not talking about retributive justice. (In the unlikely event that the people in this cell survived their imprisonment, the prospect of their captors being tried, at least at that juncture, seemed impossible.) She was instead talking about transcendent justice – that on the final day of judgement, the just would be rewarded in eternity.

Elizabeth knew that when the guards called her from her cell that last time, the words of the Bible would hold her steady in the face of fear and despair. 'Such words as "Cast your cares upon Me" or "the peace of God, which passeth all understanding", or "You shall have life eternal", never fail to give strength, courage, and hope to all believers.'[17] These would likely be the final words that she would speak before her execution. In these words, and in her knowledge of God, Elizabeth knew – with unbreakable faith – that she would be saved.

11

MISTAKEN IDENTITY

Sixteen months before the attack

NOBODY WAS UNDULY CONCERNED when Japanese soldiers took Kenneth Morgan away from his cell in the Palembang camp in early May 1942, not even when he failed to return that night. There was an obvious explanation; the Japanese had identified him as an army officer and, as such, he had been taken to the POW camp with all the other captured officers and enlisted men. Morgan – an understated stiff-upper-lip sort with a bald patch, who looked older than his forty-seven years – had earned the rank of major in the 19th Hyderabads, an infantry regiment of the British Indian Army formed after World War I. He had in fact retired in 1936, a detail of little concern to the Japanese, who probably felt he should be held with the other enemy combatants.

But the mystery of Major Kenneth Morgan's whereabouts worried Scott greatly. Scott knew more about Morgan than most. The two men had met in Singapore when Morgan was the head of the Japanese Section of the Singapore Special Branch, the job he was offered on account of his fluency in Japanese. (A noted linguist, Morgan was also fluent in Russian.) Superintendent Morgan's branch was responsible for investigating Japanese fifth column activity. Not that Morgan shared this with anyone in the prison. Nobody – outside of Scott and a couple of other internees who knew him before the war – knew that he spoke Japanese. He imagined that the Japanese would be very interested in his occupation before the war.

There was another detail about Morgan's absence that had Scott concerned. The soldiers who took Morgan off were not the regular soldiers or sentries the internees had encountered. They wore a white armband around their left arms with two characters emblazoned in red – 憲 兵. These characters – *ken* and *hei* – literally translated to 'law soldier'. The plural, *Kempei Tai*, meant 'military police'.

Sure enough, news filtered back into the camp 'that [Morgan] was being kept in a room at *Kempei* Headquarters with some local political prisoners, and that he had been seen driving about town in a car with some Japanese'.[1] Scott was filled with dread, his worst fears confirmed when another rumour swept the prison: 'Soon after the occupation of Singapore, the *kempei* [. . .] made up a list of wanted men.'[2] The prisoners referred to it as a blacklist. As sure as night followed day, Scott's name would be on that list. If Morgan – who had made every effort to keep secret his job in Singapore – was in the hands of the military police, Scott was convinced he would be arrested too. It was only a matter of when.

The *Kempei Tai* came for Scott on 30 May, four weeks after Morgan's arrest. He was told to bring his personal belongings. Like many prisoners, Scott had fallen into the habit of scrounging for clothes, shoes and other effects that might come in handy. His 'kit', an old rice sack sourced from the prison kitchen and repurposed as a holdall, consisted of a couple of old shirts given to him by others, the remains of his lifebelt, two army socks – of different shades and sizes – some notes he had taken, two personal letters and a pair of broken army boots that did not fit. He picked it up and was escorted from the jail.

There was no opportunity to farewell the men he had befriended in the camp or the passengers with whom he had rowed the dinghy across the Banka Strait. A great many would not survive captivity. Gordon Burt, the resourceful engineer and storyteller, would die of fever and beri-beri in 1945, leaving a wife and daughter. Julius Planzer was transferred out of the civilian camp – to where, nobody knew. Horace Kendall, one of the lucky men the dinghy fished from the sea after the *Giang Bee* sank, who would earn deep respect for assuming the role of 'Matron' in the hospital ward of the jail, succumbed to fever in a camp in Belalau three months before the end of the war. And the polymath William Probyn Allen, hauled aboard the dinghy with Kendall and who proved to be an expert in business and literature, fluent in multiple languages and a handy cricketer, died two months before Kendall in the same camp. Allen, who became co-editor of the Palembang *Camp News*, wrote a poem addressed to his wife at Christmas 1942 that made it to her via the Red Cross in 1944:

Last year I hung a stocking, childlike, by your bed
While you were sleeping, but this year my thoughts instead
And prayers and wishes to the stars and round moon spoken,
Are all the gifts that I can send to you for token
Of all the joy there is between us, come what may.
Have faith, my love, although the night is dark, the day
Will break and peace and good will come to men at last.
God bless and keep you always.[3]

Scott was driven to the Palembang *Kempei Tai* headquarters, sat down at a table and questioned by several English-speaking officers. The contents of his kit were emptied before him. Scott felt his pulse start to race: 'I had certain notes concealed which

I particularly did not want them to see.'[4] The notes had been folded tightly and stitched into folds in two of his shirts. They contained names and addresses of prisoners and internees in the Palembang camps that he intended to smuggle to Singapore. There was nothing in these notes that would help or hinder the Japanese war effort. That said, the very act of cataloguing this kind of information was forbidden. If they were discovered, the notes would be confiscated and Scott would be punished.

But the Japanese were disinclined to conduct a thorough search of the clothing on the table. They were transfixed by one of the two letters Scott had in the kit. Scott assumed they were analysing the letter written by his daughter Susan, penned shortly after Rosamond and the children had arrived safely in Sydney. It provided a 'straitforward [sic] written account of the harbour and hotel in Sydney'.[5] And although written by a child, it made oblique and casual references to shipping movements in the harbour and various other details. If properly analysed by Japanese intelligence, the letter might be seen to contain useful military information.

In fact, the letter that had caught the attention of the dreaded officers of the *Kempei Tai* was not from his daughter but from his son, Douglas. 'Being yet unable to write, much except his own name and mine, he had drawn his letter, and it was a mass of squiggles and cubist outlines of ships and railway trains.'[6] The *Kempei Tai* were acting as if they had stumbled on an intelligence breakthrough – 'obviously a secret plan for the invasion of some-where or other by Allied forces'[7] – that may have proved decisive. Scott had a challenging time convincing them that the master-mind behind the letter was a five-year-old boy. The *Kempei Tai* remained certain it contained vital military information, 'arguing fiercely with each other as to the precise meaning of different squiggles, most of which [Scott] could not interpret [himself]'.[8] Douglas's letter proved to be an extremely useful decoy. 'In the general hullaballoo, my notes were overlooked.'[9]

When the questioning about the contents of Douglas's letter had concluded, Scott was taken to a large, windowless gymnasium attached to the *Kempei Tai* offices. There were twelve others inside, 'Chinese and Malays suspected of sabotage, harbouring Allied troops, and other "political" crimes'.[10] The prisoners were ranged around the room. There was no sign of Morgan. A guard stood sentry at the door, closely watching the prisoners. Talking was forbidden. After several hours waiting in that stifling, airless room, several guards walked in. 'Number off!' one shouted. Nobody moved. The call to 'number off', the guard explained, was an order to form a single file. 'Number off!' he shouted again.[11] The prisoners lined up. A Chinese prisoner saw no need to rush. He ambled over and slouched into line. The guard walked over and stamped down on his bare feet. The Chinese prisoner howled in pain. Scott could see the blood pooling where the guard's hobnailed army boots had lacerated the prisoner's feet.

Scott would come in for the same treatment on several occasions in the coming days. The guards seemed intent on administering this painful punishment to every prisoner. Periodically, the guards would use the prisoners to practice their jujitsu skills. A guard would pull an unprepared prisoner to his feet and then throw him over his shoulder, slamming him into the hard gymnasium floor 'to the accompaniment of cheers from the other sentries'.[12] Forbidden from fighting back or defending themselves, the prisoners simply allowed themselves to be hurled to the floor.

In his travels through the Far East, Scott had heard about this ancient form of martial arts. The best defence, he had been told, was to go limp: 'The essence of jujitsu is to use the other man's efforts against him, and if you make no effort you cannot be thrown.'[13] Sure enough, a guard attempted to throw Scott over his shoulder. Scott relaxed his muscles and let his body sag into his attacker. He denied the guard the satisfying smack of a body being slammed down onto the floor. Scott was simply 'shoved down like a sack of potatoes'.[14] There was no fun in throwing Scott. Eventually, the guards gave up.

Scott viewed the casual violence as 'horseplay rather than deliberate cruelty'.[15] To be sure, the majority of the guards were as rough as the food was bad. But there were some 'moderately human'[16] sentries among them. A sentry who had spent several years in London and Paris, where his wife had studied, developed a particular curiosity about Scott by dint of the fact he was the only European held in the gymnasium. 'He chatted to me of Europe and Japan, and gave me cigarettes.'[17] Scott came to trust the sentry, telling him that he had 50 guilders – the money gifted to him by John Quinn, which he'd secreted away – and that he hoped he could 'buy some gear – a blanket, a shirt, pair of trousers, pair of shoes (I was barefoot), tobacco, etc: would he help?' The sentry would do what he could. The following day, an officer stumbled upon Scott and the sentry smoking together. The officer strode up to Scott, slapped him in the face and then scolded the sentry, who 'blushed scarlet'.[18] Scott abandoned hope of being able to use his guilders to buy his much needed gear. Then another guard approached Scott. He said he was the sentry's friend. Scott handed over the 50 guilders. The following day, the guard returned with some shoes, trousers and a blanket. He even presented Scott with a written receipt of all items purchased and the exact change.

Scott was an exceptional judge of character. But trusting any of the *Kempei Tai* men was an enormous gamble. These small acts of generosity, although welcome, were the exception to their rule of violence and cruelty. Sure enough, a few days later, the *Kempei Tai* showed their true colours.

It began with a simple request: a Chinese carpenter held captive on some trumped-up charge had the audacity to ask a guard for more rice. 'Certainly,' responded the guard, not the least bit perturbed. The other prisoners were astonished. An enormous

The Yong siblings. *Back row from left to right:* Annie Su-Ni, Kon Vui, Doris Su-Yung and Chau Vui. Marie Su-Tshin seated with Elizabeth Su-Moi. Singapore, c. 1938.

Rosamond Aeliz Dewar-Durie and Robert Heatlie Scott. Peking, c. 1933.

The Scott family. *From left to right:* Douglas, Rosamond, Robert, Susan. Hong Kong, c. 1940.

The newlyweds, Choy Khun Heng and Elizabeth Choy. Singapore, 16 August 1941.

The Scotts on their wedding day. Peking, 11 October 1933.

When Ivan Lyon returned to Singapore from a sea voyage to Poulo Condor – a remote island off the south coast of French Indochina – with the ravishingly beautiful Gabrielle Bouvier, the couple became the talk of Singapore society. Pictured here not long after their wedding in July 1939.

A column of smoke from burning oil tanks at Singapore Naval Base rises above the deserted streets of Singapore. The spire of St Andrew's Cathedral can be seen towards the back right of the frame. Singapore, c. January 1942.

HMS *Giang Bee*.

Two women sit on the street among debris, showing their grief for the small child whose dead body lies nearby in front of a damaged rickshaw, after a Japanese bombing raid. Singapore, c. February 1942.

Lieutenant General Arthur Percival, General Officer Commanding Malaya at the time of the Japanese attack.

Lieutenant General Yamashita Tomoyuki thumps his fist on the table as he lays out terms to Lieutenant General Arthur Percival: unconditional surrender. Ford Motor Factory, Singapore, 15 February 1942.

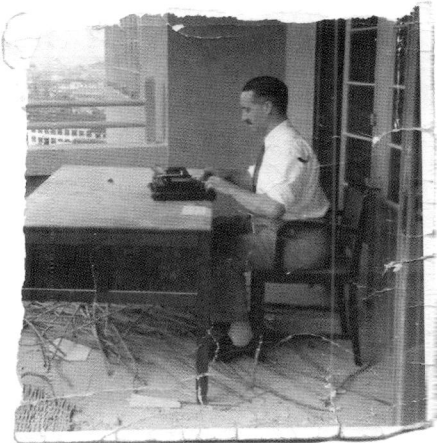

Robert Heatlie Scott at a desk on the balcony outside his office in the Cathay Building. Singapore, c. 1941.

56 — CATHAY BLDG.

AWM P04179.027_1

The Cathay Building, the tallest building in South-East Asia at the time, survived the war relatively unscathed. It was demolished in 2003. Singapore, c. 1945.

Robert Heatlie Scott, an avid smoker. Singapore, c. 1941.

The YMCA building was repurposed as headquarters, prison and torture chamber by the *Kempei Tai* during the Japanese occupation of Singapore.

Singapore's Central Police Station was one of several buildings used by the *Kempei Tai* to interrogate and incarcerate undesirables, criminals and individuals suspected of anti-Japanese activities.

The Japanese demanded total obedience from the people of Singapore during the occupation. In this photo, two *Kempei Tai* soldiers in a rickshaw will not be expected to pay a fare.

In the early days of the occupation, local Singaporeans tried to get on with their lives, as demonstrated in this bustling Chinatown market. Singapore, c. 1942.

A mass screening centre in Chinatown set up as part of *dai kensho* or the 'great inspection', designed to remove 'undesirables', mostly ethnic Chinese, at the start of the Japanese occupation. The great inspection was, in fact, a mopping-up operation for which the Chinese in Singapore provided a more fitting name: *Sook Ching*, literally 'purge through cleansing'. The atrocity resulted in the murder of at least 25,000 people and possibly as many as 50,000.

Four Japanese *Kempei Tai* officers. Three are dressed in the *Kempei Tai*'s distinctive civilian style: crisp white shirt and dapper sharkskin suit. A fourth officer wears military attire with a white armband around his left arm emblazoned with two red characters – *ken* and *hei* – literally translating to 'law soldier'.

Singapore residents bowing to Japanese soldiers.

Singaporean schoolchildren forced to enthusiastically wave the Hinomaru (Rising Sun) flags as they march towards the Syonan Gekiryo, a makeshift shrine, during Emperor Hirohito's birthday celebrations.

Members of the Japanese Propaganda Department distribute leaflets and pamphlets to Chinese and Indian civilians.

Aerial view of Changi Jail, c. 1953.

The courtyard in Changi Jail where internees were paraded on 10 October 1943.

Owing to its distinctive colour and the lifesaving supplies it delivered to the Singaporean internees in Changi Jail and Sime Road Internment Camp, this truck driven by the Swiss representative of the International Red Cross, Hans Schweizer-Iten, was dubbed the 'Blue Angel'.

Japanese officers like Captain Tanaka would drop in unannounced at the home of Hans Schweizer-Iten, whose activities were closely monitored by the occupying force. Singapore, 1 August 1942.

The Bishop of Singapore, Reverend John Leonard Wilson, and Lieutenant Andrew Ogawa, a generous enemy. Singapore, c. 1942.

Japanese currency used in Singapore was dubbed 'banana money' or 'banana notes' by dint of the image of the banana plant motif, as seen on this $10 note.

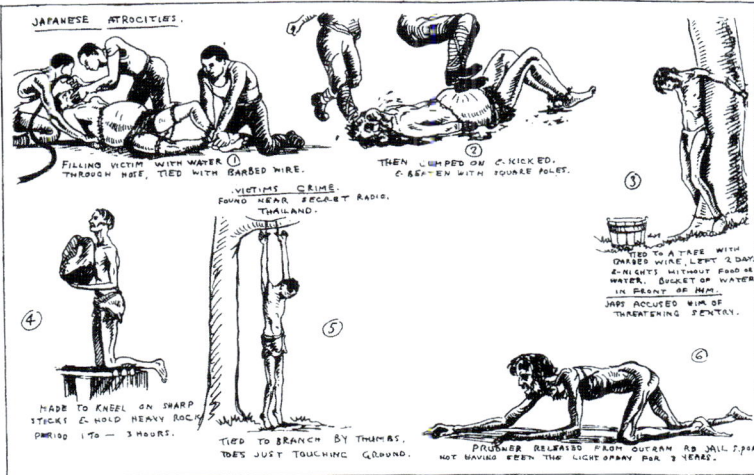

Sketches of torture positions by Leo Rawlings, who was captured at the Fall of Singapore and spent three-and-a-half years as a prisoner of the Japanese.

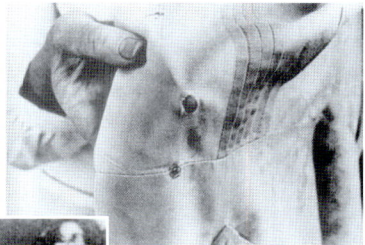

Some of the surviving nurses from the 2/13th Australian General Hospital who set out from Singapore aboard the *Vyner Brooke*. The inset is of Vivian Bullwinkel in 1945, shortly after liberation; *above right* we see the bullet hole in her uniform.

The MV *Krait* (originally known as the *Kofuku Maru*) was a Japanese trawler that was commandeered in 1942 in Singapore and operated by Services Reconnaissance Department and the Royal Australian Navy. Pictured here making her way up the Brisbane River, January 1943.

Aboard the *Krait* at Exmouth Gulf, Western Australia, September 1943. *Back row from left to right:* Wally 'Poppa' Falls, Kevin 'Cobber' Cain, Ivan Lyon, Ted Carse, James 'Paddy' McDowell. *Front row from left to right:* Andrew 'Happy' Huston, Moss Berryman, Horrie Young.

Ivan Lyon and fellow escapees aboard the *Sederhana Djohanes*. Indian Ocean, March 1942.

Members of the Jaywick team applying brown dye as *Krait* approaches the Lombok Strait. The Japanese sun-disc flag flutters at the stern of the boat.

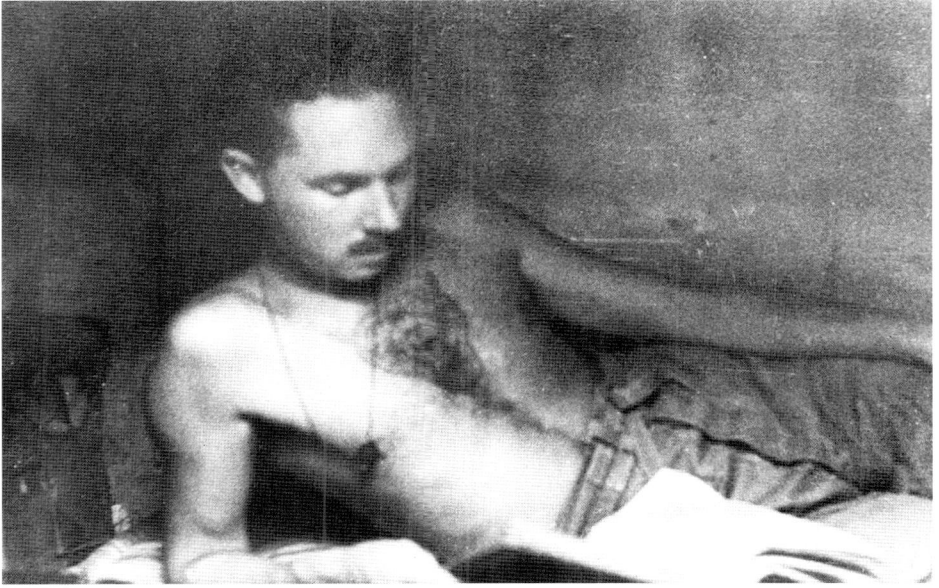

Ivan Lyon and the tiger tattoo that Gabrielle loathed.

Ivan Lyon observes shipping in the Singapore Roads from the observation post on Dongas Island, September 1943.

Commandos train in the folboats that would be used for Operation Jaywick.

A folboat with rations and equipment for two men.

The Japanese ship the *Nasusan Maru*. A ship of this class was severely damaged and unsalvageable following the successful execution of Operation Jaywick.

The five original officers of Operation Jaywick outside a tent at a training camp in January 1942. *From left to right:* Major Francis 'Gort' Chester, Major Ivan Lyon, Captain William 'Bill' Reynolds, Lieutenant Commander Donald Davidson, Sub Lieutenant Bertram Overell.

Bill Reynolds, as depicted by artist Don Russell, alongside a photograph.

To some he was charming, ebullient and genial; to others he was overwrought, superstitious and moody. The enigmatic Ivan Lyon evidently had many expressions. In this photo he appears in a whimsical mood.

Krait arrives in Refuge Bay, New South Wales. 17 January 1943.

Group portrait taken after the completion of Operation Jaywick.

Lieutenant Donald Davidson, Ivan Lyon's 2IC.

SWEETHEART - DELIGHTED TO HAVE A CHANCE TO WRITE TO YOU AT LAST.
HAVE HAD ONE LETTER FROM IAN (NOT THEN IN TOUCH WITH YOU DIRECT)
BUT NOTHING FROM YOU OR ANYONE ELSE. LONGING FOR NEWS AND
PHOTOGRAPHS OF YOU. IAN SAYS NOTHING ABOUT DAD, ALASTAIR,
AND MOLLIE, OF WHOM I OFTEN THINK. HOW ARE THEY? GIVE MY
LOVE ALSO TO YOUR FATHER AND MOTHER AND NORAH AND AUNT SON!
WONDER IF SHE IS IN ELIE? SORRY TO SAY THAT ALL OF MY
OFFICE STAFF AND CHU WHO LEFT WITH ME ARE BELIEVED DROWNED.
ONLY KNOWN SURVIVORS OF MY PARTY ARE TARRY AND MOORE OF
THE M.B.C. (TELL ERIC) AND MYSELF. GORDON IS ALSO MISSING -
TELL DOROTHY WITH ALL MY SYMPATHY. WOOTTON AND QUIN ARE SAFE.
TELL THE CHILDREN ELIZABETH AND HER HUSBAND ARE SAFE. I AM
IN GOOD HEALTH, WEIGHT ONE HUNDRED AND FIFTY FIVE POUNDS,
AND HAVE A FINE LONG BLACK BEARD! NOT SO LUCKY AS POP
WAS! LOVE TO OUR FRIENDS AND ESPECIALLY TO YOU DARLING.
I KNOW YOU MUST BE HAVING VERY TRYING TIME. HOPE YOU ARE
STAYING WITH AUNT CHRIS WHICH I THINK WOULD BE BEST FOR
THE CHILDREN AND FOR YOU. WRITE AND SEND PARCELS AS OFTEN AS
PERMITTED. LOVE - R. ROBERT HEATLIE SCOTT

During internment in Changi,
correspondence with the outside world
was limited, carefully monitored and
subject to lengthy delays. This postcard
(above) from Scott bears the censor's
stamp of approval *(below, in purple).*

Susan, Rosamond
and Douglas safely
walking the streets
of Sydney, 1942.

俘虜郵便

Service des Prisonniers de Guerre

To MRS ROSAMOND HEUZ SCOTT
(MRS. R. H. SCOTT)

% BANK OF NEW SOUTH WALES
SYDNEY, AUSTRALIA.

11" Exeter
400 Burriga Road

FROM. Enemy Civilians Internment Camp No. 1,

Bellevue Hill MALAYA.

ROBERT HEATLIE SCOTT

敵性人抑留所檢閱濟
檢閱者認印

The Japanese surrender party marching up St Andrew's Road to the Municipal Building, escorted by troops representing different units of the Allied forces.

General Itagaki Seishiro signs the instrument of surrender inside the Municipal Building in Singapore, 12 September 1945.

Robert Heatlie Scott in the witness box during the Trial of Sumida Haruzo and Twenty Others in what was more popularly known as the Double Tenth Trial. Supreme Court Building, Singapore, 20 March 1946.

The accused stand in the dock as the verdict is handed down in the concluding stages of the Double Tenth Trial. Sumida Haruzo is in the back row farthest to the left. Immediately to his left stands the sadist, Monai Todamori.

Lieutenant Colonel Sumida Haruzo with his trademark smile, dining in an undisclosed location. Date unknown.

Coverage of the Double Tenth Trial and the subsequent execution of Sumida Haruzo and other individuals found guilty of committing war crimes dominated the Singaporean press.

KEMPEI CHIEF HANGED

Lt. Col. Sumida, Singapore Kempei-tai, chief, who was hanged yesterday at Changi raol, Singapore, for his part in the notorious 'Double Tenth' case.

'Double Tenth' Men Hanged At Changi

By A Special Correspondent.

LIEUT.-Col. Sumida Haruzo, one-time chief of the Japanese Kempeitai interrogation unit in Singapore, and six of his henchmen, leading figures in the noted "Double Tenth" investigations and trial, were hanged in Changi Prison yesterday for their atrocities against 57 British and Asiatic civilians, 15 of whom died.

Their execution has all but rung down the curtain on that affair which was described as one of "unspeakable horror"—all but, because the eighth man to be sentenced to death, Toh Swee Koon, a Singapore-born Chinese, who was interpreter to the Kempeitai, is awaiting confirmation of his fate.

The Jap torturers did not have a fine sunny day for their deaths. Some of them walked to the gallows in heavy rain—after they had sung songs in their cells, shaken hands with each other and with other Japs in the condemned block.

On the gallows, hooded and bound hand and foot, they shouted "Banzai" and hailed

"unwilling participant" in the torture and death of one victim;

Staff Sergeant Morita Shozo, young ex-farmer, who felt that the use of force was necessary on several men; and

Sergeant Tsugio Sugeo, another young ex-farmer, whose interrogations eventually led to some of his victims dying.

The 15 men who died following treatment at the hands of these professional bullies who turned the prisoners of the Kempeitai into the delirsen of the East," were:

Dr. C.A. Stanley, and Dr. J.H. Bowyer, and Messrs. S. Cornelus, A.

(No. 2) Warrant Officer Monai Tadamori

(No. 4) Warrant Officer Sakamoto Shigeru

(No. 14) Sergeant Kasahara Hideo

(No. 15) Sergeant Yamauchi Satori

(No. 5) Sergeant-Major Makizono Masuo

(No. 6) Sergeant-Major Terada Takao

(No. 16) Private Murata Yoshitaro

Warrant Officer Nomura

Mugshots of the Japanese *Kempei Tai* involved in the Double Tenth atrocities who were tried for committing war crimes.

Sir Robert Heatlie Scott, Lord Lieutenant of Tweeddale, Scotland, c. 1980.

Robert Heatlie Scott came perilously close to dying on numerous occasions during and immediately after the war. Pictured here convalescing in Bangalore in October 1945, Scott required many months of rest before he fully regained his health.

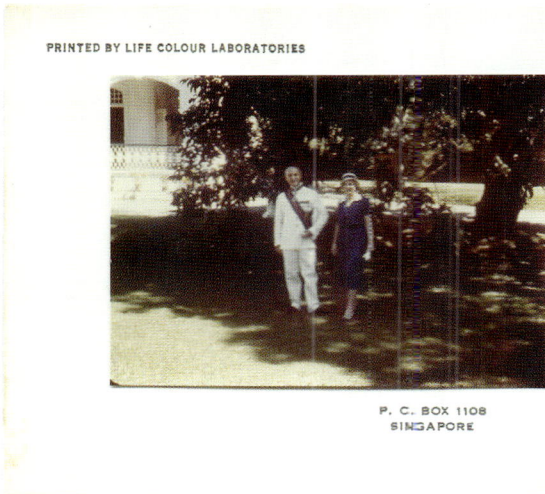

Scott returned to Singapore in 1955 as Commissioner General for the United Kingdom in South-East Asia.

Sir Robert and Lady Rosamond Scott back in Singapore, 1955.

Elizabeth Choy in London as representative of Singapore at the Coronation of Queen Elizabeth II, dressed in a satin *qipao* featuring a hand-embroidered dragon motif and an eight-word couplet in Chinese characters that read: 'Long live the Queen; may there be universal peace.' London, June 1953.

Elizabeth Choy, representing the nurses of Singapore, and Mr E.N.T. Cummings, representing former Changi internees, before presenting Princess Elizabeth, later Queen Elizabeth II, with an antique silver casket that contained a scroll listing the names of nurses who saved countless lives during the Japanese occupation. Buckingham Palace, 30 July 1946.

Mrs Choy meets the Nixons in Washington, D.C., during her lecture tour to North America in 1954.

Prince Philip, the Duke of Edinburgh, visited the School of the Blind during his official visit to Singapore in 1954. Mr Lim Yew Hock, to the Duke's left, was Chief Minister of Singapore. Elizabeth Choy was school principal.

Choy Khun Heng and Elizabeth celebrate daughter Bridget's ninth birthday in 1959, with Lynette on the left and Irene on the right.

platter of rice was brought in. The carpenter was given half. Scott sensed something sinister at play when a Malayan prisoner – 'who was in bad odour with the guards'[19] – was hauled over and told to eat the other half. Oblivious to the danger or perhaps blinded by hunger, the two prisoners scoffed down the rice. Once they were done, the two men were ordered to fight each other. If the guards sensed the two men going easy on each other, they would kick and punch them into activity. Both men fell to the ground vomiting. They were beaten savagely for messing up the floor and then made to clean it up. 'No one asked for extra food after that, though the game remained popular with some of the guards.'[20]

Although the prisoners were forbidden from talking to each other, Scott spoke to the Chinese in a mixture of Mandarin, Cantonese and Malay. He admired them greatly. Unlike the Malayans, who Scott felt 'cringed to the Japanese' to curry favour or avoid punishment, the Chinese 'were almost always dignified and independent'.[21] They made no effort to conceal the contempt and loathing they had for the Japanese, which Scott could see 'oozing from every pore'.[22] They spoke of horrifying atrocities in the early days of the occupation of Palembang. Some had witnessed friends nailed by the hands to the walls outside police stations until they perished days later. Others were tied in barbed wire to telegraph poles for all to see. The lucky ones got off with a savage public beating. 'Summary punishment of this sort,' the Chinese told Scott, 'was usually inflicted for petty theft – stealing or looting or just "scrounging".'[23] Those accused of sabotage or assisting Allied troops were arrested and never seen again. The majority, at least in the view of the Chinese prisoners who shared these gory tales with Scott, were innocent.

Stories of Japanese atrocities were unsurprising to Scott, who had seen the inhumane treatment by Japanese soldiers as the fighting intensified in those early days of the war in China. He also suspected that the Japanese had been afflicted with what he described as 'the fifth column mania'[24] that had gripped the British in Singapore prior to the capitulation. In those first frenetic weeks of the Pacific War, as the Japanese army swept down the Malay Peninsula and across the Pacific, overzealous policing ran amok through Singapore. So much time was wasted on wild goose chases. A common mistake was 'tracking down sinister flashes from a secluded spot and finding they came from one of our own ack-ack batteries'.[25] Scott recalled a lot of innocent men shot on evidence that was discredited after the fact. Those deaths were unforgivable.

But the medieval torture, public humiliation and violent deaths meted out to the Chinese in Palembang by the Japanese were in a different category. Scott was acutely aware that it was a fate that may await him. The only surprise was that he had not as yet been dragged into a room and tortured for information. It was clear that they knew he held a significant government posting in Singapore. So why the delay?

The answer to that question came from a European electrical engineer. He was brought into the gymnasium a week after Scott, who studied the new arrival with keen interest. He was the first European he had seen since being brought to the *Kempei Tai*'s gymnasium. The man seemed to be avoiding eye contact with Scott. Perhaps the Japanese had warned him not to communicate with the other white man, a theory made more plausible when the Japanese arranged a sleeping area for him on the opposite side of the room to Scott.

Not long after settling in, the European stood up. With his bag labelled 'Preiswerk' clamped under his arm, the man approached the guard who stood sentry at the only door leading out of the gymnasium. The European threw a furtive sidelong glance at Scott as he walked past. Once he received permission from the sentry to wash his clothes, the man proceeded through a small hall to a washroom. The mystery was deepening. This was one of the methods by which the prisoners communicated with each other. They would wait until a sentry's shift was approaching its end and then go to the washroom. Once the guard changed, another prisoner would fish out some dirty gear, get permission to wash his clothes and meet the other prisoner to share information. Preiswerk, if that was indeed his name, clearly 'knew the ropes'.[26]

Once the guard changed, Scott walked across the room and received permission to go to the bathroom. Scott was cautious. The mystery man knew the exact method by which the prisoners were communicating, as well as the exact time when the guard changed. Had the Japanese extracted this information from another prisoner and shared it with the European as a means of gaining Scott's trust? Was this prisoner a Japanese informer? '[I was] half expecting that he was being planted as a spy on me.'[27] In very little time, Scott dismissed any notion that this man was in league with the Japanese.

Scott never learned the man's name. He would not share it, presumably out of fear that Scott would talk and they would both be punished. Scott would refer to him as Preiswerk because of the label on his bag. He explained that he had been arrested several weeks earlier. He was taken aboard a Japanese troopship and delivered to Singapore, then driven to the *Kempei Tai* headquarters, where he was accused of being a British spy controlling all operations in the Far East. They were effectively accusing him of being near to the top of British intelligence. Preiswerk pleaded innocence. He was in fact a Swiss-born, naturalised Dutchman who worked in Palembang as an electrical engineer. But they did not believe him. They were convinced that he was the spymaster, Robert Heatlie Scott.

Just as Scott had feared, his name was on a 'blacklist [that] was circulated to camps throughout South-East Asia'.[28] But what was this nonsense about being a master spy? Whatever the reason, Scott was clearly a marked man. In their haste to arrest Scott, the Palembang *Kempei Tei* had nabbed the wrong man. This mix-up explained why Morgan – evidently on the blacklist too – was arrested by the *Kempei Tei* nearly a month before Scott, who was surely supposed to be taken away at the same time.

Preiswerk was interrogated for several days. He insisted that they had the wrong man. He did not disclose to Scott the full extent of what he had endured throughout his interrogations. But it was clear to Scott that Preiswerk suffered a 'thorough going cross examination under grim conditions'.[29] Scott was worried; the *Kempei Tai* were not only violent but also dangerously incompetent. It should not have been hard for the Japanese to establish the veracity of Preiswerk's claims. Shortly after taking control of Palembang, the Japanese kept Preiswerk in charge of the electricity company that powered the township. Preiswerk's identity was eventually established. He was shipped back to Palembang and kept under guard, presumably until an investigation into the mix-up was complete.

This led to the second and third mistakes: the fact that Preiswerk and Scott were held in the same room and the fact they found a way to talk to each other. Dreadful though Preiswerk's revelations were for Scott, it was invaluable information. Effectively, Preiswerk was negating the twin elements of shock and surprise, time-tested tools of the interrogator to unbalance the accused and trap them in a lie or a contradiction. But Preiswerk was doing more than simply giving Scott a heads-up that could be used to his advantage. He was saying, 'more or less in so many words, that he doubted if I would be allowed to survive the enquiry'.[30] He was probably also saying that Scott should consider suicide.

Preiswerk went back to the gymnasium first. They did not return together – a face-saving measure for the Japanese guard, who would have known immediately that he and the previous guard had been duped by the Europeans. If they returned separately, however, he could feign ignorance and not feel obliged to report the transgression. The prisoners would get away with it and the guard would avoid a humiliating and possibly painful rebuke from his superiors.

While Scott waited, he weighed his options: 'I considered escape, but that was out of the question. I thought quite seriously of suicide, but felt that [Rosamond], and Susan and Douglas would take a poor view of that!'[31] The eternal diplomat, fascinated with Asian cultures and the inner workings of Japan's Gestapo, also saw the situation as an opportunity: 'I was curious to know what was going to happen and wanted to learn more, at first hand, about the *Kempei*. If things got too hot, I could always fall back on suicide as a last resort.'[32]

Now that Scott had decided to confront his fate back in Singapore, he prepared a methodical approach to his imminent interrogations. He approached the situation as one would a game, the aim of which was to survive and, crucially, not tell the Japanese anything of importance. He had five points to consider:

a) Refuse to speak at all, or, if not, how much to say?
b) What must be withheld, at all costs?
c) What was the minimum number of lies to be told to make sure of (b) and how to make them convincing. (Not that I objected to telling lies to the Nips – I wanted to keep them down to a minimum merely because that reduced the chance of being caught napping on details.)
d) Whose names must be kept out of it?
e) How to answer trick questions?[33]

Scott did not make up his mind on each of these points. He had time. There was no need to have a definitive plan in place until Singapore.

On 7 June, eight days after being brought to the gymnasium, Scott was ordered to pack his kit. A young *Kempei Tei* officer and a gold-toothed private would be escorting him to Singapore. Once he had packed, Scott went around the gymnasium farewelling each Chinese prisoner in either Cantonese or Mandarin. Scott also bid adieu to Preiswerk: 'my farewells infuriated my escort, and made the sentries lose face, as I was supposed to have held no conversation with other prisoners, but I didn't care.'[34]

The Japanese handcuffed Scott. He was pushed into a car and driven to the docks. Two Chinese and two Malayans, all in handcuffs, were waiting for him. Scott would never speak with these men, as they were all kept separate. He deduced, from talking to the Japanese crew, that these men were most likely 'motor car mechanics and had probably been up to some mischief or other in the eyes of the Japanese'.[35] They were taken aboard a small oil tanker moored at the dock. Scott was the last of the captives to board. By the time he had clambered over the side with his sack, the party of four prisoners was already being led down a hatch into the hold. The gold-toothed private motioned for Scott to wait. Some of the ship's officers and crew stood by, regarding Scott with curiosity. The captain approached. In English, he invited Scott to the saloon. What was this? The private looked at Scott and then at the hatch where the officer had just taken the other four. He was uncertain how to proceed. Scott decided to go with the captain.

It was an adequately fitted out saloon, complete with comfortable chairs and a table for dining. Scott accepted a cup of freshly made tea and a cigarette from the captain. As he was discussing the expected travel time to Singapore with the captain, the officer stormed into the saloon. 'Timothy' – as Scott decided to call him, for unknown reasons – let forth a barrage of incomprehensible Japanese. The captain hushed him. 'A whispered conversation followed, the captain wanted me to stay in the saloon for the trip, and Timothy had to give way, obviously with many qualms of conscience.'[36]

With deeply wounded pride, Timothy turned to Scott: 'He shouted orders at me, waving his revolver, pointing over the side of the ship, demonstrating a man jumping overboard, and shouting "Bang! Bang!" or equivalent noises in [Japanese].'[37] Timothy was threatening to shoot Scott if he attempted to escape.

'I won't escape unless I can get away,'[38] Scott responded in English.

The captain looked askance. *Did he just say that?* The captain's English was not strong. He probably assumed he misheard Scott. Timothy, however, seemed satisfied. He left the captain and the prisoner in the saloon.

Scott came to view his voyage to Singapore as a bizarre intermission that neatly separated his war into two distinct acts – the hardships of Sumatra and the horrors of Singapore. The food aboard the tanker was excellent and the crew were extremely kind, 'especially the very fat third engineer, who had done his apprenticeship in Glasgow and then with the Canadian Pacific'.[39] Scott was treated in the manner of an honoured guest while aboard the tanker. He was lent English books to read, given an endless supply of cigarettes, provided three square meals and gifted a needle and thread to mend ripped clothes. '[T]he ship's clerk even translated the day's news into English for me, and typed it all out.'[40]

While the crew dined, Scott was permitted to walk the deck, admiring the wild beauty of the river Musi and the various tributaries he had rowed with the other castaways aboard the *Giang Bee*'s harbour dinghy. At the end of each day, the captain and Scott ate dinner together. The captain wanted to discuss the military action in the Vichy French–controlled island of Madagascar. These were the early days of the battle, the fighting having been active for barely a month. The British campaign to capture the island off the coast of Africa was of deep interest to the captain. He probably anticipated that his tanker would be required for the effort to keep the island under Axis control, the Japanese having provided naval assistance to the Vichy French. The captain produced reports that he translated and some old French maps of Madagascar. Over tea and cigarettes, the two men puzzled over the maps, struggling in vain to make out place names. None of the translations corresponded to any recognisable French towns on the island. In the smoke-filled saloon, the two men discussed in a mixture of English and Japanese the strategic benefit of capturing the island. Both sides, they agreed, had clearly recognised the advantage of controlling Madagascar's ports and thereby cutting off an important sea route to ferry troops, supplies and personnel between the European and Pacific theatres.

The captain seemed to view Scott as an equal, a peer. He was considerably more interested in the foreign prisoner than he was the *Kempei Tai* officer and private, both of whom he largely ignored. The private, who Scott nicknamed 'Toothless', was Scott's permanent minder. He was a fearful man – 'a third class private, and a complete imbecile'[41] – utterly terrified of his superior, Timothy. On one occasion, Scott declared that he needed to relieve himself. Toothless was seized with anxiety. 'He was very doubtful whether this could be permitted, his orders were to keep me in the saloon, and there he sat pointing a revolver at me the whole time, whilst I sat reading and smoking at ease.'[42] Toothless stuck his head out the saloon door, seeking a crewman to send a message to Timothy. But there was nobody around. While he faffed about, Scott indicated that the matter was becoming urgent. Evidently, the fear of humiliating the captain's honoured guest bested his fear of a reprimand from Timothy. Toothless shouted down the corridor. Scott speculated that he was seeking permission to take the prisoner to the bathroom. There was a muted response from a crewman, who, judging from his tone, hardly cared. Toothless accepted the response as an all-clear. With his revolver trained on Scott, Toothless escorted the prisoner to the water closet and stood guard.

Levelling his revolver at Scott was unnecessary. There was nowhere for him to go. Perhaps he felt that, while the tanker was navigating the Musi, he could not afford to lose sight of the prisoner. Toothless's anxiety subsided on the third day of the voyage, when the freighter made it through the mouth of the Musi and entered the open sea. The Japanese private became so relaxed that he would leave his revolver with Scott while he went for a stroll on deck. 'I used to edge up into a position to seize it quickly if by any chance one of our submarines turned up.'[43] Scott prayed that the tanker would be attacked before he landed in Singapore. Any chance of being rescued, no matter how remote – even if it meant being aboard a ship as it was torpedoed and presumably swimming to a surfaced sub – was better than returning to Singapore. 'All through the trip I had a wild hope that something would happen [. . .] Alas, nothing did.'[44]

In the last two days of the trip, Scott entertained himself by humiliating Timothy. There was nothing to it. The private had a childlike need to prove himself physically superior to Scott at every turn. At one point, they were on deck, out of sight of land, staring at the horizon. A dozen or so crew materialised. Timothy seized the chance to demonstrate he was stronger than Scott. He dropped onto the deck and completed six press-ups. Through hand motions and broken English, he challenged Scott to do the same. 'I said I was much too weak, but that when I was younger, I used to do 25 at a time, easily (I have never done more than five in my life).'[45] Timothy frowned. The gauntlet had been thrown. Honour demanded that Timothy accept the challenge of beating Scott's old record. With a reasonable crew of onlookers, Timothy dropped down and got to work. Grunting and groaning with each press-up, he started to slow down after ten and to noticeably fatigue in the teens. At twenty-two, he crumpled into a heap. 'I was roaring with laughter, but he was very offended, especially as half the ship's crew were looking on and giggling.'[46]

The tanker glided across the tepid waters of Singapore's Keppel Harbour on a typically humid June afternoon. Timothy and Toothless wore their uniform, as if preparing to parade. Once safely moored, Scott was handcuffed and brought up on deck, joining the four other handcuffed prisoners with whom he had boarded. They looked dreadful after days spent below without any fresh air. The prisoners were led down a swaying gangplank, an unnerving experience for Scott, whose cuffed hands clasped his sack over his shoulders, and with no means of holding the ropes that might prevent him from falling into the water below.

Once ashore, Scott was again separated from the other four prisoners. A car drew up and a *Kempei Tai* officer stepped out. There was another man in the car. The officer walked around and opened the door for him. Out stepped Kenneth Morgan. The officer asked Scott to identify himself. He told him that he was Robert Heatlie Scott. The officer turned to Morgan and told him to verify that he was telling the truth. Morgan said that it was true. Scott thought that 'apparently the Preiswerk episode had left its mark'.[47] It was a humiliating error. The *Kempei Tai* did not look kindly upon mistakes of any sort. Such mishaps were severely punished. Rather than creating a culture of account-ability, mistakes were hushed up to avoid loss of face, demotion or worse. This may have been the reason it took so long for the *Kempei Tai* to work out what had happened: nobody admitted to making an error.

Scott was driven with Morgan to Outram Road Gaol, formerly known as Pearl's Hill Gaol. The prison was a miserable relic of the early days of the British colonial administration. It was built in 1847 to house convicts and criminals and, in its forbidding, dark and brutal design, was a veritable cliché of all the worst elements of early-Victorian prisons. Following the capitulation, the *Kempei Tai* requisitioned the jail to incarcerate prisoners. An already grim, dismal place was made infinitely worse during their stewardship. An Australian POW named Bill Young offered his own lurid descriptions of the complex:

Passing through those great green painted, timber doors, was like entering a different era, zone, another world [. . .] [Of] the many buildings in the complex the one entered looked the largest of them all. Thick grey walls dominating, demanding attention [. . .] Inside a twenty-foot wide passage cut a swathe from floor to rooftop, all the way to the other end, barely discernible in the gloom.

Artificial light from a few naked bulbs managed to convey a hint on its forty-foot free fall from the ceiling of the hundreds of steel studded wooden doors, stretching out in three tiers on each side, and of the narrow winding stairs and walkways, that service the top two levels. White washed walls, streaked with sweaty water marked grime hung layer on layer [. . .] confirming the antiquity of the place.[48]

Morgan and Scott were forbidden from talking. They were marched inside and led upstairs to separate cells. The number painted above the solid door of Scott's cell read D168. Scott surveyed his new home:

To sleep on there were three planks, supported two feet above the ground by pillars and cross bars. The head was about two inches higher than the foot [. . .] The pillow was a short log of wood, which at any rate was better than the pillows in the Palembang prison, where they were concrete [. . .] In the corner of the cell was a small zinc bucket, as lavatory, which was emptied every two or three days. It had no lid, and was never cleaned; the stench was awful.[49]

The guard left and night fell. Scott was gripped with a terrible thirst. There was no water in the cell. In Japanese, Malay and finally in English, Scott called out 'water-tea-water',[50] at the top of his lungs. A sentry came down. Scott could see his eye through the peephole of the solid door. He banged on the door to make him shut up. Scott persisted. Eventually, the sentry actually listened to Scott's request. He scurried away, returning with a shallow tin lid full of cold tea. The tea was pushed under the base of the door. Scott slurped it down in one go. In a slow, genuinely sorrowful voice the guard spoke: 'So sorry! From the heart of Nippon! So sorry! From the heart of Nippon!'[51]

The guard's apology was sincere. Having finally got their man, the guards could not allow Scott to die. He was too valuable. With his thirst only fractionally slaked, Scott found a tolerably comfortable position on the hard, sloping bed. He rested his head on the wooden pillow and fell asleep. Tomorrow, the inquisition would begin.

12

SAM THE
SERGEANT MAJOR

Fifteen months before the attack

FOR ROB SCOTT, THE day began as it always had in his first week at Outram Road Gaol: a knock on the cell door before dawn, the appearance of two good-conduct prisoners, whom the other prisoners derogatorily referred to as 'trusties', the delivery of breakfast under the eye of a Japanese sentry, an escort out of the cell to the front gate and the handover to a *Kempei Tai* auxiliary waiting outside in a car. The auxiliary was newly arrived in Singapore. He made arrangements to be brought to the prison an hour or so earlier than necessary to allow for a spot of sightseeing. Neither the administrators at the prison nor the officers running the *Kempei Tai* headquarters knew the other's schedule, thus allowing for a trouble-free 'jaunt round town'.[1]

Scott, who had been brought in on the plan and told not to tell anyone, would direct the driver from the backseat. They would drive past the Botanic Gardens, along Lermit Road in Tanglin to look at Scott's stripped-bare house, before turning down Beach Road, past the Raffles Hotel and the Singapore Cricket Club.

The sight of uniformed Japanese soldiers patrolling the streets was jarring. But the ubiquitous Chinese rickshaw pullers and street hawkers bespoke a Singapore that, at least outwardly, had retained many of its old ways.

Scott looked admiringly at those Chinese men as they plied their trade. From the very beginning, the suffering of the Chinese had outmatched all others. Scott could well remember the early days of the siege of Singapore when a wave of Japanese bombers attacked the aerodrome at Kallang. Several bombs landed wide of the mark, striking a village amid coconut trees in the marshy areas in one of the poorest Chinese districts. When word of the tragedy reached the Cathay Building, Scott and several others who spoke Chinese were dispatched to see if they could assist.

The village comprised huts whose walls were made of earth and timber with a piece of flimsy corrugated iron that served as a roof. The destructive force of the bombs had collapsed the huts, burying those within. There were no Chinese men around. They were labourers and fishermen, all hard at work, who would soon return home to the horror of discovering their wives and children had been killed. Several air raid wardens were desperately trying to find any survivors. Scott and the others grabbed picks and shovels to help. It seemed that nobody had survived. They laid out the corpses of thirteen women and infants and covered their faces with towels. 'There was a group of children standing under the palms who had been some distance away playing when the disaster occurred,' one witness recorded. 'They were the children of the Chinese in the sheds. They were howling wildly. They could not make out what had happened. They only knew that it was something terrible.'[2]

A faint sound emerged from beneath the debris, the muffled wail of a baby. The men doubled their efforts. They carefully picked their way through the rubble, following the sound of crying. Scott was there first. Beneath a long board, Scott found a dead Chinese woman, her face mutilated and a baby still at her breast. The woman's body had borne the force of a mass of timber and earth that had fallen on them. Scott gently picked up the baby, who appeared uninjured. One of the surviving women of the village came forward and took the babe. A girl, not yet a teenager, broke away from the group standing under the palms and ran screaming towards the dead woman as she was laid alongside the other corpses. The wardens held her back. She was hysterical. Scott would never forget the sight of her: 'Never have I see such agony of grief in a child: she stood there, weeping and trembling, shaken with sobs, not saying a word.'[3] This was evidently her mother. Scott discerned that there was something else that was compounding her grief. 'Her mother had some money tied in a sash round her waist. She was afraid that it might be lost or that someone might take it away.'[4]

Scott, who understood what the girl was saying, bent down and unfastened the woman's sash and found the purse. He emptied the contents into his hand, counting out four dollars, probably the entirety of the family's savings. He handed the money to the girl, who took it. She then walked over and took her infant sibling from the arms of the woman. Scott watched as she walked back to the other group of children, the baby's crying now mollified. The girl 'looked at us with her watery eyes, sniffing slightly, and with great channels where the tears had run down her grubby little cheeks'.[5] Her face was a mask of grief, but her eyes burnt with steely resilience. It was the same expression Scott could see in the rickshaw pullers and street hawkers as he drove past on his way to interrogation. It surely gave him inspiration to endure what lay ahead.

Scott was driven to the old Colonial Secretariat, where the *Kempei Tai* established their Singaporean headquarters. As was his habit, the guard asked if Scott had eaten breakfast. He had not, Scott would lie. He would be taken to the mess and permitted to eat all the bread, butter and milk he could cram into his belly. This food – sourced from a huge booty of flour, butter and dried milk seized after the capitulation – was unpopular with the *Kempei Tai*, hence its abundance in the mess each morning. Eventually, these ingredients were replaced with the preferred Japanese breakfast staples of rice, seaweed and soya bean soup.[6]

But this morning was different. There was no breakfast even though the offer was made. The problem was Kenneth Morgan. This was the first time Morgan – retired army major and former head of the Japanese Section of the Singapore Special Branch – had been brought to the Colonial Secretariat for questioning at the same time as Scott. When the guard asked the question about whether they had eaten, Morgan answered before Scott had a chance. 'Yes, thank you,' Morgan said, 'we have had breakfast in the prison.'[7] He was politeness personified and infuriatingly honest. It took Scott every ounce of restraint not to clip him across the ears. Why decline the chance of an extra meal? Such honesty would not get you far when in the custody of the *Kempei Tai*. Scott would be sure to cure the old major of that affliction. Around thirty minutes later, Morgan and Scott were taken to separate rooms.

As ever, Scott mentally rehearsed the plan he had devised while en route to Singapore aboard the tanker. 'About 90 per cent of my work had been non-confidential, so I would tell them all about that, and try to focus their attention on it and skate away from the rest.'[8] The other 10 per cent of Scott's responsibilities – the confidential business – was tied up with his work on the Governor's War Council. As a sitting member of the council, Scott would have learnt about Allied troop dispositions in the Far East, the sites of up-country supply depots and weapon dumps in Malaya to enable an insurgency against the Japanese occupying forces, and the identity of individuals who may be interned in one of the Singapore camps and whose knowledge would be useful to the *Kempei Tai*. He would conceal this information behind omissions of truth and outright lies. If his interrogators lobbed false charges at him, he would naturally deny them. He would also flatly deny charges that were true and potentially dangerous to him. 'It whittled down to telling the truth as a general rule, but not the whole truth; telling a few lies; and supressing some of our activities and my relations with certain other departments.'[9]

So far, the strategy had worked. On the first day of his interrogation, 'the enquiry started with a flourish'.[10] No less than the commanding officer of the Singapore branch of the *Kempei Tai* – a grim-faced man of middle age – strode into the room and delivered a lecture that, from the outset, proved instructive. 'Propaganda was important, but anti-Japanese propaganda was wicked.' The man waved his finger at Scott, accusing him of 'doing anti-Japanese propaganda', meaning Scott 'was a wicked man'.[11] It was a wholly nonsensical and utterly hypocritical charge. The Japanese propaganda machine had been far more efficient, productive and successful than Britain's equivalent. Yet the commanding officer seemed sincere. Scott was clearly in the wrong. With tremendous gravity, he made an offer – an arrangement 'in the traditional spirit of Japanese *bushido*'.[12] In short, he was 'prepared to act like [a] Japanese gentlem[a]n', provided Scott 'acted like an English gentleman'.[13] If Scott misbehaved, other methods would be used to extract the information they needed. Adopting an appropriately grave tone, Scott responded: 'I would certainly do my best to act as I thought an English gentlemen ought to behave when under cross examination by the enemy in war time.'[14] The *Kempei* officer seemed satisfied. 'Later on, they accused me once or twice of breaking this promise and double crossing them (which was true), but I assured them that I was behaving exactly as I thought an English gentlemen should (which was also true).'[15]

Scott was handed over to a sergeant major, who sat down with tremendous bluster, dramatically producing a notebook filled with an enormously long list of questions. Scott nicknamed him 'Sam the Sergeant Major'. He was a man with an outsized ego, brimming with braggadocio. 'He had not set the questions himself, and some of them he couldn't even understand, and he knew nothing of Britain, the British, or about propaganda. All of which proved very useful to me.'[16] A young Japanese civilian came along to the interrogations as interpreter. In short time, Sam and Scott came to an unspoken agreement: '[H]e wanted to fill up his forms with lots of wordy information, and he got it.' Every conceivable topic was covered: 'starting with personal history – family [. . .] all about [Rosamond] – my doings in the Far East [. . .] the Ministry – its organisation – [the Ministry's] relation to other departments in the British Government – branches in the Far East – names of staff – what they did – instructions I had received from the Ministry – broadcasting – and so on.'[17]

The two men danced a pas de deux that was, at all times, led by Scott. He layered his answers with all sorts of misleading or superfluous nonsense. He was expert at inserting a piece of ostensibly tantalising information that was utterly irrelevant, fully understanding that his admissions would give rise to supplementary questions that would take the interrogation miles off course. Scott volunteered, for instance, that he had been in Australia for three weeks in November 1941, a revelation of immense excitement to Sam, who likely assumed that eventually the Japanese would absorb the great southern continent into Hirohito's empire. He tore off a blank piece of paper and scribbled down questions designed to draw out what Scott knew of Australia: 'he asked for a statement on the history, strength and equipment of the Australian army; food resources, exports of Australasia.' Scott was delighted, knowing almost nothing about Australia and even less about the Australian military. 'Here I was on sound ground because I knew so little that I could not give anything away and was able to expatiate at length.'[18]

The interpreter – 'a nice little man'[19] but weak – seemed to understand the game Scott was playing, with the run-on sentences and diatribes disguised as useful information that in fact offered nothing. But he was powerless to stop it. '[The interpreter] could not stand up to the strain of questions barked at me and my verbiose [*sic*] replies.'[20] When the interpreter dared interrupt Scott to better interpret his endless responses, Sam would subject him to a withering rebuke. The prisoner must not be prevented from talking. The interpreter's solution was for the prisoner to write down his answers, perhaps as a means of absolving himself of any responsibility when it was discovered that Scott was feeding them rubbish. Sam thought it a good idea.

Scott was happy with the progress – or lack of progress – of the interrogations, but those initial days were taxing. 'I had up to 14 hours of it daily [and was] on my guard the whole time, and still nervously assessing the situation.'[21] It was not uncommon for the session to end well into the night. Scott would be escorted out of the building where Morgan – on the occasions they were questioned on the same day – would be waiting in the car that would take them back to Outram Road. The Japanese assumed that Morgan and Scott had worked closely together in their respective roles – which they had not – and forbade the men from talking to one another, fearful that they would collude and concoct fabricated stories.

But the order was never properly conveyed to the Outram Road guards. Morgan and Scott took advantage of the bungle, sharing their experiences of each interrogation whenever possible. It was particularly useful for Scott. Morgan was repeatedly asked about Scott's responsibilities and influence as the head of the Ministry of Information's Far Eastern Bureau. Scott encouraged Morgan to continue the line he had adopted – that he had no knowledge of Scott's actual daily responsibilities – but also provided some lines that Morgan could use, which added veracity to his own partial truths and outright lies about what he had and had not done.

The bombast and relentless nature of the questioning started to take a toll. Sam might well have been easily misled, but he was tenacious. After all, Sam's 'reputation as a conscientious, zealous and ambitious detective was at stake'.[22] After a particularly long interrogation that concluded near midnight, Sam and the interpreter drove Scott back to prison. Sam said something to the interpreter, who shifted uncomfortably in his seat. The interpreter shook his head. Sam frowned and barked at him. Defeated, the interpreter turned to Scott.

'Ahem – the officer says he has seen a photograph of your wife,' he said, carefully. 'She is very beautiful. Is this so?'

'Well, *I* think so,' said Scott, taken aback. 'I don't know what others think.'

The young Japanese civilian interpreted Scott's response. Sam blinked a few times and then roared with laughter. 'When the Japanese forces capture Australia,' he said. 'I shall send a message to your wife in Sydney.'[23]

From that moment on, there was a discernible shift in the way in which the interrogations were now conducted. They took the form of an informal conversation between acquaintances. Provided Scott 'had been a good boy and there been no incidents that day – [Sam] was prepared to relax, giving [Scott] cigarettes and once or twice taking [him] to his room for a bottle of beer in the evening'.[24] Sam was clearly happy with the progress of the interrogations. He also seemed to be in Scott's thrall. The prisoner was, after all, a man who deserved to be accorded a high degree of respect. At first, Scott ascribed the deferential treatment to the high esteem the Japanese viewed those masters of propaganda: for Scott, 'a welcome change from the attitude of the British Services from 1939 to 1942, when I had so many tiresome time-wasting and futile arguments with them'.[25]

But there was something else at play. Just as Preiswerk had forewarned, the *Kempei Tai* had overestimated Scott's importance: 'They paid me the most absurd compliments. I was the "man who had turned the peoples of East Asia against them"; I was "more dangerous to Nippon than a Division of the British Army".'[26] This wildly inaccurate view ultimately boiled down to a linguistic peculiarity. In Japanese, the same word – *jōhō* – is used to describe 'information' and 'intelligence', particularly in the context of espionage. The *Kempei Tai* believed that Scott – as the head of the Far Eastern Division of the Ministry of Information – was both master propagandist and spymaster. Eager to disavow them of this notion, Scott tried to 'define the difference between "propaganda" and "secret service"'.[27]

Scott's attempts to set them straight failed. Sam simply did not believe him, in part because, as he said, 'most Japanese propagandists were also spies'.[28] He pressed home the point on what he believed were logical grounds: 'How could we distribute information unless we had previously collected it?'[29] The notion that a propagandist is exclusively engaged in the dissemination of information gleaned from espionage is a limited and wholly inaccurate view of how Scott's role worked. But there was no use in arguing the point. Assuming, from his silence, that the Japanese conclusions that Scott was a spymaster were correct, Sam revealed another piece of information that he had acquired: that he was aware of Scott's visits to Japan.

Scott was stunned. He was never going to volunteer that he had been to Japan, but he figured there was a very strong chance that they knew that he had been to the country several times before the war. Scott had been to Japan in his capacity as Vice-Consul of the Far Eastern Consulate and as Financial Adviser to the British Embassies, which maintained an office in Tokyo. Scott decided to tell the truth, that Japan's rapid modernisation, militarisation and bellicosity in Asia was always going to attract the attention of Britian. It was quite natural for Scott, a senior diplomat, to be sent to Japan to report back on the goings-on. He left out his role in trying to influence Japanese policy. But Sam waved off the explanation. Scott, he asserted, was sent to Japan as a spy and 'must obviously know who were the British agents [active in Japan], so would [he] kindly supply, at once, a complete list of names and addresses'?[30]

Scott insisted there were no active agents in Japan. It was a bold play. 'To have claimed that I didn't know would have implied that such agents existed.'[31] At the same time, Scott's assurance lent credence to Sam's conviction that Scott was privy to the goings-on at the highest levels of British espionage, which was untrue. Scott had no choice. He doubled down on the claim, declaring that he could prove there were no spies in Japan. Unsurprisingly, 'Sam was delighted'.[32]

'How can you prove it?' Sam asked.

'The Japanese attack on Malaya,' Scott said, 'took us by surprise – we weren't even able to turn out the streetlights in Singapore when the first Japanese planes came over. If we had had spies in Japan, we should have known all about it in advance.'[33]

This statement hardly disproved the existence of British spies in Japan. They might have just been totally incompetent spies. But the answer seemed to satisfy Sam: 'he asked me no more about our secret service in Japan.'[34] After a lengthy focus on British espionage in the Far East – where Scott dilated on precisely nothing for hours – the topic of the interrogation turned to Scott's role as protagonist-in-chief. At a certain point, Sam channelled all his outrage and in a voice oozing with righteous indignation declared that 'propagandists were in many ways worse than spies. They attacked the heart, as well as the brain. They twisted the pure motives of Imperial Nippon.'[35] He carried on about Japan's holy crusade to free the Asian peoples from the yoke of European imperialism. '[You have] besmirched [our] noblest and deepest ideals,'[36] he declared loftily. That Japan's occupation of large swathes of Asia was proving oppressive, cruel and violent seemed to be lost on Sam. He seemed sincere in his conviction of the purity of Japan's motives.

But Sam was building up to something. He looked squarely at Scott and with breathless indignation, waving an accusatory finger, he said: 'and [you] had done all this [. . .] not only amongst Europeans, but amongst fellow Asiatics [sic]'.[37] In Sam's view,

Scott had achieved much more than ridiculing and humiliating the Japanese race through anti-Japanese propaganda, he had overseen the ideation and distribution of these damaging, racist claims. As proof, Sam referred to anti-Japanese news bulletins broadcast through the MBC that were certainly approved by Scott's office. He listed other tools of propaganda – books, fake newsreels and films – but failed to produce any hard evidence, much to Scott's relief. In truth, Sam did not know the half of it. In the weeks leading up to the capitulation of Singapore a suite of 'fake films [were being developed] in Singapore and [additional] plans in hand for other "special" films'.[38]

These were grave charges that could only be answered with a flat-out denial. For Scott to have confessed to any part of Sam's accusations would have been suicide. 'I protested that until war with Japan broke out, our work had been anti-German and not anti-Japanese.'[39] This bald-faced lie was not easily disproven, but Sam was prepared with a retort. Firstly, it was inconceivable that Scott, the head of Britain's propaganda machine, was not taking an active role in disseminating anti-Japanese information given the Empire's military aggression and expansion through China in the preceding decade. Secondly, the defence that Scott only worked on anti-German propaganda was no defence at all. Germany and Japan were allies since the signing of the axis pact in 1940. An attack on Germany was therefore an attack on Japan. Thirdly, for Scott to cloak himself in the defence that all his activities were intended to advance Britain's interests in the Far East and had nothing to do with Japan was at best disingenuous, at worst total nonsense. Japan's mission was 'to kick the white man out of Asia, [so] anything that promoted British interests in Asia was ipso facto anti-Japanese'.[40] Fourthly, Scott 'was a liar anyway' so his denials were less than worthless. 'I must admit that the *Kempei* were correct on all four counts.'[41] Not that he was about to say as much.

Sensing he had knocked Scott off balance, Sam shifted gears. He began comparing the fighting prowess of the British and the Americans. He waxed on about the two gunboats – the USS *Wake* and the HMS *Peterel* – that happened to be on the Yangtze River and proved the only obstacles to the Japanese seizing Shanghai on 8 December 1941, shortly after the attack on Pearl Harbor. In Sam's telling of what happened, the British captain of the *Peterel* put up a spirited defence against an over-whelming Japanese force. The captain of the *Wake*, meanwhile, simply surrendered without a shot being fired. (Although it was true that the *Peterel*'s crew fought gallantly and the *Wake* sur-rendered without a fight, the only United States ship to do so in World War II, the *Wake*'s captain had unsuccessfully attempted to scuttle the vessel.) This was neither the first nor last time Scott's opinion would be sought on the actions of the British and American gunboats. He encountered 'many Japanese who admired the British commander and remarked on the contrast'.[42] Scott was always extremely cautious in his responses: 'I was always on the lookout for this sort of thing, which smelt of a desire to quote me in broadcast or otherwise.'[43]

Sure enough, Sam wanted Scott to agree that the story of the *Peterel* and the *Wake* was irrefutable proof that the Americans had no fighting traditions. Scott demurred: 'I said that our gunboat commander had followed British naval traditions; Americans had their own point of view about these things, and doubtless the American commander was acting under previously issued orders designed to prevent loss of life.'[44] Sam retorted that the Americans were cowards. Scott pointed to the American defence of Corregidor and the Philippines. Sam was forced to concede that 'in Manila the Americans had shown up very well'.[45] It was a mark of Scott's poise that – under considerable pressure and the constant threat that Sam might resort to torture to get what he needed – he not only never cracked but was able to attain the ascendency. In Sam, he was, of course, dealing with an unworthy adversary. Sam was 'an unsubtle man [. . .] too blunt to make a good detective'.[46]

Towards the end of yet another arduous day, Scott complained of a toothache. It was a delaying tactic. Remaining constantly vigilant, deftly navigating the obstacles that Sam was deploying to guide him into a trap, was exhausting. He all but demanded that he be allowed to see a dentist. To Scott's great surprise, Sam went off to ask the commanding officer for permission. While alone with the interpreter, Scott apologised insincerely for the delay his toothache would inevitably cause.

'It is all right,' said the interpreter, 'we are very glad; we are very tired!'[47]

Sure enough, Scott's request was granted. The following day, they all went to see a Chinese dentist. Scott's teeth were assessed, the dentist betraying a look of bewilderment. There was evidently no sign of decay. With Scott's check-up complete, Sam sat down in the chair and instructed the dentist to unnecessarily cap one of his teeth in gold. Meanwhile, Scott sat in the corner drinking coffee and smoking cheroots the dentist provided free of charge. Grateful for the delay the visit to the dentist provided, Scott offered the 50 guilders he was gifted in Palembang. The dentist waived the fee: how could he accept money for doing nothing? But he did accept payment from Sam for the gold. Scott was astonished: 'to do such a thing for a prisoner in custody, in front of the *Kempei*, required pluck.'[48] The Chinese dentist got his money, the interpreter and Scott had a break, and Sam's vanity was assuaged, 'so everyone was happy'.[49]

13

THE SHAKESPEARE ADVENTURE

Fourteen months before the attack

ROB SCOTT CONTINUED TO lead his interrogator in a merry dance at the old Colonial Secretariat: looping around in circles, studiously avoiding anything of importance, tediously drawing out the point, never contradicting himself and saying absolutely nothing of significance. Sam, the *Kempei Tai* sergeant major, filled his notebook with assiduously transcribed sentences of drivel. For Sam, every detail had to be jotted down. There might be a hidden gem or stunning revelation concealed in Scott's word salad. He was hyper-alert, elevating his task of extracting information from Scott to something of divine significance, at one point even sensing the hand of destiny guiding him to a breakthrough in the hunt for hidden insurgents and fifth columnists operating within Syonan.

The breakthrough occurred one morning around the beginning of Scott's daily interrogation. Sam – who 'was a bit restive'[1] – stood up and went over to the window and started drumming his fingers on the pane. Something caught his eye;

words etched onto the windowsill. Excited, Sam called the interpreter over. With great animation, the two men puzzled over the words. This building had been the nerve centre of the British administration of Singapore. The Governor maintained his office here and senior civil servants ran the colony from these very rooms. It was also the main communication hub between Singapore and London, facilitating the exchange of information, intelligence, instructions and reports. Had Sam stumbled over some sort of coded message sent from London? The interpreter wrote down the sentence on a sheet of paper and took it over to Scott.

'The officer,' said the interpreter, 'wishes to know what this means.'[2]

He pushed the paper in front of Scott, the words written in neat cursive – *Seeking the bubble reputation even in the cannon's mouth*. The words instantly transported Scott back to his school days.

'That's Shakespeare,' Scott said.[3]

The interpreter turned to Sam and, in a disappointed voice, explained that it was a quote from the great playwright. Sam was unconvinced. A Shakespearean quote etched into the windowsill by a bored civil servant had, in Sam's overheated imagination, taken on enormous significance. He was certain he had stumbled upon some secret code, a clandestine form of communication known only to the British. This, in Sam's view, was how they would organise their resistance.

Sam demanded to know about Shakespeare and the meaning of the quote. Reaching into the deep recesses of his mind, Scott recalled that the quote was from *As You Like It*. 'I gave most of the context, the seven ages of man having been drilled into my memory by having had to write them out so often as punishment lines at school.'[4]

How pertinent that this line – referring as it did to a soldier who imperils his own life to attain the 'bubble reputation' – should be the source of such fascination for Sam. This prideful, vain egotist, whose behaviour bespoke an obsession to burnish the views others had of him, now insisted that Scott write every Shakespearean poem and scene that he could recall. Scott managed to dissuade Sam of such a fruitless exercise with the help of the interpreter, who was appalled at the idea of attempting to translate Elizabethan English into modern Japanese. A compromise was reached. The interpreter would instead verify Scott's claim about the quote. Somehow, he came into possession of *As You Like It*. He spent several hours reading the play. Eventually, he found the line. Scott was correct. 'My reputation for truth telling – by that time getting a little shaky – was considerably strengthened by this comical affair. It was definitely the way gentlemen behaved in the best circles.'[5]

Sam did not see the 'Shakespeare adventure'[6] – as Scott described it – as a pointless diversion. On the contrary. He was positively beaming. He asked Scott if Shakespeare was his favourite poet. Scott said he was, in fact, more of a fan of John Keats. The next day, Sam arrived with a looted leather-bound copy of *The Complete Works of Keats*. Deprived of reading material for many months, this book would become Scott's most treasured possession. He would commit most of Keats' works to memory, an act that he would say saved him from slipping into complete misery in the dark days to come.

The interrogations became mentally exhausting for Scott. There was no break in the enquiry, not even when Scott came down with dengue fever. The questions persisted despite Scott's full-body aches, roaring temperature and nausea. 'The *Kempei* gave me some pills, but wouldn't interrupt the questioning for a trifle like that.'[7] As Scott's physical health deteriorated, not even Sam, in his zeal to complete the enquiry in good time, could deny that the interrogation was pointless. Scott could barely answer coherently. No bother. This was a chance for Sam to take stock and tally up the spectacular intelligence he had gleaned from the enquiry, which was, of course, utter claptrap.

Scott only needed to rest for half a day before his health began to return. In his cell, there was little more to do than read his copy of Keats' poems to the grim accompaniment of groaning prisoners dying in nearby cells. The Japanese in Outram Road Gaol provided no medical treatment to those suffering dysentery, beri-beri, blackwater fever or malaria. Some managed to pull through, but many did not. A Chinese prisoner in the cell next door to Scott died in agony: 'I could hear his cries and moans day and night through the walls, till one evening there was a sudden stillness, and I knew he was dead.'[8]

Scott could not say for certain whether the Japanese neglect of ill prisoners was formalised as policy. But it was certainly an attitude reflected in all the camps in which Scott was incarcerated. For those suffering chronic diseases, the situation was particularly dire. 'Cancer [sufferers] had of course little chance from the beginning: they just died, and the most they could hope for was that the camp would have enough dope of some sort to ease their suffering.'[9] The situation was equally hopeless for diabetics. Deprived of insulin, 'the men just lay in bed in the ward and slowly died of starvation before our eyes'.[10] It would later be discovered that the Japanese were hoarding insulin, most likely extracted from Red Cross parcels.

The banality of solitary confinement – of being trapped in a cell without seeing the sky – weighed on Scott. Other prisoners who had endured a longer period of incarceration were losing their minds before Scott had even arrived. One Australian soldier went insane within the first month of Scott's incarceration. Each night, he would assume the identity of the commander of the Australian Imperial Force's 8th Division, Gordon Bennett. He could be heard playing an interminable round of golf, his sententious, patrician bellows echoing through the prison corridors and keeping guards and prisoners up through the night. 'I'm General

Gordon Bennett,' he shouted. 'I'm all tee'd up!'[11] The prisoner's ranting went on for several nights, until it abruptly stopped. The general consensus was that the guards had killed him, an entirely plausible theory in Scott's view after he witnessed the maltreatment of a prisoner who was driven to insanity. 'He was manacled hand and foot to his bed, and repeatedly beaten by the guards.'[12]

Eventually, the incarcerated were permitted time outside. It was possible the decision was a preventative measure against the rapidly declining mental health of the prisoner population: 'these dark, damp cells, dirty, insanitary, with nothing – utterly nothing – to do all day and night, tended to drive you mad.'[13] The decision should not be viewed as an act of humanity; managing a lunatic asylum was considerably more complex than a prison.

Other punitive measures were relaxed, notably the prohibition of communication between prisoners. Still, one had to be careful. Scott kept his distance. While out in the yard, he counted around 120 civilians, mostly Chinese, but also several Indians, Malays and Europeans. By conversing with these people, Scott might lend credence to Sam's accusations of being the great spymaster and propagandist who had turned all of Asia against the Japanese. But he was less concerned about mingling with the thirty British and Australian prisoners. He took a few soldiers' names and enquired about the fate of their various units. Most had been cut off from their units during the fighting and had been captured attempting to escape the island following the capitulation. All of these soldiers had been sentenced to prison for the crime of escaping. They were separated from their main units, which, upon being captured, were sent to the POW camp out in Changi. This was likely a reflection of the contempt the Japanese held for those who either surrendered or escaped – both acts akin to the vile crime of cowardly avoiding to fight, which, to the Japanese, was the most heinous transgression a soldier could commit.

The fate of these poor men played on Scott's mind. He resolved to help them somehow. He got an idea when the enquiry with Sam resumed: 'I began to steal things from *Kempei* Headquarters and smuggle them into the prison for the others.'[14] It was a dangerous exercise. The likely outcome of being captured with contraband – essentially anything in his possession – would be a severe beating. Luckily for Scott, the guards barely checked him. 'I was searched each evening, but it was a slack business as a rule – which was reasonable enough, as I had been in the care of the *Kempei* all day long, and the prison police took it for granted that I could not have been up to much mischief.'[15]

Scott took full advantage of the lax security. Showing great stealth and daring, he stole some of Sam's cigarettes and matches when both interrogator and interpreter had their backs turned. He also pilfered some basic kitchen and bathroom items, such as towels and spoons. The spoons were gleefully received: 'some of the men were revolted by having to eat with fingers and just couldn't do it unless they could wash their hands.'[16] But nothing lifted morale quite like the three books of poetry Scott managed to smuggle into the prison undetected. They were part of a larger collection Sam brought into the enquiry, evidently unable to let go of his suspicion that they contained a hidden language of codes the prisoners and perhaps fifth columnists were using to communicate.

Among those three books was the collected works of Tennyson. It was a hefty volume Scott went to great trouble in getting inside the prison. It was intended for Marriott, one of the so-called 'jungle beasts' of the Argyll and Sutherland Highlanders, so named because of their ferocious and effective fighting prowess in the wild, overgrown terrain during the Malayan Campaign. The young Argyll subaltern was separated from his unit when his battalion was cut up in the Battle of Slim River. Marriot had hidden in the jungle for a month, 'got captured, refused to give away the Chinese who had helped him, was very badly beaten, court martialled, and sentenced to four years for "escaping"'.[17] Scott had met Marriot – a fellow Scotsman – in the prison yard and was left full of admiration for the young man.

There was no way Scott would risk giving the Tennyson to Marriott in the yard. The book was too bulky and cumbersome. Scott instead offered an Australian trusty bringing dinner to his cell a couple of cigarettes on the condition he deliver the book to Marriott. Scott would use the trusties as couriers to smuggle the books from cell to cell on numerous occasions, an arrangement that proved highly effective. That it took the guards nearly a year to cotton on was a measure of their lack of vigilance.

The inevitable discovery of the books precipitated a minor crisis. Several men were beaten, a predictably violent response for such a loss of face. But given the value they had provided, this was 'a cheap price to pay'.[18] The prisoners all knew the man responsible for bringing the books into the prison. Despite coming in for some brutal punishment, none of them disclosed his name, an act of courage for which Scott would be extremely grateful, particularly given what was to come.

The longer Scott was incarcerated at Outram Road Gaol, the more daring he became: 'my best effort was to take in a lighted cigarette, right past all the guards to my cell.'[19] Smoking was strictly prohibited and, like all forbidden fruit, ravenously desired. Very few prisoners managed to source cigarettes in the prison; fewer still found a match. Those lucky enough to find both had to be exceptionally careful. The guards were known to partake in spot checks, peering through the peephole of each cell door or barging into a cell unannounced. Perhaps Scott's decision to audaciously enter the prison with a lit cigarette in hand worked because it was done in plain sight. He walked past Morgan's cell, grinning at his fellow prisoner as he went. Morgan caught sight of the smouldering cigarette concealed within his hand but leaving a noticeable trail of smoke. It was like bearing witness to a schoolfriend committing some outrageous transgression right

under the headmaster's nose – and equally hilarious. It took all
Morgan's considerable restraint to prevent himself from laughing.

Scott was forced to check his cavalier attitude when the enquiry
took a sharp turn for the worse. Without warning, Sam 'produced
a bundle of violently anti-Japanese pamphlets, with illustrations
about the Japanese record in Korea and Formosa, Japanese use of
opium, and so on'.[20] Scott recognised the pamphlets because he
was the man who had suggested that they be printed. The idea
had come to him in the months leading up to the outbreak of war
in the Pacific. At that time, the Japanese were dropping their own
pamphlets across South-East Asia and the Malay Archipelago,
calling on the local people to rise up against the European occupiers. Scott's pamphlets were intended to counter that effort, to
remind the Asian people that Japan's so-called 'liberation' was
in fact a track record of brutal, inhumane conquest.

Sam demanded an explanation. Scott said nothing. Better
to wait to hear the accusation before mounting a defence. The
pamphlets, the interpreter explained, had been traced to the
Cathay Building, the building the Japanese knew had been leased
to the MBC and where Scott maintained an office. Unbeknown to
Scott, the Cathay Building had lately been repurposed to house,
among other things, the Japanese Broadcasting Department and
the Military Propaganda Department. In the frenetic moments
before evacuating Singapore, somebody neglected to destroy
the pamphlets. They hardly posed an intelligence risk for the
Allies. But for Scott their discovery was a catastrophe. Here was
incontrovertible proof that he had been engaged in the production
of anti-Japanese propaganda and, more importantly, had been
lying about it.

Sam demanded to know the people responsible for the
pamphlets. Scott had no choice but to claim responsibility.
Not only was he the one who had initiated their creation, but
the pamphlets were prepared and printed by local printers in
Singapore, rather than his office. Scott could only assume that

those people were now living under Japanese occupation. Were
he to shift responsibility to them, he would effectively be signing
their death warrant.

Sam was irate. It was 'exceedingly awkward' for Scott: 'I had
stated positively that I had done no anti-Japanese propaganda
before the outbreak of war.'[21] As a salve for Sam's grievance, Scott
doled out a series of meek excuses. The anti-Japanese material
should be viewed in the same vein as the deployment of British
forces in the Far East before the war – the natural response to
Japan's increased hostility. He prevaricated with wordy answers
and deflected the blame to his superiors by insisting the pamphlets
were 'prepared on the instructions of London'.[22] This outright lie
was grudgingly accepted, but Scott's 'reputation as a gentleman
got a nasty knock'.[23]

The pamphlet affair was an unfortunate denouement to what
had otherwise been Scott's masterclass in how to reveal nothing
in a mentally gruelling six-week enquiry. With great care, Sam,
who was elated with the volume of material he had gathered,
arranged his 'huge mass of useless information – 75 pages of
mimeographed Japanese, which, he told me with pride, was the
"biggest dossier in the office"'[24] – into a neat bundle. The dossier
would be sent directly to 'the higher authorities',[25] Sam's smug
bearing indicating that the information 'would carry him to high
office'.[26] Scott took no satisfaction in having duped 'poor Sam'.[27]
It was not that he cared a jot for his inquisitor, but rather a
recollection of the warning he had received from Preiswerk, the
Swiss engineer mistaken for Scott: no man facing the sorts of
charges that the *Kempei Tai* had levelled against Scott would
be permitted to survive. 'I had an uneasy feeling that when the
[senior officers] got down to [reading the dossier] in their own
time, and waded through it, and found that its value was nil,
they would be after me again.'[28]

At the end of Sam's enquiry, Scott was transferred out of
Outram Road Gaol along with Morgan, whose interrogation

had ended three weeks earlier. Morgan revealed that he too was suspected of espionage and 'for working agents all over China for and on behalf of R.H. Scott'.[29] On the final day of his interrogation, Morgan saw his name next to Scott's in the notebook on the table before him. Both their names were underlined in red pen. Although never found guilty in a legal sense – the enquiries into each man were not, after all, trials – the Japanese concluded that both men were responsible for heinous crimes. Yet there was lingering uncertainty, not in regard to their criminality, but as to whether the *Kempei Tai* had extracted every last morsel of knowledge from these key figures. It was this uncertainty that very likely saved them from execution.

Both men were nonetheless extremely dangerous and could not simply be permitted to mingle with other prisoners. Outram Road Gaol was deemed inadequate to prevent these two criminals from getting up to more mischief. They were bundled into a car and driven east to Changi jail, where they would be placed in solitary confinement.

14

TO CAST GOOD SEED

Four weeks after the attack

IN KUDAT, NORTH BORNEO, Chinese families kept a tradition of arranged marriages until the generation before Elizabeth Choy was born. The missionary schools, which were now educating young girls as well as boys, may have – intentionally or not – contributed to the end of that tradition. The young women these schools produced were independently minded and determined to shape their own destiny. Arranged marriages did not fit with such aspirations. Elizabeth's father was nonetheless in favour of the practice. He would tell his eldest daughter that 'the arranged marriages were quite successful and happy'.[1] Although Elizabeth's marriage was not arranged, it was certainly a match that was encouraged by the elder generation.

Elizabeth first met Choy Khun Heng through his sister, a close friend and classmate at the convent school. They would walk home together after school, Elizabeth routinely stopping in for something to eat before continuing on. She paid little attention to the shy and understated boy with a talent for mathematics who would become her husband. But she could not ignore her future mother-in-law, who doted upon this charming and polite young Hakka lady from the wilds of Borneo, affectionately calling Elizabeth her Chinese birth name, Su Moi. 'The old lady took a fancy to me and looked after me very well, giving me lunch every day, and eventually she told me I would make a very good wife for her second son.'[2] Elizabeth was initially underwhelmed. But the sight of the old lady's look of despondency at Elizabeth's evident lack of interest in her son moved something in Elizabeth. 'I said, "All right, I will marry your son," and at least make one old lady happy.'[3]

It was a long engagement, the couple eventually marrying nearly a decade after they first met, four months before war broke out in the Pacific. The double wedding – Elizabeth's brother, Kon Vui, married on the same day to save the extended family back in Borneo two trips to Singapore – 'was a very grand affair, the reception was held in the Victoria Memorial Hall, and there were five hundred guests'.[4] From the outset, Choy and Elizabeth's marriage could never be characterised as a heady, passionate romance. But the two were devoted to each other.

In the canteen at Miyako hospital, life for the Choys was busy. The smuggling operation was becoming more sophisticated, drawing other internees in Changi into its orbit. Norman Coulson, a water engineer originally from Newcastle upon Tyne who worked in the Public Works Department in Singapore before the war, played a crucial role. Deemed to have a job central to maintaining critical infrastructure, Coulson was not interned. He was a regular guest at the Bishop of Singapore's residence, where he would play cards and dine. Bishop Wilson asked Coulson, who was often called out to Changi to repair damaged pipes, if he was willing to help smuggle even more money into the jail. Coulson's pipes proved the perfect receptacle in which to smuggle cash and other supplies. The pipes were watertight, easily transportable and inconspicuous.

Coulson supplied pipes directly to the bishop, who stuffed them with cash. They were then handed to secretary K.T. Alexander to give to the Choys, who handed them to courier John Long on his next hospital run.

Everybody, including a large number of Japanese, seemed to be aware of the scale of goods and money being trafficked from the canteen to Changi. Visitors would come with a parcel, letter, trinket, cash or keepsake to be delivered to an internee. Elizabeth was always accommodating, handing over the items to John Long. 'Anybody who wanted to [. . .] pass anything onto a friend would come to us. We said, "All right."'[5] It was in her nature to help those in need, irrespective of the risks. 'Anybody in trouble I would help. Everything we did was to help people.'[6] She lived the Christian proverb, 'Cast good seed into the sea and an island will grow.'* For Elizabeth, genuine fulfilment in life was a by-product of helping others. 'Many people in this world are running around looking for happiness, but I think the fundamental law for happiness is to forget yourself and help others, and then happiness automatically comes to you.'[7]

Whenever possible, Long would share with Elizabeth some of the goings-on in Changi. In this way, she learnt about the fate of some of the more well-known internees. Elizabeth felt great pangs of pity for the Governor of the Straits Settlement and High Commissioner of the Malay States, Sir Shenton Thomas, and his wife, Lady Thomas, who – Long had told her – were kept in different cell blocks and forbidden from seeing each other.** To have endured such hardship alone seemed particularly cruel.

---

*   This proverb appears on the (out-of-print) transcript of her interview with Shirle Gordon, see Shirle Gordon, 'The Autobiography of Elizabeth Choy Su-Mei'.

** Sir Shenton Thomas would ultimately be shipped out to Korea and then on to Japan. Lady Thomas remained in Singapore throughout the Japanese occupation.

Elizabeth arranged for 'medicine and daily necessities'[8] to be delivered to Lady Thomas, to ease her suffering.

To be sure, the risks the Choys were taking in helping the internees were enormous. But their concerns were mitigated by the level of complicity of the Japanese, whose involvement in the smuggling was becoming increasingly transparent. On his ambulance runs, John Long would occasionally bring patients whose maladies were relatively minor. He took them to the canteen to meet the Choys and even some of the Japanese sentries. On one such occasion, Long took along the former Chief Surveyor of Singapore, Thomas Kitching, with eight dysentery cases to Miyako. Kitching wrote about the experience in his diary:

We travel 10 miles via Timpines to [Miyako] I see one car and one bus during the whole journey. [Another internee named Dr T.H Bowyer and Long take] me to the 'shop', a place in the hospital run by a Chinese employee and his wife, both very nice. A [Japanese] sentry comes up too with a Jap-Malay dictionary. He speaks scarcely at all, but we sit down at the same table – Bowyer, Spragg, [Long], Elizabeth, the wife, and myself. I have two Tiger beers (aha! at last!), soup, omelette, pork and beans. I can't pay, but [the Choys] absolutely refuse any payment in any case.[9]

Without warning, around mid-October 1943, roughly a year after it opened, the Miyako canteen was abruptly closed. The Choys were instructed to set up a new canteen at Tan Tock Seng Hospital, which had been renamed Hakuai Byōin, literally 'Universal Love Hospital'.[10] Tan Tock Seng, as everyone continued to call it, served as the main civilian hospital at the time. The crucial link between Changi and the outside world was severed. Changi internees in need of medical assistance would now be sent to the shockingly substandard hospice at Sime Road Camp. There were also whispers of an incident that had occurred at

Changi. Details were sketchy, but the rumours involved *Kempei Tai* soldiers and officers carrying out some sort of raid. Nothing good could come of that.

The raid on Changi coincided with a beefed-up *Kempei Tai* presence through the Chinese neighbourhoods. *Kempei Tai* soldiers were raiding houses in the middle of the night, searching for anything suspicious and sometimes dragging someone off for questioning. Elizabeth did not panic. Even if the Miyako canteen closure was part of these *Kempei* activities, she was confident that she and her husband had not really done anything wrong. Their work at the canteen had served a 'humanitarian purpose'.[11] Elizabeth did not look inside Coulson's pipes once they were handed over to her by the bishop's secretary. She assumed they were filled with 'food [. . .] maybe a bit of news or letters or notes [. . .] innocent things, money to buy things'.[12] In time, she would learn that the British were smuggling material into Changi that was strictly prohibited.

Two weeks after setting up the canteen at Tan Tock Seng, Choy Khun Heng disappeared. He had left home early to open up. When Elizabeth arrived, Choy was not there. The doctors and nurses who worked at the hospital offered no explanation. Elizabeth approached a Japanese sentry, asking if he knew her husband's whereabouts. He told her that he had been taken for questioning at the YMCA, the building that now served as the headquarters of the *Kempei Tai*.

Elizabeth returned to work while frantically puzzling out what to do next. She needed help. But who could she ask? Since the canteen at Miyako was shut, Elizabeth was no longer connected with K.T. Alexander or John Long, essentially her only contacts. The hospital staff were of no use, most of them determined to stay clear of Elizabeth, who was clearly persona non grata. That left her only one choice.

After finishing work at the canteen, Elizabeth walked from Tan Tock Seng to the YMCA, pushing through the front door and eyeing the guard at the front office. Elizabeth introduced herself and explained that her husband had been taken. She all but demanded to see him. She said that she knew that he was here. The guard shook his head. Elizabeth persisted. What had happened to him?

'No,' the guard said, in a voice that brooked no argument. 'We don't know.'[13]

This was pointless. Elizabeth turned to leave, despondent but not yet defeated. She walked across the road and sat down on the grass verge directly opposite the building where she was convinced her husband was being held. There she waited, watching the Kempei Tai officers file in and out through the front door, hoping for an explanation of Choy Khun Heng's whereabouts. At dusk, a soldier appeared and ordered her to leave. Remaining here was not only futile, it was dangerous. She stood up and left.

For two weeks, Elizabeth existed in a state of constant anxiety. In order to provide money for her family, she had to continue work, but her mind was constantly occupied with the where-abouts of her husband. Seventeen days after Choy had vanished, a man dressed in a sharkskin suit appeared at the family house in Mackenzie Road and requested to speak to Elizabeth.

'Do you want to see your husband?' he asked. There was no acknowledgement from this Kempei Tai officer that Elizabeth had been lied to. Not that she cared. Choy was alive. That was all that mattered. 'Yes,' she said. 'Of course I do.'

'Alright, come.' The guard made to turn and then stopped. 'You said that your husband would be cold [without] a blanket. You bring a blanket to see him.'[14]

Elizabeth did not think it a strange suggestion. The joyous reve-lation that her husband was alive had distracted her. She hurried back inside, grabbed a thick woollen blanket and returned to meet the officer out on the street. The two walked in silence to the YMCA. On arrival, the officer instructed Elizabeth to hand over all her possessions to one of the duty officers. Elizabeth's heart skipped a beat. Why did they need her possessions? Several guards had surrounded her. When she did not respond to the demand, a guard stepped forward and roughly removed the watch from her wrist and the jewellery from her fingers and around her neck. Elizabeth made an attempt to retrieve the comb from her bag, but before she could open the handbag, it was snatched away from her. She was left with nothing but the blanket.

The guards led her inside the building. It was dank and humid within. She was led down a hall and taken to a cell of wooden bars. There was a small gap at the base of the prison bars that Elizabeth would later learn was where food was delivered and where prisoners entered and exited the cell. Inside, Elizabeth counted twenty people. All but one of the detainees were male. They were squatting or sitting in deathly silence, all facing the corridor. There was no space to move. The prisoners were downcast and fearful. Some had a haunted look. In one corner, a tap hung over an open commode that was caked in brown and green lichen. This was the source of the stench in the room.

Elizabeth was told to enter. She crawled through the narrow gap at the cell's base. The prisoners made space for her, but all averted her eyes. She knew instantly not to speak. Her mind went to the same place it always did in a crisis – concern for others. She knew she would not be returning to Mackenzie Road anytime soon. When she failed to appear, how would her father – frail, sick and emotionally devastated at the death of his favourite son – react to her disappearance? A dreadful scream from above wrenched her back into the present. None of the other detainees reacted. They had heard much worse before.

Hours passed. Elizabeth waited, sitting cross-legged, not daring to move. The only sound that broke the silence was the blood-curdling screams that continued to echo through the corridors and cells of the building. She sensed the other detainees becoming restless. There was increased fidgeting and shuffling. This was not fear. It was anticipation. A guard appeared, pushing bowls of food through the gap at the base of the cell. The detainees distributed the bowls to the others. Elizabeth finished her first prison meal of rice, a few vegetable scraps and a tiny portion of meat, in two modest mouthfuls. A bucket filled with liquid was passed into the cell along with a single mug. Elizabeth watched as one person held the bucket while another scooped up a mugful of the liquid. They would drink the mug of liquid in one or two slurps before handing it to the person sitting next to them. The heat and humidity in that room was oppressive. Whatever the substance of the drink, it was gratefully accepted. Eventually, the mug was handed to Elizabeth. The mug was filthy, caked in dirt and bits of hardened grit, and the liquid inside the bucket was tepid and brown. Without hesitating, Elizabeth dipped her mug inside and drank down bland, lukewarm tea. She handed the mug to the next person, holding the bucket for him.

After she had endured several hours of silence, unable to move or talk, a guard appeared outside the cell. He pointed at Elizabeth and told her to come forward. She steeled herself for what was to come. She would not show fear. *Sit up straight.* That was the message she would deliver her students when she caught them slouching. She would meet whatever fate awaited her outside this cell with grace and poise. She placed the blanket on the ground and shuffled past the other detainees, crawling through the narrow gap beneath the prison bars. She stood up, pushed her shoulders back and followed the guards along a corridor and up a flight of stairs. The guard guided her into a room. The door slammed behind her. Her first interrogation was about to begin.

15

THE MAN IN THE TOWER

Fourteen months before the attack

CHANGI JAIL ROSE UP amid the rubber plantations, coconut trees and jungle that covered the largely flat landscape of Singapore's eastern peninsula. Japanese bombers had left the building alone, having learnt it was being used as an internment camp for Japanese civilians. As such, the walls and roofs of the jail were intact and without so much as a 'shrapnel scar'.[1] Construction had finished only six years prior to the outbreak of war to incarcerate prisoners serving long-term sentences. Although newly built, the structure called to mind a medieval castle with great grey blocks of cells, an ominous tower and two encircling walls surmounted at intervals with watchtowers. The inner wall of the jail was 25 feet in height, the outer wall twice as high. The entire complex covered around 11 acres.*

---

* The Changi area was the site of two related but distinct camps: the Changi internment camp, which housed civilians, and the Changi POW camp, which primarily held military personnel captured by the Japanese. The Changi jail was the facility used to incarcerate internees. The Changi POW camp was a sprawling complex comprising several repurposed British barracks.

At the main entrance, a steel portcullis powered by electricity would be raised, permitting access for guards, visitors and inmates through a large gate and into a hall under the tower. The hall funnelled into a kind of bottleneck that led to a nexus of two corridors, each leading to one of the jail's two massive three-storey buildings. These were each divided into two self-contained cell blocks with their own exercise yard, dining room and workshop. The jail's architects contrived to build a fortress that was escape-proof; 'every corridor, every window, has its iron grille, while massive steel doors cut off the interconnecting blocks and floors.'[2]

Rob Scott and Kenneth Morgan were driven inside. They were escorted through the entrance and processed outside a guardroom adjacent to a room assigned to internees who acted as camp officials. Japanese guards told Scott and Morgan that they would not be allowed into the open air. They were forbidden from any interaction with any other internee before being led up a staircase to the upper levels of the tower. They were separated, taken into their own cell and placed in solitary confinement.

The cell Scott was all but certain would be his home for the remainder of the war – and perhaps for the term of his natural life – was a considerable improvement on his accommodation at Outram Road Gaol. It was 'fairly large, about fourteen feet square; one quarter of which was cut off to form a bathroom'.[3] The bathroom was an absolute luxury, complete with an 'Asiatic type push-and-pull'[4], a tap with actual running water and a wash-stand. The cell had two windows boarded up with cardboard. Once alone, Scott set about manufacturing peepholes. Being located just inside the main wall of the prison, the view was pretty miserable: 'I looked across this road at a thirty-foot-high wall, which blocked any further view.'[5] He would nonetheless come to appreciate the view for the distractions it offered. The road that his room overlooked led to the entrance to the prison, which was only a few yards from his cell. 'This was one of my main pastimes in "solitary" – watching the front gate: Japanese arriving and leaving, working parties of civilians going to cut wood, going out with carts to fetch wood, going out to garden, and so on.'[6]

There came a rap on Scott's cell door around an hour after his arrival. An internee entered with a tray of warm food, a packet of cigarettes and matches. The internee looked at Scott and nodded. Behind him stood a sentry, who kept close watch. The internee was an Australian named Charles Edward Hopkins. 'Hoppy', as he was popularly known, walked over and placed the tray on the ground in front of Scott.

'Sir Shenton sends his love,' whispered Hoppy.[7] He turned and walked out, the sentry closing the cell door.

Scott surely felt warmth bloom from within. Owing to his high station within Singapore's civil administration, Scott had met Governor Shenton Thomas on numerous occasions, including as a sitting member of the Governor's War Council. Notwithstanding the frustrations he felt with the civil administration over which the Governor presided and the obtuseness of his war council, Scott always admired Sir Shenton. Knowing that he was here in Changi was surely comforting.

The problem was how to get a message to the Governor. He would tackle that problem later. Scott's focus was on the food. He had been delivered a generous serving of rice and mince. There was even a pudding. He devoured both dinner and dessert, concluding the food 'was excellent'.[8] The inclusion of a fork and spoon – knives naturally not permitted – was a welcome return to a more civilised way of dining after months of eating with his hands. Evidently the treatment of internees in Changi was considerably better than what he had experienced elsewhere. Scott rightly suspected that this was the consequence of the internees essentially running the camp. 'The Japanese [military] supplied nothing: no drugs, eating utensils, beds, mosquito nets, garden tools, or any mortal thing, except basic rations – rice, root

vegetables, a little oil and cooking fat, a little salt fish or sometimes beef, and a few other odds and ends.'[9] Only later would
Scott discover the sophisticated and organised society that had
emerged within Changi in the first year of the occupation.

Scott pulled a cigarette from the packet Hoppy had handed
him. When he opened the box of matches, a note fell out. It read:
'Who are you? What has happened?' Scott was suddenly aware
of his appearance: 'I looked like a scarecrow when I arrived.'[10]
Having lost his shaving kit when the *Giang Bee* went down, Scott
had no means of trimming his beard, which was an effulgent
mass of knots that had grown a life of its own: 'a great busy
affair half way down my chest, like a French parish priest'.[11]
His clothes were torn and messy and he had dropped weight. His
wild-man appearance had caused a stir in the camp. Who was
this strange fellow who was so important the Japanese had sent
him to the tower? 'As I was hustled straight from the entrance
arch into my cell, only a few internees, all strangers to me, had
seen me come in.'[12]

Scott turned in for the night, buoyed by Hoppy's message and
the prospect of being able to correspond with the rest of the camp.
His mood was dampened somewhat when he realised the cell
offered nowhere to sleep, not even the slanted wooden planks that
he enjoyed at Outram Road Gaol. Instead, he was forced to 'lie
on the cement floor, cold, damp, and draughty'.[13] By now, Scott
had grown used to such discomforts. He was surrendering to sleep
when he felt something on his leg. It seemed that Scott was not
alone in the cell – he shared it with all manner of bugs. The latest
discomfort to which he would need to become accustomed was
trying to sleep while cockroaches scurried all over him.

Scott was up early the next morning. He prepared to write a
response to Hoppy. The Japanese had permitted a lined exercise
book and pencils, an extraordinary indulgence that put him on
edge. That the internees managed to smuggle a note inside a

matchbox raised questions. How had the Japanese sentries missed it? Was it incompetence or a means of coaxing information from him? And if so, was this internee in on it? At this point, Scott knew nothing of the man, not even his name. The internees who delivered the food back at Outram Road Gaol were trusties. If this internee was a trusty, then using him to courier a message was fraught with risk. No man who won favour with the Japanese could be trusted.

Scott knew he had to go carefully. The safest option was to ignore the questions scrawled on the note altogether. But that was never going to happen. Scott had no idea how long he would be confined to his cell. His experience in Outram Road Gaol had revealed how quickly isolation and an unoccupied mind led to madness. The chance to correspond through Hoppy was the mental rail onto which he could grasp to prevent his mind from slipping. He would answer the questions in the note, one at a time, and make sure not to include anything sensitive or incriminating.

When the cell door opened, Scott stood up. He had positioned himself next to the tray. Hoppy came over with a new tray holding a bowl of *kunji* – porridge made from rice flour and maize flour. The sentry kept watch at the door to guard against any bold escape attempt, just as Scott had hoped. Scott waited until Hoppy was handing him the tray of food. With his lips partially concealed behind that luxuriant beard, he mouthed his name in a voice barely above a whisper. Hoppy showed no outward sign that the name meant anything to him or even that he heard Scott. He bent down, picked up the tray and left.

Hoppy returned several hours later with a meal of rice and mince. There was a corked bottle of water on the tray. It was an odd addition to his meal. Scott's cell had running water. As he handed Scott the tray, Hoppy whispered something about the cork. Once he was alone, Scott uncorked the bottle. A note was crammed inside the cork. It was a greeting from Chris Dawson, a civil servant Scott had encountered before the evacuation.

While in solitary, Scott would communicate by way of messages in bottles. The notes contained names of some camp internees with whom Scott was familiar, bits of information about Changi and scraps of news about the war. God knew how they heard about the war. Scott could only assume that the news was sourced from the guards or perhaps from an internee fluent in Japanese who overheard conversations. Later he would learn that the news was from a considerably more reliable source. At this point, he did not care from where it came: 'Chris' [news] accounts were my great standby.'[14]

Scott would reply to each message, making use of the hollowed-out cork to conceal scraps of paper that would be taken out of the cell. The bottle would then be returned with the next meal, with a new note stashed in the cork, which he would promptly destroy after reading. As such, we cannot know exactly what Scott wrote or what he received. It was very likely he provided a summary of his attempted escape aboard the *Giang Bee*, notable military and civilian captives he had encountered and perhaps the conditions in the camps in Palembang and Outram Road Gaol. Given what we know of what was brought into his cell, Scott clearly requested books, news and anything else that could occupy his mind.

Hoppy – whose name Scott now knew through the smuggled correspondence – took tremendous risks for Scott. He had inventive ways of providing reading material for Scott. On several occasions, he would bring peanuts carried within sheets of American newspapers. 'The sentry, who had to inspect all food, would examine the peanuts and overlook the wrapping (after all, peanuts had to be wrapped up in something).'[15] These were old papers printed before the war. But Scott devoured them all the same, just as he churned through the books that Hoppy somehow managed to smuggle into the cell.

Other methods were invented to keep Scott apprised of how the war was unfolding. His cell was situated close to an enormous fuse box. The camp electricians, all internees, were regularly called on to replace burnt-out fuses. The electricians would park their truck outside Scott's window and sing tunes with altered lyrics that included news updates: 'It's a long way to Tipperary – *Akyab has fallen* . . .'[16] Such news updates were discontinued on account of the two sentries manning the entrance some 20 yards away who started to show signs of suspicion. Nevertheless, the care and concern shown by Hoppy and the others was deeply moving: 'the men's representative (head of the internees, elected by the whole camp) and the Camp generally were always agitating about me and [Kenneth] Morgan. Protest after protest was made to the Japanese, who bluntly stated (when permission was asked to send us bedding), "these men are not internees".'[17] Therefore, they were not entitled to any more comforts.

A month after arriving at Changi, Scott developed a serious ear infection, a common Changi ailment referred to as Singapore Ear. 'It is very painful, the ears swell up and discharge a filthy pus, and are uncomfortable to sleep on.'[18] If untreated, the ears would eventually become completely blocked, rendering the sufferer partially or wholly deaf. Scott's repeated requests to see a doctor were ignored for five months. By January 1943 when he was finally given medical attention, the infection had clearly healed. The doctor – who knew that Scott's ears were fine – painted his ears with mercurochrome, a topical antiseptic that was burgundy in colour. The doctor made such a mess that it looked as if both Scott's ears were discharging blood. As the Japanese now assumed Scott was suffering some heinous infection, the doctor was now permitted to visit on several more occasions until the mercurochrome faded. The Sikh sentry – who had replaced the Japanese sentry – could not speak a word of English, thus allowing doctor and patient to have 'a little chat under pretence of discussing [Scott's] non-existent symptoms'.[19]

The doctor assured Scott that the camp was continuing to advocate for his release from solitary. Scott never made any complaints to the Japanese, fearful that such an action would invite unwanted attention and a new round of interrogations. But requests for something to sleep on and more reading material were granted: 'I got a bed – of wooden planks – and a mattress and a pillow; and books began to come in with permission of the Japanese.'[20] The camp library supplied the books, which were delivered to Scott's cell by way of a Japanese interpreter, who had to read each book to make sure no secret codes or messages were being sent in. After a few weeks, he got sick of it. Having grown accustomed to the steady supply of reading material, the abruptness with which the library service was discontinued was a shock. 'The steady improvement was very heartening and the set back in October, when the books stopped, was depressing.'[21]

By now, Scott had been in Changi for ten weeks. The circumstances and novelties of his incarceration – including the smuggled news from Chris Dawson, the better-than-average food, the books and the other bits of reading material brought into his cell – had worn off. Scott was feeling indolent. In the absence of any distractions brought into his cell, Scott built a strict routine. His day was divided into three parts, and each segment commenced with cleaning himself at the washstand There were two exercise periods, three smoking sessions, time allotted for mending and washing out the cell, and time given over to reading and memorising the works of Keats. There were games he invented too, most commonly 'a mental ten years' diary: where was I ten years ago today – nine years ago today – etc. etc. – and what was I doing and whom did I meet?'[22] He also found solace in his notebook. Rather than the risky enterprise of journaling his experience, Scott devoted pages to memory games. He wrote down every book title of which he could think, categorised into genre – children's, cookery, reference, hobbies, wines and more. There were names of friends and their addresses, restaurants of London, a glossary of dog training terms and techniques, recipes, diet programs and anything else that came into his mind.

At other times, Scott would watch the comings and goings at the front gate through the peepholes he had made in the cardboarded windows. 'One of the events of my life in "solitary" was to see the monthly parade of women and children leaving the camp to walk to the seashore a mile or so away, for a swim.'[23] Among the smartly dressed women and children off for their monthly picnic, Scott would reliably spy Lady Thomas – Governor Sir Shenton Thomas's wife – and Chris Dawson's wife, Jill. They would linger at the rear of the parade. When the sentries were looking away, the two women would turn to face Scott's window and smile and wave. For that little stunt, which they never failed to perform, Scott believed that they were 'inviting a face-slapping at least; it meant a lot to me'.[24]

After six weeks, the library service resumed. The arrival of fresh titles was an enormous relief and coincided with an easing of restrictions. Hoppy managed to arrange for a barber to visit. Scott was handed a mirror and was at once appalled and impressed with his dishevelled beard. He was happy enough for his hair to be trimmed, but he would not allow the beard to be removed. Not yet. Scott also received his first visitor, one of Rosamond's closest friends. She arrived unexpectedly, beaming at the sight of Scott, having convinced the Japanese that he was in fact her legal guardian. She delivered Scott a slice of cake.

Seven months after Scott entered solitary, the Changi Commandant paid him a visit. His name was Asahi. He spoke excellent English, having lived and worked in London before the war as the Japanese Commercial Attaché. This was not the first time Scott had a hosted a Japanese officer in his cell. A couple of *Kempei Tai* officers paid him a visit, seeking information about various Japanese men Scott might have known in Singapore. There were suspicions that some Japanese discovered in India who had lived in Singapore before the war might have been operating as agents for the Allies. 'I was naturally totally unable to be of any assistance!'[25]

Commandant Asahi cast a stern eye over Scott. 'Do you wish for anything?' he asked.

Scott was nearly rendered speechless. There were many things he wanted. He said the first thing that came to his head. 'I have not been in the open air for over seven months: may I take open air exercise daily?'

Asahi looked confused. 'But would you like to join the other internees?'

'Of course,' Scott said, without hesitation.

'Well, you may – if you sign a promise.'

Scott was convinced that this was a lure intended to entice him into a confession. 'What sort of a promise?' he asked.

'I promise not to break the peace of the camp,' he said.

It took every ounce of restraint not to burst out laughing. Scott managed to effect his most serious tone: 'Yes, I think I can sign such a promise.'[26]

Asahi led Scott out of his cell. The date was 19 February 1943. It was the first time he had left his cell in 220 days. Asahi conceded that he did not know the reason Scott had been placed in solitary confinement. Scott believed he was telling the truth. But it was a striking admission. Was this decision – to keep Asahi out of the loop – a security precaution, a way of compartmentalising intelligence to prevent careless dissemination? Or were certain officers of the *Kempei Tai* determined to keep Scott for themselves, to hitch their own promotions to the secrets he possessed, as it were? Neither, at least in Scott's view, who believed it was yet another 'interesting example of Japanese administrative inefficiency, and lack of coordination between departments'.[27] When Scott had arrived, there was a different commandant in place; when Asahi arrived, no record of Scott existed. He was releasing Scott of his own volition.

Scott followed Asahi into an office, Kenneth Morgan arriving shortly thereafter. They were both made to sign sworn statements that they would not attempt to escape. Since the attempted escape of four Australian POWs held in a barracks to the north of the jail, which was part of the Changi complex, many POWs and internees were compelled to sign a pledge of non-escape. The so-called Selarang Barracks Square Incident led to the illegal execution of the four POWs. The 1929 Geneva Convention on the Treatment of POWs recognised a prisoner's right to escape. Although not a signatory to the Geneva Convention, Japan was nonetheless obliged to adhere to certain principles of humanitarian treatment under international law. In having Scott and Morgan sign the pledge, the Japanese were forcing the two men, in effect, to waive their international rights. Scott hesitated before signing, but only for a moment: 'escape, I had long since decided, was out of the question, especially from solitary confinement.'[28]

After both men both signed, they were handed over to the camp authorities – the internees – and taken directly to the camp hospital. 'To all the others in the camp, interment was *durance vile*. To us it was freedom.'[29]

Changi Prison plan

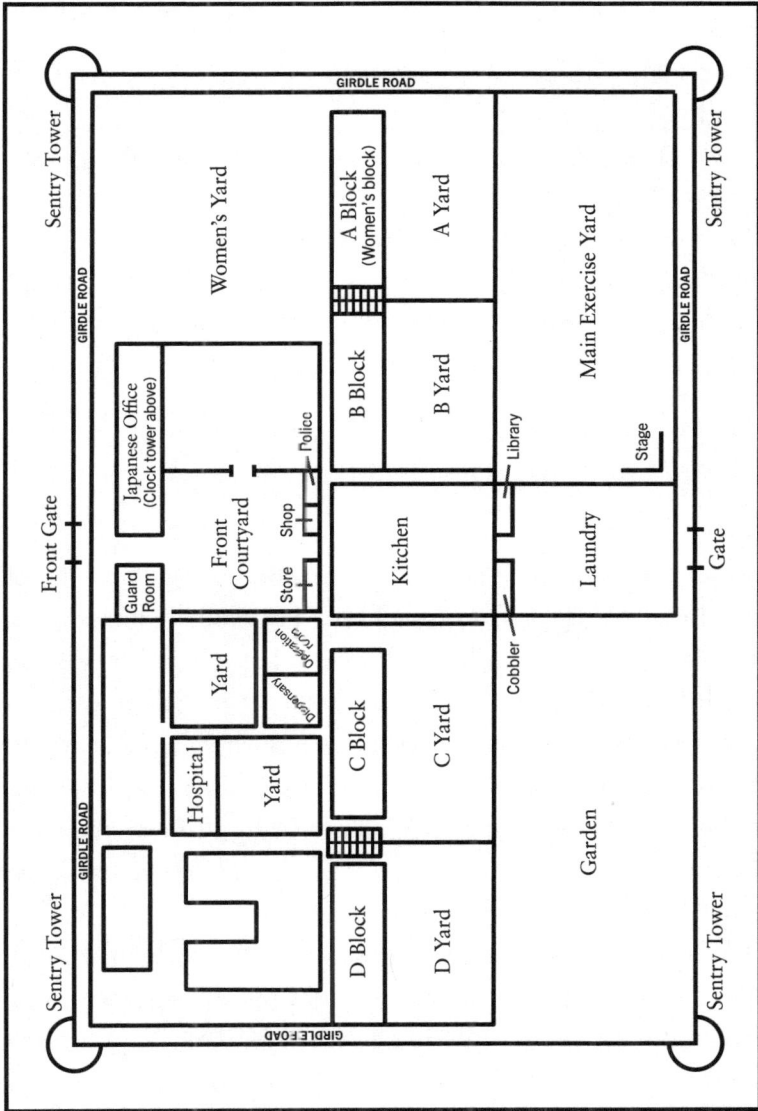

Changi Prison plan

- Sentry Tower
- GIRDLE ROAD
- Front Gate
- Sentry Tower
- Women's Yard
- Japanese Office (Clock tower above)
- A Block (Women's block)
- A Yard
- B Block
- B Yard
- Main Exercise Yard
- Front Courtyard
- Police
- Shop
- Store
- Guard Room
- Kitchen
- Library
- Stage
- Laundry
- Gate
- Dispensary
- Operation Room
- Yard
- Hospital
- Yard
- C Block
- C Yard
- Cobbler
- Garden
- D Block
- D Yard
- Sentry Tower
- GIRDLE ROAD
- Sentry Tower

16

THE BLACK MARKET

Ten months before the attack

ONE INTERNEE NOTED THAT Rob Scott emerged from solitary confinement 'surprisingly well and cheerful',[1] a phenomenon he ascribed to his restful period alone in his cell. Solitary was never restful. Scott's good health and buoyant mood were the consequence of being among people, many of them friends and former colleagues, in a facility that was a considerable improvement on the hardships, deprivations and indignities of the camps in Palembang and Outram Road Gaol. Changi Prison was, comparatively, a place of unimaginable luxuries.

Although its aesthetic was severe, grey, brutal and ugly, Changi was light-years ahead in regard to prisoner amenities. Every one of the hundreds of cells in Changi had a latrine in working order, in addition to plumbed-in toilets conveniently situated throughout the cell blocks. The internees enjoyed daily showers, washed their clothes in a spacious and well-equipped laundry, borrowed books from a library with shelves holding 5000 titles, and cooked meals in a large kitchen 'equipped with the most up-to-date steam-cooking equipment, all complete and in working order'.[2] Nonetheless, the prison, which was designed to incarcerate 700 people, was extremely overcrowded. At the start of the occupation, there were 3000 internees in Changi jail; that number would swell to 3400 within two years. Scott was assigned a bed in a room previously used to flog misbehaving prisoners before the war, which now accommodated twelve men.

But unlike the camps of Sumatra and the misery in Outram Road Gaol, where the prisoners wallowed in despair, the Changi internees seemed, if not content, then relieved at their situation; some were upbeat. There was a sense that living in this jail was probably the best possible outcome for a European in Singapore. George L. Peet, who was Scott's colleague in the Ministry and who was interned after the capitulation, observed:

> Those walls from the inside appeared to us not as restraints on our freedom, as barriers shutting us from the pleasures of normal life, but rather as defence against a hostile and dangerous world. It was no hardship to be imprisoned at that time, for we felt comparatively safe in the camp, whereas we knew that for us Singapore had become a different place, one in which we had no part, where we were regarded with the utmost suspicion.[3]

Not everyone felt the same. There was, as Peet observed, 'that trying type of internee who spent half his leisure time brooding on our grievances, real or imaginary, [who] was continuingly comforting his mean little soul with the thought that special revenge would be expected after the war for our having been put in gaol, instead of [. . .] in hotels or in our own house in the suburbs of Singapore, for there were actually people among us who argued, quite passionately, those were not unreasonable expectations'.[4] When reminded that these complaints were being voiced by people interned in the very place where the British administration in Singapore had interned Japanese civilians, they were unmoved: 'they still refused to admit that sauce for the Nipponese goose was sauce for the British gander.'[5] Scott agreed with Peet: 'Changi Gaol was by far the most suitable building in which [the Japanese] could have confined us and we were fortunate to have been put there.'[6]

Yet for Scott, the notion that the worst was behind him felt delusional. Keeping a low profile was all but impossible. He had attained a certain celebrity among the other internees – as the 'Man in the Tower' – and felt that the gaze of the *Kempei Tai* would inevitably be trained upon him again. If he was correct, his next interrogator could be considerably more violent and considerably less buffoonish than Sam. Another chat with the *Kempei Tai* was something Scott wanted to avoid. But how? He had seen how fearful the Japanese were of cholera outbreaks at the camp in Palembang. Perhaps he could manufacture the symptoms to keep the guards at bay. He sought the advice of Changi's doctors. There was no shortage of men to consult; more than 100 doctors were interned at Changi. They told him that, 'unfortunately, the only diseases likely to influence the Japanese are things like cholera and dysentery, subject to checking by objective tests'.[7]

If a disease of the body could not be faked, what about a disease of the mind? Would the *Kempei Tai* bother to interrogate a man who had lost his marbles? In their unequivocal advice, the doctors were as one: don't do it. One doctor suggested Scott borrow *The Road to En-Dor* from the camp library. The book was an autobiographical account of the wartime experiences of E.H. Jones, a Welsh soldier in a Turkish POW camp in the previous war. Jones relates how he and an Australian prisoner feigned insanity in the hopes of being repatriated. The plan worked, but not before the two men suffered enormous physical and psychological torment from their captors.[8] The book had the desired effect on Scott. It seemed highly probable that if he were to attempt the same strategy, he would suffer a similar fate:

'I had not forgotten the wretch I had seen manacled in [Outram Road] not many months earlier.'[9]

After abandoning the idea of faking insanity, Scott committed to the typical internee's life in Changi. The camp was divided into four blocks. There were, at this juncture, around 2800 men and 370 women, fifty-five children and six infants in the camp.[10] Block A was the women's camp, cut off from the rest of the camp with walls and locked doors. Blocks B, C and D were open to each other, and the male internees moved freely between them. The upper levels of each block commanded spectacular views across Singapore. One side of the prison offered an unimpeded view across the fields of rubber and coconut trees, to the distinct jungle-clad hill of Bukit Timah. On a clear day, the mighty eminence of Mount Pulai in Malaya could be seen soaring into the tropical clouds in the far distance. The other side of the prison provided a view onto what one internee called, 'a glorious panorama of sea and coast curving into the eastern end of the Straits of Johore'.[11]

As for security, the Japanese policed the prison with a light touch. The Japanese sentries charged with keeping an eye on the internees were more like supervisors than fearsome guards. The camp seemed to be almost entirely run by internees. Perhaps most startling was the amount of money on the premises. The place was awash with cash, and where there is a lot of money and a high demand for goods in an unregulated environment, there is a black market. Everyone was in on it – the guards, the internees, the administrators and the civilians employed to work in the jail. Scott also discovered that 'if you had money, there were plenty of things to be bought'.[12]

When Changi's Central Committee turned to the Church as a financier, they probably hoped that the money that would provide the foundations of their financial system – with its $5 monthly allowance to all internees – would not be as susceptible to corruption and racketeering. But such an outcome was unavoidable. Besides, the money ultimately achieved what they had hoped it would do. It provided the bedrock of a highly functional mini society, which spurred the internees into action. There was a camp organisation with designated leadership and committees, an office, registry, shop, kitchen, stores, carpenters, gardeners, hospital, tinsmiths, classes for children and educational opportunities for adults. Almost everyone had a role to play and a job of work to earn money.

Scott took his turn hauling wood carts and did an enormous amount of gardening. He even worked as a barber. While carefully trimming one internee's hair, Scott's customer observed: 'This is an odd hobby, Scott. Where did you learn to be a barber?'

'I didn't,' Scott said, 'I'm learning now.'[13]

The money Scott earned, combined with his monthly allowance, was enough to buy 300 small cheroots, thirty eggs or 15 ounces of locally made pipe tobacco. The shop also supplied bananas, palm sugar, tinned stuffs and more. Scott still had the $37 in Singaporean currency that he took with him before leaving the Cathay Building and boarding the *Giang Bee*. The money should have attained talismanic properties in Scott's mind. Not only had those notes remained dry during the sea voyage in the dinghy after the sinking of the *Giang Bee*, Scott managed to keep the money hidden despite multiple examinations by guards on his way into the camps of Palembang and Singapore. That money was a good luck charm.

Evidently Scott did not see it that way. At the first opportunity to spend it, the money went fast. He bought sweets and extra tobacco and sundry other items, and very quickly found himself in need of more cash. The Dutch guilders that John Quinn had gifted him back in Palembang would also have vanished had it been accepted as legal tender. His inability to swap the guilders, whose trading value was equivalent per unit of currency to Singaporean money, was acutely frustrating. An opportunity to engage in a currency exchange came from the unlikeliest of individuals – the Camp Commandant.

Scott and Morgan were a source of ongoing fascination to Asahi. His curiosity was fuelled by an enduring interest in all things British, which harked back to his days as the Japanese attaché in London. A highly compartmentalised approach to information sharing and a hopelessly inefficient system of communication and record keeping meant that Asahi did not have the slightest notion of the identity of these evidently important individuals; he also had nobody to ask. Except, that is, for the two men themselves. Asahi summoned them for an interview. The Commandant spent much of the time waxing on about his career, his time in Singapore and the 'marvellous way he ran the internment camp',[14] which, in Scott's estimation, was to do absolutely nothing for the internees and just let them run the camp themselves. It was an approach best defined as wilful neglect, in Scott's view, and 'judging by Japanese standards, this was indeed a liberal and humane policy'.[15]

Scott's assessment of Asahi's approach to the administration of Changi was accurate, if a little harsh. In reality, the Commandant's light touch afforded the internees privileges that were unthinkable in other Japanese internment and POW camps throughout the Far East. Take, for example, his positively enlightened approach to allowing the internees time outside the jail as an antidote to the grey misery of Changi's walls. He ordered the guards to wire off a large area directly outside the prison, within which the prisoners could 'go for a stroll or read or talk in pleasant and restful surroundings with trees and grass around us instead of the eternal concrete'.[16] Additionally, Asahi offered the internees the twice-weekly chance to walk to a nearby rubber estate to collect wood for the camp, plus the monthly sojourn to the beach for a swim.

Asahi's management of Changi was not only relatively humane, it was tactically wise: happier internees were easier to control and less likely to raise a rebellion. But for all these privileges, Scott rightly remained distrustful of Asahi's motives in summoning the two men for a meeting. He was, after all, the enemy. Both internees treated the meeting as an interrogation, batting away his enquires about their roles before the war and implying that they both held low-level positions in the Strait Settlements government. Asahi did not press them further. He seemed more interested in other matters. 'At the end of the interview, he asked Morgan and myself to answer a series of questions in writing: what had caused the war, how long would it last, how would it end, did the internees have any complaints.'[17] Asahi assured the two men that their answers would not be used against them. Scott was now an expert at detecting when an interrogator used deception to set an unwitting suspect on a glide path to confession. But he sensed there was no trickery here. Asahi was genuinely interested in their opinions of the war's origins, and, perhaps most importantly, what they thought of his prison camp.

The two men set about writing up every conceivable complaint that they could imagine. They knew it would likely come to nothing, but any opportunity to improve the lot of the prison population was worth a shot. They may have had a better chance of affecting some change had Scott not also written a devastating critique of the circumstances that gave rise to the war in the Pacific, levelling the blame entirely on Japan. '[I] prophesied that [Japan] would find herself much hampered by her conquests, "like a boxer who has seized the silver cups before the fight starts."'[18] For good measure, he predicted Germany's defeat in the spring of 1944 and Japan's unconditional surrender in the autumn of 1945.

On delivering their list of complaints in writing to Asahi, Scott hazarded a request: 'I asked him if he would change my Dutch guilders into Singapore money.'[19] Asahi promised that he would look into it. Scott was under no illusions. The promise would surely be broken after Asahi read Scott's savage appraisal of the prison. Scott remained sceptical when a Japanese sentry arrived at his dorm with a message from the Commandant, assuring him that an exchange for his guilders could be made.

Nevertheless, Scott – who reasoned that he had absolutely nothing to lose, given the guilders were worthless – handed over the Dutch money. Astonishingly, the sentry returned and counted over the correct amount of Singaporean banana notes, named as such owing to the motifs of banana trees on $10 bills. 'This little fund I soon blew on a pair of flannel trousers, smokes, sweets, exercise books, pencils and eggs.'[20]

Scott came to wonder if Asahi was, in fact, a very decent man and that in facilitating the exchange of money he 'was seeking to make up for having kept Morgan and me locked up for so long'.[21] It is also possible that Asahi wanted to win Scott and Morgan's trust as a means of exerting control. Clearly these two men had clout within the camp. That was obvious from the heartfelt and persistent advocacy to improve their conditions and the demands from the Camp Committee to release them from solitary confinement. Whoever these men were, whatever they had done to end up in solitary, did not matter. To the rest of the camp, they were leaders. Making an enemy of these two men was a very foolish idea. They might attempt to organise a mass escape or raise an unruly mob. Such events posed no mortal threat to Asahi, but a bloody, violent riot in Changi would be ruinous for his career. So, like the seasoned attaché he had once been, he took a diplomatic approach.

It was the same approach he took to the huge sums of money being smuggled into the camp. Asahi knew about the cash circulating through the camp – how could he not? – and turned a blind eye. He was probably also in favour of the basic financial system that the injection of capital had created, with its attendant benefits of internees feeling a sense of social contribution and self-worth from having a job to do. Other downstream consequences of introducing a flow of money into the camp included keeping the guards happy, many of whom were clearly turning a sizeable profit. The British had stockpiled huge quantities of tinned food, having anticipated a long siege. The godowns and provision shops throughout the municipal area 'were bursting with tinned food-stuffs when the Japanese captured it'.[22] After the capitulation, widespread looting resulted in the tinned supplies ending up in the hands of individuals who turned black marketeers. Much of the stockpile was seized by Japanese soldiers, who cut a deal with Changi's sentries, who 'used to bring sackfuls [sic] of tinned goods at night, sell them to racketeers in the camp, who in turn retailed them to their customers'.[23]

But the Japanese were by no means the only people financially benefiting from Changi's commercial opportunities. Talk of the Bishop of Singapore's injection of hundreds of thousands of borrowed cash into the internees' coffers had inspired others in the Swiss community to get a piece of the action. There were more ways to get their money out of Singapore than by loaning huge sums of money to the Church. The most profitable method was providing supplies on credit. Changi was not self-sufficient. Some vegetables could be grown in the areas Asahi had cordoned off outside the walls, but most supplies had to be sourced from outside the camp. The Swiss businessman Hans Schweizer-Iten – the individual who had arranged the loan of vast sums of money to the Church, cash that continued to be smuggled into Changi – had, for a long time, lobbied the Japanese to recognise him as the Singaporean representative of the International Red Cross. Were his request granted, he would be permitted to routinely carry out an inspection of Changi and assess what supplies were needed. The Japanese would never grant the international aid organisation the right to function in Singapore, therefore Schweizer-Iten never officially became the representative of the Red Cross. (In fact, the International Red Cross was not permitted to carry out an inspection of Changi until the end of the war.)

But owing to the chronic shortage of supplies and the very real risk of starvation or an epidemic of disease sweeping through Changi, the Japanese accepted a compromise. Although prohibited from inspecting the camp and reporting on whatever he may have inadvertently seen while dealing with the Japanese camp administrators, Schweizer-Iten – with the help of other Swiss and Chinese employees of the trading company Diethelm & Co., where Schweizer-Iten was employed as managing director – was allowed to deliver supplies to the camp. It would prove to be at once an act of humanitarian aid that almost certainly saved thousands of lives and a highly lucrative wheeze.

Schweizer-Iten purchased all manner of things in bulk – tinned milk, tinned food, tobacco, rice, eating utensils, gardening tools, towels, blankets, clothing, mosquito nets and other consumer goods stored in the Diethelm warehouses – and then delivered it all to the camp in a clapped-out faded azure lorry. Every purchased item was provided on credit to the internees, entirely financed by the Swiss community, 'to be repaid after the war with six per cent interest'[24] – around the pre-war rate of exchange. For the Swiss, Changi had become an alchemist's cauldron that turned soon-to-be-worthless Singapore banana notes into Swiss francs that would be collected at the end of the war at a very tidy profit. Scott marvelled at the scheme, which was indisputably ingenious despite carrying the odour of something unseemly; these large profits were, after all, generated from desperately hungry internees. The internees were not complaining – they nicknamed Schweizer-Iten's old lorry that regularly turned up at Changi's front gate heavily laden with lifesaving supplies 'The Blue Angel' – and neither was Scott: 'They made fortunes out of it, the amount involved finally ran into millions of dollars; but we can't grumble, as they saved the camp, and moreover they often had arguments with the Nips and ran big risks to keep the supplies flowing.'[25]

Eventually, Asahi put a stop to Schweizer-Iten's supply runs, eager no doubt to control the distribution of food and materials that were becoming increasingly scarce. When his visits to Changi were discontinued, Schweizer-Iten was permitted to drive his lorry to Sime Road Camp to deliver much-needed food and supplies to the internees for much of the rest of the occupation.

He would later be suspected of being a spy and was subjected to numerous and lengthy interrogations by the *Kempei Tai*, some lasting as long as ten hours. Although never tortured or incarcerated, Schweizer-Iten was put under enormous pressure to confess to spying and to reveal the names of internees who were working against the Japanese. He denied the accusation that he was spy, and it redounds to his enormous credit that he never incriminated any internees to save his own skin.*

The end of Schweizer-Iten's deliveries was preceded by a change in guard. The Japanese military guards – 'who had regarded their duties in the internment camp merely as a pleasurable interlude in active service'[26] – were replaced almost entirely with Sikhs towards the end of 1942, mostly warders or former policemen when Singapore was British. The Sikhs were less approachable and more forbidding than the Japanese guards; they were also less corruptible. George L. Peet observed that 'they were far too much in awe of the Japanese authorities to risk any illicit trafficking, so there were no black-market goods forthcoming from that quarter.'[27]

With a limited supply of goods smuggled into the jail, prices skyrocketed. The internees came to rely almost entirely on the money that was brought into the camp to pay for extras. Like any black market, Changi's financial system was not self-sustaining. There was obviously no system of taxation or tithing to create some sort of centralised bank that could redistribute the money. The cash that circulated within the camp was continually run down as the Japanese took their healthy cut and the racketeers hoarded their earnings. The only solution was bringing in more and more banana notes from outside – and that depended on the Choys.

---

* Hans Schweizer-Iten would survive the war, eventually migrating to Perth with his wife, where he became a publican, a founding member of the Western Australian Cancer Council and President of the Western Australian Swiss Club. He is remembered as a courageous advocate of the internees in Singapore during World War II, whose actions almost certainly prevented the death by starvation or malnourishment of thousands of men, women and children.

17

THE SUSPECTED INSURGENT

Two months after the attack

ELIZABETH CHOY'S FIRST INTERROGATION took place in a musty room of paint-peeling walls on the first floor of the YMCA building. At its centre was a table with two chairs: otherwise, it was a featureless, bleak square box with an atmosphere of decay. A *Kempei Tai* officer aged in his thirties was seated on one side of the table. He looked up at Elizabeth and instructed her in English to sit.

'Do you know Robert Heatlie Scott?' he asked.

'Yes.' The officer made a note.

'Do you know John Long?'

'Yes.'[1]

The interrogation continued in this fashion, with the guard asking whether Elizabeth knew several other individuals, including Coulson and Bishop Wilson. Elizabeth knew them all. They were the names of every contact Elizabeth and her husband had made, directly and indirectly, during their time at the Miyako canteen. She answered honestly, responding to each name in the affirmative.

'Do you know that they're all here?' asked the officer.

'No,' said Elizabeth. They were certainly not in her cell, but they could very well be in other cells. It was impossible to know. The interrogator was sending her a message: whatever she answered, he would be checking off against whatever her accomplices said.

'You better tell me truth,' he said. '[Because] we know the whole story.'

'Why didn't you tell me earlier?' said Elizabeth. 'If it's something to do with sending in food [. . .] I can tell you [that], yes, we sent food in to help the people who are interned. We send medicine in. We send money in.'

'Because you are anti-Japanese,' he said.

'No.'

'You are pro-British.'

'No,' she said. 'Anybody in trouble I would help. Everything we did was to help people.'[2]

The officer asked further questions about the canteen, specifically relating to the materials, money and supplies handed to the ambulance driver John Long. Elizabeth answered honestly, focusing on her own activities, always careful not to name other individuals so as to avoid their arrest. The interrogation went on for an interminable period, the officer taking careful notes. He stood up without warning and abruptly left the room. Guards came inside and took Elizabeth back to the cell.

Elizabeth's first interrogation was unsettling. But it was neither violent nor degrading. She crawled back into the cell, daring to hope that once her story was verified, she and her husband would be released. She settled back into a spot on the floor where she had left her blanket. Another meal of rice with lukewarm tea was delivered. Once the food was eaten and the mug and the bucket were passed back through the gate, a guard ordered the prisoners to sleep. Almost in unison, the detainees all lay down. Elizabeth contorted her body into a shape so that she was not pressing too closely against the person next to her. It was no use. They were hemmed in, sardine-like. Those devilish lights made sleep almost impossible. But the others who had been here longer managed to drift off. Sounds became more pronounced. She could hear the heavy breathing of a sleeping man; a colicky baby wailing in the distance; the scratching of the bugs that crawled on the walls of the cell. They were all frightened into silence at the sound of a man's tortured scream that pierced the stuffy night air.

A guard summoned Elizabeth early the next morning. She was led back to the same cell where she was interrogated the previous day. The door was closed behind her. A different *Kempei Tai* officer was sat at the table. It was otherwise eerily similar to the day before – the same oppressive humidity, the sweaty stench of the room, the grimly sparse interior of the cell. The officer told her to sit before he began asking questions. He read out the same roll call of names that Elizabeth was quizzed about the day before. Again, she was asked to verify if she knew each person. They were trying to catch her in a lie. She was asked to disclose specific details about her involvement in smuggling food and supplies into the camp. There was now a particular emphasis on John Long and the functional role she and her husband had played in getting money into Changi. The interrogator also wanted to know the details of her involvement in smuggling radio parts into the camp. Elizabeth saw no danger in telling the truth. After all, getting supplies and money into that jail served the same objective – relieving the misery of the poor souls incarcerated within. As for the radio parts, she knew nothing about it.

Once she had finished her explanation, the officer accused her of being pro-British and anti-Japanese. Elizabeth denied the accusation, just as she had done the day before. She was only helping those in need. The officer ended the interrogation. Elizabeth returned to her cell, rattled. Being accused of being pro-British and anti-Japanese would, if proven, carried a severe punishment. Her actions did not, in her view, reveal any sort of allegiance. If anything, they were revealing of her character: she would, after all, do the same thing for anyone, irrespective of race, creed, religion or nationality. She would even extend that generosity to the Japanese, whose occupation of Singapore and treatment of her family and her community had brought such misery. That was the truth, and the truth – she reminded herself – would set her free.

But the interrogator's question regarding radio parts was deeply concerning. Everybody knew that having a radio was strictly forbidden. Had she unwittingly been guilty of smuggling radio parts into Changi? Elizabeth wrestled with these uneasy thoughts. She found no solace in the company of the other prisoners. In these days before she learnt how to sign, the sense of isolation was overwhelming. This was surely the cruellest irony of her present circumstances: Elizabeth was in the most crowded living conditions imaginable and yet had never felt so alone.

18

THE NEWS BULLETIN

Five months before the attack

THE INTERNEES WERE OPERATING several short-wave radios in the camp before Rob Scott arrived at Changi. To minimise the risk of their discovery, they were built into stools and hospital equipment, their smallest components having been smuggled in the pipes sourced from the engineer Norman Coulson. They were so well concealed that nobody knew exactly how many radios there were: 'maybe four, maybe six'.[1] Some even doubted there were any radios, believing the news made its way into the camp from Chinese contacts on the outside.

But the Changi radios were no myth. News was shared from the owners of each radio set to friends, then spread more widely. Like any good story, each rehashed news item was infused with rumour, innuendo, hyperbole and outright lies. 'By the time an item had been passed on through half a dozen mouths it was usually so twisted as to be unrecognisable, and when it met itself coming via another route there was no resemblance.'[2]

The radios should have boosted morale, giving the internees a sense of connection to the outside world. But nobody really knew what news was true and what was false, save the owners of the radio sets. Scott believed that, rather than being uplifting, the news was negatively impacting the internees. He reasoned that something had to be done: 'There was a general desire to overhaul [how news was shared] and to try to coordinate the receivers to avoid competition and overlapping.'[3]

In consultation with the central committee, Scott banded together with four others to form a Main News Committee. The Director of the Far Eastern Bureau of the Ministry of Information had come full circle, back to disseminating the news, albeit on a much smaller scale. Scott was appointed head of the news committee, whose members included Dr Hugh McIntyre, an osteopath from New Zealand feted for setting up a makeshift clinic in Changi and treating the rheumatism that flared among the older internees; John Long, who would add to his ambulance driving responsibilities; Walter Stevenson, a Scottish electrical engineer; and Lionel Earl, who had been employed in the Malayan Civil Service.

The news committee relied on two radio sets. Stevenson and McIntyre were responsible for one set and Long and some trusted friends ran the other. At night, the two radio parties would listen to bulletins out of San Francisco, but the main source of information was the BBC. Notes and summaries of each bulletin were compiled and then delivered – by way of scouts and messengers – early each morning to Earl and Scott, who were co-editors. The two men transformed an unadorned sheet of news from the notes into a daily bulletin that would be shared across the camp each evening. Three copies were made and then all four prepared for distribution.

In parallel to the news committee, Scott ran the Main Distribution Committee, along with Earl, Long and two other internees. The distribution of the news proved to be a more complex operation than the news gathering. By lunchtime, a member of the distribution committee had delivered a copy of the news to a designated distributor in each of the four blocks of the internment camp, including the women's block. The news sheets were never passed on beyond these four distributors. They would read the sheet and commit the stories to memory, before destroying their copy to limit the possibility of the Japanese discovering the operation. The distributor would then pass on the news orally to ten nominated sub-distributors in the male blocks and five in the women's block. Each sub-distributor managed a floor or section that covered roughly 100 internees. The sub-distributors would then whisper the news to around ten floor distributors, whose patch generally totalled ten people. Scott reckoned that 'by about tea time, the entire camp was covered'.[4]

The news bulletin, as the daily update became known among the internees, quickly earned a reputation for reliability. Upon being informed of some piece of war news from a source other than one of the floor distributors, internees would ask: 'Where did you hear that? In the news bulletin? I won't believe it till I hear it in the bulletin.'[5] In addition to the daily news bulletins, Walter Stevenson would write a summary of Wickham Steed's Friday commentaries broadcast on the BBC. Steed was one of the most prominent and influential English journalists of the early twentieth century, and his talks were extremely popular among the camp.

Scott was vigilant in maintaining secrecy. 'The organisation',[6] as he described the work of the news and distribution committees, was compartmentalised into silos. Even those who were directly involved in the news sharing generally only knew one other person in the chain. They certainly did not know the members of the committee or the identity of the man who sat at the top. 'Inside the organisation men did not know each other unless they were in direct contact; and outside the organisation the ordinary internee knew no one except the sub distributor on his floor.'[7] To avoid calling attention to themselves, Scott insisted that every person assigned to a committee was to keep up their day jobs: 'We all [have] our ordinary work to do. I my gardening and barbering, Mac his twisting of spines, Long driving his ambulance, Lionel doing his job as block secretary; and so on all down the line.'[8]

Despite efforts to safeguard the news operation from the Japanese, the organisation had its weak points. Nothing, in Scott's view, was more dangerous than getting the radio parts into Changi: 'Smuggling in spares [for the radio sets] was a constant worry.'[9] There were also personnel issues. 'Some distributors could not trust their memory, and despite our strict orders to the contrary some of them would keep rough notes of the bulletins, which they then mislaid in library books and all over the place.'[10] Unnerved by the careless and forgetful behaviour of the distributors, Scott arranged for chalk and slates to be smuggled into the camp as a workaround. The slates would less likely go missing and the writing on them could be rubbed out at the first sign of danger. But scrawling the news on a portable chalkboard was tricky and led to inaccuracy. Scott abandoned the slates and reinstated the old system of disseminating the news with a firm reminder that copies were to be destroyed the moment they had been read. He was fighting a lost cause. Even committee member Stevenson broke the rule. He kept a master copy of summaries of the Steed copies in a book marked 'W.S.', the initials that he shared with the popular journalist.

Irrespective of the risks of capture, an accurate daily news bulletin lifted morale just as Scott had predicted. Also, the internees had a way of knowing if the Japanese ever caught wind of the news bulletins: 'an ingenious arrangement for tapping the main telephone line from the Japanese Commandant's office to the city.'[11] If the Commandant got wind of the existence of radio equipment, he would have no choice but to phone the *Kempei Tai* for support. Owing to a shortage of Japanese-speaking internees, the phone tap could not be listened to twenty-four hours a day.

But it did give Scott confidence that they would likely have a warning of an imminent *Kempei Tai* raid.

In Scott's opinion, the complex work of the news and distribution committees, with all its moving parts and components, 'went swimmingly'.[12] Altogether, life in Changi was very tolerable: 'I had my gardening and other fatigues [which referred to the compulsory chores and labour each internee was assigned to do]; enough food; books to read; the news to edit; lectures and plays and concerts to go to.'[13] He took up Dutch and made good progress. In his spare time, Scott set about making a chess set. He successfully arranged for a pocketknife to be smuggled into the camp along with pieces of wood. He even found a fellow chess player; 'a friend who was as bad as I was'.[14]

Scott also participated in the Relatives Meeting, where male internees were permitted to visit family in the women's block. The meeting in the rose garden – 'a valiant [. . .] effort by the women to turn part of a prison yard into a remnant of civilisation'[15] – took place every Monday from noon until one o'clock. 'There the men sat at little tables, guzzling coffee and cakes provided by their female "relatives" (wives, sisters, fiancées, and – to the annoyance of the genuine relations – a tidy group of "guardians").'[16] Scott had been admitted to this group on account of being named by Elizabeth Petrie, one of Rosamond's old friends, as her guardian. Without a shred of evidence to support the claim, the Japanese allowed it. He was given the coveted 'blue ticket' that gave him admission to the women's cell.

This was not the only interaction Scott enjoyed with the women's camp. There was also Question Hour, a favourite of Scott's, where so-called male experts spent an hour answering questions on all manner of topics – to, as Scott archly referred, 'instruct the female mind'.[17] The equivalent concession was not granted to the female internees, a fact the women made light of by asking absurd questions; Scott 'was once called on to explain how handwriting showed character in a ten-minute Question

Hour talk'.[18] Whether intended or not, the Question Hour was entertainment rather than instruction, descending to the ridiculous and therefore considerably more worthwhile for both speakers and attendees.

Scott was even propositioned by one female attendee after one visit. She smuggled a note through the same distribution network used to deliver the news bulletin, which had lately functioned as a means of corresponding between the male and female blocks. 'Dear Mr Scott,' she wrote, 'I enjoyed your talk very much. Can you tell me what you think of my curves? And are my lines right [. . .]?' Scott responded in kind: 'Your curves are interesting and deserve further research [. . .] the slope of the lines shows an inclination to fall, which however appears to have been repressed recently [. . .]' There were other sentences dripping with innuendo that Scott would not commit to the historical record. But when he sent his note back to his admirer, the sub-distributor and floor distributor read it. 'The joke was, as I heard later, that my diagnosis of her character was unfortunately only too accurate, and, as the note had to pass through several hands before reaching her, half the women's camp knew what I had told her!'[19]

When considering the totality of his internment and imprisonment during the war, Scott described the experience as a 'Grand Guignol hotchpotch of black and white patches [and Changi] was one of the white patches'.[20] But a storm was gathering. In June, Asahi summoned Scott back to his office. Months had passed since his last meeting with the Commandant. Scott was not especially concerned. If the Japanese had somehow learnt of his network of news distributors, Scott would more likely be facing a *Kempei Tai* interrogator. Perhaps the Commandant had received a message for Scott, perhaps a signal from Rosamond. He hoped his family was okay.

Instead, the Commandant merely wanted to ask him some questions. They were so unremarkable that Scott forgot them as soon as he left the office. Bewildered, he returned to his block and went about his business. The only element to the meeting that could be said to be slightly unusual was the presence of a third man. He was dressed sharply in a sharkskin suit, saying nothing, closely observing Scott. The Commandant did not introduce the stranger to Scott. It was as if he was not even there. The man was middle-aged, bullet-headed, shorter than average but powerfully built; he exuded an intense vitality through his constant smile. A jackal's smile.

19

THE SMILING TORTURER

Six months before the attack

A MAJOR LATELY APPOINTED as head of the Syonan-to branch of the *Kempei Tai* should strike a bearing that was grim, violent, ruthless, depraved or something else in keeping with the unit's sinister reputation. Major Sumida Haruzo was instead an irrepressibly jolly individual. His sentences were forever on the cusp of spilling into laughter; his constant smile was variously described as brilliant, radiant and seraphic. He greeted acquaintances and enemies with the sort of warm bonhomie generally reserved for a best friend or cherished family member.

In another departure from the caricature of the *Kempei Tai* officer, Sumida hated administering torture. He held the view that the experience of torturing a person was far worse for the torturer than the victim. He even claimed that 'it [was] more painful to drive a nail into someone's foot than to suffer such an impaling'.[1] Sumida clearly believed that the use of torture against a suspected enemy of Japan was morally justified, given the atrocities for which he would ultimately be held responsible.

His distaste for inflicting pain on someone simply made him feel squeamish.

Of course, the personality traits that defined Sumida made his squeamishness relatively easy to overcome. He was a mixture of two complementary characteristics: a political doctrinaire, who would on occasion interrupt the flow of an interrogation with a lengthy sermon about the righteousness of Japan's cause, and a ruthlessly ambitious careerist who would let nothing stand in the way of his professional advancement. Sumida's ardent belief in the divine nature of Hirohito's mission certainly aided his steady rise in an organisation that viewed itself, as one historian described it, as 'the visible arm of the law, the guardians of the law, the public censors and overseers of private morals and thought'.[2] But to get anywhere in the *Kempei Tai*, Sumida knew that understanding how to use torture in an interrogation without killing a suspect was no less important than understanding counterespionage, the use of explosives, fifth-column organisation, code-breaking and methods of burglary.[3] He would, in short, have to become an expert at hurting people.

Sumida's first victims were likely tortured while he was on civilian duty in Japan in 1935, having been posted to the *Kempei Tai* with the rank of captain after a decade of service in the army. It was during this period that he fine-tuned his craft on communists, pacificists, criminals and other undesirables. Like all newly admitted officers in the unit, he learnt how to inflict maximum pain with a blunt instrument or a heavy rope, without delivering a fatal blow. He became proficient at knowing the length of time a man could be held underwater to be rendered unconscious but not beyond the point of being revived. He even became accomplished at the use of the battery, knowing the appropriate voltage to deliver terrifying pain without electrocuting his victim to death.

Sumida evidently became an exceptional torturer; those who saw him in action described him as 'very extreme'.[4] But administering pain was something he viewed as burdensome and unpleasant. Eventually, once he attained the rank of major, Sumida rarely tortured suspects, instead delegating this unsavoury work to his subordinates. While stationed in Syonan, he claimed that he only ever 'beat one man with a wooden stick about ten times'.[5] Sumida may not have been lying. There does not exist a conclusive or verifiable record of him torturing anyone, remarkable given the enormous number of Chinese and Europeans who would be brutally interrogated during his tenure as unit commander in Syonan.*

Avoiding the use of torture was partly informed by Sumida's changing attitude to the efficacy of the practice as a means of extracting information. There were, he learnt, many ways to elicit information from suspects and some were arguably more effective than inflicting pain. In the parlance of the modern detective story, Sumida came to assume the role of 'good cop' in an interrogation, apeing the part of the concerned confidant – with his warm demeanour and effervescent smile – to the hapless accused in order to draw out a confession. He was also thorough in his investigations, revealing unnervingly intimate details about the accused, linking them to activities that could only have been revealed by informants and insisting that denying the crime for which they were accused was futile. The threat of torture, he believed, was as useful as torture itself, which sometimes had the deleterious effect of rendering a man insensible and incoherent in his answers or tempting him into lies to avoid further agony. Sumida would instead begin an interrogation with an invitation for the suspect to voluntarily confess. If he encountered a particularly recalcitrant suspect, he would talk about the 'second way'[6]

---

* Whether Sumida Haruzo actively participated in the torture of suspects while in command of the Syonan branch of the *Kempei Tai* is difficult to discern. Survivors claimed he did, but it is probable that they were seeking to directly implicate him in an effort to bring him to justice. It is impossible to prove. Those men he more likely would have tortured did not survive the war.

to obtain information while gesturing at the other, unsmiling *Kempei Tai* man. Such threats had a way of loosening tongues.

Sumida's holistic approach to detection and interrogation was clearly successful. Not long after transferring from his regular army unit, he was posted with the rank of captain to the *Kemptei Tai* training school in Tokyo. After successfully discharging general duties in Japan, he was deployed to the Occupied Territories. At the outbreak of the Pacific War, he was in Peking, in northern China, training *Kempei Tai* graduates in military police work. Finally, he was given the plum role of Commanding Officer of the *Kempei Tai* at the naval base in Maizuru, where he was promoted to major. His skills as a teacher and administrator evidently did not go unnoticed by his superiors. His many qualities led to his most prestigious posting yet, head of the Syonan-to branch of the *Kempei Tai*. The appointment was a great honour and a heavy responsibility.

All was not well in Syonan-to. The island, Sumida quickly learnt, was 'essentially a town for the consumption of goods'.[7] The soil was not sufficient to grow crops or establish farms to raise livestock. Everything had to be imported: vegetables, fruit and particularly rice. Prior to the war, two-thirds of Malaya's annual rice requirements were imported. From the moment the bombs were dropped on Pearl Harbor, very little rice made it to Singapore.[8] The municipal area, moreover, was extremely crowded. Notwithstanding the population dip following the evacuations of many Europeans before the invasion and large numbers of Chinese murdered in the *Sook Ching* massacre, huge numbers of Japanese forces stationed on the island, as well as civilians attached to the army and the administration, actually increased the total population. This in turn increased the demand for basic supplies that had to be shipped in. With resources being diverted to troops on the front line and supply lines constantly disrupted, food became scarce. Adding to the pressure were opportunistic wholesale food distributors who obtained supplies at controlled prices but did not observe price ceilings when selling to retailers. And why would they? Suddenly their wares were in high demand. They increased their margins to the retailers, who passed that cost on to the desperately hungry consumer.

To address a shortage of money to pay for goods, the Japanese administration frantically printed banana notes that only succeeded in putting upward pressure on inflation. At the time of capitulation, 10 cents would buy you a *kati* – approximately 1.3 pounds or 600 grams – of rice. By the middle of 1942, the same quantity of rice would cost $5. The cost jumped again to $8 per *kati* by 1943 and would, by the end of the war, reach as high as $12. Hunger was endemic. Over the same period, a dozen eggs went from 50 cents before the occupation to $432.60 at the cessation of hostilities. In quick time, sections of the population began to starve. Hyperinflation not only impacted food. As Rob Scott observed:

> A sack of old newspapers in the summer of 1942 was worth close on fifty [dollars]; by 1944 a tyre for a motor truck fetched $400 and a bicycle tyre $15. In 1945 these prices were vastly higher, a good fountain pen costing $120.[9]

The people did their best with the little they had. For protein, they raised chicken and ducks in their homes. Cockroaches were used to fatten them up in place of grain, which was non-existent. The Japanese handed out tapioca and tapioca noodles and distributed a Malayan cookbook full of tapioca recipes, while suggesting alternative food substitutes for more orthodox ingredients. Bread made of millet in place of wheat was handed out to the people. 'It was just like our eraser,' said one Syonan resident of the bread substitute. 'When you throw it, it can bounce.'[10] These measures were not enacted by the Japanese out of a heartfelt concern for the public, but because of one immutable fact: a starving population is an enormous threat to an occupying force. 'The most important factor in gaining the support of the [people] was not the ideals associated with Greater East Asia but stability,' observed one historian, 'and the key to that was food.'[11]

With food both scare and expensive, the population became restless. Low-level sabotage, including the cutting of telephone wires, and an uptick in robberies – a classic sign of civil unrest – gave rise to a perception among the occupying force that control was being lost. In truth, these were hardly the sorts of activities that foretold of Japan losing control. Nonetheless, the Japanese felt they had good reason to be alarmed. And the situation was only going to get worse. On arrival, Sumida had been told that the rationing of food, controls on the distribution of clothing, a general ban of the sale of iron and other resources that could be seized and repurposed in aid of the war effort, as well as controls around the use of automobiles would be introduced. These measures would create a climate of profound disquiet and desperation: the perfect conditions in which communists, guerillas and other anti-Japanese elements would thrive.

Fuelling Sumida's anxiety about an emergent fifth column was the discovery of radio sets in houses throughout Syonan. Few things were deemed a greater threat to order and stability than these deadly devices. A pipeline of enemy propaganda could be publicly broadcast along with uncensored updates about the war; this at a time when Japan's indomitable hold over its possessions in the Pacific was beginning to weaken. There had been setbacks in the New Guinea campaign against the Australians, the army had withdrawn from Guadalcanal in the face of fierce fighting with the Americans, the Japanese Navy lost the decisive Battle of the Bismarck Sea and there was increased guerrilla activity in Burma. All of this was being gleefully reported in the enemy's broadcasts.

Maintaining control over such a large society that feared and loathed the governing authority with a relatively small occupying force required more than the threat of violence. Control largely depended on the belief that Japan could not be defeated. A decade of stunning military victories in Manchuria, China, Malaya, the Philippines and the Dutch East Indies created perceptions that the Japanese military was invincible. Radio broadcasts of Japanese military defeats pricked that aura of invincibility. They could, moreover, act as a kind of malignant energy source, fuelling a minor crime wave into a full-blown insurgency.

The plan was to act pre-emptively, to excise the tumour before it metastasised into something fatal. A fresh approach was needed. The seeds of discontent had been allowed to germinate into something toxic under the watch of the existing leadership of the *Kempei Tai*, so Sumida was brought in to tidy things up. He would serve under Colonel Kojima Masanori, the commanding officer of No. 3 *Kempei Tai* unit, who was responsible for Malaya (including Syanon-to) and the Riau Archipelago. Sumida's brief was to investigate anti-Japanese sentiment in Syonan, while overseeing standard *Kempei Tai* duties – maintaining security across the island and policing Japanese soldiers and civilians. He was placed in charge of 360 personnel, sent reems of reports compiled over the previous fourteen months by other *Kempei Tai* officers, given an office at the upper floors of the YMCA building and handed the keys to a plush accommodation near the harbour. Sumida – described by some as possessing a 'cunning brain'[12] capable of conjuring fantastic narratives from threads of evidence – began to form a picture of the situation in Syonan, and it was decidedly bleak for the Japanese.

It was his opinion that, around the time he arrived in Syonan, the situation was 'on the point of transition from better to worse'.[13] Sumida held a dim view of his predecessor, believing him to have missed the telltale signs of an organised conspiracy to undermine the Japanese from within. The more obvious examples of sabotage may have been duly reported. But much was ignored. Where the occupying force suffered any misfortune or mishap, Sumida saw

the work of a highly organised fifth column. Wrote one prominent politician of Sumida's paranoid deductions: '[a] Japanese
official was run over in the street – he must have been murdered
by anti-Japanese elements. A Japanese solider was injured in a
drunken brawl – it must have been a calculated defiance of the
Imperial Army.'[14] All the other common incidents and accidents
that afflict any society in both peacetime and war were now seen
as calculated and malicious, executed with exquisite precision by
the enemy within.

Sumida's belief that these acts were all coordinated attacks
raised many questions: where were these operations planned?
Who was involved? Who financed them? Most importantly, who
directed them? The obvious first place to look for answers was
within the Chinese community. Sumida needed informants, and
fortunately the practice of gathering intelligence through insider
knowledge was well in train before Sumida arrived. Informants
had been heavily relied upon to identify those individuals involved
in the China Relief Fund during *Sook Ching*. Sumida embarked
on a recruitment drive to replenish his stocks of Chinese spies.
Opportunists and outlaws were all too happy to cooperate for
money and food. Some of the more sadistically inclined seemed
eager to accuse an innocent person with impunity. Others saw
in informing on their countrymen a way of settling old scores or
taking down rivals. Most, however, were desperate cases: outcasts
and homeless, forced to turn to prostitution and crime after the
capitulation, and who saw in becoming an informant a chance
to survive.

But Sumida knew that the cooperation of Chinese informants
did not mean the information they provided could necessarily
be trusted. These people were, in his view, often destitute or
corrupt – hardly the sorts of individuals you could rely upon
to be honest. The key, then, was to force people into informing
through outright threats. The consequences for an informant
of double-crossing, exaggerating or fibbing to the Japanese was

extremely grave. When informants were brought into the fold, lying was far too dangerous a proposition to even contemplate for themselves and their families.

Sumida's most significant breakthrough came from exploiting the enmities between Chinese nationalists and communists. The great majority of Chinese in Syonan identified with the national- ist government of Chiang Kai-shek. It was through informants in this group that Sumida discovered the existence of a radio transceiver in an old tomb operated by Chinese communists. The transmitter was deemed powerful enough to send signals to the British in India. A stunning revelation. The discovery suggested a coordinated campaign between the British and the Chinese com- munists to conduct guerilla operations within Syonan. What if the communists were doing more than simply carrying out low-level sabotage on behalf of the British? What if the radio was being used to pass intelligence *to* the British?

There is no record of the *Kempei Tai* conducting any inter- rogations of those suspected of operating the transmitter in the tomb, and for good reason – the transmitter did not appear to work. It had been operated before the war. In all probability, the men who operated it were killed in *Sook Ching*. But Sumida found ways to mould facts in a way that supported his established views, to conjure fantastic narratives from tenuous and often competing truths and half-truths. According to his twisted logic, that the transmitter was broken merely proved that he was dealing with a cunning adversary. The Chinese, he reasoned, probably got wind of his investigation and sought to destroy the device as a means of throwing Sumida off the scent.

Sumida was not so easily fooled. He believed he had found proof that those seemingly disparate and random acts of sabotage were in fact being directed by the British in India. His mind was made up: the situation in Syonan was far worse than initially believed. The real threat was not the Chinese, who, in Sumida's view, were puppets, functionaries and footsoldiers serving the true danger – the British. The transmitter's destruction meant that the Chinese had another means of communicating with the British. Sumida's conviction, now fully formed, held that the Chinese must be taking instruction from the British internees in Changi.

In retrospect, it all seemed so obvious. The internment camp was full of senior bureaucrats whose connections into each of the ethnic communities of Syonan were well established. Many of these internees could speak Mandarin. Some had lived here for years, decades even. There were also engineers and technicians among their ranks, no doubt skilled in the manufacture of time-fused bombs and incendiaries, who could provide technical advice to would-be insurgents. As one historian points out, there were also 'the British Government officials, the Foreign Office and the Colonial Office representatives who could institute propaganda'.[15] Sumida had made what he believed was a breakthrough.

Kempei Tai staff, disguised as Japanese guards, were sent to gather intelligence about the goings-on in Changi. Their reports appalled Sumida. Changi, it seemed, was hardly run by the Japanese at all. The British were given permission to appoint leaders for each of the four blocks, they ran well-organised committees that sounded like intelligence briefings, and there was also a thriving black market in which the Japanese guards participated. Their profiteering, in Sumida's mind, amounted to complicity with the enemy. More staggering were the liberties the Commandant granted the prison population. Numerous internees were permitted to leave Changi and venture into the municipal areas. Such excursions provided ample opportunities to conspire with Chinese contacts.

Sumida sourced a complete list of internees in the jail. One name stuck out: Robert Heatlie Scott, Director of the Far Eastern Division of the Ministry of Information. Sumida dug deeper, finding the bloated report compiled by a woefully inept sergeant who interrogated Scott nearly a year earlier. It was a dossier full of misleading and pointless observations: a meandering tome of little

worth beyond Scott's confession that he had disseminated propaganda before the war. Its author concluded that Scott, despite
repeated denials, was a spy. Like the very best spies, Scott was
clearly skilled in saying much and revealing nothing. That would
have been clear in the transcripts of the interview.

Sumida was elated. He had what he needed, the final piece
of the puzzle. Scott – the propagandist and the spy – was the
lynchpin in the enemy's effort to destabilise Syonan. His methods
were admittedly ingenious, the plan devilishly clever in its sim-
plicity. Safely concealed behind the walls of Changi – hidden
it plain sight, as it were – Scott would meet with other leaders
of the insurgency (no doubt operating under the guise of some
unthreatening committee) and agree on targets for various
sabotage operations. Scott's men would be sent out of the camp,
seemingly undertaking harmless errands, where they would meet
with Chinese contacts. Instructions were then communicated to
insurgents.

Sumida formed another theory: Scott was communicating
directly with the British in India by way of radios hidden in
Changi. If proven, the consequences for the Japanese were devastating. In war, trusted information sourced from behind lines – in
the very seat of the Southern Army's headquarters, no less – was
potentially lethal for an occupying force. The mind boggled at
what the British now knew about the occupation of Syonan. Scott
could have sent word back to India regarding Syonan's defences,
troop strength, the morale of the civilian population, food avail-
ability, even shipping movements in the harbour. The British in
India were likely relaying instructions from London concerning
all manner of guerrilla operations. They may even be giving word
to prepare the local people for an Allied invasion.

To Sumida, Scott represented the gravest threat imaginable.
He had to be stopped. He decided to visit Changi. He would make
his own assessment of the fitness of the Commandment, the lax
security of the prison and the extent of the freedoms the internees

enjoyed. Sumida would also insist on a meeting with Scott. He wanted to look into the eyes of his adversary. Around this time, in his office in the YMCA building, Sumida drew up a chart with civilian names and prominent British internees. It looked like a family tree, lines connecting certain individuals to others, and notes scribbled next to other names, tying them to specific incidents. At the top of that chart, Sumida wrote the name of his investigation's number one suspect: Robert Heatlie Scott. The most dangerous man in Syonan.

20
THE SADIST

Two months after the attack

ELIZABETH CHOY HAD, by now, been interrogated several times. She had not as yet been tortured. But there was an uptick in the severity of her treatment at each subsequent interrogation. She had been forced to kneel in uncomfortable positions and was occasionally shoved. Questions were often shouted at her by furious officers standing inches from her face. She maintained her poise, never confessing to the false accusations made against her, no matter the physical intimidation. But it was clear that the Japanese would not stop until they had extracted a confession.

Around three weeks after being imprisoned in the YMCA, Elizabeth was called from her cell and led into an interrogation room. She shuddered at the sight of the man seated at the table waiting for her inside. Other detainees had pointed him out when he had passed the cell, whispering that he was a sadist. At this point, she did not yet know his name, but he certainly knew hers. This was Sergeant Monai Tadamori's first interrogation of the teacher who ran the Miyako canteen. She had proven surprisingly defiant. Sumida always sent the hard cases to Monai.

Elizabeth did not give in to fear. She maintained her dignity – shoulders back, chin raised, face a mask of quiet resolution. Monai rose from his seat. He extended his arm in a gentlemanly fashion to the seat opposite. Elizabeth moved cautiously over to the chair and sat down. Monai started talking. His voice was gentle, calming. An interpreter matched his calming tone. Monai, through the interpreter, enquired about her health. He mentioned the weather and the humidity. Elizabeth felt unbalanced. This was not what she had expected. At one point, she found herself chuckling at his heavily sarcastic observation about the accommodation meeting her expectation. He seemed to Elizabeth almost apologetic that she had been caught up in this situation. He would do his best to put this sorry episode behind them so that she could be released to her family. Perhaps the other detainees had got this man wrong.

Monai moved around to other side of the table, continuing to talk in a friendly tone. He rested his weight on the table right next to Elizabeth. She never actually saw him raise his arm, but she felt the full force of the blow. A brilliant explosion of light and pain billowed from the right side of her face. She looked up at Monai in shock. His mask was removed.

'Are you anti-Japanese?' Monai barked. Elizabeth said nothing. She was stunned. His eyes were expressionless, his face blank. Monai slapped her again, nearly knocking Elizabeth off her chair.

'No,' Elizabeth said, in between gasps.

This time, Monai clenched his fist. The blow caught Elizabeth across the cheek, just below her eye.

'Are you pro-British?' Monai asked.

'No,' said Elizabeth.[1]

Something new boiled within Elizabeth. She felt raw hatred for this man: 'I would have killed him if I could.'[2] The physical treatment was shocking. But it was his deceptive character, his insincerity, that Elizabeth found repellent. Monai asked more questions. Elizabeth said nothing: 'I refused to answer his questions.'[3]

Monai grabbed Elizabeth and pulled her into a standing position. They were facing each other, his face inches from hers. Monai took hold of the top of her dress and wrenched it down, exposing Elizabeth's breasts. But Elizabeth did not flinch. She had been forced to relieve herself in the commode in a cell packed with strangers. Where others had found the experience degrading and humiliating, Elizabeth was unconcerned. There was no shame in relieving oneself publicly when there was no way of avoiding it. She wondered if her insouciance, her ease with being naked, harked back to her childhood in the jungles of Borneo, where nudity was perfectly natural. If Monai expected her to break for having her breasts exposed, he was mistaken.

'You know Duncan Wallace?' asked Monai.

Wallace was a manager of the Chartered Bank before being taken prisoner in Changi. Elizabeth had heard his name mentioned but had not met him.

'Where did he keep the money?' asked Monai.

'I don't know,' Elizabeth responded.

'But . . . surely he must have told you,' said Monai, his tone disbelieving. 'You must know.'

'I heard,' Elizabeth started. 'It was rumoured that days before the surrender, they burnt all the bank notes.'

Monai shook his head. 'No, no, they have hidden them somewhere.'

'I don't know that,' she said.[4]

Monai was visibly agitated. He forced her over to a hard concrete slab and made her kneel before him. He persisted with his questioning of the whereabouts of the money. Elizabeth told him the truth. She did not know.

Monai moved away from the topic and started talking about

ships in the harbour. This was new. What ships? What harbour? He wanted to know what Elizabeth knew about it. She shook her head; she didn't know what he was talking about.

'Oh, you won't tell the truth,' said Monai. 'All right, we are going to kill you.'

'I've told you the truth,' said Elizabeth. 'I cannot tell you any more.'[5]

Monai returned to the table, picked up his belongings and abruptly left. The interpreter followed. Guards came in, lifted her up and dragged her back to the cell. She was not permitted to cover her breasts. Elizabeth's boiling rage had ebbed away. Fear had taken over. Monai was not done with her. They would meet again and next time it would be more violent, particularly if she could not answer his questions. She had already admitted to helping smuggle money into Changi. But what was this talk of ships in the harbour? Something big had happened. What exactly, Elizabeth could not say.

PART II

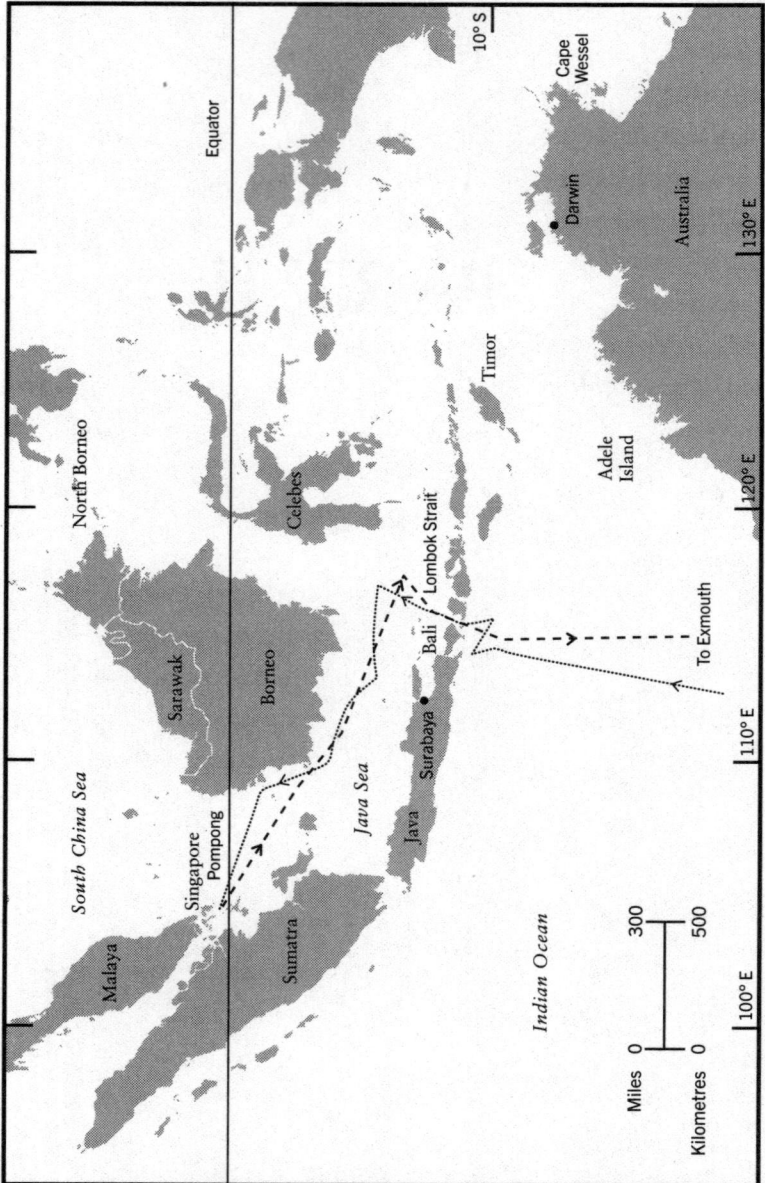

Ocean route of the *Krait*

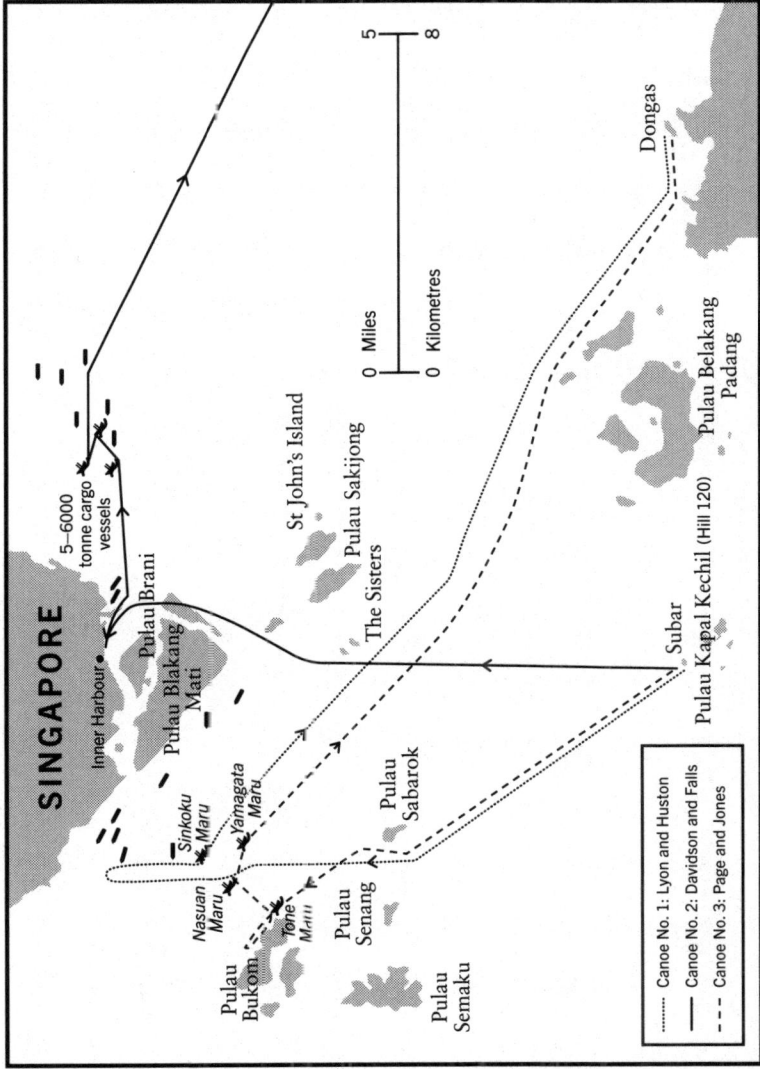

Singapore Area – Operation Jaywick Attack Courses and Location of Shipping

21

THE ATTACK

CAPTAIN IVAN LYON SET OFF in the two-man collapsible folding kayak known as a folboat on the night of 25 September 1943 from a tiny bracken-covered island called Subar. Seated in front of Lyon was his bowman, Able Seaman Andrew Huston, universally known as 'Happy Huston' because nobody could remember seeing him smile.

Lyon's folboat – designated Canoe No. 1 – belonged to a raiding party comprising six men and three two-man folboats. They were all dressed in black suits of waterproof silk, two pairs of black cotton socks and black sandshoes. Each man was armed with a .38 revolver with 100 rounds of ammunition and a large knife. A compass and first-aid kit were attached to their belts, and they each carried a single cyanide pill in the event of capture. Safely tucked inside the folboat were 80 pounds (36 kilograms) of magnetic limpet mines. The six raiders were approaching the final phase of an operation codenamed Jaywick: their mission to destroy Japanese shipping in Singapore Harbour.

Historically speaking, Lyon – who conceived, planned and took command of Operation Jaywick – looms as an enigma: a spectral, ambiguous figure on whom everyone has a different take. Born in 1915, he is described variously as overwrought, aloof, womanising, mercurial, sullen, wilful and superstitious, but also as charming, vivacious, fun, daring, romantic and audacious. This Harrow-educated scion of the heralded Strathmore clan, who shared a common ancestor with Queen Elizabeth – formerly Lady Elizabeth Bowes-Lyon – was fluent in French and expert in Scottish sword dancing and the Highland fling, and the same man who, after an afternoon in Singapore sinking copious Tiger beers, visited a Serangoon Road tattooist with friends and paid for a red, blue and yellow tiger to be emblazoned across his chest.

These contrasts to his personality were reflected in Lyon's physical appearance. Standing a shade under six feet, Lyon's slender and fine, almost feminine, features concealed a robust masculinity. No less contrasting were his facial expressions – in one instant he was ruminative to the point of being sombre, the next moment a childlike toothy grin set his face alight. Whatever thoughts and emotions were bubbling beneath the surface of this man as he paddled towards the blacked-out targets ahead, Lyon surely felt the spirit of an avenging angel.

In September 1941, Lyon was transferred from the Gordon Highlanders – his regular unit, with which he had been posted to Singapore since 1938 – to the storied Special Operations Executive (SOE). Sometimes referred to as Churchill's Secret Army or the Ministry of Ungentlemanly Warfare, SOE was formed in 1940 to conduct espionage, sabotage and reconnaissance in all territories occupied or attacked by the Axis powers. SOE's Far Eastern headquarters was located in the Cathay Building in Singapore, the eleven-storey 'skyscraper' in which Lyon almost certainly crossed paths with Robert Heatlie Scott. Among many things, SOE was involved in training stay-behind parties of Malayan, Indian and Chinese guerillas in the likely event of Japan declaring war and sweeping down the Malay Peninsula. According to historian Lynette Silver, Lyon's duties also included the 'assassination of a large number of enemy agents'.[1] These were mostly Vichy French agents sent from Indochina who were working with the Japanese to destabilise British-held territories.

When war broke out in the Pacific, Lyon helped slip guerrillas behind the lines in Malaya and organised supply dumps with food, medicine and munitions. Lyon and Lieutenant Herbert 'Jock' Campbell, another SOE recruit, set off in a small sailing craft to establish a route connecting Singapore to Sumatra by way of a chain of islands to enable supplies to be sent to stay-behind parties. The route would also offer a path for the infiltration or exfiltration of guerrillas, or so it was hoped. Campbell and Lyon essentially island-hopped the Riau Archipelago, winning the loyalty and cooperation of village headmen with cash bribes and leaving them tins of emergency rations, along with instructions for guerrillas on how to get to the next island in the chain.

When Singapore's fall was imminent, the route became a path to safety. Lyon was evacuated with other SOE personnel and dropped off on Durian Island, 50 miles south-east of Singapore with a young corporal from the Royal Medical Corps named Ronald 'Taffy' Morris. While Morris set up camp, Lyon sailed to nearby islands in a dinghy, directing headmen he had paid off again to direct all evacuees who landed in their village to Durian. A stream of evacuees out of Singapore arrived on the island within days. While Morris tended to the sick or those who had suffered shrapnel wounds during the battle, Lyon provided food, supplies and instructions. He told them to sail to a village at the mouth of the Indragiri River in Sumatra, where they would be met by Jock Campbell, who would arrange their transport upstream to the inland port of Rengat. From there, they would be guided through the Sumatran mountains to Padang, on the west coast, where a vessel would ferry them across the Indian Ocean to Ceylon or India.

Lyon and Morris would assist many hundreds of evacuees over the ensuing two weeks. Once the last of the evacuees had been sent off, the two men set sail in their dinghy on the 40-mile voyage south to the mouth of the Indragiri. It proved a harrowing journey. After sailing within several hundred feet of a Japanese destroyer and narrowly avoiding being revealed by a searchlight from a patrol boat, the dinghy was very nearly swamped in a tropical storm. They made it to the Indragiri the following day, taking delivery of a motorboat for Rengat before hiking to the west coast, where they undertook the journey across the vast Indian Ocean in separate vessels. Lyon secured passage with fifteen others aboard a large, barely seaworthy *prau*, eventually being picked up in sight of Ceylon by the *Anglo-Canadian*, a merchant vessel of 5000 tons, which took them to Bombay. Throughout the remainder of the journey, Lyon stewed over the humiliation of the British capitulation of Singapore, which had been more than just his home for over four years. It was the island where he had started a family with his beautiful wife.

Even in the rumour-filled, tight-knit, self-replicating and interconnected society that were the European colonies of the Far East, Gabrielle Bouvier seemed to garner more attention than was reasonable for someone who lived on Poulo Condor, a remote island off the south coast of French Indochina. As the daughter of the island's governor, Commandant Bouvier – a decorated veteran of World War I – she certainly had status. Her name, moreover, shimmered with scandal as the very young divorcée who had a child from her first marriage. But it was the rumours of her looks that enlivened Lyon's romantic spirit: the chestnut-haired Gabrielle was said to be ravishingly beautiful.

Lyon, who before the war regularly sailed the islands of the Riau Archipelago in a 20-foot sloop named *Vinette*, decided on venturing north to meet the French beauty. Upon making landfall in Poulo Condor, Lyon was invited to dine with the Commandant and his family. Whatever initial suspicions the Commandant had about Lyon's intentions were assuaged by the Gordon Highlander's wit and charm. Bouvier surely approved of the match. Lyon was a highly educated British officer of noble lineage who had come to rescue his daughter and remove from her name the stain of divorce. What's more, he could speak French.

Gabrielle was less impressed. Lyon drank too much for her liking and she was wary of his grand romantic gesture of sailing from Singapore to meet her, perhaps still wounded for having been swept off her feet and into an ill-fated marriage once before. There was also the matter of his tattoo. Lyon 'had no inhibitions about'[2] displaying the tiger and Gabrielle 'loathed it'.[3] Inevitably, the wilful Lyon won her over. They were married several months later in Saigon in July 1939. The stunning Gabrielle – who had left her daughter, Christienne, with her parents – and the dashing Gordon Highlander caused a sensation on arriving in Singapore. At first they lived in a bungalow off Orchard Road before moving to a more secluded house on the beach near Changi. The couple was swamped with dinner invitations. In September 1941, Gabrielle gave birth to a boy named Clive.

Lyon's period of bliss was practically over before it began as war clouds gathered over the Pacific. To ensure his family's safety, he secured passage to Australia for Clive and Gabrielle aboard a troopship, Christienne remaining with her grandparents in Poulo Condor. Despite his immense relief when receiving word that his young family had disembarked in Fremantle, Lyon felt bitter resentment towards the Japanese for having denied him the chance to build a future in the home he'd made with Gabrielle. As the *Anglo-Canadian* neared her destination, an audacious mission to strike back at the Japanese was taking shape in his mind.

The idea originated in a conversation back in Rengat, shortly after Lyon's motorboat collided with a wholly unprepossessing 70-foot Japanese vessel named *Kofuku Maru*. She was a long, narrow boat, 11 feet across the beam. Her prominent wheelhouse amidships gave way to a slightly raised platform above the engine room with side windowpanes that reached back to her stern, over which was slung a roof of tattered canvas. The stink emanating from her hold suggested the *Kofuku Maru* was built for fishing.

The captain of the vessel, a forty-nine-year-old merchant seaman named William 'Bill' Reynolds, was preparing to disembark when Lyon rammed into his boat. He emerged from the wheelhouse bristling with indignation, and delivered Lyon a withering rebuke. Not the least bit perturbed, Lyon moored alongside and requested permission to board the *Kofuku Maru* with a bottle of medicinal whisky sourced from within the hold of the motorboat. Reynolds' fury evaporated at the sight of the bottle. Over several glasses, Lyon coaxed Reynolds into sharing the story of the fishing boat.

The day after Japan attacked Pearl Harbor, the *Kofuku Maru* was impounded in Telok Ayer Basin in Singapore, where she had been moored. With the British facing imminent defeat, Reynolds managed to obtain the vessel and, with a hastily assembled Chinese crew, sailed through waters churning with evacuating ships beneath skies thick with enemy aircraft. Despite its ungainly, gullet-thin appearance, the *Kofoku Maru* proved surprisingly seaworthy. For a boat of her size, she was also capable of holding a large number of passengers. Reynolds had already picked up hundreds of castaways left stranded on islands surrounding Singapore and delivered them safely to Rengat.

Remarkably, the *Kofuku Maru* had, at least to that point, gone unmolested and seemingly unnoticed. Japanese ship captains and aircraft pilots evidently determined that she was friend, not foe. This revelation galvanised Reynolds into continuing his rescue operations. When he deemed more rescues impossible, he resolved to sail to India via the Malacca Strait. It was a bold plan. The Malacca Strait – a narrow stretch of water bisecting Malaya and Singapore – was a notoriously deadly sea passage where Sumatran cut-throats and pirates held sway. The Strait would now almost certainly be heavily patrolled by the Japanese. But Reynolds was confident that he could, as one historian puts it, 'run the blockade by sailing through it'.[4] Lyon and Reynolds agreed that, should they somehow survive, they would meet in India and see if the little fishing boat could somehow be used to take the fight back to the Japanese.

Puncturing the belief that the boat's cloak of invisibility was foolproof, the *Kofuku Maru* was engaged in a gunfight with a Japanese patrol boat a little over a week later. Reynolds and his crew managed to fight them off with a Lewis machine gun and rifles. Despite the near miss, Reynolds was not the least bit dissuaded from continuing his rescue work. Over a period of a month, he would rescue more than 1500 people in ten separate operations. When the last rescue run was complete, he sailed the *Kofuku Maru* through the Malacca Strait without mishap.

By the time Reynolds was reunited with the rail-thin British Gordon Highlander in Bombay, the deadly operation was all but fully formed in Ivan Lyon's mind. He pitched his idea to Reynolds, who was instantly enraptured. 'Basically,' Lynette Silver outlines, 'it involved sneaking back into Singapore with a team of highly trained operatives to secrete incendiary devices on shore installations and place top-secret, delayed-action, magnetic limpet mines on the hulls of enemy vessels.'[5] Preparations, planning, recruitment and training would all take place in India, from where the attack would be staged. Lyon managed to get in front of General Sir Archibald Wavell, Commander-in-Chief of the British forces in India, who approved of the plan with one amendment: the attack would be staged from Australia. Wavell's amendment made sense, given the Indian Ocean was aswarm with Japanese vessels. But the change upended Lyon's plans for very personal reasons.

After the meeting with Wavell, Lyon sent an urgent telegram to Gabrielle to remain in Fremantle. He was too late. Gabrielle and Clive were already steaming for Bombay aboard SS *Nankin* after Lyon had telegrammed them to join him in India. No matter, Ivan could reunite with his family in India and then find transport back to Australia. Several days later, the *Nankin* disappeared without trace. The consensus was that an enemy submarine had sunk her in the Indian Ocean. No survivors were reported.

The mission to strike back against the Japanese now took on a personal dimension for Ivan Lyon. He found a berth on a transport to Australia, grief-stricken and enraged, with a monomaniacal focus on delivering a blow to the Japanese. He codenamed his mission 'Jaywick', a word derived from a cleaning product used in Singapore toilets. Jay Wick was said to be 'a powerful deodoriser which removed noxious smells'.[6]

With fierce intensity, Lyon set about securing permission to make Operation Jaywick a reality. Wavell may have approved the mission, but funding, equipment, training facilities, ordnance and personnel would need to come from the Australian military. In a feat of astonishing charm, networking, negotiation and shear bloody-mindedness, Lyon would ultimately receive a sub-stantial sum of money from SOE and support from the Royal Australian Navy. The money enabled Lyon to maintain a head-quarters in a well-appointed flat in Sydney's Potts Point and establish a training camp at Refuge Bay, well north of the city, dubbed Camp X.

Reynolds, meanwhile, remained in India to supervise an engine overhaul of his vessel, which he renamed the *Krait* (pronounced 'Krite') after a deadly Indian snake, a species expert at hiding in rodent holes, debris or loose soil by day and emerging at night to strike its prey. Although the boat's new name evoked the mission's tactics of stealth and concealment, the efficient lethality of the snake did not quite match the performance of the *Krait*'s engines, which, even after an overhaul, would repeatedly break down and create delays. The *Krait* finally arrived at Camp X on 17 January 1943. Operation Jaywick would comprise eleven Australian and three British personnel, including Lyon, promoted to the rank of major, who was commanding officer.* Reynolds was unavailable for the mission and was replaced by Hubert Edward 'Ted' Carse, a lieutenant in the naval reserve with a prodigious thirst for beer. Lyon appointed Lieutenant Donald Davidson – a lean, hard-as-nails Scotsman in his mid-thirties who had migrated to Australia to work as a jackaroo as a young adult, and who had enlisted in the Royal Navy – as his second-in-command. Davidson led recruits in a gruelling training regime at Camp X, which was 'carried out for eighteen hours a day in all weathers and any time of day or night'.[7] Beer, cigarettes and women were all banned. The men were subjected to gruelling swimming and running sessions, and then schooled in the critical arts of being a commando: how to paddle a canoe silently, how to vanish into the landscape, how to strip and reassemble a weapon in the dark, how to garrotte a man in total silence, how to open his throat with a dagger. They were also taught how to sabotage a vessel with a magnetic limpet mine.

Aspects of the mission were shared with the recruits, but Jaywick's target was kept secret until the *Krait* left Exmouth Gulf, in Western Australia. The men were mustered on deck the day after very nearly capsizing in a violent storm shortly after slipping beyond sight of land. They were told they were destined for Singapore. Most of the crew, who had framed a market and were taking bets on the likely target, had tipped Java or Surabaya. That Singapore was the destination was staggering news.

If the sole purpose of this mission was tactical in nature – that

---

* Operation Jaywick is often grouped into the various World War II covert operations carried out by the 'Z Special Unit'. In fact, the Z Special Unit tended to the administrative needs of army personnel seconded to Special Operations Australia (whose cover name was Services Reconnaissance Department, or SRD) operations. Z Special Unit was often recorded on the service records and discharge papers of these SRD recruits and, as such, this is the unit to which many thought they belonged after the war. In fact, all SRD army recruits were attached to their parent unit throughout the war.

is, to destroy Japanese shipping and nothing more – then the wisest money was on Rabaul, a crucial base for the Japanese as they waged an offensive through the Solomons. Of all the Japanese bases within the *Krait*'s range, it was in Rabaul where a Japanese light cruiser, destroyer, minesweeper or even a highly prized aircraft carrier might be found. Not only was Singapore 2500 miles from Exmouth Gulf and deep within Japanese-controlled waters, ships moored in Keppel Harbour were more likely to be supply vessels, transports, freighters and oil tankers whose destruction would hardly hamper Japan's ability to wage war in the Pacific.

But this was more than just a mission about sinking ships. The strategic purpose of Jaywick was propaganda. Most people had never heard of Rabaul; everyone knew Singapore and what it meant for Britain to surrender her island fortress in the East. As Lynette Silver observes: 'Properly handled, a raid on Singapore would not only force the Japanese to redeploy their troops to cover their coastal bases, it would create an enormous morale boost for Britain and Australia.'[8]

For Ivan Lyon, the attack on Singapore remained deeply personal. He regarded the capitulation of Singapore as a disgrace, an embarrassment. He was also still grieving the loss of his wife and young son. Unbeknown to Lyon, Gabrielle and Clive were in fact alive. The *Nankin* was not destroyed but taken as a prize by the German raider KMS *Thor*. All the *Nankin*'s passengers were shipped to Japan and interned in a camp at Fukushima. Even if Lyon knew that his family was safe and would survive the war, he still would have felt the sting and the shame of Singapore's loss. That he thought they were dead merely buttressed his fury with grief.

After the crew had been told the target, a homemade Japanese flag was flown from the stern. The men covered themselves in brown dye to look more Japanese and dressed in sarongs as Ted Carse, the navigator, set a course for Lombok Strait. Six days after departing Exmouth Gulf, the *Krait* approached Nusa Besar island – known today as Nusa Penida or the Island of Temples – at the mouth of the strait. Despite, as Lyon reported, 'conditions of perfect visibility',[9] the *Krait* set a course for the narrows, running headlong into a tidal surge. Carse pushed the engine to maximum revs, but the tide was overpowering. The *Krait* started losing ground. It took four hours to sail beyond Nusa Besar's four-mile coastline. Although sparsely populated during Dutch rule, the island was a hive of Japanese activity with 'numerous controlled fires on the hillsides [. . .] and both moving and fixed lights'.[10]

At dawn, 'barely into the Northern Narrows',[11] Carse calculated that they were 7 miles east of Lombok and 9 miles west of Bali. It was an anxious morning as the *Krait* made an agonisingly slow pace through this pass, in sight of those on both shorelines. Eventually they found cover in the haze that is peculiar to this region during the monsoon season, before setting a course northwest, wending between some of the uninhabited tropical islands of the western Malay Archipelago at a slovenly six knots. When a stiff breeze lifted the haze, the *Krait* was once more exposed. Crucially, two Japanese float planes left them alone after passing overhead at close range to inspect, evidently concluding that the *Krait* was indeed a Japanese fishing boat.

On 17 September, they anchored off Panjang island, roughly 30 nautical miles from Singapore. The raiding party was offloaded with their folboats – which they all referred to as canoes – operational gear and enough food and water to last a month. Carse set sail in the *Krait* for Borneo with instructions to rendezvous with the raiding party at Pompong Island on the night of 1 October. Lyon's team had to get into Singapore, sink as many ships as possible and then paddle a staggering 53 nautical miles or roughly 100 kilometres in twelve days. The schedule did not concern Lyon, who ordered a three-day rest. The raiding party planned to set off after dark on 20 September, but the departure was delayed by the appearance of a 70-foot patrol boat that chugged past a mile off the coast. Unperturbed, the commandoes entered the water after dark. They were edging ever closer to the attack phase of the operation.

Over two separate nights, they paddled towards Singapore, camping at various islands in between, eventually landing on Dongas Island a tick after midnight on the morning of 23 September. It was tough going. In addition to unseen currents and capricious wind shifts that would herald rain bursts and storms, Lyon noted that 'the canoes when loaded with food and water for a week, operational stores and men [carried] a total cargo of approximately 700 lbs [approximately 300 kg and] were very low in the water and sluggish'.[12] Dongas, an island less than 8 miles from Keppel Harbour, was chosen as the operational post. The island met all the party's requirements: 'the high ground on the North side provided an excellent view of the Roads [and] drinking water was found in a disused well.'[13]

For five days, Lyon kept a keen watch on the goings-on across Singapore Strait: 'there was no black-out in Singapore and the lights of cars driving down Beach Road could be clearly seen.'[14] Lyon noted that a mast had been erected above the Cathay Building, a signal station had been built on St John's Island and that there was a hive of activity to the west, where the clang of steel and roar of engine 'suggested either ship repair or building'.[15] Otherwise, everything seemed unnervingly unchanged, as if life was progressing as normal and the war was some abstract thing that no longer troubled the people of the island. There was nothing from this distance that bespoke the hardships and horrors the population of the island were in fact enduring.

Shipping activity was frenetic: 'Ships arrived from the East, either singly or in groups – none of these exceeded five ships and only one group was escorted. All were heavily laden and proceeded direct to their anchorage.'[16] Lyon observed no less than 100,000 tons of shipping at any one time moving through the Roads – a stretch of water off the southern coast of Singapore used extensively by vessels to load or unload cargo, await clearance to enter Keppel Harbour or seek shelter – over the five days that the party kept watch. Late in the afternoon, numerous ships totalling around 65,000 tons assembled directly opposite Dongas, awaiting a mooring or a place to anchor in the harbour. The time had come.

The three canoes pushed off the beach at Dongas at eight o'clock at night on 24 September, proceeding for the target area in an arrow formation. Almost at once they ran into trouble. The tide was against them. They dug their paddles deep into the onrush of water, inching their way across Singapore Strait for five hours before abandoning the attack. To have continued would have been suicide. There was not enough time to cover the remaining distance, attach limpet mines to ships and get back to Dongas before dawn. Two canoes returned to Dongas just before daylight, but Lyon's canoe was swept to the south of the island, where he and Huston spent 'an unhappy day sitting in the rain'[17] amid some boulders, hiding from the local inhabitants of Dongas, awaiting nightfall to return to their hide.

Davidson had a hot meal ready for Lyon and Huston by the time the two commandoes reunited with the rest of the raiding party. The failed first attempt, although a near-fatal miscalculation of the strength of the tide, proved instructive. Even if the tides were favourable, it was clear that the probability of making it across the Singapore Strait and back after attaching the mines all before daybreak was improbable. Dongas was too far from the target areas. They needed to launch the attack from closer in. Davidson suggested Subar, an island 8 miles to the west that was considerably closer.

After a day of rest, the raiding party set off for Subar before dawn on 26 September. There was neither a beach nor a source of fresh water on Subar, but the island provided 'an excellent vantage point from which to observe activities in Singapore'.[18] Lyon, Davidson and Lieutenant Robert Page, the leaders of each of the canoes, assigned themselves specific target areas. Given the size of the vessels they would be attacking and the near darkness in which the mission was to be executed – they had coincided the attack with the new moon – they wanted to avoid doubling or tripling up on the same target. Examination Anchorage was assigned to Lyon; Page would take care of ships moored at Bukom Island; and Davidson would hunt in Keppel Harbour.

The three canoes left Subar at sunset, lining up in an arrow formation as they pushed off from the beach. A manageable cross tide on their starboard quarters was easily negotiated, barely requiring them to make an adjustment to their strokes. A few hundred yards from Subar, Davidson steered his canoe east for Keppel Harbour and was swallowed in the night. Lyon and Page continued on together. A searchlight from the nearby island of Blakang Mati* 'shone uncomfortably close'.[19] The commandoes kept still while the searchlight illuminated the water around them, a stationary object considerably harder for the eye to detect at night than one that was moving. The searchlight moved off. They continued on.

As planned, the two canoes parted at Jong Island. Lyon and Huston maintained their course into the inky darkness, their well-practised strokes all but inaudible as they paddled through the black water. They paddled into Examination Anchorage at 10.30 p.m. Back on Subar, Lyon had sighted ten ships lying at anchor through his telescope. But at night the ships were 'blacked out and completely invisible against the background of hills'.[20] They eventually sighted a ship before realising that it 'belonged to Page'.[21] The hour was late; dawn was approaching. They needed to allow themselves enough time to get back to Dongas before sunrise. Lyon settled on one of two tankers that he could make out by a slightly less conspicuous red light that replaced the more common white navigation light fixed around the anchor

---

* Blakang Mati is today a resort island known as Sentosa.

to prevent collisions. The target selected was the *Sinkoku Maru*, a hefty 10,000-ton tanker that would require multiple mines to destroy.

As bowman, Huston held the canoe steady against the ship while Lyon retrieved the first demolition charge. The attack used an explosive called a Mk 1 Limpet mine, a metal demolition charge weighing 4 kilograms (8.8 pounds). The mine comprised a rectangular metal casing that contained 1 kilogram (2.2 pounds) of compressed TNT. Six horseshoe-shaped magnets were attached to the charge that would cling to the iron hulls of a ship. Three limpets were to be clamped in the same vicinity to inflict maximum damage, each mine capable of punching a jagged 3-foot hole into the side of a ship. The three mines were connected by a detonating cord. To increase the probability that the mines sunk the ship, a collapsible rod 6 feet in length was used to clamp the mines below the waterline. Once attached, the mines were armed by pulling a pin attached to the detonation cord, activating a delayed fuse that would allow the raiders plenty of time to escape.

Given the tanker's immense size, the full complement of mines would be needed to sink her or, more realistically, remove her from service. Lyon attached the first group of three limpets to the propeller shaft. Once the fuse was activated, Lyon signalled to Huston to venture forward. They drew alongside the tanker, pausing in the approximate location of the engine room to attach the second group of three mines without trouble. While retrieving the first of the second group of three limpets, Huston frantically signalled to Lyon to halt. Lyon looked up and saw a man staring directly at him from an open porthole 10 feet above. The commandoes kept absolutely still. The man gazed at them for an indeterminate period, before knocking his head on his bedside lamp as he withdrew his head. Perhaps he'd heard the metallic thud as the magnets of each limpet connected with his ship's iron hull. Maybe the presence of the canoe outside his cabin had disturbed the gentle lapping of the water. Or perhaps the man was simply enjoying a breath of fresh air. All that could be known for certain is that he had seen nothing. Lyon resumed his work, arming the final mines and then setting off on the 12-mile paddle to Dongas.

Page and his bowman, Arthur 'Joe' Jones, reached the wharves of Bukom Island, 3 miles south of Singapore, around an hour before Lyon and Huston mined the tanker. They spent an hour scoping the scene and settling on a target. A large barge illuminated by arc lights cast a gloomy pall over shadowy figures who were 'working amongst what appeared to be cauldrons of steam'.[22] The two men paddled on, Page making out the outline of a sentry standing guard on the well-lit wharves near the bow of a tanker. The only ship they deemed suitable to attack was a freighter. They attached three limpets to it and then made for the next target, another freighter of 4000 tons with a greyish-black hull that was anchored a mile from Bukom. With the tide now running west to east, they drifted easily to a third target – another freighter of similar tonnage, around 350 feet in length – which Page and Jones mined amidships aft. Once the limpets were attached, the two men dumped whatever they could into the sea to allow for a faster getaway and set a course for Dongas.

Of the three folboats that comprised the raiding party, none could have said to have taken greater risks than Davidson and his partner, Wally Falls, nicknamed 'Poppa' by dint of being the oldest NCO in Jaywick at the age of twenty-three. They took their canoe to the east of Blakang Mati, right into the teeth of Empire Dock in Singapore. As they made their way to the target area, a tugboat with her navigation lights illuminating the thick steam billowing from her chimney appeared from nowhere. The commandoes frantically increased their paddle cadence, narrowly averting being run down. The tug carried on oblivious.

Davidson and Falls gulped a few steadying breaths and resumed course. The Blakang Mati searchlight shone well above

their heads seeking enemy approaches farther out to sea. Davidson
and Falls crossed the unmanned and open boom gate – a defens-
ive net strung across the narrow stretch of water to block ships
from entering – and inspected the main wharf, which was empty.
Davidson deemed that the shipping moored to the wharves of
Empire Dock was not only too well lit to risk attack but also too
small to waste the limpets on.

They paddled back past the boom and made for the Roads,
their eyes feasting on 'many excellent targets'.[23] Davidson selected
three ships of between 5000 and 6000 tons, two of which were
heavily laden with cargo and the third of which appeared empty.
They attacked the ships on the port side, the seaward side, to avoid
being revealed by Singapore's bright lights. Davidson kept time by
the clock of Victoria Hall, which chimed every fifteen minutes.
When the clock chimed 1.15 a.m., the pair paddled clear into
the Riau Strait and set course for Pompong, where they would
rendezvous with *Krait*.

Lyon and Huston landed on Dongas at 5.15 a.m. on
27 September at the very moment the first mines exploded. Page
and Jones, who had landed half an hour earlier, joined them
moments later. The four men looked on as Singapore Harbour
was set ablaze. Over the following hours, the harbour become a
hive of frenetic activity as patrol boats combed the Roads, while
ships fortunate to have escaped the attack weighed anchor. Lyon
could see smoke belching into the sky from the tanker he and
Huston had mined. Page noted, with tremendous satisfaction, that
the bow of one of the freighters he had attacked was pointing
skyward. The blast of ships' sirens drew the local villagers of
Dongas onto the shoreline. The four men pulled their canoes
under the cover of mangroves to wait out the day, observing the
chaos unfolding across Singapore Strait. At dusk, they would set
a course for Pompong in waters soon to be thick with Japanese
patrols.

22

THE NUMBER ONE WORK

THE ATTACK AWOKE Major Sumida Haruzo before daybreak on 26 September. Sumida, whose apartment was situated near Keppel Harbour, described the first detonation as 'quite a large explosion'.[1] He got dressed and made his way onto the street where a guard permanently stationed outside his residence called for a driver. He was driven directly to the YMCA: 'As soon as I arrived at my office that morning I was told that several Japanese cargo boats, including oil tankers, were exploded in the port.'[2] Sumida had his orderly telephone the waterfront *Kempei Tai*, who confirmed the reports. Nobody had been captured and there were only theories as to the identity of the culprits. Sumida rang off. He did not need to hear theories. To him, it was obvious. The attack involved insurgents from Singapore or one of the outlying islands and was masterminded by Robert Heatlie Scott.

Sumida was summoned to Army Headquarters in the Cathay Building. Field Marshal Terauchi Hisaichi, commanding officer of the Southern Army, Colonel Kojima Masanori, commander and overseer of *Kempei Tai* operations in Malaya and the Riau Archipelago, and Lieutenant Hinomoto, commander of the Syonan-to waterfront *Kempei Tai* were all present. Numerous other army officers and adjutants were also in attendance, as well as Japanese administrators concerned with port affairs. They each took turns to provide updates. By and large they all agreed on the particulars: 'in the early morning five "A" ships blew up in the harbour of Singapore and [. . .] two ships sunk.'[3] The ships that 'blew up' were believed to be salvageable, but it was too soon to say for certain.

Aircraft sent to reconnoitre the Malacca Strait and the southern approaches to Singapore had seen no sign of enemy shipping. Crewed vessels in the vicinity and dockworkers had not seen anything either. As such, Sumida recalled, 'it was concluded that the explosions were not caused by torpedo attacks, but by some explosive, something detonated. It was thought that probably during the night someone had approached these ships on small boats and explosives were attached to these ships and later detonated.'[4] The exact number of men killed or wounded in the attack is unknown. Sumida claimed there were no casualties, which was possible given the attack 'happened to be a Saturday and all the cargo had been landed and the crew was ashore for a day off'.[5]

That there was no sign of enemy activity was not the least bit surprising to Sumida. This attack, he believed, had come from within. When his opinion was sought by a senior officer, Sumida was unequivocal: 'I felt that the state of peace and order and this serious incident were related and that a thorough measure should be taken in order to prevent the recurrence of such [a] grievous incident.'[6] Sumida also asserted his belief that the attack had been masterminded and funded from within Changi. This was not the first time he had voiced this theory to his superiors, having sought approval to raid Changi weeks earlier. But his requests were denied; he lacked the definitive proof he needed to start arresting Scott and his accomplices. Sumida boiled with frustration. The longer he waited, the worse the situation would become. Syonan, he was convinced, was on the verge of rebellion.

Every measure intended to ease the population's misery was undermined with a policy that imposed some other restriction that made life tougher. Back in August, the long-anticipated controls on the distribution of clothing and staple materials were enforced. Industry was also hit, with a ban on the distribution and sale of heavy machinery and anything made of iron. These materials were needed for the war effort. With food and jobs becoming increasingly scare, the people took matters into their own hands. In their desperation, they scavenged and stole. Crime, particularly robberies, became rampant. Sumida observed that 'the unfavourable war situation for the Japanese and the menace and inconvenience to life would make all the civilians [. . .] begin to fall away from the Japanese and [. . .] I made observations that quite a large number, or I should say most of the inhabitants in Malaya and [Syonan], were becoming unfriendly to the Japanese'.[7] Syonan was a tinderbox. Scott and his men in Changi were offering these disaffected people a match to set it alight.

During the hot and humid month before the attack, more catastrophes were visited upon the occupying force. A suspicious fire destroyed a military warehouse down near the docks. Shortly thereafter, a Japanese freighter sailing out of Penang caught fire and sank. These incidents were believed to have been carried out by communist insurgents. Although occurring in different places, they were symptoms of a cancer that originated in Changi and metastasised all the way up the Malay Peninsula.

Sumida installed a man in Changi to spy on Scott. It was learnt that Scott was running some sort of espionage ring from within Changi under the guise of a news committee. Direr still, news about the war – up to date and accurate – appeared to be circulating through the camp. This suggested that Sumida's long-held concern was proving true: the internees had smuggled radios into the camp. If there were radios in the camp, then it was possible Scott was communicating directly with the British in India.

Sometime in August, Sumida filed his report to his commanding officer, Colonel Kojima, in which he laid out the rationale for raiding Changi:

> Some of the internees at Changi often came out to town to do shopping, and through this freedom they could have done something if they had intended to do so. The second reason was the presence of Mr Scott in Changi. He was the former head of the Information Bureau and [. . .] he would start anti-Japanese activity of an espionage character. Some of the guards at Changi lived in the city and went to work there [and] these people might be involved in some sort of activity if there was any.[8]

When it came to approving the raid, Kojima demurred. The reason the raid was delayed is impossible to know for certain. The suspected existence of short-wave radios and the presence of a senior British propagandist and probable spy were certainly grounds to turn the place over and make arrests. Perhaps Kojima felt that if he acted hastily, he might not see the bigger picture. He needed more than circumstantial evidence of short-wave radios, a web of spies, operatives, saboteurs and insurgents working for Scott. The proof he desired continued to elude the investigators. 'No definitive date [for a raid] was set,' Sumida would say, 'but we were expecting to obtain enough information and start by December.'[9] He resolved to keep an eye on Scott and his men in Changi.

Now, with at least two ships confirmed to have sunk, and others smouldering on the surface and possibly unsalvageable, delaying the raid on Changi appeared to have been a terrible lapse. A raid would have led to Scott's arrest, the discovery of the radios and the attack on the harbour would have been thwarted. With Field Marshal Terauchi eyeballing him and awaiting his theory on the attack, Sumida asserted his view on who was responsible. The explanation he provided in that meeting cannot be known. But a subsequent signal sent from army headquarters and intercepted by the Allies revealed that Sumida's theory became Terauchi's established position: it was 'a clever plan by Malayans working under the supervision of Caucasians directing behind the scenes'.[10]

At the end of the conference, Sumida returned to the YMCA. At noon, a signal was sent to Kojima from Terauchi:

> The Commander of the 3rd *Kempei Tai* Southern Army will clean up the enemy elements in Singapore and in Prai [the coastal regions of the Malayan Peninsula facing Penang Island] and take measures promptly to counteract any acts against the Japanese forces.[11]

That Prai was included as an area to be mopped up suggests that Sumida's view – that Malayan guerrillas were involved in the attack, and that it may have been staged from a region further north – had also swayed Terauchi. Given the scale of the attack, Kojima suggested the order be revised to include not just Singapore and Prai but all of Malaya. Another order was issued that night with Kojima's suggested amendments. Kojima then met with Sumida and handed him his written orders. Sumida recalled:

> It stated that I should promptly take measures against the plottings of the enemy elements according to the following plans. The first of these plans was to obtain information concerning the sinking by explosion of the ships in the port of Singapore and to arrest people suspected to be concerned with the matter. Secondly the investigation of the Changi camp and arrest of the suspected persons there. Thirdly the

arrest of suspected persons allegedly engaged in espionage. Fourthly, the arrest of all other enemy elements not included above.[12]

In his investigation, Sumida would now have the unlimited powers he craved to prove his theory about Scott and the spy ring he had been running from his cell in Changi. The investigation was called *Ichigo Hosaku*, or the Number One Work, a title immensely satisfying to Sumida's ego. It nonetheless conveyed in no uncertain terms the expectation to deliver results. After all, there was nothing more important in Syonan at that time than finding the culprits responsible for the attack in the harbour. The pressure on Sumida was huge.

Resisting the urge to act hastily, Sumida instead methodically planned the raid on Changi. A party of thirty *Kempei Tai* would be needed. These men would be divided into four platoons. Each of these platoons was given ten reinforcements drawn from an army unit that was staging through Syonan en route to Burma. Each platoon was assigned a block of the prison that they would search once all the internees were called onto the parade ground. Sumida also arranged for a large group of English-speaking interpreters to accompany the raiding party. They included multilingual Chinese professionals pressed into service by the *Kempei Tai* and English-speaking Japanese nationals employed in large Japanese commercial firms. Prison staff would be largely sidelined. If Sumida had his way, the prison staff would be removed altogether. They could not be trusted. But he needed as much manpower as he could muster. A large number of men on hand would limit the possibility that the British internees could destroy evidence when they realised the jig was up.

A list of nineteen names was drawn up. At the top of the list, Sumida wrote Robert Heatlie Scott. Another list of names of Chinese suspects living freely within Syonan or working inside Changi was also circulated. To avoid the risk of Scott and his men being forewarned of the raid, the arrests of Chinese living outside of Changi would occur at the same time or shortly after the arrests of the internees.

Lending legitimacy and perhaps greater urgency to the raid came a report from informers that 'raised up the curtain of the Changi case'.[13] Three informers – including a Chinese man named Feng Khoo, who worked a desk job in Changi, and two Eurasian internees, Charley Dias and a woman known only as Renee – had been shadowing a Chinese registry clerk who also worked at Changi. His name was Khoo Hock Choo. All three reported seeing him smuggle items to British internees. The *Kempei Tai* moved fast, first arresting Khoo's brother, 'in whose possession was found a radio set'.[14] Like many other Chinese arrested in the anxious weeks ahead, Khoo's brother was seized in the early-morning hours before sunrise. 'When you were taken in by the Kempeitai,' said one Chinese prisoner, 'normally at half past three or five o'clock Tokyo [time], you are in your pyjamas. [. . .] You're not allowed to dress, not allowed to change. And you're put in a [cell] where the sentries could see inside.'[15]

For Sumida, Khoo's smuggling of materials to Changi in addition to his brother's radio set was the silver bullet that proved Chinese intermediaries were doing the bidding of their British overlords. In fact, all that could be proven was that Khoo, like every other man working at Changi and practically every internee, was active in Changi's thriving black market. As for his brother's radio, nobody seemed to care that the radio set could only receive broadcasts rather than transmit them. This detail was either missed or totally ignored; it did comport with Sumida's premediated conclusions.

Sumida had all that he needed. He set out his justification for the raid around three points that were presented to his superiors. In Changi Internment Camp, he wrote:

a) were hidden a short-wave wireless receiver and transmission sets which were strictly prohibited by the Japanese Army;

b) an espionage organisation was strongly suspected;

c) anti-Japanese elements within the prison were in contact [with the Chinese] and were gathering large sums of money for their movements.[16]

The raid was scheduled for 10 October: 10/10. An auspicious date for the nationalist Chinese, the Double Tenth Day marked the anniversary of the Wuchang Uprising, which ultimately led to the collapse of the imperial Qing Dynasty, bringing to an end more than a thousand years of imperial rule. From 1912, the year after the uprising, 10 October would become a public holiday in China and a day of exuberant celebration. For many Chinese in Syonan and the internees of Changi, the Double Tenth would hereafter be remembered as the beginning of the horror.

Ivan Lyon, Robert Page and their two respective bowmen in the two folboats spent much of the day of the attack observing the chaos and confusion in Singapore and the harbour. Shortly after the first mines detonated, the Japanese blacked out Singapore – possibly suspecting the explosions were the result of a bombing raid. Lyon could see and hear explosions for around forty-five minutes, each boom accompanied by the intermittent wails of ships' horns as anxious captains in surrounding vessels blasted their sirens. Lyon noted several ships 'under-weigh and cruising slowing up and down the harbour'[17] and numerous aircraft taking off from the aerodrome at Kallang, a short distance from Singapore's central hub. The aircraft headed north-west to reconnoitre the Malacca Strait. They returned two hours later to inspect the southern approaches into Singapore. Japanese Zeros and other light aircraft patrolled the skies throughout the day. The commandoes retreated farther into Dongas's interior, where the canopy was thickest, to keep out of sight of the air reconnaissance and the countless launches sent to patrol the Roads, the Singapore Strait and the waters north of nearby Batam Island. They waited patiently, carefully observing every detail of the Japanese reaction. Clearly, the enemy had no idea of what had hit them.

Against all expectations, the four commandoes encountered no searchlights or patrols on the first leg of their journey to Pompong to rendezvous with the *Krait*. The only threat was a small steamship anchored at the north of the Bulan Strait: 'we drifted past it on the tide without being observed.'[18] They continued without incident to Bulat and thence to Panjang, paddling the last mile through a violent storm. The storm cleared up through the night before a bank of dark cumulus barrelled towards them from the west later in the day. Lyon had hoped to cover half of the 28-mile journey to Pompong that night. The date was 30 September. Ted Carse, who was skippering the *Krait*, was making his way from the waters west of Borneo to the rendezvous point to pick up the raiding party 'between dusk and dawn on the 1–2 October'.[19]

But to blithely set off into a storm, having narrowly avoided being swamped during the storm of the previous night, was too risky. Lyon made the critical decision to postpone the departure, forcing them to make the final stretch to Pompong by day – a decision 'amply justified by the violence that later developed'.[20] Waves surged up the beaches and detonated against Panjang's rockier outcrops, the storm setting the night sky ablaze with lightning while whipping up a wind that brought down trees and took fallen branches out to sea.

They left at dawn, a stiff headwind rendering the herculean task before them even more arduous. Several aircraft flew directly overhead throughout the day but either misidentified the blackened shapes below as local fishermen or did not even see them. In the early afternoon, in excellent visibility, the raiders paddled past a Japanese observation post situated on a remote island. The folboats were apparently unseen. They took a one-hour break at an island called Torte before covering the final 16 miles of the journey in shifting winds and unpredictable currents, making it to Pompong three hours before dawn on 2 October – some twenty-one hours after leaving Panjang.

The two folboats circumnavigated the island in search of the *Krait*. There was no sign of her. Unable to paddle any further, the raiders landed on Pompong and collapsed on the beach. The first rays of sunlight stirred one, who woke the others. Dangerously exposed, they quickly dragged their folboats into the jungle, when they sighted the *Krait*: she was 'about two miles away heading down the Temiang Strait'.[21]

After mining the ships in Keppel Harbour, Lieutenant Donald Davidson and Able Seaman Wally Falls paddled across the Singapore Strait towards Dongas. They heard the explosions but their view of Singapore was impeded by the western coast of Batam, where they decided to make camp for the day, setting off at dusk along a circuitous route through a chain of islands. They narrowly avoided a Japanese patrol and were caught in the same storm that had forced the other two canoes to bunker down in Panjang for the night. Davidson and Falls kept the bow of their canoe pointed into the waves as the tempest brought 'a deluge of rain, thunder and lightning and [lashed] the sea into a fury'.[22] The storm blew itself out after two horrendous hours, the two men fighting their immense fatigue and struggling to an island called Abang Besar, where they rested for the day. They made for Pompong the next night, reaching the rendezvous a day ahead of schedule.

Davidson was not unduly panicked when there was no sign of the other four commandoes. There were innumerable reasons why Lyon, Huston, Page and Jones missed the rendezvous. Carse, who had been drinking heavily while the six raiders had completed the mission, was anxious to make for Exmouth Gulf. The constant strain of sailing the *Krait* aimlessly in Japanese-controlled waters in two weeks of relentless heat broken intermittently by dangerous storms had taken its toll. Carse's nerves were further frayed when Davidson decided that they would return to Pompong on the night of 3 October and wait until dawn the following day, effectively giving the raiders a further twenty-four hours. Carse overruled. As navigator, he had the call. Besides, Lyon had been insistent that the *Krait* was to not linger in Pompong if the raiding party missed the rendezvous. A row broke out, Davidson managing to talk Carse around with the aid of his .38.

Lyon – who was making preparations to commandeer a local vessel and sail to India once the monsoon abated – sighted the dark shadow of the *Krait* making her way back to Pompong around eight o'clock on the night of 3 October. He was not entirely surprised that the *Krait* returned, having discovered Davidson's campsite and assumed he would come back. The two folboats were launched and the four raiders paddled out to reunite with their comrades.

The journey across the Java Sea was uneventful, save for the appearance of a flying boat that took no notice of them. As planned, they entered the Lombok Strait at dusk with a 'feeling of complete confidence'.[23] This tricky passage of water, whose vicious tides had been so troublesome weeks earlier, would be the site of one final twist. Around midnight, with the moon risen and a southerly stirring up the waves, the lookouts sighted a ship looming on the horizon off their port beam, the sea curling white at her bow clearly visible in the moonlight.

The ship was around 250 feet in length, a minesweeper with raked bows and a single gun on her raised forecastle that had been guarding the northern narrows of the strait; she was on a ramming course with the *Krait*. Lyon ordered the men below and to ready their weapons as the minesweeper turned hard to port, drawing abeam of the *Krait* and settling on a parallel course around 100 yards off her port quarter. Lyon entered the wheelhouse alongside Carse, standing near a plunging detonator connected by wires to enough gelignite and plastic explosive to destroy the *Krait* and, if they got the timing right, punch a gaping hole in the minesweeper. If the detonator malfunctioned, he had the cyanide pills at hand to give to his men. Whatever happened, Lyon would not allow the Japanese to take his men prisoner. He would sooner kill them all than have their secrets extracted through torture before their inevitable execution.

For eight excruciating minutes the minesweeper paced *Krait* before abruptly increasing her speed and then turning away on a course to Lombok. The reason why the minesweeper did not challenge the *Krait* is a matter of conjecture. That the close encounter occurred just on midnight was, at least in Ted Carse's thinking, telling: 'Whether it was because of the approach to the change of watches and the officer of the first watch had had a bad day and wanted to go to his bunk or they had got into trouble with some high-ranking officials over stopping similar boats to ours, we can't tell, but it was certainly a miracle.'[24] Carse guided the *Krait* through the Lombok Strait into the Indian Ocean, relieved to no longer be 'skulking by the by-ways and corners of the sea'.[25]

The next day, Lyon ordered the Japanese flag flying at the stern to be taken down. They arrived at Exmouth Gulf a week later. In forty-eight days, they had traversed a distance of 5000 miles without casualty, ostensibly having sunk or damaged seven ships. It was an astonishing accomplishment. Lyon and Page were flown to Melbourne to be debriefed before reuniting with the other Jaywick members in Brisbane for a party thrown in their honour. Prior to an exuberant celebration, a photograph of the entire team was organised. Lyon, Page and Davidson are among those seated at the front. Underscoring their steely-eyed expressions burns a look of smouldering anger.

On their return to Australia, they were all sworn to secrecy so as not to jeopardise similar operations that would now have the go-ahead. This was a departure from Jaywick's original purpose.

Sinking or damaging enemy vessels was no mean feat. But destroying oil tankers, freighters and cargo vessels was akin to delivering a bloody nose rather than a knockout blow. The location of the attack was more significant than the ships targeted. Singapore was a heavily defended seaport, deep in Japanese-controlled territory and a place of immense symbolic importance to the Japanese and the Allies.

Aside from the loss of prestige that comes with an attack on a symbolically significant base, Jaywick's strategic value was effectively sending the enemy a message: commando units could penetrate deep inside their territory and execute raids with impunity. Although improbable, the hope was that the Japanese may pull back resources and personnel from the frontlines to fortify other naval bases to guard against this capability. This ambition was never given a chance to succeed because the Japanese never knew that the attack was carried out by a commando unit. Without anyone claiming responsibility, moreover, the Japanese turned their vengeful gaze to enemies – real and imagined – who lurked within.

23

THE DOUBLE TENTH INCIDENT

JOHN LONG – THE BRITISH ENGINEER, ambulance driver, news committee member and former employee of the Shell company – was probably the first internee to hear of the attack at Singapore Harbour. He caught the gist of the attack, subsequently confirmed by former Chinese colleagues at Shell Petroleum with whom Long was still in contact, while on a hospital run to Miyako. Details were scant, but it was clear that several ships, including tankers, had been sunk by incendiaries of some sort. Long shared the news with others in Changi. The internees were aware of small groups of clandestine British troops operating up-country, installed prior to the capitulation of Singapore. Most assumed that these men had trained a group of Malayan guerrillas who had infiltrated Singapore and then fixed magnetic bombs on the ships. Scott alone believed that the saboteurs came from the sea, but his other suppositions were incorrect; he contended a raiding party comprised of disgruntled Javanese guerrillas had exacted vengeance on the oppressive and violent Japanese.[1]

The attack coincided with an uptick in Japanese activity within the camp and an increase in phone calls made and received from the Commandant's office. Scott had heard that 'a week [prior to the attack], a big conference had been held in the office, attended by many strange Japanese'.[2] Scott believed, like most of the other internees, that the Japanese were going to relocate them to another camp. This theory was first floated by an internee who revealed that he had been instructed to draw a large-scale map of the prison with every cell marked with the names of those who occupied them. This man, who had worked as an architect before the war, was deemed the best person for the job. As such, when the Japanese spread word that the entire camp was to parade in the main yard the following morning at exactly nine o'clock, nobody was unduly concerned; the order supported the theory that the Japanese meant to relocate the camp – they were probably taking a headcount. After all, the numbers of internees in the camp were in constant flux. New arrivals came in from Malaya and elsewhere while others died or were transferred to Miyako owing to illness. The camp leadership oversaw an office that assiduously kept a record of all internees, but the Japanese records were a mess, 'so it was unsurprising that they should want to take a count'.[3] Whatever other theories were voiced as to the reason for the parade, nobody linked the order to what had happened in the harbour.

The entire camp assembled in the main yard several minutes before the appointed hour. The serried ranks of internees turned out in their thousands, grouped according to their block. It was Sunday 10 October, the Double Tenth – a day of national significance to the Chinese and the day before Rob Scott's tenth wedding anniversary.

Rob Scott and Rosamond Aeliz Dewar-Durie first met somewhere on a sea voyage between England and China in the winter of 1933. Scott was returning from leave; Rosamond was embarking on the adventure of a lifetime. Her brother – a lieutenant of the Argyll and Sutherland Highlanders who was attached to the British Legation in China for language study – had encouraged her to set sail for the Far East in a letter. He told her that she could take up secretarial work alongside his own wife in Peking. Rosamond thought it a splendid idea. She saved up and bought two day dresses, two evening dresses, two hats and a one-way ticket to China. For a woman in her early twenties to embark on such a grand adventure was a marked departure from the societal norms and expectations regarding roles for women of the era. Rosamond was far from typical.

Born in the Persian city of Ahvaz (located in modern-day Iran) in 1911, Rosamond endured an at times difficult childhood. Her parents separated and she was sent, at a very young age, to an English boarding school. The challenges of her formative years moulded her into a young woman of considerable resilience; to Rosamond, a journey to parts unknown on a ship where she did not know a soul was not in the least bit daunting. In fact, quite the opposite. She would, in subsequent years, relate to her family that the journey was exciting. The passengers 'really knew how to party'[4] and while onboard she would meet her future husband.

Rob Scott, the extremely charming, very handsome and highly eligible bachelor, was attracting considerable attention among the female passengers. Rosamond contrived chance meetings on deck. Yet there was no indication that a passionate yearning for Rosamond was stirring in Scott on the odd occasions the two conversed. She temporarily paused her pursuits of him, having no interest in joining all those other hens pecking away at this man for his attention. She would bide her time.

The actual romance was kindled later in the voyage, during a stopover in Hong Kong. A large portion of the passengers attended a mixed round-robin tournament at the beautifully manicured lawns of the tennis courts adjoined to the Hong Kong Cricket Club. Independently, Scott and Rosamond decided to enter the tournament, eventually facing off against each other. At some point, Scott sent down an ace. This sort of thing had happened regularly in the tournament – Scott serving a little too hard, his hapless opponent flailing away with her racket and striking nothing but air. He would insist they replay the point. Normally, his opponent would demurely decline his kind offer, seizing the opportunity of not making herself out to be a fusspot as a means of impressing her handsome adversary. So, after acing Rosamond, Scott apologised and offered to replay the point. But rather than wave away the apology, Rosamond responded that in fact she definitely had *not* been ready and accepted his offer. From that moment on, the young Persian-born lady had the British diplomat's undivided attention. At subsequent parties and expat soirees, the roles were reversed: Scott was now seeking out Rosamond.

They were married on a typically mild and clear autumn day at the British Legation Chapel in Peking on 11 October 1933. The altar was decorated with yellow chrysanthemums and palms, Scott stylishly dressed in a formal black frockcoat with silk-faced lapels, waistcoat and Ascot cravat, Rosamond resplendent in an 'empire gown of white satin with a girdle of pearls and a square train. Her tulle veil fell from a cap of seed pearls [and] she carried a bouquet of white carnations and maiden-hair fern.'[5] The pageantry of the previous day's Double Tenth celebrations – with banners depicting the Chinese characters denoting the Double Tenth adorning public buildings, flag-raising ceremonies, military parades, dance troupes performing to traditional song, and Chinese minstrels clashing cymbals, striking gongs and keeping a frenetic beat on the ancient bass drum to drive the dragon's writhing antics as fireworks lit up the night sky – surely made it feel as if the whole of China was celebrating Rosamond and Scott's imminent nuptials.

They honeymooned in Peking's Western Hills the weekend after the wedding and enjoyed a second, more substantial

honeymoon in January, when Scott took a furlough on completion of his time with Sir Miles Lampson. The married couple
dovetailed a visit to Scott's sister in Uganda into a motor tour
of the continent. They bought a clapped-out old car in Nairobi,
drove to Uganda, made it through the Belgian Congo, broke
down in the French colony of Ubangi-Shari, and motored north
to Cairo, having somehow revived the engine and kept it alive
the entire length and breadth of the Sudan and Egypt.

As Scott waited in the Changi yard for the headcount to start,
his thoughts were surely fixed on his wife. The splendour of their
wedding, following as it did the festive Peking celebrations of
the Double Tenth, were a far cry from the grim grey walls and
grilles that covered the windows of Changi's ugly cell blocks
looming ominously before him. The mood of this Double Tenth
was decidedly different. It was soon to become decidedly worse.

If anything brought him back to the present, it was the steadily
rising heat of the day. The guards were late. It was already well
past nine o'clock, the hour they had been told to form up in the
yard. He hoped the headcount would not take long. Scott looked
around for any signs of activity. Something was amiss. For the
first time since stepping onto the yard he noticed that there were
no Sikh guards. Among all the sentries, the Sikhs had been the
most visible to the internees in recent months and had all but
taken over guard duties by the time of the Double Tenth. Scott
generally held a favourable view of the Sikhs, always immaculately dressed in their distinctive turbans, who he described as
'quite decent'[6] in their treatment of the internees. That the Sikhs
were not assisting in the roll call was odd. This was precisely the
sort of duty to which a sentry was suited.

The internees began to stir uncomfortably in the unforgiv-
ing sun, shuffling side-to-side, waiting for something to happen.
Around ten o'clock, a Japanese man walked into the yard, flanked
by a large force of *Kempei Tai* men and armed troops. This was

Asahi's replacement, the new commandant, whose name was Suzuki. He stood before the ranks of men and, in a booming voice, shouted all manner of accusations at the assembled internees in Japanese. A translator attempted to be heard above the ceaseless shouts of his superior. To most, his translations were inaudible. But one man caught the end of one of the translated sentences: 'will be severely punished'.[7] While Suzuki continued his verbal barrage, armed guards spread out across the yard, surrounding the internees. The doors and entrances leading into each block were closed. The jail was in lockdown. Once all the guards were in place, the Commandant cleared his throat. He looked down at a sheet of paper, evidently a list of names. The first name to be called was Robert Heatlie Scott.

Two *Kempei Tai* guards seized Scott, while a third patted him down. His luxuriant beard was combed with sweaty fingers in a vain effort to find something – anything – incriminating. To the assembled internees, the sight of Scott being seized and frisked was utterly bewildering. Who was this man? What exactly had he done to deserve such treatment? That only a couple of dozen internees among the thousands knew Scott's identity proved that the effort to keep his identity a secret was a success. Clearly, however, the Japanese had never lost track of him.

Other names were called out. They were, as one internee observed, 'electricians, merchants, doctors, Eurasians, a ship's butcher'.[8] They had different backgrounds and professions, and were even drawn from different cell blocks, and were called out in an 'apparently haphazard'[9] fashion. Scott knew that their names had not been drawn at random. Most had been members of at least one of the committees of the camp. Of the men on the news committee, only Walter Stevenson and Scott were called. Evidently, the Japanese did not know everything. But it was clear that they had been watching and listening more closely than first imagined.

Satisfied that Scott had nothing on his person, the guards led him inside the building with the others who were seized.

Nineteen men were arrested on that first day and were all taken to various rooms. Around an hour later, the remaining internees were returned to their respective blocks and ordered to parade in their assigned yards. Sentries bearing rifles with bayonets roamed the blocks and turned over every cell and room in the camp. Scott's room was given a very thorough examination: 'It so happened that I had nothing there except notes of Wickham Steed's speech.'[10] The notes were written in a private code of Scott's own making, scrawled on a piece of dirty old newspaper in which he kept his filthy pipe cleaner. One witness noticed that the Japanese guards 'took one glance at the paper, screwed their noses (it literally stank of stale tobacco) and threw it away'.[11]

Periodically, an internee would be summoned forward to claim ownership of an object – a letter, a document, a map – that was discovered in his room. Once identified and claimed as his own, the internee would be ordered back in line. There was never any punishment meted out for owning such items. To the internees, the parameters of the search were confined to finding 'any evidence of connection with the outside'.[12] As such, typewriters, torches, medical bags, maps, documents and money were all impounded. The Japanese, it seemed, were intent on finding evidence of a conspiracy perpetrated by those arrested. The internees were kept on the parade grounds for the entire day. Those who collapsed from heatstroke were left unconscious in the sun. The only respite came when a thunderstorm broke across the camp, drenching the internees in rain. Darkness fell. Exhausted, dehydrated and hungry, the internees were ordered back to their cells at around nine o'clock that night. The *Kempei Tai* continued their search of the camp the following day.

The term 'the Double Tenth' entered the parlance of the camp, describing a definitive moment in the lives of those interned in Changi when everything changed. Rice rations were reduced, performances and lectures were cancelled and fatigue parties sent to collect wood and other essentials from outside the camp were suspended. Activities such as bridge and reading were curtailed due to restrictions placed on the use of lights, and other recreational programs were suspended indefinitely. Worst of all, the Changi internees came to experience intense hunger for the first time since the war began. The Japanese had cancelled all nonessential items from entering the camp, including supplementary foodstuffs that had been purchased by the central committee using smuggled cash to bolster the meagre prison rations. As one internee observed, 'queues of hungry people lined up for rice and *kunji*, and these were quickly put on the official "seconds" lists. The midday soup became a thin brew, with little in it except green vegetables, the bread from the outside bakery no longer came in, and through time the evening *kunji* disappeared, so that all we had at that meal was a small piece of soya bread.'[13] Compounding the internees' hunger, morale plummeted. Without the news and distribution committees, there were no reliable updates on the war. Rumour, misinformation, lies and distortions once again swept through the jail. Nobody knew what to believe. The internees were in a state of constant fear. Over the coming weeks, *Kempei Tai* guards would carry out arrests. Seemingly at random, internees were seized and 'taken away for what fate we know not'.[14]

After being marched off the parade ground on the day of the raid and witnessing the ransacking of his cell, Rob Scott was kept in solitary confinement. At nightfall, he was roughly bundled into a car and driven to the old town along the long stretch of road that carved through the darkened jungle covering much of the east of the island. They eventually drove across the bridge over the river and approached Fort Canning, following the road that led to the grand Municipal Building, an area of Singapore Scott knew well. Shortly after midnight, on the day of his tenth wedding anniversary, Scott arrived outside a three-storey Edwardian building on Stamford Road: his new home, the YMCA.

24

CONFESSIONS

Two weeks after the attack

PAPERS, BOOKS, WIRES, TOOLS, radio sets, money and other contraband discovered in Changi's cells during the raid were packed up and delivered to Sumida's office in the YMCA. It was an intelligence windfall, revealing a clever system of news sharing, numerous radio devices to receive the news, a sophisticated spy organisation and a breathtaking level of criminality. Sumida's men also discovered around $400,000 in banana notes in the prison, much of it hidden in the cell of the banker, Walter Thomas Yoxall, who had been arrested on the day of the raid. Sumida knew about the black market operating in Changi, but this was a staggering sum of money.

Sumida kept the investigation focused on three main areas. Firstly, the organisational structure and leadership of the espionage ring. Secondly, the system of finance within the internment camp that was surely funding anti-Japanese operations throughout the island and probably in Malaya. Thirdly, the existence of several radio sets. Each of the internees arrested in Changi and the Eurasians and Chinese arrested on the outside were, in the main, questioned in relation to one of these three areas. These suspects would be assigned their own interrogators – sometimes one, usually several – who had their own interpreters drawn from *Kempei Tai* staff or Chinese and Malayan interpreters handpicked from Japanese businesses trading in Syonan. There would be overlap, internees or fifth columnists inevitably being involved in more than one aspect of the three areas, but this system of categorising crimes provided a framework from which Sumida could keep track of the investigation.

Warrant Officer Sakamoto Shigeru led the investigation into the radio sets and assigned several junior staff and interpreters. Staff Sergeant Shin led interrogations into the organisation's finances with the assistance of the Malayan interpreter Miyazaki Kasuo. The all-important internal organisation and leadership of the spy ring would be assigned to Staff Sergeant Makita, Staff Sergeant Miyakawa and Sumida himself. Warrant Officer Monai Tadamori, the interrogator who unfailingly delivered results and who was often described as being 'the favoured and right hand man of the chief',[1] would take a leading role in this area of the investigation too. They would primarily use the American-born interpreter Nigo Masayoshi and several others as needed.

Once allocated to one of the specific groups, Sumida's men set themselves to their task with frightening vigour, releasing all the pent-up energy and frustration of weeks and months of inaction. Sakamoto's team delivered the first breakthrough. Sumida had assigned Sakamoto the task of interrogating Mr S. Cornelius, a Eurasian man employed in the Atlas Ice Works. Cornelius – who was not a Changi internee – had been on the *Kempei Tai*'s radar after informers had ratted him out as a smuggler. It was claimed that he was involved in receiving and delivering letters to the friends and family of internees still living in Syonan. An Indian named Joseph Francis, who was the driver of a senior camp officer who routinely ventured into Syonan on business, would meet Cornelius at a prearranged place. Francis would take delivery of the letters and hand over a bunch of replies written by the internees. The letters were taken into Changi and distributed. Sumida wondered if he was smuggling other contraband.

Corporals Toichiro and Takaya were given the task of interrogating Cornelius. Toichiro and Takaya were both pushing forty and regularly passed over for promotion. They were dogsbodies, generally assigned menial tasks and administrative duties and thoroughly fed up with their lot. They delighted in having been given such an important job. The interrogation of Cornelius took place inside a drab building in Smith Street that had lately been occupied by the *Kempei Tai*. Takaya, a known hothead who was conversant in Malay, did not bother to use his interpreter. While Cornelius tried to make sense of his interrogator's accent, Takaya 'got hold of a wooden stick some four or five feet long and three-quarters of an inch thick'[2] and flogged Cornelius in the buttocks and lower back at least fifteen times. Exhausted, Takaya rested, sharing a cigarette with Toichiro. They decided to wait for an interpreter, rightly concluding that Takaya's Malay was not up to scratch.

But instead of an interpreter, they got Sumida. The Commander wanted to see for himself how the interrogation – one of the first of the Number One Work – was progressing. He waited around for several minutes, and then ordered the interrogation to continue. Judging from the intensity of Cornelius's screams, the prisoners in surrounding rooms adjudged the violence had increased in tempo. Between them, Toichiro and Takaya flogged Cornelius with the stick at least thirty times. Eventually, bits and pieces of information started to trickle out from him. He was, as Sumida suspected, not only smuggling letters into Changi. He also confessed to smuggling $200 into the camp. But Toichiro and Takaya sensed Cornelius was holding something back. A tap connected to a hose was turned on. They forced the end of the nozzle into Cornelius' mouth. Immobilised from the flogging,

Cornelius lay on his back, full to bursting with water. One of the interrogators then stomped hard on his stomach, causing Cornelius to vomit. Utterly spent, he confirmed that, yes, he had in fact been smuggling radio parts into Changi.

Buoyed by their success, the two Japanese interrogators were eager to extract even more information through torture. The sort of violence meted out to Cornelius from this point on is not known for certain, but probably involved more flogging and more water treatment. Toichiro claimed that Cornelius was still conscious at the end of the interrogation. He was offered a cigarette. This was a custom of interrogators after subjecting a man to water torture. Said one victim offered a cigarette in similar circumstances, 'If [the tortured man] is given a cigarette to smoke and can smoke it, it still appears that he is healthy and well.'[3] Cornelius declined the cigarette. He died a few hours later after being dragged back to his cell.

Sumida savagely reprimanded the two corporals. The good work in securing a confession to smuggling radio parts into Changi had been completely undone by their excessive treatment. A veritable goldmine of information had now been lost. Perhaps the Indian driver Francis would have more information. He was arrested on 11 October and taken straight to Smith Street. Under extreme torture, Francis corroborated Cornelius's story and even added fascinating detail as to how it had all played out.

Months earlier, Francis had told Cornelius that the British leadership within Changi required radio parts. Cornelius was only too happy to assist. After sourcing the radio parts, Cornelius gave them to Francis, who concealed them inside the car and drove directly into the camp. The vehicle, which belonged to the Commandant, was never properly searched. Once within the camp walls, it 'would conveniently develop some engine trouble necessitating the attention of the internees in the Camp Workshop'.[4] They would remove the radio parts and deliver them to a select group of internees.

This was good intelligence, but the interrogators were unsatisfied; Francis knew more than he was letting on. They flogged him mercilessly until he confessed to smuggling a transmitter into Changi. Sumida was surely overjoyed. The transmitter's existence all but proved that the internees were sending and receiving messages from the British in India. The only problem was that the 'confessions' of Francis and Cornelius were mostly made up. The only component of the story that was ever corroborated by other internees was that Cornelius had arranged for some letters to be delivered to Changi in addition to giving $200 to Francis to smuggle into the jail, an act of charity that cost him his life. Cornelius left behind a wife and two young children. Sumida seemed to have forgotten that if you subject a man to extreme pain, eventually he will confess to anything.

Francis would be kept in Smith Street for another eight months, periodically interrogated and tortured when his story did not stack up. In May 1944, he was dragged from his cell and dumped on the street and told that he was free to go. A passerby helped him up and loaded him into the back of a trishaw. He was ridden to his brother's house in Bencoolen Street. Francis died from his injuries a year later.

25

CELL ONE

Two weeks after the attack

SCOTT HAD VISITED THE 'Y' before the war. The rooms within had been renovated since the Japanese had taken residence. 'Part of the ground floor, including the billiard room, had been made into cells, three big ones, sixteen feet square, and two small, nine feet square.'[1] The three large cells running along the back of the building were accessible by an L-shaped corridor, the two smaller cells opening to the shorter leg of the L. There was a third room at the very end of the corridor, used to store prisoners' kit. Each cell was numbered one to five, 'one to three being the big ones, four and five the small'.[2] The door that led into the corridor looked straight into cell two, where at least one but usually two sentries would sit day and night, unless patrolling the corridor.

Scott was led to cell one. The constant glare of the ceiling light revealed the hollowed-out faces of eleven prisoners who crouched on their haunches on the bug-infested floor. A pitifully small window fitted with wooden bars situated high on the wall provided no breeze. The sharply rising hill at the back of the Y created a natural barrier, rendering this side of the building unventilated. The air inside the cell was fuggy and close, a revolting stink rising from the open commode in the corner having no means of escape. From above, Scott heard the sound of screaming – dreadful, bloodcurdling screams of agony. Equally disturbing were the unchanged expressions of the other inmates, who, at least outwardly, were unmoved by the suffering of a fellow prisoner. Clearly, the sound of torture was a constant refrain in this hellish place.

Scott was pushed into the cell and told to sit and not to talk to anyone. His cellmates made space for him. In time, he would come to know them through a combination of barely audible whispers and an ingenious system of sign language which the multilingual Scott had no trouble picking up. His cellmates were Chinese, save for two Indians and one Malay. These men were inside for an assortment of offences, some absurdly minor. Several Chinese men were rickshaw drivers who were flogged daily for overcharging customers. This, Scott would later discover, was a common punishment meted out by the Japanese as a cost-of-living measure. 'They [the *Kempei Tai*] published orders prescribing maximum rickshaw fares, but as the city was flooded with worthless notes, twenty cents meant nothing.'[3] The Japanese authorities tended to turn a blind eye to what they unfairly viewed as price gouging. Unless, of course, a driver was foolish enough to overcharge a *Kempei Tei* man. Such an offence would earn a night-long flogging, or worse.

There were other individuals accused of serious crimes whose lives hung by a thread, such as the old Chinese fisherman. When Scott arrived, the fisherman was in a dreadful state. The occupants of a Japanese patrol boat arrested him after chancing on his boat at night. He'd been fishing late with his lamp, as was the local custom. He'd even produced a net and small haul of fish to prove he was telling the truth. But the Japanese were not convinced. This man was likely signalling to other fifth columnists preparing another raid on the harbour. The fisherman stubbornly refused to confess. At least, that was how the Japanese saw things. He was strapped to a ladder, his head pushed into a tub full of water, which he was made to swallow until his stomach was distended. Once he was nearly unconscious, they would drag him outside and savagely kick him in the stomach and kidneys until he vomited blood. Despite his emaciated state, the fisherman could no longer swallow food, as it caused too much pain. He offered his rations to Scott and the others. After a couple of months of this treatment, the *Kempei Tai* 'finally convinced themselves that he was harmless, and let him go, more dead than alive'.[4]

Aside from Scott himself, perhaps there was no man in greater danger than the Malayan chauffeur who had run down a Japanese soldier and killed him. The fact that the soldier was blind drunk was immaterial. The death of a soldier at the hands of any non-Japanese, irrespective of where the fault lay, had to be harshly punished. 'The Malay was kept in the cells for a fortnight [and] flogged daily till he was almost insensible.'[5] Each night, he would be dragged back to his cell, 'his back, arms and trousers a mass of blood'.[6] Having made their point, the *Kempei Tai* brought him a clean white suit and turned him loose.

There was also a woman in Scott's cell. It was bad enough that she had to endure the beastly discomforts and indignities of life in the YMCA – the foul bugs, the stench and humidity, the meagre servings of revolting food, the tepid tea, the rough sleeping without bedding, performing her 'most intimate toilet in front of a lot of strange men' and the 'sentries on guard who strolled about when the mood took them'[7] – but to subject this woman to the bloodcurdling screams of her brother, tortured days on end upstairs, seemed another level of cruelty. Each agonised howl caused her to wince and crouch low, her voice barely a whisper: 'my brother, my brother.'[8]

Her name was Germaine. Her husband, a Swiss businessman, had been locked up in Central Police Station, held without charge.

Her brother was yet another suspected Chinese saboteur. Scott never discovered the exact nature of the charges levelled against the three, possibly because none were ever laid. It seemed the Japanese believed Germaine's brother and husband to be involved in some conspiracy. Germaine was being kept as leverage, her brother's torturers threatening to harm or kill her if he did not confess. Compounding Germaine's horror, a *Kempei Tai* sergeant had taken a liking to her. Throughout her imprisonment, the guard called her out of the cell at all hours of the night. She would be returned some time the following day. At first, Scott wrongly assumed she went up for questioning, until Germaine confided in him that she was the Japanese sergeant's comfort woman.

'She spoke excellent English,' Scott noted, 'and told me that she was very fond of both her husband and the sergeant, but fondest of all of her brother.'[9] Germaine's affection for the Japanese sergeant – a man who was participating in the torture of her brother and clearly benefiting from her husband's incarceration – might seem incomprehensible. Germaine very likely saw the whole affair as a sordid transaction: in exchange for sex, the sergeant gave Germaine respite from the misery of her cell. She may also have deemed it prudent to profess her affection for the sergeant to her cellmates for her own safety. All of these men would be interrogated if they had not already been so. Who knew what they would be asked or what they would say when taken upstairs?

Germaine's term of incarceration lasted seven months. As her body began to waste away, the Japanese sergeant's appearances became more infrequent until his visits stopped altogether. She would survive, but she never saw her husband again. He died of an unspecified illness, most likely from neglect and ill-treatment while imprisoned. She was released around the same time as her brother. Scott saw him before he was let go: he 'was so terribly tortured that I doubt whether he is still alive'.[10]

She was not the only woman to come into cell one. Ten days after his imprisonment, Scott would meet Mrs Cornelius, who had been brought to the YMCA with her husband. She shared the cell with Scott and spent the following day cringing and crying out for her husband, whose screams echoed throughout the building for eight hours, until they fell abruptly silent. He was dragged back down to another cell, 'his body, from the waist upwards, was black and blue; from the left side of his stomach to this right shoulder extended a weal caused by his having been beaten with a wet rope'.[11] He was dumped on the cell floor. Someone heard him utter, 'Christ, what a beating.'[12] He reached out towards the commode, most likely gesturing for a cup of water from the tap. He fell unconscious, arms splayed out, and died.

The *Kempei Tai* left Cornelius in the cell until the following afternoon. Extracting his body from the narrow entrance to the cell was a macabre affair. Rigor mortis had set in by the time he was taken away. The guards violently wrenched his arms so that the body could be forced out of the cell. To the prisoners in the cell, the sound of Cornelius' arms breaking was as horrifying as the raucous laughter of the guards. Mercifully, Mrs Cornelius did not witness her husband's corpse debased and defiled. She was kept in her cell for six months, never once questioned, left to ponder his fate. She suffered dysentery and came perilously close to death, but somehow pulled through. 'Then they just let her go,' Scott wrote, 'quite casually, leaving it to her to find out that her husband had died months earlier.'[13] She was forced to find her own transport home, where her children would be waiting for their parents.

But the most interesting prisoner to Scott was a young Chinese female accused of being a communist. She was among a group ratted on by a Chinese youth. The youth, who was also in Scott's cell, was very pleased with himself, while the other Chinese would have nothing to do with him. It quickly became clear why: 'He had been mixed up in communist youth circles, and was now denouncing his friends, and apparently thoroughly enjoying it.'[14] In exchange for being an informer, the young man was given good meals, clean clothing and cigarettes. He was even taken out periodically to dance halls, and presumably offered comfort women. But the *Kempei Tai* sensed he was holding something back. They would get what they wanted through other methods: 'They flung saucerfuls [*sic*] of petrol and kerosene on his legs and ankles, and sometimes on his stomach, and set fire to them, raising enormous blisters. They also filled his stomach with petrol – he reeked of it for days.'[15] Having assured the guards that he had revealed all that he knew, the prisoner seemed able to recall more details of the group's anti-Japanese activities while being burnt. More youths were brought in, including the girl.

Aside from some mild questioning that did not appear to involve torture, the young woman was initially left alone. She confided in Scott that she thought she would be alright. Scott thought her confidence was misplaced. Being communist was bad enough. But to be communist *and* Chinese was, in the eyes of the Japanese, to be something loathsome and abhorrent, grotesque even. Later, during his interrogation, Scott would learn something of the *Kempei Tai*'s attitude to the Chinese. 'Do you regard Chinese as human beings?' his interrogator asked. Astonished, Scott answered that of course he did. 'That is wrong,' the interrogator retorted. 'We Nipponese do not look on Chinese as human. They are good for nothing except making money. They are not entitled to any consideration whatsoever.'[16]

The girl wallowed in the cell for weeks, until her name was called. The guard told her that she would not be returning to her cell. 'She was overjoyed, smiled and waved goodbye to us all and went off to the office for the usual leaving formalities.'[17] An hour later the girl returned in tears. She was roped together with the other six communists, including the badly burnt informer. They were being paraded before the other prisoners as a final humiliation and perhaps as a warning to others. This was the spectacle they had to endure before being taken to face justice: a show trial in which their fate had been predetermined, where conviction was certain and execution inevitable. Scott watched as they were led outside. They were never heard from again.

Walter Stevenson was the first of the Changi internees arrested on the Double Tenth to be tortured. The interrogation took place in the room directly above Rob Scott's cell. The ceiling was thin. Every sound was distinct. Scott could hear the dull thud followed by a groan or cry when Stevenson was kicked. He heard the whistle and smack of the bamboo stick as it was ferociously whipped across Stevenson's body. He heard the slosh and struggle for air as Stevenson's head was forced into a bucket of water. At the end of each session, Stevenson was brought back downstairs and walked slowly past Scott's cell. He was in a dreadful state. 'He had open wounds, ulcers, sores on his hands and feet and body.'[18] Scott offered him a kind word, risking severe punishment for breaking the strict rule of no speaking. Stevenson nodded and smiled, even enquiring of Scott's health. He was putting on a brave show. But no man could withstand such treatment without breaking.

The sound of Stevenson's suffering was somehow a more heightened, visceral experience than bearing visual witness. The Japanese surely knew as much. Torturing Stevenson directly above Scott's cell, walking him past Scott's cell after each session and even allowing the two men to briefly converse was very likely a deliberate tactic intended to send a message that the same treatment awaited Scott. It was an effective tactic insofar as Scott found the sounds of Stevenson's ordeal 'nerve shattering'.[19] But it was also a miscalculation. Scott heard every question that Stevenson was asked. He knew exactly what Stevenson had revealed about the news committee, the names they managed to prise out of him and the precise means by which information was distributed across the camp.

Equally important, Scott was able to form a picture of the case the Japanese had built against the internees. He learnt that 'behind the *Kempei* actions lay a suspicion that the camp harboured the headquarters of a big spy, sabotage, and counter propaganda organisation, in wireless communication with India'. This was worse than Scott had imagined, not because any of it was true but because it was so ludicrous: 'This absurd suspicion amounted almost to a certainty in their minds.'[20] Scott had known the day he was brought into the YMCA that he was regarded as a senior figure of this fantastic conspiracy. That was obvious the moment his name was called first during those initial arrests on the Double Tenth. But he had no inkling then of the seriousness of the crimes of which he was suspected.

Stevenson was tortured for at least three straight days, then sporadically over the course of the next four weeks. He showed titanic fortitude to stick to the truth, denying every charge of spying, sabotage and counter-propaganda. There were ample opportunities for Stevenson to end his suffering, to widen the net of the conspiracy by naming names or validating the charges through confession. His obdurate refusal to do so, even in the face of appalling and depraved violence, left a big impression on Scott. He stuck to the truth and provided parameters Scott would use to tailor his own responses when he was inevitably taken upstairs for questioning.

On 10 November, barely capable of walking, Stevenson was transferred to Central Police Station and tortured on at least two subsequent occasions with electricity. Quite unnecessarily, the guards kept him cuffed in his cell. 'After he had received electric treatment,' said a cellmate in Central, 'he could not stand to take his meal. He was very weak.'[21] Burn marks were visible on his face and thighs where the live cables were placed. A short time after Stevenson was transferred to Central, dysentery swept through the prisoner population, and he became wretchedly sick. A Japanese doctor visited him twice and gave him two injections

of God knew what. A fellow prisoner, Dr Bowyer, was permitted
to see him. Bowyer warned the Japanese that if Stevenson was
not moved to a hospital he would be dead within twenty-four
hours. Stevenson was dead three hours later.

Information gleaned from the interrogation of Stevenson broad-
ened the investigation. The *Kempei Tai* did not so much turn
their gaze away from the internees in Changi as much as widen
the lens of their search. Scott's cell of a dozen people doubled
in number. The majority of new arrivals came from the Chinese
community, where enemies were always presumed to exist. There
were Malays and Eurasians too, including a former journalist who
had been operating his short-wave radio throughout the entirety
of the Occupation. He confided in Scott that he spent much of
his time 'listening to personal messages broadcast from New
Delhi for internees and prisoners of war in Singapore'.[22] He had
smuggled several thousand such messages into the camps before
being caught, arrested and tortured. The charge was working as
a spy for the British master spy in Changi, Robert Heatlie Scott.
    But Sumida had a problem. Stevenson's interrogation had
certainly yielded information, but nothing like the devastating
revelations he expected. Scott, for instance, was described as
merely the head of a news-distributing committee within Changi,
Stevenson admitted to the smuggling of short-wave radio sets
into the camp and that Allied broadcasts were printed and distributed throughout the camp – a serious crime, to be sure, but
nothing that rose to the level of espionage or insurgency. The case
against Scott as the master spy remained entirely circumstantial.
It was clear that Scott possessed the wherewithal to orchestrate
espionage operations. He was a diplomat who spoke multiple
languages, had spent time in Japan and China, was a significant figure in the British administration before the war and had
even confessed to leading a team of propagandists. To Sumida,
this lack of evidence merely proved the cunning and skill of his

adversary; that there was no evidence that tied him directly to any specific act of sabotage, in a sense, validated Scott's standing as a highly skilled spymaster.

Sumida continued to hold back on interrogating Scott. He wanted a more complete picture of his crimes before that process began. He instead set his sights on another individual whose name was repeatedly mentioned in unconnected interrogations. That name was John Long. How Long had avoided arrest on the Double Tenth seemed, in retrospect, an astonishing oversight. He was formerly employed by the Shell Company and maintained contact with former colleagues who would have good knowledge of the activities down at the harbour. For over a year, he had been venturing out of Changi under the auspices of driving sick internees in his ambulance to Miyako, but was no doubt up to no good. And, crucially, Sumida learned that he was a member of the news committee and therefore almost certainly one of Scott's lieutenants. Sumida had Long arrested six days after the initial Double Tenth raid.

The task of interrogating Long would fall to Sumida's most trusted man. Sergeant Monai Tadamori did not disappoint.

26

THE TORMENT OF DR STANLEY

Three weeks after the attack

MONAI TODAMORI WAS A rising star of the *Kempei Tai*. He was part of a consignment of fifteen other *Kempei Tai* staff sent down from Bangkok at Sumida's request in May 1943 to help clamp down on the increase in anti-Japanese activity. Aged in his early thirties, Monai was smart, determined, ambitious and fanatical. It had been a different story before the war. He was a merchant who owned a struggling food shop that barely yielded the profit he needed to feed his wife and three very young children. Joining the military provided a solution. In 1934, at the age of twenty-three, with the war in China poised to expand, he enlisted as a second-class private in the *Kempei Tai*. Like so many men who held jobs deemed to be of a lower status in Japan's rigid class hierarchy, the instant prestige and repute that came with wearing military uniform, complete with the flashy red and white armband of the much-feared military police, was surely intoxicating. Monai committed himself to military life with unyielding zeal, discovering a talent for interrogation and a taste for violence.

By the time he was posted to Syonan, Monai was a staff sergeant with a violent reputation. 'Monai was a brute even to the Japanese,' said one of the men assigned to interpret for him. 'Everyone feared him.'[1] But his methods delivered results. In Monai, Sumida would find a man who lived up to his reputation. By the end of May, he moved Monai out of the Criminal Section – which investigated looting, damage to property and black-market activities – and appointed him leader of the Third Section, 'which was chiefly concerned with counter espionage work'.[2] In this position, he would have ample opportunity to indulge his violent impulses.

Monai spared none of the *Kempei Tai*'s psychological tricks and physical torments to coax John Long into talking. It worked all too well: 'In response to flattery, and more in response to torture, [Long] signed practically anything [Monai] asked.'[3] Monai reported back to Sumida that Long confessed to smuggling huge quantities of money – a fact that could easily be corroborated – and also personal communiqués, medical supplies and radio parts. He also admitted to being 'connected in some espionage activity [in relation to] petroleum with the co-operation of the inhabitants of the island'.[4] But it was Long's insight into the intricate network of spies inside and outside Changi that elevated his interrogation to something akin to a turning point in the Number One Work. The evidence gleaned from Long's 'confessions' led to a flurry of arrests in Changi and the Chinese community, including of thirteen internees who were brought to either the YMCA or Smith Street.

Among the more noteworthy men arrested was the Bishop of Singapore, Reverend John Wilson. Long revealed the bishop's critical role in funnelling cash into Changi. He stated that most of Yoxall's enormous cache of money was brought in through Wilson's smuggling operation. Having chosen silence rather than to lie or bear false witness, the bishop came in for a torrid time. His silence also had unintended consequences. Without anyone disputing or refuting Long's more outlandish claims, Long's statements came to be viewed by Sumida as empirical fact.

Before the end of October, Long confirmed Monai's hypothesis that a sophisticated spy ring was in existence in Changi and led by Robert Heatlie Scott. He had claimed that intermediaries would pass on Scott's orders to insurgents to conduct sabotage operations. He listed the names of Changi internees who were involved in the spy ring and even confessed to the 'fact' that Scott and other senior members of the spy ring within Changi were responsible for organising and coordinating the attack on Singapore Harbour. Details concerning the whereabouts of the all-important transmitter that had been used to signal the British in India were admittedly sketchy. To Sumida, it seemed plausible that Long could not be sure of the transmitter's location.

The Indian driver Francis had similarly confessed to the existence of a transmitter. Like Long, Francis stopped short of providing the transmitter's whereabouts; he seemed not to know. This was yet another demonstration of the sophisticated operation Scott had put in place. In the time-honoured tradition of espionage, the spy ring operating in Changi had been compartmentalised, whereby Long and Francis and others serving functionary roles were told only what they needed to know. It was a sensible precaution to limit the damage of someone spilling secrets of their own accord or, should they be captured, under pressure. The point was that Long stated unequivocally that the transmitter existed.

Long also confirmed what Sumida suspected all along: that Chinese conspirators were involved in Scott's operations. On 29 October 1943 – around the time Long had finished revealing the names of individuals outside Changi who were central to the smuggling operation – Sumida ordered the arrest of the bookkeeper, suspected spy and Long's contact in Miyako, Choy Khun Heng. Choy had bought radio sets on Long's instruction – or so Long claimed – and they were smuggled into the camp.

Choy was arrested by two Japanese *Kempei Tai* soldiers –
one of them being Sergeant Sugimoto Kozo – in the canteen at
Tan Tock Seng Hospital. Sugimoto accused him of sending radio
parts and money into Changi. Choy said nothing. Revealing
his role would lead to the arrest of many people, including his
wife. He was taken to Central Police Station, where he lived
on meagre rice rations for days before being transferred back
to the YMCA. He was led to an interrogation room and left
alone for a few hours. Eventually, four soldiers entered the room.
Sergeant Major Morita Shozo, a brute of a man, was the officer
assigned to extract a confession from Choy. Morita repeated the
accusations levelled against Choy, that he was a key functionary
in an elaborate conspiracy to smuggle radio parts into Changi
Prison and that he had bought radio parts for Long. 'I showed
him parts of a wireless set found in Changi,' Morita later said.
'Choy made repeated denials and I felt the use of force would
be necessary.'[5]

Choy continued to remain silent. Morita's men stepped
forward and grabbed hold of Choy, dragging him out of the room
and pushing him down a narrow hall and into another room. In
the middle sat a heavy plank of wood fitted with a triangular
bar. Neatly arranged across the floor were iron rods, bamboo
sticks and several lengths of rope. In one corner of the room was
a large tub filled with water.

Choy's shirt was ripped off his body. He was then taken over
to the plank of wood and forced into a kneeling position. The
guards fixed the triangular bar between Choy's knees, which
kept him balanced. Ropes were then fastened around his ankles
and his wrists were tied behind his back, preventing his arms
from taking the weight off his body. Each soldier then picked
up one of the items on the ground. Choy was repeatedly told
to confess to his crimes. Each time he denied the accusations
levelled against him, a soldier would strike him with a bamboo
stick or an iron rod.

After several whacks, Choy begged his torturers to stop. They would only stop, they said, when he made a full confession. To confess to those crimes would mean death. Choy simply shook his head, and so the torture continued. At the point he was beginning to lose feeling in his legs and arms, Choy's bonds were cut. He collapsed onto the hard ground. He was dragged over to the tub of water. His head was pushed into the water and held down until he lost consciousness. He was pulled out of the tub and turned onto his back. After he was revived, Shozo demanded that he confess to his crimes. Choy shook his head. Two soldiers knelt down next to Choy and held him down. A third, Monai, forced Choy to open his mouth while Morita poured in water through a tube, forcing him to drink. The tube was eventually taken away. Monai then stepped forward and stamped viciously on Choy's distended stomach.

It was eleven o'clock in the morning when Choy's torture began. It did not finish until six o'clock that evening. He had remained kneeling on the plank for two-hour stretches at time, periodically relieved from the agony of bearing his weight on knees only to be subjected to the water treatment. Throughout his ordeal, he continued to deny Shozo's accusations. Monai and the other guards dragged him into the cell. Before they pulled the door shut, they told him they would see him tomorrow. Choy would receive the same punishment for the next twenty days.

Sumida's focus was now firmly on the information furnished from John Long, whose 'confessions' yielded, among many things, the names of the men who sat on the news committee. Rob Scott, Lionel Earl, Walter Stevenson and Long himself were already in custody. The only man yet to be arrested was Dr Hugh McIntyre. Sumida arranged for McIntyre's arrest on 24 October and then set his men upon him. The interrogation of McIntyre would turn up even more lines of enquiry.

McIntyre's 'confessions' proved particularly devastating for Dr C. Stanley, a married man of fifty years of age, interned at Changi. Stanley was one of the doctors Scott consulted shortly after leaving solitary confinement, back when he was contemplating feigning insanity. Sumida had Stanley in his sights from early in the investigation after a homemade electric clock was found in his cell in Changi. The discovery of the clock prompted a thorough examination of Stanley's cell, which uncovered a secret compartment inside of which were manuals and an operator's key. 'The *Kempei* put two and two together,' wrote Scott, 'and added it up to make a radio transmitter.'[6] There was, of course, no transmitter. Stanley's radio could receive signals but not send them.

Sumida saw it differently. That Stanley had manufactured the clock within his cell with very limited materials suggested he was a resourceful man of considerable skill in electronics and engineering. Was it not reasonable to assume that such a man could also build a small transmitter? Sumida had Stanley sent to Central Police Station, where he wallowed for a month. Meanwhile, Sumida built a case against him. He ordered more pressure to be exerted on McIntyre, who was by now utterly pliant and spilling it all, offering lurid descriptions of the imagined and sophisticated spy ring operating within Changi. It was all a fantasy intended to please the interrogators and stop the torture. When that information failed to appease his interrogators, McIntyre invented a process by which messages were developed and then sent. As ever, it began with Rob Scott, who would gather all the information from his sources and determine what needed to be signalled. Scott would then pass a message to Earl, who in turn passed the message to Henry Bryning, an electrical engineer with no involvement in any of Changi's committees but who was suspicious on account of his profession. McIntyre confirmed that Bryning would then give the message to Stanley, who would signal it to the British Headquarters in India.[7]

The information gleaned from McIntyre's torture sealed the doctor's fate: Stanley was Scott's signalman. Sumida concluded that nobody was better placed to know the information that Scott possessed than the man charged with signalling his messages. Once unlocked, Stanley's mind would reveal the crucial pieces of evidence that would ultimately bring Scott undone. Stanley was transferred to the YMCA. Sumida instructed Monai to find out what Stanley knew. Stanley was placed in one of the larger cells. Samuel Travis, an employee of Henry Waugh & Co. – a British trading house based in Singapore that imported consumer goods – was the only other European in the cell with Stanley. Travis had been arrested a week after the Double Tenth. He was savagely beaten in the Changi tower and accused of being a spy and owning a transmitter, all of which was false. After being transferred to the YMCA, Travis endured one horrifying week of violence without confessing. The Japanese all but gave up on him. His interrogation had concluded by the time Stanley arrived.

'[Stanley] arrived on about 13th November 1943,' Travis wrote. 'He looked very ill and told me he had been suffering from "flu and fever".'[8] Stanley was taken upstairs on his first day and questioned for three hours. Monai led the questioning. Nigo, the overweight *Kempei Tai* auxiliary who spoke English with an American accent, was brought in as interpreter. Monai set out the case against Stanley. He told him that they knew all about the news distributing committee and the fact that the committee also functioned as a signalling unit for an espionage ring. They also knew of Stanley's pivotal function as the man who would transmit signals either directly to India or to intermediaries. Finally, they knew about the document that Rob Scott had handed him in late September, which essentially gave the go-ahead for the raid on Singapore Harbour. Monai praised Stanley's heroism for his involvement in the raid. Now it was time to own up to it.

Stanley confirmed the existence of a news distributing committee. Every other accusation was false. After Nigo had translated

Stanley's response, Monai warned that refusing to talk would delay the release of all the other prisoners brought from Changi. Stanley surely spotted the lie a mile away. Confirming Monai's false accusations would only further imperil the lives of the prisoners and very likely result in further arrests. Stanley insisted he had no involvement in the destruction of the ships in the harbour. Monai told him that he would have the night to think about it.

They left him alone on the second day, a classic *Kempei Tai* misdirection to fill the prisoner with false hope that perhaps the interrogators had decided to let him off. On day three, Stanley entered hell. Monai asked if Stanley had thought over their conversation. He said he could not provide information about the attack on the harbour because he had nothing to do with it. Two guards moved towards Stanley and forced him off his chair. He was made to 'kneel on a duck-board with a billet of firewood tied between his legs'.[9] He was held in this position for an entire day. For the next five days, Stanley was taken back upstairs and forced to kneel in the same fashion for the entire day while being sporadically beaten by the guards. After a week of this treatment, Stanley was brought back to his cell at night with a pronounced limp. He crawled into the cell, finding a spot next to Travis, barely able to sit upright. Travis helped with the tea and rice that was brought in. He lay down at night, whispering what he had endured to Travis, before falling unconscious.

Stanley surely knew that the confession the Japanese sought would very likely result in multiple executions. They had not broken him. Sumida ordered Monai to increase the pressure. For three straight days, the guards set upon Stanley with sticks, iron bars, wet knotted ropes, belts with buckles and brass rods. The kneeling treatment continued, but with the added refinement of stomping on Stanley's feet. He was also given the water treatment. Stanley returned sodden and 'in a dazed condition [. . .] his feet were very swollen and cut and his face was bruised and pulpy'.[10]

On the fourth day, he could no longer walk. The guards carried him back to the cell on a rattan chair and toppled him onto the floor outside the cell. He slithered into the cell and fell unconscious. But still he resisted.

On the next day, Stanley's screams were more pronounced and piercing. Bishop Wilson heard Stanley's 'voice crying out in agony denying charges made against him'.[11] When he came back down, he was nearly defeated. Vivid red weals and blackened skin could be seen on his face and torso where live electrical wires were pressed into his skin. Travis sensed that Stanley's extraordinary resilience was breaking. Still he held on. The following day, Travis could hear the screaming once more. Stanley was brought back on a trestle table made of canvas. The table where he had been tied down and electrocuted. His face was hollowed out, his soul shattered. 'At this stage,' wrote Travis, 'he had been forced into signing a confession and wanted to commit suicide as it was totally untrue and he could not stand the electric table.'[12]

Having Stanley confess to signalling British headquarters in India was a significant milestone in the investigation. But Sumida craved more. He wanted to know what was actually being sent. The investigation was on the verge of a major breakthrough. Stanley was brought back upstairs by an interpreter named Tsujio. Monai and Nigo – the other interpreter – were waiting for him. Stanley was ordered to sit. Monai explained that the questioning into Stanley had entered a new phase. Now that Stanley had signed the confession, there was no point in holding back information. The time had come to disclose the contents of every message he signalled.

Stanley looked around. His interrogators were seated on the other side of a small table and the door was unguarded – now was his chance. He had planned this moment the previous night. The only question was whether his body still worked. Stanley leapt to his feet and ran. He had made it to the door, Tsujio and Nigo in pursuit. Stanley scrambled along the corridor, limping heavily.

He could see the open archway that led out to the balcony, around 32 feet (10 metres) distance. That archway surely symbolised many things for Stanley: defiance of Monai and his thugs, freedom from the agonies of that room, atonement for having falsely confessed. It would all be over through that archway.

He was not there yet. The guards were catching up. They might be fitter and stronger, but Stanley held a single advantage. Unless they wanted to join Stanley in death, the guards would have to abruptly slow their pace as they approached the balcony. Sensing the dilemma, they desperately lunged for him, extending their arms, clasping for his tattered shirt. But they were too late. Stanley made it through the arch onto the balcony and then threw himself over the low railing.

He was only leaping from the first floor, around 13 feet (4 metres) from the ground; by no means a height that would guarantee death. Stanley must have reasoned that the surest way to kill himself from such a height was to meet the ground head-first. He angled his body in such a way so that his head would meet the ground. But death eluded him. A mound of hard earth, excavated from an adjacent block and deposited under the very point where Stanley had launched himself, effectively raised the ground around six and a half feet (2 metres) from its normal height. Stanley 'landed somewhere between the top and bottom of the mound, on the side'.[13]

Monai arrived outside shortly after Stanley jumped from the balcony. He found Stanley lying motionless. His eyes were blinking but he made no sound. Monai shouted for the guards. Nigo told Stanley to stand. He said he could not move. Something was broken. Someone found a wooden board inside the YMCA that was hastily repurposed as a stretcher. Stanley was roughly lifted onto the board and taken back to his cell. They tipped him onto the floor outside the cell.

Travis was horrified at the sight of his friend. Risking a thrashing, Travis insisted that a doctor be summoned to conduct an examination. Nigo stepped forward and kicked 'Dr Stanley as hard as he could in the crotch'.[14]

Stanley explained to Travis what had happened. He told him that he had probably broken his pelvis, which was why his legs were completely useless. The next morning, an English-speaking Japanese doctor came to examine Stanley. Travis insisted that he be taken to hospital. The doctor 'looked at him and said that he was not ill enough'.[15] The guards returned hours later and took him upstairs. Travis could hear Stanley's screams. This continued for several days. The last time they brought Stanley back, he was wearing nothing but a tattered vest. From the burn marks, Travis could see that electricity had been applied to his armpits, the back of his knees, in between his toes and his genitalia.

Delirious and slipping in and out of consciousness, Stanley indicated he needed to relieve himself. Travis helped him onto the pedestal. The fluid that oozed from Stanley's penis was viscous and vivid red in colour. The doctor came back with a thin canvas mattress. With the help of two Chinese prisoners, Travis was told to carry him from the cell. They gently lifted Stanley's broken body onto the bed. Other than his vest, he was utterly exposed. They walked him out the front door of the building and placed the stretcher in the back of a van. The *Kempei Tai* sentry overseeing the operation turned to the driver and said, 'Kandang Kerbau.'[16]

Late in the evening of 29 November 1943, a Singaporean doctor of Eurasian descent was finishing his rounds in the Kandang Kerbau hospital. The doctor's name was Benjamin Henry Sheares, a highly regarded obstetrician appointed as the medical officer at the hospital following the capitulation.* Dr Sheares was finishing his rounds when he came upon the corpse

---

*   Dr Benjamin Henry Sheares would pioneer the lower Caesarean section to replace the upper Caesarean section. The revised procedure would be attributed to lowering mortality and morbidity rates among pregnant women. Following his retirement from medicine, Sheares served three terms as President of Singapore, from 1971 to 1981.

lying on the stretcher outside the admissions room. A blanket was pulled up to the dead man's neck, leaving only his face exposed. Sheares took a closer look. Although the body was disfigured, bruised and emaciated, Sheares recognised Dr Stanley. The two men had encountered each other on regular occasions in this very hospital over the preceding decade. Japanese officers appeared at Dr Sheares' side and told him to clear off. Sheares knew that little good would come of protesting. 'A few minutes later,' he would say, 'the Japanese matron came to me and told me not to mention a word of having seen the body of a European outside the admission room.'[17]

The following morning, the Chinese clerk named Toh Swee Khun, forced to work as an interpreter for the *Kempei Tai*, entered the undertaker Walter Neubronner's shop. He was relaying a message. Neubronner had known Toh for fifteen years. There were no pleasantries exchanged. Toh told Neubronner that he was to follow him to the YMCA. Neubronner was unconcerned. Since the capitulation, the Japanese had been calling on his services with some regularity. His firm was one of the few Singaporean businesses untroubled by the occupation. Neubronner and Toh were driven to Stamford Road. 'I accompanied [Toh] to the top floor of the YMCA and saw a senior officer sitting in a big chair,' wrote Neubronner.[18] With Toh interpreting, Sumida asked Neubronner to quote for both a coffin and for arranging the burial of a corpse lying in Kandang Kerbau. Neubronner stated his price. Sumida accepted.

A Japanese officer accompanied Neubronner to the hospital that evening. 'On arriving with the coffin,' Neubronner recalled, 'I went into the mortuary and saw the body of a European.'[19] Dr Stanley's corpse was uncovered and arranged alongside the bodies of a Chinese man and three children. Neubronner could see that Stanley had come in for rough treatment: 'I noticed some blue marks on both his cheeks and his two hands were badly bruised all over, as well as both his legs.'[20] With the help of an orderly, Neubronner lifted Stanley's body into the coffin. As he was about to screw the lid shut, the Japanese officer ordered him to nail the coffin shut. The only possible reason to nail down the lid of a coffin was to make exhumation that much more difficult. Neubronner did as instructed. The burial took place the following day. Sumida and an officer from Changi attended.

'Who was this man?' Neubronner dared ask the two Japanese officers, his pen at the ready to complete the death certificate.

The Changi officer, pointing at Neubronner's papers, said: 'No name given, no certificate, no paper.'[21]

The coffin was pushed into the freshly dug grave. No words were spoken. The Japanese officers left. Neubronner waited until the burial was complete. As he watched the soil being shovelled over the coffin, Neubronner reflected that the funeral was 'performed like burying a dog'.[22]

27

AN UNRAVELLING
INVESTIGATION

Four weeks after the attack

SUMIDA REGARDED STANLEY'S DEATH an undeniable setback. He had essentially confirmed what Long had claimed. (Stanley recanted on his confessions, an inconvenience which Sumida explained away as an aberration.) And yet, infuriatingly, Stanley had died before revealing the transmitter's whereabouts. Sumida was holding back the interrogation of Robert Heatlie Scott until the investigation was essentially wrapped up. He had confessions but he wanted physical evidence; the transmitter was the silver bullet of the entire case. Under torture, the British internees had confirmed Sumida's central thesis: that Scott was communicating with the British in India and had conceived, directed and funded the attack on Japanese shipping in the harbour. There was physical evidence of the conspiracy in the form of large reserves of cash to fund the attack, radio sets to receive information and written documents – albeit indecipherable – most likely used to communicate messages in secret code.

But the transmitter – that crucial piece of radio technology that would prove beyond doubt that Scott was sending messages to the

British and, perhaps, sending instructions to Chinese insurgents and Malayan guerrillas – continued to elude the investigators. Sumida pored over the reports of the interrogations, searching for something he may have missed. He zeroed in on the interrogation of Khoo Hock Choo, the registry clerk accused of handing radio parts to internees. Khoo had been arrested on the Double Tenth and taken directly to Smith Street. He came in for some frightful punishment. A few days after his arrest, Khoo was dragged to an interrogation room where four toughs were waiting for him. They made him kneel on a sharp pole while an interrogator sat on his shoulders and started riding him like a horse. Another man stepped forward and punched him in the stomach, sending him sprawling across the floor, after which the men present 'grabbed a pole 5 foot long [1.5 metres] made of solid wood, and all four took turns beating [him]'.[1] This went on for twelve hours before Khoo passed out. He woke up in a pool of his own blood.

Three days later, Khoo was accused of being a British agent and 'would be treated the way all British agents deserved'.[2] He was lowered headfirst into a bath and pulled out at the point of losing consciousness. He was allowed one breath, and then dipped back in. Khoo lost count of how many times he was dunked in the bath. 'When I was brought out everything was blurred,' said Khoo. 'I heard voices [. . .] and one of them jumped on my stomach, with the result that everything gushed out.'[3] Despite his agony, he had revealed nothing of note. He had not even given up a name. To Sumida, Khoo's resilience was at once admirable and frustrating. Sumida became fixated on the idea that Khoo was holding something back, that he knew where the transmitter was located. Khoo was brought back to the YMCA and Sumida set his best man the task of finding out what he knew. Khoo would not be able to hide his secrets from Monai.

Rather than start the interrogation with more violence, Monai enticed Khoo into revealing what he knew in exchange for his freedom and a job. 'I was brought to a room where [Monai] was,' said Khoo. 'He offered me an armchair, and said I could have my release if I would name Europeans whom I had been in contact in Changi. I told him I did not know any, and he then said he would reward me and give me work in the Military Police department.'[4] Khoo said nothing. He just stared at him. Monai screamed at him that he would be executed. Khoo was hauled into a cell. It was overcrowded and filthy and similar in size and smell to his cell in Smith Street. There were seventeen men and three women – a young Chinese communist girl, a Eurasian lady and Chinese woman named Elizabeth Choy.

Monai reported back to Sumida. It was clear that Khoo was prepared to face death rather than spill secrets. They could apply further pressure on him, but it was unlikely they would get much more out of him. Once again, Sumida marvelled at the cunning and deviousness of his adversary, Robert Scott. Like the best leaders, Scott knew the men he could trust not to share his most devastating secrets. Just like Stanley – who had sent Scott's signals and held out telling them where the transmitter was located – Khoo was clearly one such man, the kind that would die before talking. To break such an individual, Sumida needed a different plan. Rather than ordering further torturing of Khoo, Sumida built a strategy around catching him in a lie. Sumida looked over his record. The people who had informed on Khoo had said they had seen him handing radio parts to internees. One of the internees they named was William Thorpe Cherry, a government printer who had been serving in the auxiliary fire service during the bombing campaign of Singapore and who was currently languishing in the YMCA.

Cherry was forty-seven years of age and in truth looked older. He wore thick spectacles and false teeth, which were confiscated on arrival. After being accused of being 'the number one spy in Malaya'[5] – a claim Cherry strongly denied – he was kicked, slapped and punched, subjected to water torture, beatings with rods, ropes and bamboo poles. During one interrogation, a burning cigar was pressed against his thighs. After a week with no results, Cherry was sent to Smith Street. He was taken directly to an interrogation room where a battery with leads hummed in the centre of the room. Cherry recalled that an interrogator 'plugged a lead in to the mains and touched my bare back with the exposed ends of the wire. The shock threw me about 15 feet [4.5 metres] across the room from a sitting position.'[6]

Cherry was then moved around from the YMCA, Smith Street and Central Station, the constant relocation keeping him disoriented. Along the way, he suffered every imaginable indignity and agony. By mid-December, when Cherry was in Smith Street, Monai dragged him out of his cell. Cherry, who could barely walk, was blindfolded and put up against a wall. 'I then heard [Monai] giving orders to the execution squad, which consisted of six men,' Cherry recounted. '[He] then came to me and asked if I had anything more to say, and I said, "Nothing."' While preparing for imminent death, Cherry heard his executioners working the bolts of their rifles as if they were reloading. Eventually, there was a murmuring of voices. '[Monai] came up to me again and said the execution would be postponed till the next day and I was given pencil and paper to write a last letter to my mother.'[7] It was a mock execution; another classic *Kempei Tai* strategy.

What Cherry revealed to the Japanese subsequent to this harrowing ordeal is unclear. Monai claimed that Cherry confessed 'to have employed an outsider to obtain short-wave receiving sets to be used outside the camp and engaged on similar work'.[8] Cherry refuted this claim, stating that throughout the ordeal he denied every accusation that was put to him. Although he did concede that his 'memory [was] a little vague as to exactly what happened to [him] in detail from around December'.[9] Cherry possibly confessed to certain accusations as a means of staying the torturers' hand and did not want to admit to it later out of fear of being unfairly accused of cowardice.

But one thing is almost certain – William Cherry had nothing to do with anything. He was not involved in any of the Changi committees, nor did he appear to have much – if any – involvement in the black market. He was that rarest of things in Changi: a law-abiding internee. That Cherry was brought in for interrogation was almost certainly a case of mistaken identity. Neither Khoo nor Cherry ever recalled meeting each other and certainly never engaged in a handover of radio parts. Not that Sumida saw it that way. Gaps in the investigation that could not logically be explained simply served as further proof of Scott's genius.

In fact, the torture of William Cherry was emblematic of an investigation that was unravelling. The three essential areas of Sumida's enquiry – the leadership of the spy ring, and the source of the money and the radio sets – had become so overlapped and confused that everything had morphed into an unwieldy mass of conflicting information. Sumida clung desperately to his conspiracy theory: Cherry might not have known the transmitter's location, but he was a key component in the intricate machine that Scott had built. Without any evidence, Sumida concluded that Cherry was giving messages to pass to Khoo, who in turn passed them to his brother Tien, who 'was found to have distributed messages based on radio news he listened-in'.[10] In other words, Cherry was running a propagandist (Tien) through an intermediary (his brother Choo) in an effort to stir up the Chinese population against the Japanese. Cherry's job as a government printer may have lent credence to the theory, since such a job made him skilled in the art of mass communication. It was yet another theory based on conjecture, shoddy intelligence, false assumptions, misinterpretations and a steadfast belief that British control over the Chinese, even during the occupation, was absolute.

Sumida's increasingly outlandish conclusions reveal the pressure he was under. In the Japanese military, an order was less an instruction to be followed than a command that was divinely ordained. Nobody understood this better than the zealous officers of the *Kempei Tai*. Historian Raymond Lamont-Brown describes it best: 'As all Japanese were brought up to recognise blind duty to one's superiors and, ultimately, to the emperor, all military orders were considered to be in his name. Consequently, an order to execute, torture or mistreat POWs was deemed an imperial command to be carried out without hesitation.'[11] In this context, the Number One Work was not merely an investigation into the attack on the harbour, it was a command to bring those responsible to justice. The distinction is important. An investigation, at least in the conventional sense, is the gathering of information and evidence, after upon which a charge is made and then tested in a court of law. But Sumida's investigation was essentially over the moment he reported his findings to Colonel Kojima and Field Marshal Terauchi in the Cathay Building on the day of the attack. When he laid out his case against Scott and the Changi internees, Sumida was effectively presenting his findings.

But that did not mean he was absolved of having to provide evidence. The burden now rested on Sumida to conjure up the physical material that proved his claims about espionage rings, transmitters, fifth columnists, communists and all the rest of it. Sumida was effectively required to retrofit the evidence – whether it be physical material or confessions – to suit his claims, rather than using the evidence as the foundation upon which a case could be built. The evidence found thus far – radio receivers, money, documents – was incriminating. But he still lacked the transmitter: that crucial piece that would tie the whole case up in a neat bow. Until then, he would be relying solely on internees confessing to the transmitter's existence without knowing its location. Sumida was now adamant that only one man knew the location of the transmitter. The time to face his adversary was fast approaching. Before that happened, there was another whose links to the master spy needed thorough examination. Perhaps her knowledge could shed a new light on the Number One Work. To date, she had proved recalcitrant. Sumida sent Monai to find out what she knew.

28

THE BATTERY

Six weeks after the attack

SINCE ELIZABETH CHOY'S FRIGHTENING encounter with Monai, she had been interrogated by other *Kempei Tai* personnel. Although she had not been physically assaulted, the questions were asked aggressively and were worryingly fixated on the notion that she was involved in the attack on the harbour. How the Japanese thought Elizabeth – a schoolteacher lately employed in the canteen at Miyako – had the means and capability to destroy Japanese ships was beyond her. She continued to pray to God for guidance. All the while, Sorby Adams' favourite song – 'The Bonnie Banks o' Loch Lomond' – played pleasantly in her mind, keeping her uplifted and steady in the midst of all this madness.

Elizabeth was called from her cell several days after her last interrogation. In the intervening days, she had begun to hope that the ordeal was over, that the passing of time without an interrogation indicated that the Japanese had concluded she was innocent. But she knew in her heart that this would not be so: 'when I was in that place I really thought I would never get out.'[1]

She was led upstairs and into a room where Monai was waiting for her. Beside him was a wooden frame, a bucket of water and a nest of electric cables. Unlike Monai's first interrogation of Elizabeth, now he dispensed any false charm as she was man-handled into a chair.

Over an interminable period, Monai subjected Elizabeth to a barrage of questions. The usual subjects were covered – the money, the radio parts, her ties to Robert Heatlie Scott – but the focus was the destruction of the ships. Elizabeth denied everything. Monai asked her again, his temper frayed, his voice combative. When Elizabeth denied any knowledge, he reached across the table and slapped her. Unlike the boiling rage and indignation that welled up within her the last time Monai hit her, Elizabeth instead felt herself go cold with dread. Everything about Monai's bearing indicated that this treatment would not stop until he got the answers he wanted.

Eventually, Monai barked orders to a couple of guards. Elizabeth was grabbed by her arms and hauled over to the rough wooden frame on the floor. The frame was rough with splinters that pierced into her knees. The guards forced her into a kneeling position and then tied Elizabeth's arms behind her back. Once she was bound, Monai wrenched down her dress, exposing her breasts. Monai was fuming, demanding Elizabeth tell her the truth.

'I've told you the truth,' Elizabeth pleaded. 'I cannot tell you any more.'

'You must tell us the truth [about the ships], otherwise we will kill you.'

Death was ever present in the YMCA. But never before had any of the guards or interrogators explicitly threatened to kill Elizabeth.

'No,' she said. '[I] don't know anything.'

'Then we are going to execute you.'

'Well, if you have to execute me for telling you the truth, I can't help it,' she said. 'Go ahead.'[2]

Elizabeth kept her head up, her mouth firmly set in defiance. Monai walked behind her and tightened the ropes that bound her to the frame. She was now firmly fixed in place. She could not go forwards, backwards or sideways without the ropes biting into her skin. To avoid the pain, she had to remain still. But holding this position for any length of time was exhausting.

Monai sloshed the bucket of water over Elizabeth. Fear rippled through her body. What was this? Monai then walked over to a small black box and flicked a switch. The box emitted a low buzz. He picked up two cables; one electrode was attached by a clip to Elizabeth's foot. The other – a bare wire that made a crackling noise – was waved in front of Elizabeth. Without warning, he pressed the wire into her breast. Elizabeth's back arched. Her mouth fell open as if to scream, but in her agony, no sound emerged. After a few moments her whole body began to convulse. When Monai removed the wire from Elizabeth's body a piercing scream emerged from deep within her. Monai repeated the questions, demanding she confess her involvement in the destruction of the ships. But Elizabeth was incapable of speaking. Tears streamed from her eyes and mucus poured from her nose and mouth. Her mind was still processing the agony that had just speared through her body.

'The battery', as the *Kempei Tai* referred to the use of electricity as a form of torture, was usually deployed as a means of breaking particularly resilient prisoners. Electrodes or bare wires attached to a battery-operated or hand-cranked generator capable of producing a substantial electrical current were pressed to sensitive places such as genitals, ears, the mouth or breasts. The battery had the advantage of leaving minor signs of injury like burn marks, allowing a degree of plausible deniability should there ever be accusations of inhumane treatment. The real damage was psychological. After one short session with the battery, a victim would say almost anything to avoid further punishment.

For the interrogator, using the battery brought with it the risk of killing the prisoner. The likelihood of inducing a cardiac arrest or respiratory failure was very real, particularly when the battery was applied to a weakened, sick, elderly or infirm prisoner. Even a younger prisoner in relatively good health could be killed or rendered permanently insensible should the officer controlling the interrogation session overdo it.

Monai was anxious not to kill Elizabeth, nor did he want to destroy her mind, at least not before he'd extracted a confession. He evidently concluded that she was particularly strong-willed and could bear more pain than the average person, physically and psychologically. After allowing her to catch her breath, he pressed the wire against her skin once more. Elizabeth body convulsed with terrifying violence. Her mind was scrambling, losing its grip on reality. When Monai pulled the wire away, the room was rent in half with her agonised screams.

Over fifteen to twenty minutes, Monai used the battery on Elizabeth six times.[3] When he was done, the guards untied the ropes that bound Elizabeth. She crumpled onto the frame. The guards picked her up and dragged her back to the chair. Monai told her that it would all be over if she confessed to being anti-Japanese and revealed the details of her involvement in the destruction of the ships in the harbour.

Elizabeth was not registering his questions. Her mind had become fixed on the most prosaic of problems – she was in need of a handkerchief. When Monai had been giving her the electric shock, tears and mucous had streamed down her face. Amid the agony in the aftermath of her torture, while being bombarded with more questions from one of the cruellest officers and facing a mortal threat to her life, Elizabeth just wanted something to wipe her face. Despite all that Monai had taken from her, there were things he could not touch: her unimpeachable integrity, her undeniable courage, but also her sense of dignity and self-respect.

'You tell us [everything] and we'll forgive you,' said Monai.

Elizabeth came back to her senses. There was nothing that she had done to the Japanese for which she required forgiveness. She shook her head – no. Monai may well have yearned to have the guards tie her up to the frame and subject her to more of the battery treatment. But indulging that desire would probably kill her. There was no need to rush. Besides, he had something special in store. Monai told the guards to take her back to her cell. Before she was carried away, Monai told her he would see her tomorrow. Elizabeth was taken through the door. She shrugged away the guards as they walked her down the corridor. She would make it back to the cell unaided. Elizabeth walked past Rob Scott, held her head high, her back straight, her torn clothes revealing bruises and burn marks. 'She was,' he surmised, 'a remarkably plucky lady.'[4]

Once outside her cell, Elizabeth bent down and slid under the prison bars and shuffled to the spot among the packed throng that had been saved for her. Elizabeth did not register the reaction of her cellmates at the sight of her. Surely, they knew what had happened. Doubtless, they had heard her piercing screams. But this was not the time to enquire of her health. The guards stood sentry outside the cell, watching closely. The immediate aftermath of a brutal interrogation was a time of acute vulnerability for a prisoner. This was where they let down their guard, where caution was thrown to the wind. She might start talking and let something slip.

Elizabeth was oblivious. She had been gripped by a sudden, deep urge to eat: the type of hunger that ruled her every thought. From outside, the unmistakable sound of the itinerant noodle seller's call reached her ears. She could hear the beating of his bamboo slabs – *tock, tock, tock* – as he sold his goods. It seemed he was passing directly under the cell. Elizabeth's sense of imprisonment had never felt so acute. Just beyond her cell wall was food and freedom. It seemed so impossibly close and yet it could not have been further away. She lay there packed in between her fellow cellmates, tormented by her hunger, shutting out thoughts of the horrors that tomorrow might bring. For an interminable time, the noodle seller's summons echoed through the stuffy cell air – *tock, tock, tock.*

Elizabeth heard a guard calling her name. She was being summoned from her cell. She could hardly believe it. Had she even slept? Elizabeth was not ready to face another session. But to protest was utterly pointless. She shuffled forward. After crawling under the prison bars she stood upright, slightly shaky; no doubt the lingering effect of Monai's interrogation. She was led back to the interrogation room.

Monai was waiting for her. Alongside him was another officer – this was Sergeant Major Makizono Masuo. There was an air of purpose about the two men, a sense of vicious intent. Guards bound Elizabeth to the frame. She was forced to kneel on the splintered wooden planks. Pain shot through the weeping wounds on her knees and shins that had been bruised and lacerated from the previous day's punishment. Elizabeth waited for the inevitable questions. But they did not come. In her peripheral vision, Elizabeth saw the cell door open. More men walked in. She heard her name spoken. A familiar voice. She looked up. Looking back down at her with heartbroken eyes was her husband.

29

A DEADLY GAME

Six weeks after the attack

THE GUARDS CAME FOR Rob Scott at around two o'clock in the afternoon three weeks after he was arrested in Changi. He was taken from his cell and led through a door to a nearby interrogation room. Following Dr Stanley's attempted suicide, high-value prisoners like Scott would be interviewed on the ground floor. For Scott, the effect of walking any distance was dizzying. He had barely stood, much less walked, in twenty-five days. He fought to keep his mind focused. The Japanese, of course, held a distinct advantage. They had prised information, much of it fabricated, from other prisoners. They had access to the wordy (albeit useless) report written by Sam some fifteen months earlier. They also had Scott in a position of physical vulnerability; he was under-nourished and exhausted.

But he was not completely unprepared. Scott had learnt much through whispered exchanges with other prisoners and the sounds of interrogations emanating from the rooms above his cell. The near impossible task of 'keep[ing] in touch with all that was going on – who were arrested, how they were treated and where they were being kept'[1] had not been in vain. He had, for instance, discovered 'that in a room on the third floor was a large map of Singapore island, with "ROBERT HEATLIE SCOTT" marked on top'.[2] He learnt of some nonsense about a transmitter found in a Chinese tomb and that he was deemed a key organiser in a conspiracy that involved some Chinese.

Scott knew that he would be tortured. He regarded this inevitability as if it were an enemy tactic that needed to be countered. Torture posed a threat insofar as it could corrupt his mind to act in a fashion that would please his interrogators and deviate from his strategy. But torture was not to be feared. Fear was a potent emotion that would work against him. Should fear overwhelm him, then he risked telling the Japanese just about anything. There could be no surer way of defeat and probably death than for that to happen. He just needed to maintain consistency and clarity in his responses. Nothing he said could deviate from what he had previously told Sam. When he was subjected to pain, he would simply have to endure and stick to his answers.

There were two *Kempei Tai* officers, an NCO and an interpreter, waiting for Scott in the interrogation room. The interpreter's name was Shimada. He stood to one side of a square table around which the three officers sat with Sakamoto Shigeru, a warrant officer in his early thirties. Deep lines were etched beneath Sakamoto's eyes and his nose was flattened and crooked, as if it had been broken in a fight. Sakamoto had organised the search for radio parts, documents and other contraband in Changi on the Double Tenth. Scott had seen him when the internees were paraded in the yard and his name was called out.

Sergeant Monai Tadamori was sat opposite Sakamoto. Monai had closely cropped hair that accentuated the angularity of his face. He moved in slow, deliberate movements, watching Scott carefully with his expressionless eyes. Monai had been assigned to Scott's case. Any subsequent questioning to this initial interrogation would be handled by Monai. At the head of the table sat Major Sumida Haruzo. Sumida was flashing his broadest smile as Scott walked into the room. There was nothing malicious or sinister in his smile. It was not the smile of a villain, but more of the sort that you would see on the face of an old friend greeting you at a reunion after a long absence. Sumida had lost none of the vitality he exuded when Scott saw him in the Changi Commandant's office months earlier.

Sumida waved at the empty seat directly before Scott. He offered several biscuits to Scott, who gladly accepted them. The rock-hard texture and bland taste made Scott wonder if they were dog biscuits. Sumida explained that, at this point, Scott was not accused of committing a crime. That would come later. Sumida began the interrogation with questions about his name, his family, the addresses where he had lived in Tokyo, China and Singapore. Scott answered truthfully.

'Your replies are exactly the same as those you gave last year,' Sumida said, referring to Sam's hopelessly inept interrogation.

'But of course they are the same,' said Scott. 'I am telling the truth, and it is easy to remember the truth.'

Sumida pounced: 'But you have a good memory, haven't you?' Scott had been anticipating this moment:

If you say 'Yes', you can never afterwards avoid answering a question by saying that you can't remember what happened. If you say 'No' then, when you say you can't remember something, they reply you yourself admitted that your memory was bad – so it is quite possible that what you are denying did actually happen, but you have forgotten – and as they know positively it did happen [. . .] and as your memory is poor, you might as well admit it and have done with it.[3]

'I have an excellent memory,' Scott responded.

'So when questioned you will never be able to plead that you cannot answer because you have forgotten?'

This was Scott's last chance. He could not claim a lapsing memory as a tactic to avoid answering a tricky question. But provided everything he said was watertight and consistent, maintaining that he had an excellent memory would lend greater credibility to his answers. Scott decided to wholly commit to the strategy.

'Certainly not,' he said, 'my memory is first class, so when I tell you something is so or is not so there can be no question about it, and you need not waste time by further enquiries.'[4]

Scott's statement hung heavily in the air. Sumida did not appear to like it. But he let it pass. He then laid out the case against Scott.

The *Kempei Tai* knew all about Scott's anti-Japanese propaganda work in Japan, China and Singapore. They knew about his network of spies in Changi, his contacts in the Chinese community, they even knew about his transmitter in the Chinese tomb. He was accused of being the master spy who had overseen and coordinated sabotage operations against the Japanese in Singapore. There was no use in denying any of it. The case compiled against Scott was beyond compelling and his guilt was plain for all to see. Nevertheless, for Scott's case to precede to trial, Sumida required a confession to be signed. This was Japanese custom and had nothing to do with the fact that the case lacked material evidence. That no evidence against Scott had been discovered 'merely showed that [Scott] was an uncommonly clever crook [who had concealed] evidence from the *Kempei*, the finest police force in the world'.[5]

Sumida encouraged Scott to confess and save everyone trouble. He even offered Scott cigarettes and bully beef in exchange for a confession. Scott declined, as Sumida surely knew he would. Sumida explained that there were three methods to extract evidence and secure a confession from Scott: 'by psychology, by material evidence, and by combining the two.'[6] Scott hardly needed Sumida to explain that the first method – psychology – was a euphemism for torture. In Sumida's estimation, the second method was dull: 'any fool could convict a criminal if he found independent evidence.'[7] As a rule, Sumida's preference was the third method. Owing to the conspicuous lack of physical evidence to support the accusations, the first method was the only viable option. As the investigating officer, Monai had discretionary power to use whatever method he deemed fit to get what he needed and was not responsible for whatever happened to the prisoner.

Scott's look of disgust prompted Sumida to add, 'You must understand that there are differences between the Nipponese and British legal systems.'[8]

'There certainly are!' Scott replied.[9] A look of thunder came over Sumida. It was probably Scott's apparent lack of fear that annoyed him. Scott asked what would happen if he said nothing.

'It is essential that you make a confession,' replied Sumida. 'Under our law, you cannot be tried until you confess. For that reason, I have authority to use any degree of force to extract a confession and so have all my subordinates.'[10] Scott said that Sumida's methods of investigation amounted to compelling men to sign false confessions. 'No,' Sumida countered, 'the Kempei never [make] a mistake.' Scott said they were making a mistake at this moment if they thought these 'fantastic accusations were true'. Sumida smiled. He knew he was right, he said. They knew about Scott: 'they had me under observation for months.'[11]

Sumida moved on to the most devastating and absurd charge – that Scott was having his contacts send messages to British headquarters in India by way of the transmitter in the Chinese tomb. Scott asked when these messages were sent. Sumida consulted his papers and stated a date.

Scott shook his head. 'How could I have run a transmitter when I was in solitary confinement?' he asked.

Sumida rose up in his chair and slammed the table with his fist. 'I am conducting this enquiry! Not you! I am to ask the questions! You may not! Besides,' he said, his voice trailing off almost mournfully, 'I was about to ask you the same question myself.'[12] Sumida was hopeful that Scott would freely admit to the existence of the transmitter that Stanley was using at Scott's instructions before revealing its whereabouts. When he said nothing, Sumida turned his attention to the attack on Japanese shipping in the harbour. The sudden change in topic caught Scott off guard. This was the first time he had been linked to the attack. It was confirmation of the suspicion he'd held since the Double Tenth raid: that the interrogations of the Changi internees were driven by the attack on the Japanese tankers he had first heard about from John Long.

Sumida made casual reference to 'how slight the damage really was',[13] which brought the ghost of an unbidden grin to Scott's face. He remembered himself and took on a neutral expression. But it was too late. They had seen. Internally, Scott castigated himself. By now, they had been going for several hours. The four Japanese men had been watching him 'like hawks'.[14] They were looking for a tell – a physical action that betrayed a lie or a bluff. Precisely for this reason, Scott had been at pains to control his entire body throughout. He was conscious of the fact that, 'however much you may control your hands, face, and feet, the muscles of the knees tend to contract under stress'.[15] But it was his face that had let him down. He was certain that the grin had given him away. That he had nothing to do with the raid hardly mattered. Simply knowing that it had happened implicated him in the plot.

Sure enough, Sumida asked questions about Scott's knowledge of the attack – how it was carried out, who was involved and where the explosives were sourced. Scott denied any knowledge of the raid. Strictly speaking, this was a lie. Scott knew about the attack after the fact. But such an admission would open a line of enquiry about how he knew, which would implicate John Long and his contacts at the canteen.

'I want to ask you about the least important charge of all – radio,' said Sumida. He had preceded this statement with a lofty claim about how much he already knew. 'You ran a short-wave radio in the camp?'

'Yes,' said Scott.

'What are the names of your colleagues?'[16]

Sumida wanted the names of the news and distribution committees. Scott did not believe for a minute that this was, as Sumida claimed, an unimportant charge. He was asking Scott to provide the names of his accomplices in this imagined conspiracy. He knew that Sumida was aware of at least some of the members of the committees; he had heard Stevenson give names under torture. He could simply repeat those names. But if he omitted the name of an individual that Sumida had discovered from another source, then Scott would be deemed a liar. If, however, he furnished every name, then he might unnecessarily be endangering multiple lives. Scott had to tread carefully. Too much information would endanger others' lives; not enough would endanger his own.

Scott said, 'I will not tell you.' He was 'quaking inwardly'[17] when he said it.

Sumida threw back his head and laughed. He gleefully welcomed the answer. To get Scott to reveal the identity of each man on the committee, Sumida would make him a deal: 'He offered to tell me the names, if I would promise to confirm whether they were or were not the men involved.'[18] To Scott, this was an opportunity to prove himself both cooperative and truthful. Judging from Sumida's confidence, Scott was certain that his interrogator had the names – that this was a scare tactic, a way to demonstrate how much he already knew. It was a game of poker; Scott was being asked to show his hand. Scott nodded. He was going all in. Sumida pushed a piece of paper and a pen over to Scott. He wrote down the names. The two lists tallied.

'There you are!' Sumida shouted with triumph. 'The *Kempei* never bluff! That will show you that we mean what we say when we tell you we know all about you.'[19] Sumida waxed on about the irregularity of sharing information with a prisoner. Sumida, who was at pains throughout the interrogation to remind Scott that he was answerable to authorities more senior than those in Syonan, said it 'would get me into trouble in Tokyo if it were known' what he had just done, 'so I can tell you no more, except that we know all about your other activities, just as we did about the radio; the sooner you confess the better for everyone'.[20]

Clearly perceiving that he had just injured his adversary, Sumida embarked on an analysis of the war's origins, joyously castigating the pitiful defence of Singapore. 'Britain has made mistakes,' Sumida said with a smirk.[21] Always on the lookout to sidetrack his interrogator, Scott decided to respond: 'so has Japan – Pearl Harbour [*sic*]';[22] Scott argued that the decision to cripple the United States Navy was a fatal miscalculation. Sumida took the bait. They went back-and-forth, Sumida betraying knowledge of Japan's current tactical approach of the war and overall strategy – to seize control of Burma in order to tighten the stranglehold on supplies into China while consolidating its control over occupied territories so that Hirohito's government could negotiate from a position of great strength – and Scott countering that 'Japan underestimated the immense industrial and military potential of the United States and the speed which this could be released given a stimulus powerful enough to rouse the entire nation. Pearl [Harbor] provided that impetus.'[23] Sumida shook his head: 'Twelve months, was all we need.'[24] The statement was said with finality, but Scott saw another chance to turn the questioning from himself. 'But it's now nearly two years,' he said. 'The plan has failed.'[25] Sumida set off on a two-hour diatribe about Japan's divine right to rule Asia, declaiming on the 'history of the relations between Japan and the Western Powers and Russia'.[26] He was taking a sort of victory lap, conveying a sense of inevitability about his defeat of Scott before sending him back to his cell.

But Scott had led Sumida on a merry dance. With respect to the actual investigation, the interrogation yielded no useful information beyond what was already known: 'that there were several short-wave receiving sets [. . .] and the Allied broadcasts were listened-in to, and Mr Scott and others edited what was received. And typewritten copies were passed round to the internees [and] that there was a committee, called the news-editing committee, and they had conferences or meetings.'[27] The slowly dawning realisation that Scott had seized control of the interrogation, had become the authority in the room, surely infuriated Sumida. But he tamped down his desire to have Monai inflict physical pain on Scott. In the end, Sumida's encounter with Scott served to deepen his respect for this very worthy adversary. Sumida had to be patient. It would be an honour to destroy this man: 'I knew from the first that the case was going to be difficult.'[28]

An idea popped into Sumida's head. He had proof that Scott's news committee met four days before the attack. If a message was going to be transmitted from the Chinese tomb – or, more likely, Stanley's undiscovered transmitter in Changi – to British headquarters, it surely would have been discussed then.

And what of the money? Sumida's investigation into the internees' finances had stalled and this was a key pillar of the Number One Work. If more than $400,000 in cash was found in Changi, how much money had already been sent out to fund fifth-column activities? Walter Yoxall, in whose cell the money was discovered, was the first suspect interviewed in respect of this area of enquiry. Yoxall, an employee of the Hongkong and Shanghai Bank's Singapore branch, had been appointed camp treasurer. As he truthfully confessed in his first two interrogations, Yoxall was 'in charge of the accumulated funds which we had got together in order to purchase extra food and suchlike'.[29]

Sumida believed that Yoxall's explanation was a convenient cover story. The attack on the harbour involved the acquisition of explosives powerful enough to damage and sink ships. Such munitions did not come cheap. That money, and all the rest that had already been spent, was put to work in the most devious ways and Yoxall knew how it was done. Sumida ordered his men to extract that information out of Yoxall by any means necessary. He was first asked questions unrelated to camp funds – for instance, 'how the internees at the gaol were getting broadcast news'.[30] Yoxall could not answer because he honestly did not know. He was the camp treasurer. Outside matters related to money and accounting, he knew nothing. The guards were not having it.

'As the Japanese found they were not getting very much information out of me they began torturing me,' Yoxall wrote. 'It consisted of beatings with sticks and wet knotted ropes, kicking and punching. I was also subjected to the water torture, and with the water still inside me I was left for several hours underneath the tap with the water dripping on my distended stomach.'[31] When this failed to yield information, Yoxall's torturers took turns jumping on his feet, legs and thighs while he was kneeling on sharp planks of wood. But Yoxall revealed nothing.

Yoxall's mind was capable of calling up people and incidents with incredible precision. Beyond controlling the funds that enabled Changi's black market, Yoxall never did anything drastically incriminating. He never made a mistake or misstep in the interrogation either, even when he was forced to repeatedly recount the same information under torture. In the end, it was Yoxall's steel-trap mind and powers of recall – including the fact that he could remember the exact amount of money smuggled into Changi, which tallied with his assiduously kept bookkeeping records – that prompted Sumida to shift his focus to how the money was funnelled into the camp. Perhaps individuals further up the supply chain knew more than they were letting on.

The money trail started with Bishop John Leonard Wilson. As it turned out, both Yoxall and the bishop's assistant – K.T. Alexander – had kept assiduous records of the cashflow.* When Sumida and Monai compared Yoxall's and the bishop's bookkeeping, there was a key difference in the sums. The bishop and his people had calculated a difference of $10,000 between the church's records and Yoxall's books. This piece of intelligence put the focus squarely on the Choys, the first recipients of the church money. Before Sumida subjected the Chinese canteen worker and his wife to more pressure, he would lean on the Choys' Changi contact – the ambulance driver John Long. Long had proven himself a most cooperative prisoner. He would be able to help Sumida corner the Choys.

---

*   The historical record is unclear on whether Alexander had named the source of the borrowed funds in the church's books. Whether Sumida discovered that the bishop's financier was a neutral Swiss did not matter. There was nothing that could be done about that anyway.

30

LYING AND SURVIVING

Six weeks after the attack

JOHN LONG DID NOT DISAPPOINT. He told Monai that Scott handed him envelopes with the single letter C on them with instructions to give them to the Choys. Long was forbidden from opening the letters but he was certain that one of them instructed the Choys to take $10,000 and deliver the money directly to the saboteurs to purchase the explosives. Monai was relishing his chance to interrogate Elizabeth Choy again. But even when presented with this revelation, he knew that she would need more encouragement to divulge her involvement. This was a woman who could withstand the battery. Cornering her with a morsel of information about an alleged letter she had received from Scott would hardly make her crack. He suggested to Sumida that Choy Khun Heng join his wife's interrogation.

Choy had been transferred to the YMCA five weeks earlier and placed in a cell far from Elizabeth. Neither had any idea that they were in the same building. Sergeant Major Morita Shozo – the officer assigned to extract information from Choy – followed him to the YMCA. The water torture to which Shozo subjected Choy in the early days of his incarceration at the Central Police Station was suspended at the YMCA. Instead, Choy was regularly made to kneel on a rough plank of wood with a triangular iron bar behind his knees and told to remain still. If he moved, a guard or officer stamped viciously on the triangular bar, burnt Choy with cigarettes or lashed him with ropes, iron rods and bamboo sticks.

But Choy's interrogations produced no results. Other than acknowledging his role in providing Long with money and supplies to ease the suffering of the Changi internees, Choy denied working for Scott as a spy. When pressed for names, Choy provided none, instead claiming he knew nobody in Changi other than Long. He also insisted that he was not acting with any other member of the Chinese community.

Infuriated at this lack of progress, Sumida changed course. He sent in Monai to get answers. Unlike Shozo, whose brief did not exceed finding names, Monai's focus was on the destruction of ships in Singapore harbour. Choy clearly did not have the training to plant high explosives on ships, but he had the resources to buy them – the missing $10,000. Naturally, Choy denied everything, so Monai introduced him to the battery. He was tied to a frame and forced to kneel on splintered wooden planks, whereupon one electrode connected to a generator was attached to his foot and the other – an exposed wire – was pressed to his exposed skin.

After a short pause in his interrogations, Choy was summoned from his cell and led to an interrogation room. He was mentally preparing himself for more abuse and agony. He was quite sure his body – now racked with beri-beri – would not be able to bear it. But he would continue to tell the truth, even if it killed him. When the door opened, he could not comprehend what he was seeing. What was Elizabeth doing here? He took her in – her short, tattered black frock, her bare feet. He could well imagine her pain from kneeling on that rough, splintered wood, having suffered the same discomforts himself. She also seemed 'very nervous and very weak'.[1] They must have used the battery on her.

For her part, Elizabeth thought Choy was at death's door. Always a lean man, Choy was now dramatically underweight 'from beriberi, diarrhoea and lung trouble'.[2] There were also signs that violence had been inflicted upon his body. Monai could only have brought her husband in at this moment for one reason: to torture him before her eyes. Elizabeth had suffered brutal violence, depravity, cruelty, pain and undernourishment, but had maintained her dignity throughout. She had not confessed to any of the lies levelled at her, notwithstanding the promise of freedom. But could she continue to resist the torturers when maintaining her innocence would directly lead to her husband's torture?

Before either husband or wife could say anything to each other, the guards pulled Choy's arms behind him and bound his wrists together. He was forced to kneel alongside his wife. Monai claimed to have proof that they were both involved in the smuggling of money into Changi, the destruction of the ships in the harbour and a conspiracy to carry out more sabotage. Sergeant Major Makizono Masuo joined in, naming individuals the two interrogators claimed had implicated the couple. The missing thousands that never made it to Changi were also mentioned. The Choys, Monai asserted, had given that money to saboteurs with instructions to buy the explosives that were used to destroy the ships in the harbour and they had done it on the orders of Robert Heatlie Scott. Monai went into detail about the letter from Scott that was marked C. Both Choy and Elizabeth knew nothing of the letter. It did not exist – Long had fabricated the whole thing.

Monai was prepared for this answer. He nodded to a guard, who left the room. He returned minutes later with John Long. Choy accused Long of lying. Long, physically beaten and mentally on the verge of collapse, stuck to the charge. He told them both to confess and then was led back to his cell. Clearly, Long had been viciously tortured into writing such a false statement. But his outrageous lie, which cast him as Scott's innocent messenger, effectively deflected the agony that he had endured onto others.

Monai demanded the Choys confess. They both refused. Monai and Makizono then went to work on Choy. They punched and kicked him, all the while demanding that he 'admit that [he] was blowing up ships'.[3] After a savage thirty-minute beating, Choy collapsed to the ground. Monai switched on the generator and picked up the leads. Elizabeth was horrified. They were going to electrocute him before her eyes. It had been bad enough watching him being beaten, and yet she knew well that the battery would take him into an entirely different universe of pain. But instead of walking towards her husband, lying prone on the ground, Monai looked down at Elizabeth. The electricity was not for her husband – it was for her.

Monai attached the electrode to her foot and, with the live cable inches from her face, told her that she would be spared the agony if she confessed. She said that she had done nothing wrong. Monai expected she would say as much. It hardly mattered. Elizabeth was the one who would feel the physical pain, but it was her husband he was targeting. Choy was sure to start talking when he witnessed his wife writhing in agony.

Monai stepped forward and pressed the wire into the heel of one of Elizabeth's bare feet. Her back arched and her body spasmed. She heard someone scream – a blood-curdling, horrifying sound. It took her mind a moment to catch up to the fact that she was hearing herself. After a few moments' respite, Monai pressed the wire into her leg, after which he applied the wire to each hand. In the intervals between the administration of the torture, he would tell her to confess. Elizabeth said nothing. She was beyond speaking. Monai turned to Choy. He told him that his wife's suffering would be over if he confessed.

'Stick to the truth!' Elizabeth gasped. 'It's a lie! Stick to the truth! Don't mind me!'[4]

Choy begged Monai to stop. Monai ignored him, pressing the wire into Elizabeth once more. Choy estimated that the electrocution of his wife went on for about fifteen minutes. Monai held the wire to her body for longer durations than the previous day, confident, perhaps, that Elizabeth could physically withstand the torture. In her agony, Elizabeth would have gladly welcomed death. For Choy, the sight of his wife's torture was soul-destroying. Something broke inside him on that day.

Elizabeth was eventually untied. Without the support of the frame, she collapsed on the ground. Choy was not permitted to approach her.

'Now,' said Monai, 'both of you confess, we'll let you go. If not, we'll execute both of you.'

Elizabeth could only shake her head.

Monai turned to Choy.

'I've nothing to tell you,' he said.

'Alright,' Monai said. 'Then tomorrow you will both be executed.'[5]

The next time Elizabeth would be called out of her cell, Monai explained, she would be taken to Johore and at eight o'clock would 'have her head chopped off'.[6] Choy, who Monai assured would be present for his wife's execution, would then be beheaded at ten o'clock.

The officers and guards then all abruptly left the room. Choy shuffled over and held his wife. They were left alone to contemplate the value they placed on their own lives. They agreed: 'If we were executed, we died for the truth; it would be an honourable death.'[7] They knew a confession would have dire consequences for all the others whom the Japanese had implicated in their far-fetched conspiracy.

Monai and Makizono and several guards returned after twenty minutes. Choy and Elizabeth said their goodbyes. The guards picked Elizabeth up and dragged her out of the cell. Monai told Choy to sit at the table. Already weakened from the

savage beating, hollowed out at the sight of his wife being electrocuted, horrified at the prospect of witnessing his wife's execution,
Choy summoned the little strength he had left and stood up,
collapsing onto the chair. Monai laid a piece of paper and a pen
on the table and was told to write a farewell letter to Elizabeth.
It was another cruel ploy of the *Kempei Tai*, a way of making
their impending execution – a prospect that seemed abstract and
incomprehensible – very real. Choy wrote a farewell to his wife.
When he had finished the letter, Monai told him that, should
he confess, he would be set free along with his wife. But Choy's
mind was made up: 'We would die for a good cause, but would
not give away names of our friends.'[8]

The mystery of the missing $10,000 would not be solved until
after the war. Yoxall had indeed received $10,000 less than
than the bishop and his assistant had borrowed. Reverend John
Hayter, Assistant Chaplain of St Andrew's Cathedral and one of
the priests who avoided internment in the first year of the occupation, discovered what had happened. 'At a certain point,' Hayter
wrote, 'word had been sent out to the Choys from the Gaol that
no further money was needed for the time being. By ill luck the
missing money was already on its way.'[9] The money was intercepted by a third party, an internee who often received the money
from Long once it had been smuggled into Changi and who
would pass it onto Yoxall. Having known that the money was
not presently required, the internee 'passed [it] direct to a group
of people who were able to, and did, buy extra medical supplies
for use in the Gaol'.[10] The money, having never made it to Yoxall,
was never recorded in his books.

Monai reported the steadfast denials of the Choys to Sumida.
The canteen workers, he told Sumida, had not wavered; not
even the prospect of imminent death coaxed a confession.
Perhaps they were telling the truth. Monai suggested to Sumida
that he interrogate Long again. He wanted to test his growing

suspicion that Long was merely telling him what he wanted to hear to avoid punishment. Sumida agreed. After further interrogation of Long, Monai reported his findings to Sumida: 'I found later from Mr. Long [. . .] that he had wanted to please the investigator and had told a lie about the messages.'[11]

31

A BROKEN MAN

Six weeks after the attack

SUMIDA RELUCTANTLY EXONERATED THE Choys from any involvement in the attack on the harbour. But he was not ready to let them go. He remained doggedly committed to the idea that Robert Heatlie Scott was a master spy and had probably organised the attack. The Choys might yet be able to provide information that could sink Scott. In the meantime, Sumida sought out another source who supported Long's claims about Scott. Long may have lied about the letter, but Sumida was not ready to accept that he had made everything up. Sumida found a corroborating witness in notes of the interrogation of the osteopath Dr Hugh McIntyre. A member of the news committee, McIntyre had been arrested two weeks after the Double Tenth raid and taken to the YMCA. Prior to his arrest, Sumida and his men had found out that McIntyre's list of patients prior to the war included Rear Admiral Spooner and his wife and Air Vice Marshal Babington. He also provided medical advice to Sir George Sansom – British diplomat, Japanophile, adviser to the

British Navy and Robert Scott's predecessor on the Governor's War Council.[1]

McIntyre's first interrogation was a civilised affair. He was politely asked to provide details about his work, his patients prior to the war and his involvement in the camp news committee. The Japanese interrogator then asked McIntyre if John Long, Lionel Earl and Walter Stevenson were also members of the committee. McIntyre confirmed that they were, but did not mention Scott. It would prove a devastating decision. McIntyre was told: 'We want you to wait for a little time.'[2] He was probably being invited to weigh his decision not to volunteer his connection to Scott. He remained silent and was eventually taken down to the cells.

On the way to his cell, McIntyre spotted Stevenson, who attempted to communicate with him through sign language. Two guards noticed and savagely beat Stevenson to the ground before doing the same to McIntyre. Stevenson was taken back upstairs to an interrogation room along with Lionel Earl. The guards, meanwhile, hauled McIntyre into a cell with at least sixteen others. By coincidence, he was placed in a position that gave him a line of sight to Scott, who was in a cell off the corridor that ran perpendicular to his own cell. 'Scott made a signal to me which I found difficult to interpret,' McIntyre wrote, 'but I arrived at the conclusion that he meant it was possible to keep fairly dumb if nothing else.'[3] McIntyre could not, however, keep silent.

The guards returned an hour later and took McIntyre back upstairs. Staff Sergeant Makita, a short-statured, thick-necked bull of a man, was leading the interrogation. 'In the examination room, the atmosphere had changed,' McIntyre recalled. 'The equipment of the room then was a chair and some ropes and a couple of thugs who threw me into the chair and tied my hands behind it. The interpreter then asked, "Why didn't you say that Scott was a Member of that Committee?"'

'You didn't ask me,' McIntyre responded.[4]

Makita waited for the interpreter to translate the prisoner's words and then approached McIntyre in a threatening manner. Rather than strike him, Makita asked several more relatively innocuous questions, before saying: 'We will give you sufficient time to think this matter over, the charge against you is espionage. You and Scott are the two principals and you are allowing yourself to be used by Scott for his purposes. We will give you 24 hours to think about things and then talk.'[5]

By seeding the idea in McIntyre's mind that he was being betrayed, Makita was deploying the interrogator's time-honoured divide-and-conquer technique. At two o'clock the following morning, McIntyre was brought back upstairs. The guards led him into the room where Makita was waiting for him with five *Kempei Tai* auxiliaries. McIntyre was shoved into a chair.

'How did Scott convey his instruction to you?' barked Makita.

'He didn't convey any instruction to me,' said McIntyre.

'We know you are the missing link between Scott and the people in Singapore,' Makita said. 'We have got you already on this Radio charge – you are a principal in this and you are the man to suffer for that. We give you a chance now to escape with your life.'[6]

McIntyre denied everything. Makita ordered that the men tie McIntyre's arms behind his back. A noose was placed over McIntyre's neck and tied off to a ring on the ceiling. A third rope was then used to bind his ankles. It was only through a tremendous amount of exertion that McIntyre kept the pressure of the rope off his neck. Makita, meanwhile, was stripped to the waist, having removed his coat and singlet, and was holding a wooden pole whose diameter was two inches square. With all his force, Makita struck McIntyre on the legs and arms with the pole, causing him to lose his balance, the noose cutting off his airways and causing him to black out.

A bucket of water was poured over McIntyre's head. He was pulled to his feet. His legs gave way and he toppled over. He noticed the shattered remains of Makita's wooden pole scattered across the floor. The ropes around McIntyre's arms were untied but the noose remained around his neck. 'I sat on the floor,' McIntyre recalled, 'and they brought me a cup of coffee of which I was rather suspicious.'[7] Makita and his men left him and returned an hour later. He was asked the same questions, which McIntyre defiantly refused to answer. Once again, he was tied up, the noose was pulled through the ring and Makita, his torso glistening with sweat, set upon him with a new wooden rod.

McIntyre began to lose track of time. He estimated the beating went for another couple of hours because he recalled seeing the changing colour of the sky through the cell window. He fell unconscious, waking up covered in blood and with a splitting headache. Guards were staring down at him. Through the cell window, the sky was dark again. Had he lost an entire day? He became aware of a throbbing ache in his left arm. He looked down and saw a puncture wound. His right hand shot up to feel it. 'The guards pulled my right hand away. They then took me back to the old room and forced some tablets of ephedrine between my teeth, held my nose and gave me a mouthful of water.'[8] McIntyre concluded the drug was ephedrine on the basis of its stimulating effect.

An hour later, the interrogation resumed. When it was done, McIntyre was dragged downstairs and dumped in a cell. 'One of the Chinese in the cell attempted to put some water on my shirt which was torn and stuck to my back, which was black and blue from head to heels.'[9] There was no respite. The guards came for McIntyre the next day. They forced him to place his foot onto a block of wood. Makita picked up a metal pole and brought it down on McIntyre's foot with all his fury. 'He did that to both my feet and they did the same thing to both my hands'[10] The blows fractured multiple fingers, rendering both hands useless for several days.

Sumida followed the interrogation of McIntyre closely. Monai's suspicions of Long were correct. He was confessing to everything, even when two pieces of information contradicted each other. In stark contrast, McIntyre's denials in the face of extreme physical pressure appeared to impress Sumida. His statements were deemed more reliable. But physical torture was not delivering results. Sumida decided to pivot the interrogation to psychological torment. This was a task at which Sumida excelled.

'The next day,' McIntyre reported, 'they took me up again. They tied me up as before and Makita was present as well as the man we learned to recognise as the head of the Gestapo.'[11] Smiling brightly, Sumida turned to the interpreter and instructed him to tell McIntyre that the accusations that he faced were more serious than he realised. Once again, the question was put to McIntyre as to the order that Scott had given him and, once again, McIntyre said that there was no order. How had he conveyed messages from Scott to Singapore? No messages were conveyed, he responded. There was a short pause before Sumida asked where in Changi the transmitter was located. This was a new question and one that surely unsettled McIntyre. What exactly did they think he had been doing? 'I told them I did not know anything at all and that I had told them the whole story of the radio reception organisation and distribution [committee] as I knew it.'[12]

'How did [you] know?' Sumida asked.[13]

McIntyre knew that Sumida was referring to the attack on the ships. Whatever McIntyre said did not satisfy Sumida, who accused him of being obstinate. McIntyre insisted that he would answer all questions: 'They did not say anything more but simply handed me a sheet of paper and a pencil.'[14] McIntyre told them he was unable to write because they had broken his fingers. Sumida ignored him. He explained to McIntyre that this would be his only chance to write a letter to his relatives. His execution was imminent. There was no point in writing a letter, McIntyre explained. He had no idea of the whereabouts of his family. They had been evacuated prior to the capitulation.

'Ah, yes, but we know,' Sumida said in English. Talking directly to McIntyre without the aid of a translator somehow lent the remark greater authenticity. McIntyre was shaken.

'My wife, as far as I know, is not an internee,' MacIntyre said.

'She is in our hands,' Sumida said. 'Unless you answer these questions your wife will be brought back here and she will be examined.'[15]

The interpreter repeated the question about the order that Scott gave McIntyre and how he found out about the destruction of the ships in the harbour. McIntyre maintained his ignorance. Guards dragged him downstairs and gave him the water treatment. At one point, he stopped breathing. 'When I came to, I was lying on the floor again in the room upstairs and they appeared to have been doing artificial respiration.'[16]

McIntyre was offered coffee, which he declined. The Japanese insisted. A guard moved behind him and held his head still while another held his nose. A mug of coffee was forced between his lips and he was made to swallow. 'I then realised that every time they offered me coffee like that it was drugged because I knew nothing more until the following morning.'[17]

He awoke to a feeling of weightlessness. Guards were carrying him upstairs. Feeling groggy, he was sat on a chair with his hands tied behind his back. The slant of the sunlight through the windows indicated late afternoon. Makita started talking. 'There is something you know about the ships,' the interpreter said, 'about what happened on the 27th of September.'

McIntyre said he did not know anything about it.

'We will give you a lead,' the interpreter said. 'It is the day of the explosions on the Japanese ships.'[18]

McIntyre knew nothing about it. Rather than press him for answers, they 'worked themselves up into a spasm of frenzied fanaticism'. They spoke of the divine might of the Japanese Army and the Navy, the cruelty the British had exacted against all Asians, and the reality 'that Japan was the Saviour of the world'.[19]

The appropriate response was for McIntyre to look enraptured. He instead paid them the most cutting insult: he fell asleep.

The following day, McIntyre was once again taken upstairs. He was told it was his very last chance to confess to being directly involved in the sinking of the ships in the harbour. He denied all knowledge of the attack. They took him downstairs and bundled him into a waiting car. They drove the backstreets of Singapore, passing buildings and houses that were only vaguely familiar to McIntyre: 'I only recognised the drive up round Hill Street.'[20]

The car pulled up in a courtyard. It was a foreboding place that backed onto high walls made of wood. McIntyre was ordered out of the car. He was led through a gate that was promptly slammed shut, taken across a gravelled yard and put up against a wall. 'Presently six Japanese soldiers came out with rifles,' recalled McIntyre. 'The guard then came over to me and tied my feet and my hands behind me.' The interpreter told McIntyre that 'this was the way Nippon treated people who had acted towards her as [McIntyre] had done, and refused to make reparations'.[21]

The six soldiers formed up in a line. The interpreter asked McIntyre if he wanted to be blindfolded: 'I said "No".'[22] They blindfolded him anyway, with a multicoloured handkerchief. Orders were shouted in Japanese. McIntyre heard 'the clicking of rifle bolts and then one final order'.[23]

McIntyre's next recollection was lying on a stretcher, having either fainted or been knocked out cold. He was kept in a room on his own upstairs in the YMCA without a bucket, forced to endure the humiliation of having to urinate directly onto the floor while being surveilled. He would recall that 'the treatment after that was of a passive nature except for occasional face slapping and buffeting about'.[24] He was even allowed to attend to ill internees.

McIntyre's recollections following the mock execution differ markedly from the Japanese version. The *Kempei Tai* would claim that McIntyre fully cooperated with the investigation practically from the beginning. The Japanese never denied that McIntyre was subjected to torture. They did, however, dispute that he was drugged – a claim that is impossible to verify – and that he was subjected to a sham firing squad, an incident that almost certainly *did* happen, given the numerous reports from others who endured the same experience. By the time Makita and his thugs had worked over McIntyre, the interrogation was handed over to Monai.

Monai claimed that McIntyre was a defeated man who confessed that a few days before the attack, following a meeting with the news committee, Robert Heatlie Scott handed him a document that said: 'In Singapore harbour there are many Japanese ships now. This is a good chance.'[25] McIntyre was to pass this message on to Long, who in turn instructed Bryning to share it with Stevenson, who wired the message to British Headquarters in India. It was McIntyre's belief – at least in Monai's telling of the story – that 'by the time of the next [news committee] meeting on 30 September the news of the sinking of the Japanese boats had seeped into the camp, and he confessed that he thought that this was the result of the message'.[26] Monai took credit for extracting these critical details from McIntyre: 'This [information] I got without so much as touching McIntyre with a finger and he said: "If you had hit me or beaten me as the other interrogators before you, I would not have told this to you, even if I were to die."'

Monai made other claims, some of them totally implausible. For instance, after making his confession, McIntyre apparently said to Monai that 'you beat me with your gentlemanliness and kind attitude'.[27] Gentlemanly and kind were not words any victims used to describe Monai. McIntyre also said, according to Monai, that 'another reason I told you this is that by telling you the truth many people who were arrested will be released sooner'. McIntyre was then said to have started weeping. 'I am only afraid that you may consider me betraying my own countrymen, but I have to recognise facts as facts.'[28]

But none of what McIntyre 'confessed' to Monai were facts. The very notion, moreover, that McIntyre could believe that in providing Monai with this information he would secure the release of prisoners was delusional. So, then, did it ever happen? In the highly detailed affidavit that McIntyre submitted to the court in the trial of the Japanese responsible for the Double Tenth incident, he makes no mention of being interrogated by Monai at all. After being lined up in front of the firing squad, blindfolded and then suddenly falling unconscious, McIntyre stated: 'I have a very hazy recollection of what happened after that.'[29] Of course, if Monai was telling the truth or even part of the truth, McIntyre would not admit to making such false claims. To do so would be to acknowledge that he was partly responsible for the arrest and torture of innocent internees, like poor Henry Bryning.

Bryning was unconnected to any illegal activity within Changi. His name was not mentioned by any other prisoner during interrogation. He was arrested ten days after McIntyre, a date which coincides within a day or so of when Monai claims McIntyre made his statements. If we therefore accept, which it would seem we must, that McIntyre did make such statements, then he corroborated much of Long's claims and, as such, lent a measure of plausibility to Sumida's conspiracy theory.

The questions that Stanley and Bryning were asked or what they told their interrogators cannot be known. Stanley was tortured to death and Bryning would die of dysentery three months after his arrest. Nevertheless, on the basis of the statements Monai made to various internees, including Scott, the questions put to John Long are easier to discern, because he 'revealed a good deal, on many subjects, in response to flattery, and more in response to torture. In the end he signed practically anything they asked, bringing about the arrest of many internees and townsfolk.'[30] Scott would know better than most the statements and so-called confessions Long made. After all, they would become the basis of the case against him. But in the end, McIntyre's information would prove equally devastating.

32

UNENDING HORROR

Four months after the attack

ROBERT HEATLIE SCOTT'S FIRST interrogation – a sixteen-hour ordeal that finished at six o'clock in the morning – was followed by an appalling day. He was forbidden from lying down. He attempted to sleep while squatting, but to no avail. In the waking nightmare of that day, Scott willed the hours away until he was permitted to lie down and succumb to his fatigue. In the late afternoon, the sentry appeared outside the cell and called Scott's name. It was typical for the torture to begin in this fashion – at a moment of sleep-deprived vulnerability. Nauseatingly tired, Scott was led to the interrogation room. Monai and the interpreter Shimada were the only two men in the room. Scott was told to sit down at the very table he'd been interrogated at several hours earlier.

'Had the camp news committee discussed the sabotaging of the tankers at [the] Committee meeting on September 23?' asked Monai.[1] Scott said they had not. Monai nodded and told the guard to take Scott back to his cell. Evidently, Monai was asking a question that Sumida had forgotten to ask himself. Scott barely had time to process the single-question interrogation before the sentry appeared at his side to take him to a new home – cell number five. This cell was around nine feet by nine feet, smaller than his previous cell by some way. Changing cells brought no physical relief. The floor was filthy, bugs clung to the walls, the commode discharged a familiar foul stench, and it was no less stuffy and airless. The window opened to a different side of the building, but it gave onto a well-protected verandah. The cell's sole advantage was being situated around the corner from where the sentries sat. Scott was out of sight and could chance talking with his cellmates. There were six other men inside; none of them were Changi internees, nor had they been arrested in connection with the Double Tenth raid. Scott was being isolated from those he knew to prevent collusion.

Scott's new cellmates each had an interesting story to tell: 'I passed the time by listening to the life stories and crimes of my companions, Chinese, Eurasians and Japanese, thus acquiring much miscellaneous information about odds and ends.'[2] The conversations kept at bay the bitter ennui of inaction and boredom, and the dread of his inevitable torture. The greatest source of entertainment came from the unlikeliest of cellmates, a Japanese artillery officer arrested for a drunken bayonet duel with another officer. He provided a visceral account of jungle fighting. Scott recalled:

His tales were full of incident and carried conviction. He made caustic comments on the ease with which Japanese fast mobile troops in Malaya, unburdened by heavy kit or any food at all, ambushed British, Indian and Australian soldiers laden with bully beef and equipment, captured them, ate their supplies, forced them to go on as porters, and, if it was inconvenient to send them to a Prisoner of War Depot, shot them when the stores had been consumed.[3]

Scott also met a well-educated Japanese civilian who managed a telegraph office and who had been accused of large-scale corruption. Exactly what he had done was not made clear. But the man freely admitted his guilt. Scott found him 'an interesting and agreeable man, who discussed economics and world problems'.[4] One night, Scott noticed the man furiously scratching away at his throat. In the dim moonlight coming through the window, Scott could see glistening blood running over his hands and dripping onto his shirt. The civilian had managed to smuggle a razor blade into the cell. The blade had been concealed in his socks – Japanese prisoners being permitted to cover their feet. The sight of him attempting suicide was 'an unusual experience'[5] for Scott, but not unsurprising. Scott knew not to interfere. This man would very likely be tortured and executed. But he had already suffered the gravest punishment – the loss of face that had attended his arrest.

During his stints in Tokyo, Scott had learnt much of Japanese concepts of honour and the crucial role they played in guiding personal and communal lives. This was an enduring legacy of *bushido*, or the way of the warrior, a strict code of conduct that promulgated the virtues of loyalty, courage and self-discipline. This disgraced Japanese man, feverishly sawing away at his throat, was not trying to kill himself to escape torture, but to restore honour to himself and his family. He very likely viewed the act as akin to performing *seppuku*, the highly ritualised suicide practised by samurai after committing grave offences or failures. *Seppuku* had a set of prescribed steps, culminating in the samurai disembowelling himself with a large knife. In the absence of a knife, the Japanese prisoner in cell five had to make do with a razor blade to the throat. But his suicide attempt was unsuccessful: 'Failing in this, he cut out his tongue [. . .] the blood made a nasty mess all over the floor on his place and mine – we were lying cheek by jowl.'[6]

*

The torture of Robert Heatlie Scott began in February 1944, three months after his one-question interrogation with Monai. Scott was called from his cell quite unexpectedly. He was taken to a small room at the back of the YMCA guarded by a sentry. The room resembled a birdcage 'with an open side of wooden pillars, so that the sentry could see the whole of the cell at a glance'.[7] Scott was instructed to squat, Japanese fashion, in front of the sentry. While he squatted, billets of firewood, sticks, rods, broomsticks, canes, ashtrays and other objects were brought into the room and placed on the floor around him. Scott remained in a squatting position for hours.

Eventually, Monai entered the room. He was accompanied by two interpreters, the small, thin Shimada and the fat Nigo, who spoke English with an American accent. Through Shimada, Monai instructed Scott to kneel on a rack of sharp wooden slats. Monai began the interview by having two of Scott's fingers tied tightly together with thick string. The other end of the string was then tied off to an iron bar across a window high above. The string was pulled taut so that Scott's arm was fully extended, 'so that the shoulder joint was nearly dislocated'.[8]

Monai reminded Scott that, in accordance with Japanese practice, he required a confession before they could proceed to trial. He repeated the charges that Sumida had first laid out against Scott: sabotage, spying, anti-Japanese propaganda and running radios in Changi. Monai included an additional charge of planning and ordering the raid on the Japanese ships in Singapore harbour. Outwardly, Scott remained poised. Inwardly he was surely worried. In previous interrogations, he had managed to talk his way through, deflecting questions through obfuscation, misinformation and dissembling. He was always able to outwit his interrogators through reason, claims of ignorance, denial or flat-out lying. His gift for reading people, evaluating their character – fine-tuned after years as a diplomat – had proven useful. These tactics were exceedingly effective against Sam, who was guided down roads paved with useless information and arrived at the end with the impression that he had unearthed golden intelligence.

But this was different: 'Now I was dealing with a senior and very experienced detective officer.'[9] The general atmosphere within the room was combative. From the outset, the interrogation was violent. Monai countered every denial with a physical blow to nearly every part of Scott's body and head, using the instruments that had been laid across the room. At one point, a stick was broken across his face. Periodically, Monai would stamp down on Scott's bare feet. This went on for two hours until the string tied around Scott's fingers was cut. He collapsed into a crumpled heap on the hard floor. Monai kicked him, ordering that he resume the squatting position. Exhausted, Scott pulled himself up and managed to squat. Monai and the two interpreters left, leaving the sentry to keep watch. They all returned half an hour later to resume the interrogation. Scott was forced to kneel on the sharp wooden slats, and this time when Monai did not get the answers that he wanted, he would jump onto the soles of Scott's feet.[10]

During the ordeal, Scott reflected on the staggering claims that Monai was making about him. Clearly, since his last interrogation, 'the Kempei [had been] collecting, by flattery and torture, a mass of conflicting and sometimes false evidence'.[11] Monai delighted in telling Scott the names of his fellow internees who had confessed, detailing the specific accusations they had levelled against him. He even showed Scott Long's handwritten 'confessions'. It was likely done to torment Scott by revealing that his friends and acquaintances in Changi had betrayed him.

Inasmuch as it was designed to elicit a false confession from Scott, Monai's tactic failed. But these revelations left Scott enraged. He would nickname McIntyre 'Adolf' and described him as having 'cracked fairly easily under examination'.[12] But it was Long's written confession that particularly rankled Scott.

Long's smuggling efforts were unambiguously perilous. Everyone knew that, if caught, he ran the very real risk of being severely punished. He was a central figure in a smuggling operation that was a lifeline for the Changi internees. As courier, he brought thousands of dollars into the camp as well as letters, supplies and other comforts. He was also a vital conduit of information, Scott himself describing him as 'one of our channels for contacting Singapore residents'.[13]

But Long's so-called confessions led to an enormous amount of suffering. Scott was among those who bore the brunt of his signed statements and admissions. Scott derisorily referred to Long as someone who had 'signed practically anything they asked'[14] to avoid being tortured. Scott probably felt he had a right to feel indignant. He was enduring the same physical and psychological abuse as Long did, had suffered the same indignities in the YMCA cells, and yet he managed to keep quiet.

By monitoring the changing colour of the sky through the cell window, Scott calculated that he had been there for six days. Monai's interrogation was relentless. He would take intermittent breaks that would vary in length from thirty minutes to two hours before the interrogation would resume. Questions were straight to the point and the answers had to be likewise. Monai set traps, repeating questions, taking inexplicable deviations, gaslighting Scott with claims that Scott had made contradictory remarks. Scott avoided most traps; some he did not.

Monai, who preferred working at night, created a chaotic and exacting interrogation schedule that was designed to drive Scott into a state of extreme fatigue:

I would be called out about 11 p.m. or any hour of the night or day, put on a rack for a couple of hours in silence; then twenty minutes of questions; an hour's beating and shouting; more questioning. Sometimes he would dismiss me for the night about 2.30 a.m. call me out again at 3, dismiss me at 4, call me out again at 5 a.m.[15]

Monai would sometimes engage Scott in an ideological joust, dressing up his racist beliefs in Japan's right to rule in high-minded axioms about freedom and the right of all Asians to self-rule. 'We must bring freedom to all Asiatic races in the first place,' he declared, 'that is, of course, first get rid of the white man, then allow Asiatic races to govern themselves.'

Sometimes, Scott would take the bait. 'Do you mean *absolute* freedom?' he once responded. 'Supposing for example Chinese or Indian interests conflicted with Japanese interest – supposing they wanted to turn out all Japanese, as well as all Europeans?'

'That could not happen,' Monai retorted. 'Naturally, we should always retain general control – freedom of course means freedom to develop on lines which we shall lay down, as we are the leaders of Asia.'[16]

Monai's racism, his arrogance, riled Scott. He knew better than to bite back. But his suffering, his hunger, his physical pain and fatigue, and his utter weariness of Monai's fanaticism under-mined his better judgement. 'Do you want to turn all Asiatics?' His voice surely full of emotion. 'That is impossible – you tried to do that with the Formosans and the Koreans, stamping out their customs and dress and habits and language; and you failed. How can you hope to succeed with Indians and Malays and Chinese?'[17]

Scott could see that his logic annoyed Monai, which brought him satisfaction, until Monai took out his frustration with violence. He would then end the conversation with a final racist rant: 'We shall not attempt world domination till we have enough Japanese – we need 100 million, and we shall have them in twenty years' time. We can use the other [Asians]. But we cannot depend on them. The Chinese love money, the Malays love pleasure, and the Indians are liars. Only the Japanese have the character necessary to govern the whole world.'[18]

During Monai's breaks, Scott would be ordered to assume a squatting position in front of the guard. At no point was he able to rest or lie down. Scott's food rations were halved for the first four days of his interrogation, before being suspended entirely. He would be allowed to eat when he confessed. Scott guarded against slipping into madness by anchoring his thoughts to the great poet whose collected works he had been gifted by Sam the Sergeant Major: 'in silence Keats came in again to distract my mind and pass the time.'[19]

But Scott was rarely left alone for long. While Monai rested, Nigo would take his turn on Scott. The interpreter was a source of curiosity to Scott. To begin with, he was conspicuously overweight. In an environment where food scarcity rendered every physique rake thin – Japanese guards included – Nigo was a physical oddity. Also, his English – which he spoke with an American accent – was flawless. Born and raised in Los Angeles, Nigo was interned with other Japanese nationals in a camp in Arizona at the outbreak of war. Along with his mother, Nigo was among numerous Japanese exchanged for American civilians caught behind enemy lines when the fighting started. These exchanges were a means by which senior diplomats and their families could be brought home. How Nigo managed to qualify for exchange is unclear. It seems he was among the few selected for his linguistic skills.

Nigo departed New Jersey aboard the exchange ship MS *Gripsholm*, a liner charted by the US State Department to ferry Japanese and German nationals to exchange points. The ship took Nigo to Singapore, landing on 2 November 1943, by which time the Number One Work was in full swing. Sumida needed interpreters. 'After my arrival in Singapore,' Nigo said, 'I was given a job as a civilian interpreter in the *Kempei Tai* Branch at the YMCA.'[20] As a fluent English speaker, Nigo was assigned to officers leading the interrogations of the high-value prisoners, including Stanley, the Bishop of Singapore and Yoxall.

The views these men had of Nigo vary. Some would state that he offered kindness, even providing water to tortured victims when the *Kempei Tai* guards and officers were looking away. Others, like Scott, would say differently.

Unlike other interpreters Scott had encountered, Nigo took an active role in his torture: 'On those occasions when [Monai] was out of the room, [Nigo] carried on the same beating on much the same lines, which I thought was particularly pointless.'[21] Nigo made the interrogation infinitely worse, recognising when Scott was mincing words or making contradictory statements, and physically punished him for it. Given Scott's profile as the master spy, Nigo may have felt compelled to actively participate in Scott's torture beyond his role as interpreter. After all, Sumida would be keeping a very close eye on this interrogation. Nigo's safety was not necessarily assured. He was a citizen of a country at war with Japan. Perhaps the kindnesses he had offered other prisoners had been noted by the guards and he had been warned. Or perhaps he wanted to prove himself as a bone fide Nipponese, committed to Hirohito's divine mission. Whether out of fear or heartfelt patriotism, Nigo beat Scott with the instruments scattered throughout the room. He adopted a method of punishment, preferred by *Kempei Tai* torturers and no doubt observed during interrogations, of attacking the same spot on the victim's body. He probably noticed Monai striking Scott's knee with a broom stick. Nigo picked up a club, striking it viciously 'till it was like a young football'.[22]

After his week-long torture, Scott had formed a thesis on his captors:

> The *Kempei* have the mentality of spoilt boys of fourteen, headstrong, selfish, brutal; very *very* sorry for themselves when they are ill or hurt but enjoying inflicting pain on others [. . .] Like children, they are sensitive to criticism: it is incomprehensible that anyone should impugn their motives

or not share their ideals and point of view, which by them, as by children, are held in all sincerity.[23]

Scott saw these grown men as typifying the adolescent mind in the overwhelmingly poor judgements they formed of all non-Japanese people, whom they regarded as alien. This, in Scott's view, was 'because they have no background of travel, general experience, and education; no sense of proportion; no tolerance. School boys judging adults.'[24]

The characterisation of the *Kempei Tai* as children seemed particularly salient to Scott when considering the ludicrous fantasies that sprang forth from their overheated imaginations. Notwithstanding his senior rank and abilities as a detective, Scott believed that Sumida typified this characterisation, observing: 'his mind teems with images of fighter pilots, Red Indians round the corner, ambushes in every lane, spies, wonderful inventions, hidden treasure, sinister, diabolically clever strangers.'[25] To Scott, Sumida and all his men 'seemed to live in a world of melodrama, where everyone and everything was suspect, all foreigners were spies [. . .] and the wilder the story the more fascinatingly probable it became'.[26]

Despite his ordeal, Scott did not give in to hatred of the Japanese. Even in this moment of abject misery, he recalled the more endearing characteristics of the Japanese: their penchant for playing with children, love of animals and flashes of a sense of humour. He remembered the time in Palembang when he witnessed a sentry 'put down his bayonet, and weep, when an internee [. . .] showed him a picture of his children; for the sentry, too, had not seen his children for years'. The Japanese, in Scott's view, were not men that were 'lacking any spark of humanity'.[27]

A notable exception to this rule was Monai Tadamori. This mirthless, cruel fanatic seemed to take a perverse pleasure in the suffering he inflicted on others. He was, in Scott's estimation, an 'out-an-out sadist'.[28] Sumida's right-hand man took Scott to places of physical pain that were barely imaginable. The agony he experienced coupled with an extreme fatigue surely loosened his grip on sanity. But Scott clung to a single hope – the investigation was on shaky ground: 'They had collected too much evidence and did not know what was true and what was false.'[29] With each passing day, Scott noticed doubt creeping into the faces of his torturers: 'as it progressed, I began to sense a lack of certainty and assurance however much they blustered and shouted that they knew all and that I must sign forthwith or be further tortured till I died.' The game Scott had been playing since his capture had entered a new phase: 'It became, in my mind, a race with time: could I, by denials, convince them that they were after a mare's nest, or at any rate so discredit evidence collected as to shake their faith in it – before I collapsed?'[30]

Scott's torment was not simply physical. The psychological pain – or 'third degree methods', as Scott described them – was no less horrific. 'One of their most cruel threats was telling me that many of my friends had been arrested. Some had died, and others were dying; the camp was being rigorously punished; (all these statements were, I knew, true); the only way to save them and the camp was for me to confess at once.'[31] Scott's refusal to make a false confession – which was an extraordinary demonstration of bravery – was solely motivated by his conviction that Monai was being dishonest. Falsely confessing would not end the investigation, it would only serve to lengthen and broaden it. More innocent men and women, inside and outside Changi, would be drawn into its death spiral. And so Scott clung to the truth and maintained his innocence.

Monai returned to the cell after a short break. His order was to secure a full confession from Scott. In that objective he was failing. This was not a man accustomed to failure. Scott's wrist was tied off to the bar across the window and pulled taut. His fatigued legs could barely keep him upright. Should he fall, his shoulder would dislocate. Monai asked questions. At this point, Scott was only capable of answering with grunts and shakes of his head. Monai would set upon him with the instruments. He would grab hold of his beard and wrench a handful of whiskers. He would stamp on Scott's already severely injured feet, deepening existing wounds to such an extent that ligaments and bone were exposed. When the session was over, Monai went to consult with Sumida. He was physically exhausted and defeated. Scott had beaten him; he had beaten them all.

Sumida was unsurprised when Monai reported that Scott did not confess. His adversary was not only cunning and devious, he was brave, too. Just like the Choys, Scott's resilience and resistance in the face of unfathomable agony had proven that there was no connection between the blowing up of the ships in Singapore Harbour and the activities of the internees in Changi. Other prisoners had made written confessions under torture. Those confessions were worth less than the paper they were written on. Scott and the Choys, and many others, had proven those confessions false by simply keeping their answers consistent. If there was a definite moment that Sumida decided to bring the investigation to an end, it was almost certainly during Monai's final report of the interrogation of Scott. The supposed master spy who had orchestrated all anti-Japanese activities in Syonan, including the blowing up of the ships, was clearly innocent, at least of the serious crimes with which he was charged. Sumida's ever-fertile mind was now at work, puzzling out a way to tidy up the Number One Work and save face. Meanwhile, he sent Monai back to the examination room with one final, disgraceful order – a last-ditch effort to extract a confession.

Had Scott full command of his senses, he would have noticed something different about Monai. Something, perhaps, in his measured demeanour, his authoritative bearing: a man poised to carry out a solemn duty. Scott may have also noticed that Monai was attired in uniform, his sword strapped to his belt. A piece of paper and a pencil were laid on the ground in front of Scott. Scott was ordered to write a farewell letter to his wife before his execution. Beaten, fatigued, barely conscious, Scott did not react: 'I was by then in such a state that the sentence left me unmoved.'[32]

Scott's indifference to his fate clearly surprised Monai. Perhaps the prisoner did not understand. Monai was more explicit, stating the date and the place where his execution would take place. Scott kept still. Monai pulled out his sword. He held it before Scott and ordered him to run his finger along the blade to 'test its keenness'.[33] Scott's face remained expressionless, inscrutable. This was not what Monai expected. These white men feared death. But Monai did not see a terrified man. Though his body was a bruised and broken ruin, Scott appeared calm. Death had no hold over him: 'In a way, I welcomed the prospect,' Scott would go on to reflect.[34]

Just before leaving the examination room, Monai told Scott he would see him tomorrow at his execution. Scott was forced to remain awake for another night. Of all the long nights he had endured since his miraculous escape on the *Giang Bee* – the epic journey aboard the dinghy, his capture and internment in Sumatra, his journey back to Singapore and his internment in Outram Road Gaol and Changi Jail, and his brutal incarceration in the YMCA – this was surely the longest. His agony that night was not out of fear of his impending death. Scott sensed almost beyond a doubt that Monai was bluffing. He was fearful that if his life was to be spared, 'the examination would be continued'.[35]

Sumida could hardly have been surprised that threatening Scott with execution did not elicit a confession. Scott's continued defiance and undeniable courage had quashed Sumida's claims. Without a confession, Scott could not be brought to trial, at least not on the charges for which he had been accused. Beyond the money and the radio receivers – whose existence had been plausibly explained – there was a complete lack of genuinely incriminating evidence. Changi had been turned upside down and no transmitter had been found. Sumida knew when he had been beaten.

Scott was returned to his cell the following morning. He would be interviewed several more times over the subsequent three weeks, but without violence. Scott's suspicions – 'that the *Kempei*'s faith in their evidence had been shaken'[36] – were proven true. The interviews covered the same territory, but the officers conducting the interrogations were not invested in the process; there was no fight left in these dogs. Finally, one day towards the end of March 1944, six months after being arrested, Scott was interrogated for the last time. Not that he believed it was over. They told him, 'We have left you alone for a few days. The case has been under review and will now be reopened from the beginning. We shall start all over again, and this time we shall continue through to the death. We shall begin tomorrow; you have today to think it over.'[37]

Scott had no reason to think they were bluffing. But he held his nerve. Sure enough, the statement proved either a pitiful final fishing expedition for information or yet another degrading and callous scare tactic. Either way, it was an act of cruelty perpetrated by a murderous military unit. As the days passed and nothing came of the threat, Scott knew he had prevailed. 'They failed,' he wrote. 'I was the last to be examined [. . .] I won, but only by a short head.'[38]

The investigation had taken Scott beyond the limit of his physical endurance. After several months of incarceration in a filthy cell, limited mobility, starvation rations and then a week of extreme torture, Scott began to lose his hold on life. The untreated gash across the sole of his foot had become infected. He worryingly went off his food, and then his body began to swell: 'I contracted serious oedema, the whole body grossly swollen from the feet to the heart and lungs.'[39] Poor diet and remaining stationary for extended periods are among the causes of oedema. Squatting for indeterminate periods and kneeling on the rack while being tortured certainly did not help. Scott's swelling, however, was probably caused by a lack of nutrients in his inadequate rice diet. This poor diet had led to beri-beri, which explained the pain in his limbs, confusion and irregular heartbeat. The punching and beating with sticks and rods to his face had not helped his appearance. From face to foot, Scott was a bloated, blackened grotesquerie, utterly unrecognisable even to those who knew him well.

Limping back to his cell after his final interview, no doubt still wondering if the *Kempei* officer was bluffing about the resumption of his torture, Scott tripped over. It took an enormous effort to get to his knees. When he looked up, he was staring into the face of a Chinese woman through the wooden bars of another cell. This was the second time Rob Scott laid eyes on Elizabeth Choy. A day earlier, Elizabeth had been stripped, severely beaten and electrocuted. Not that Scott could tell from looking at her. In that dirty cell, surrounded by a mass of miserable men, Elizabeth comported herself with grace and poise, her head high and shoulders back. Perhaps her strength inspired him. Without any help from the guard, Scott managed to get to his feet. Legs heavy, short on breath, pain in every joint in his body, Scott turned and resumed his slow, painful journey back to his cell.

33

THE DEATH HOUSES
OF SAGO LANE

THE SLUM IN THE Sago Lane district of Chinatown was among the worst in Singapore. Crumbling tenement houses accommodating hundreds of people spilled onto squalid, filthy streets. Entire families occupied single bedrooms that, owing to their size, were known as cubicles. Located near the sea, the district was prone to flooding in the monsoon season. Those families who occupied the ground-level rooms of the buildings that lined the filthy streets would have to move their furniture and possessions to the upper levels to avoid the knee-deep rainwater that would surge into their homes. When the water receded, the floors would be layered with the direst mud, drawing plagues of mosquitoes and insects.

Elizabeth Choy visited the slum in 1957, having heard about a child in need of her help. During her four-year stint as the first principal for the Singapore School for the Blind, Elizabeth made it a habit to visit the slums and *kampungs* – the old villages of thatched roofs, timber and dirt floors located outside the municipal areas of Singapore – to find the blind children. Her mission was to persuade the children's parents or guardians to let them attend the school as boarders. 'Of course, to them, the whole thing sounded absurd. Some of them [asked], "What, send the child to school? How can they study when they have no sight?"'[1] Elizabeth would calmly explain that there were special ways to teach them to read with their fingers; that there was hope for their child.

One child from Sago Lane, whose name was Chan Poh Lin, was beset with multiple challenges. Not only was she blind and crushingly poor, she was also deaf. The daughter of a hawker (who was largely uninterested in his only child because of her sex and disability) and a hardworking waitress, Poh Lin lost her hearing aged twelve and then lost her sight two years later. After making some enquiries, Elizabeth was directed to the cubicle in which Poh Lin's family lived. She scaled the steep, narrow stairs between floors and walked through the narrow passageways, eventually finding the girl locked in her world of silent darkness in a blacked-out room. Nobody really knew whether Poh Lin felt anguished, sorrowful or indifferent to her situation. As Elizabeth Choy's biographer noted, 'she just kept crouched in one corner of the family's cubicle, out of people's way and ate whatever food her mother fed her'.[2] Elizabeth kept her emotion in check: 'I looked into this dark cubicle and saw just one wooden bed, and a tiny passage just wide enough to walk through. So I asked the parents, "Where does this girl sleep?" And her mother said, "Well, she sleeps under the bed." The place was so dark that you had to find the way by groping about, and whether your eyes were shut or open made no difference.'[3]

Moved by Elizabeth's concern and impressed with her conviction, Poh Lin's mother allowed her daughter to be enrolled at the School for the Blind. Poh Lin's progress at school was impressive. She learned braille and how to understand people through various methods involving her sense of touch. She read about the life of Helen Keller – the blind and deaf American who became a prolific author, essayist and campaigner for women's rights, labour rights and an advocate for people with disabilities – who quickly became an inspiration. Poh Lin's life underwent further transformation following a visit from John Wilson, Director of the Royal Commonwealth Society for the Blind. Wilson – who completely lost his sight aged thirteen when a school chemistry experiment went horribly wrong – was deeply moved by this girl who 'wanted to learn like Helen Keller, to speak English like the Queen of England, to meet everyone in the world'.[4] Wilson pulled some strings and arranged for her to study at the Perkins School for the Blind in Massachusetts for six years on a full scholarship. The Perkins School was the same institution where Helen Keller was educated. Poh Lin would learn how to speak English by feeling and touching a speaker's lips and throat. She topped the school in mathematics and became president of the sports club. She would meet Mahatma Gandhi. Poh Lin would remain in the United States for thirteen years. During that time, she would meet her hero, Helen Keller, at her home in Connecticut, the press dubbing Poh Lin the 'Helen Keller of the East'.

Every two years, Poh Lin returned to Singapore to visit her family. On one occasion, Elizabeth accompanied her back to Sago Lane. Poh Lin told Elizabeth that she planned to one day teach at the School for the Blind, which she did for seventeen years. On arrival at Poh Lin's home, they passed one of Sago Lane's 'death houses'. These unprepossessing buildings were owned by businesses that rented them out to families whose loved ones were critically ill. Business for the death house owners was good. They essentially provided affordable palliative care in a space big enough for relatives and friends to visit a loved one before they died. For a fee, the company would also provide attendants – who Elizabeth did not believe were medically trained – to tend to the sick relative. They also offered a solution to the nightmare of having to get a coffin up the narrow stairs and ladders to the upper storeys, and the bigger nightmare of bringing it down when it contained a corpse.

The mood in the death houses, in Elizabeth's opinion, was quite naturally mournful but also 'very colourful'.[5] Elizabeth could speak from a place of deep wisdom on the subjects of death and grief. From a young age she had known the transient nature of life and the speed with which death could be delivered. In the remote village where she was raised, Elizabeth would watch the Dusan and Kadazan headhunters return from afar, having dispensed justice: 'I could see very well, heads dangling; on my left one hero and on my right another. They [headhunters] would walk proudly past the [family] bungalow [. . .] carrying long spears on their shoulders.'[6] The elders told her that these heads belonged to transgressors, criminals, warmongers, bad men. The headhunters were seen as protectors, enforcers of justice: 'if a man could show more heads around his *kampung* or outside his hut, that was a brave man and daring enough to go and punish the evil-doers.'[7] Those men killed violently. But Elizabeth saw something honourable in the old customs of the Dusan and Kadazan: 'That was their way of seeing that justice was done.'[8]

Elizabeth was not frightened of the head-hunters. But she did fear death: 'I remember in my younger days [. . .] there were very few deaths, but each death was accompanied by a lot of wailing and not very pleasant noise such as clashing of cymbals and gongs.'[9] By now, of course, Elizabeth had seen more death than she had ever imagined. The spectre of death no longer scared her: 'death to me is nothing.'[10] When her sister took her last breath at the age of thirty-one – leaving behind three children aged five, three and one – Elizabeth observed that she was full of faith and trust in God. Elizabeth held the hand of her sister, whom she had effectively raised as her own daughter, and listened as she said: 'Ah, well, I am going to where my father and grandfather are.'[11] She did not mention their mother because she was only a one-year-old when she died. When it was over, Elizabeth thought her sister died in a state of grace and beauty.

There was neither grace nor beauty in the manner of the death of so many people at the YMCA. There was only agony, suffering and misery. Despite his grotesquely swollen face, Elizabeth Choy recognised Robert Heatlie Scott sprawled on the floor outside her cell. He was made of stern stuff. That was evident in his effort to stand up, to walk on, to hold his head erect with pride – a rare demonstration of dignity salvaged in the face of cruel and savage violence. But how much could one man suffer? Surely he was close to death. She felt utterly heartbroken for him. It was the same way she felt for the *towkay*, the eminent businessmen accustomed to a hitherto luxurious life who found themselves holed up in miserable conditions in Changi, the YMCA or Smith Street. Scott, she believed, was of a similar ilk. He was a man of influence in Singapore, a leader of great repute who played a key part in the affairs of the island. Elizabeth thought it quite natural that such a man would find the deprivation and depravity of the YMCA harder to bear than her. In her estimation, the horror of this place was worst for such men because they were not used to hardship. She felt herself blessed for the hardscrabble upbringing that had wrought in her such resilience. As Elizabeth's father observed, 'if anybody could take it, [Elizabeth] could take it.'[12]

Elizabeth grouped her own husband into this category of men whose background and upbringing rendered them ill-prepared for prison: 'All his life was pampered when he was young. Not like me. We were from the pioneering days of Sabah. We were hardy.'[13] And what of her husband? Even if Monai had not come good on his threat, Choy Khun Heng was surely dead. Elizabeth had looked into his eyes after the devil Monai had pressed the live wire into her. She could see that his spirit was broken. Thoughts of her husband, nightmares of her torture, the suffering in that hellish place were taking her down. Elizabeth recommitted herself to serving others, and used sign language to learn of the hardships and concerns of her cellmates. But the weight of their stories only pulled her down deeper. Khoo Hock Choo described being laid on his back under a tap, having a hessian bag forced over his head while the tap was turned on full. He thought he would drown. Another time he was tied to a wooden board, arms and legs pinioned while two *Kempei Tai* guards battered him with wooden planks. Tan Yew Cheng had been beaten with a pointed metal rod, told to kneel in an uncomfortable position for hours on end and subjected to the white-hot agony of the battery. He was told that if he did not confess to being a spy, he would be killed.[14] There were other prisoners summoned from the cell in relatively good physical shape who would be dragged back unconscious, covered in blood and bruises. Others would return without any evidence of physical violence, but with the haunted look of the deeply traumatised: pale faces, sunken eyes, vacant expressions. They would retreat into their own minds. Some of these poor defeated souls would not return from their next interrogation.

Elizabeth could not unburden herself of the abject misery and suffering of the people around her. She could no longer retreat to happy memories teaching the students at St Andrew's. She could no longer hear the sweet melody of 'The Bonnie Banks o' Loch Lomond'. She could no longer sense the presence of her late mother. Even her deep faith – constant and unbreakable – could not keep her from sliding into despair. Elizabeth was under-weight and underfed, and her appetite ebbed away. She forwent her meagre food rations, preferring to gift her thrice-daily rice portion to others rather than eat it herself. Her body was wasting. When she ran her fingers through her hair, she would pull out clumps. If she wrapped her hands around her waist, her long fingers from opposite hands met easily, forming a fragile circle. Her shoulders drooped and her eyelids could barely stay open; her skeletal frame sagged under the heavy weight of constant exhaustion.

The Japanese guards took note of her loss of appetite. Incredibly, a message was sent to Elizabeth's family: 'Will you [provide] some food for Mrs Choy?'[15] If she was not going to eat the food that the Japanese provided, perhaps she would be more receptive to food supplied from home. Why, after subjecting her to unimaginable agonies and very nearly killing her in the process, were the *Kempei Tai* suddenly concerned for her health? It has long been speculated that the Japanese harboured a grudging respect for Elizabeth, and such extra food rations were a tacit acknowledgement of her courage and resilience, deeply admired virtues in Japanese culture. And yet every man in Sumida's unit was profoundly racist towards the Chinese, irrespective of sex or character. The closest any officer came to paying her an actual compliment was comparing her to an official at Scotland Yard – presumably a nod to the immovable, tough archetype of the British bobby that Elizabeth embodied. Elizabeth had beaten them, but that did not make them admire her.

The decision to find her more food, to keep her alive, was driven by self-interest. Sumida knew that the torture of an innocent woman – and not just any woman, but a schoolteacher, a much-admired member of her congregation, a pillar of the Chinese community – would foment public outrage. Allowing such a woman to die while in custody might lead to civil disturbance, even rioting. In all probability, he was also considering how her death would seem in a court at the end of the war. And so Elizabeth started receiving more substantial rations of food sent from her family. Not that it helped. She continued to prioritise the welfare of others over herself: 'Every day, some [extra] food would be sent to me and of course I shared with others.'[16]

If she would not eat, she must be released. On 26 May 1944, Elizabeth was summoned from her cell. Her cellmates made a path for her. She shuffled forward and then slid under the gap at the base of the bars one final time. She stood up – ramrod-straight, chin high – and followed a guard, who led her through the corridor and back to the front office of the YMCA. She thought she was, at long last, being taken to Johore to be beheaded as Monai had promised. Death held no sway over her: 'Death now to me is nothing.'[17]

'We are going to let you go,' said a guard perched behind a desk at the front of the building. 'We believe what you did [had a] humanitarian purpose.'[18]

The *Kempei Tai* decided that Elizabeth's smuggling activity was about saving lives. This conclusion was surely reached two months earlier in March – if not earlier – at the end of the brutal week-long interrogation of Robert Heatlie Scott. Once the case against Scott, accusing him of being a master spy and leader of a fifth column, fell apart, so did his imagined link to Elizabeth. She was obviously not involved in the attack on the ships in the harbour or any other sabotage. 'You are just wanting to help,' the guard said.[19] He handed Elizabeth her handbag and the other possessions that she had surrendered before entering the building. 'You can go,' he said, busying himself with some papers on his desk, as if Elizabeth had never been there.[20] She looked at her belongings in a state of shock. After imprisoning Elizabeth for 193 days – beating her, starving her, electrocuting her, humiliating her and torturing her in front of her husband – the *Kempei Tai* had concluded that she was just trying to help. She may well have wanted to lash out in outraged protest at the injustice of it all. But she was too smart to act in such a way. Such behaviour risked being returned to a cell.

Elizabeth walked out of the building. She stopped and looked left and right. The outside world was unchanged. Cyclists and trishaw drivers rode past, the call of street hawkers and the snapping clappers of the mee-man echoed through the streets. Pedestrians kept a respectful distance from the soldiers who patrolled the streets. Elizabeth turned for home. Nobody paid her any mind, despite her shabby appearance – she was still dressed in the filthy frock she had put on more than six months earlier. She was invisible. They could not have imagined what horrors she had endured. Not that she cared anyway: 'When I was in that place,

I really thought I would never get out. And ever since the day of my release, I have considered myself as having an extra lease on life, and for that reason I don't care what happens to me now, nothing can hurt me. I feel I have reached the bottom of things, and after that nothing can ever touch me, really.'[21]

34

SWINDLERS, THIEVES, LIARS AND MURDERERS

Seven months after the attack

ROB SCOTT WAS DYING. On 10 April 1944, six months after being brought to the YMCA, he was transferred to Miyako, the hospital 12 miles from the city. Sumida's decision to send Scott to hospital was, as ever, driven by self-interest. Should Sumida ever be called to account for all that he had done, then it was better his victims die in a hospital than in a cell or interrogation room. He could even point to his attempts to save their lives by providing medical assistance. Scott was carried into the hospital on a stretcher. It was his first time in the former lunatic asylum and he had not counted on its size: 'Miyako is an enormous hospital. It was built of numbers of one-storey wards, very large, about 100 feet long by thirty feet wide.'[1] He was taken to a ward with barred windows that overlooked a verandah no patients could access. The *Kempei Tai* had repurposed this ward to treat prisoners and their own personnel. There were around two dozen men in the ward at that time, including several internees, Chinese and Indian prisoners and a handful of Japanese.

Food was scarce. The orderlies stole most of the food rationed out to the patients. What remained was limited, bland and barely edible. Medical treatment, such as it was, was minimal: 'There was a timid young Chinese doctor, Chu, who made the daily round accompanied by the Japanese sentry. Chu was terrified to speak to prisoners, especially Europeans; he would make a cursory examination, prescribe medicines [. . .] and hurry out.'[2] More often than not, Miyako's dispensary did not have the medicines Chu prescribed because they had been sold on the black market. All the same, Scott felt that Chu did his best: 'In his frightened way, he did try to help us. But he knew that drugs were short, corruption universal, the whole staff on the point of revolt because they were underpaid and half starved, and that there was not much he could do.'[3]

Death was ever present in that grim, dirty ward. The lavatories were fetid and foul. There were no bedsheets. Mattresses were sweat-soaked and streaked with faeces. But it was a lack of nursing care that was the greatest threat to survival. 'If a man was too weak to feed himself, he just died of starvation, unless there was some able-bodied patient in the ward humane enough to help him, and honest enough not to eat the other man's food himself.'[4] A creeping cynicism took hold of Scott. Throughout his internment and incarceration, he had seen troubling exhibitions of selfishness and petty greed. He had seen proud British men toady up to their Japanese captors in an effort to win favours. He had even known female internees to have shared a bed with a Japanese. All of it was done to live. Personal integrity, dignity and humanity were overridden by an instinct to survive.

There was a heartening show of kindness and care between the patients who had been interned in Changi. They banded together in that ward, looking after each other as best they could. Where possible, they also attempted to help others. Scott was particularly impressed by an internee named Bobby Burns – who was himself a 'mass of festering sores and wounds'[5] – who took it upon himself to wash, nurse and ultimately save the life of a Chinese shoemaker who had lost the use of his hands. And Dr Bowyer, the internee arrested and tortured at the Central Police Station on the charge of plotting the recapture of Singapore, who, despite ill health, set about scrubbing the toilets. Men like these two helped Scott as much as they could. Slowly his health improved.

But the seeming indifference that too many able-bodied men showed towards the suffering and plight of others in that ward was deeply dispiriting to Scott. This was particularly the case with the townsfolk. For them, providing care came at a cost. Only a very few patients had something to trade. 'In Miyako, certain prisoners were allowed by the Japanese to receive food parcels from outside. Others got money smuggled in through one of the orderlies and could buy – at extortionate rates – curry puffs, maize bread, bananas, etc., through the orderlies or from peddlers who slipped up to the grill outside our veranda when no was looking.'[6] That meant if a man admitted to Miyako had neither money nor food, his chances of survival were practically nil. For this reason, Scott observed, the highest rate of mortality was among the Chinese who came from the Central Police Station. The majority of these men suffered dysentery or dry beri-beri, a disease that affects the central nervous system, where 'the body shrivels to a skeleton, till you can see every bone, and even see the backbone from the front: legs and arms are match sticks'.[7] They would be dead not long after admission. As Scott's health improved, he did what he could to help the seriously ill, but his path to recovery was slow. Standing for any length of time was an enormous struggle. He was simply too ill to do much at all.

A few days after being admitted to Miyako, Scott was approached by a Chinese man. Emaciated, dishevelled and nursing injuries sustained at the hands of multiple torturers, Choy Khun Heng had become a nervous and diminished version of his former self. Like his wife, Elizabeth, Choy's name had been repeatedly brought up during Scott's interrogation. This was the man with whom Scott had supposedly conspired to blow up the ships in the harbour. John Long had been Choy's contact in Miyako. This was not entirely new information to Scott. He had had discerned, from whispered conversations with other prisoners and through sign language in the YMCA, that Long's 'confessions' had been particularly catastrophic for the Chinese community.

But what Choy revealed to Scott was worse than he had imagined: '[Choy] told me the story of Long swearing that I had sent Choy messages. [Long] alleged in writing, that I used to give him envelopes with the single letter "C" on them, and that his duty was merely to hand them to Choy; he did not know the contents.' Nothing, though, was more appalling than Choy's claim that Long refused to retract the false confession during his wife's torture: '[Choy] told me how he, with his wife, had confronted Long in the presence of interpreters; how Long had stuck to the charge; how he and Elizabeth Choy had been tortured.'[8]

Several days later, Long was admitted to Miyako, the first time the two men had seen each other in six months. Scott fumed at the sight of him and immediately approached Choy. 'Come on,' he said, 'let's confront Long – I want to get his version of your story.'[9] Choy was not a combative man but reluctantly went along with it. Together, the two men cornered Long. Scott bluntly asked the questions. To his astonishment, 'Long admitted the whole story, confirming Choy in every particular'.[10] Long must have seen Scott's look of disbelief. 'My conscience is clear,'[11] Long said, defiantly.

Long was not a popular figure in that ward. There were at least five other men who held him personally responsible for their arrest and their torture. The group, which was loftily self-titled the Singapore Re-Establishing Committee, comprised the Tasmanian Stanley Middlebrook, Dr Bowyer, Wulfrum Penseler, Leslie Gorsuch, a one-eyed rubber broker named Alan Ker and Long. Middlebrook, like Gorsuch, was employed in the Malayan Civil Service and evidently thought it prudent to discuss measures that could be taken to prevent Singapore from collapsing into a state of lawlessness in the event the Japanese were driven out of Malaya. Bowyer was invited onto the committee to offer thoughts on maintaining public health. Like Long, Penseler and Ker – the general manager of an Australian-owned goldmine in Malaya and the director of American Rubber Products, respectively – had standing in the business community and their contacts might prove useful in restoring order.

The committee met twice in 1942 at a time, at least to them, when the prospect of Britain's retaking of Singapore seemed good. As Scott observed: 'The Committee died a natural death when it was realised that the war was going to be a long affair.'[12] Sumida's imagination went to work the moment he learned of the committee's existence through Long. This was not a group of men engaged in an informal conversation about security and public health measures to be implemented should Britain take back Singapore by force. This was a group conspiring to undermine Japan's occupation by organising an insurgency and developing military strategies that would be communicated to British forces. Back at the YMCA, Sumida had his interrogators put pressure on Long and he confirmed Sumida's suspicions: the committee's work was indeed 'a sinister conspiracy'.[13]

Long not only corroborated Sumida's stated belief in the work of the committee, he provided names over the ensuing weeks. One by one they were arrested. All strenuously denied Long's version of events. Sumida was particularly interested in Middlebrook, who, it was discovered, was fluent in several Chinese dialects. Middlebrook's cell was turned over and several scraps of paper with mysterious and barely legible Chinese characters that made peculiar allusions to Malayan characters were found. Were these guerrillas in Malaya ordered to carry out attacks? Nothing of the sort. Middlebrook maintained a dilletante's fascination with Malayan history and politics. The scraps of paper were, in fact, first-hand accounts written more than six decades earlier about an early Chinese administrator of Kuala Lumpur named Yap Ah Loy. Yap's role in modernising Kuala Lumpur in the mid-nineteenth century was, in Middlebrook's view, worthy of a book, a project he intended to work on while interned. Sumida did not believe it for a second and had Middlebrook savagely tortured.

When it was over, Middlebrook was transferred to Sime Road Camp covered in 'large black scars such as one sees from unhealed ulcers',[14] all over his legs, shins, back and buttocks. There was also a red mark around his ankle, suggesting that he had been fettered. The night before he died, he said one final coherent sentence: 'They have been devils to me – they have treated me like fiends – I will tell you all about it and we must get it into writing as soon as we can.'[15] Middlebrook fell into a coma and died hours later.

Scott found it particularly infuriating that Long did not appear to be the least bit sorry for what he had said, that his *conscience was clear*. Scott wrote: 'I asked how on earth he could say that, when he had just admitted that he had lied to the *Kempei*, and that men and women had been tortured for the lies he told.'[16] Long clearly did not appreciate having his character impugned in such a fashion. In a voice that brooked no further discussion and a tone that bordered on aggressive, he repeated that his conscience was clear and walked off. Scott bristled: 'He did not have [the] grace even to apologise to Choy for having been the cause of Elizabeth's tortures.'[17] This was contemptible and something Scott would never forgive: 'I thought that the most disgraceful black mark against Long – worse than anything else he did – not even a word of regret.'[18]

For Scott, not everything Choy told him was bleak. Learning first-hand the story of the Choys' canteen and the risks they took in smuggling messages, supplies, radio parts and hundreds of thousands of dollars was inspiring. He was particularly affected by Elizabeth's courageous refusal to give anyone up to save herself, describing it as 'one of the most gallant incidents in the whole case. Squalid and sordid as some aspects of this futile tragedy were, they were relieved by courage such as this.'[19] He rightly believed that the fortitude of many internees and individuals in the Chinese community, particularly the Choys, diminished the *Kempei*'s conviction in the plausibility of their ludicrous case: 'As denials by A were backed independently by denials from B, and then by C, they could not but doubt whether the evidence already obtained was reliable.'[20] Not only had the Choys kept the internees alive in Changi through their smuggling activities, they had also saved many prisoners of the *Kempei Tai* through raw grit and breathtaking fortitude.

On 23 April 1944, a *Kempei* sergeant delivered two letters and a parcel to Scott in Miyako. The first letter he looked at was written in an unmistakable hand: Rosamond's. The letter had been opened – no doubt checked by Japanese sensors – but no pages were removed nor text redacted. The Japanese censor clearly did not perceive any threat from a letter jointly written by two young children. To Scott, the letter from his family 'was a godsend'.[21] This was the first he had heard from them since being returned to Singapore from Sumatra two years earlier.

Reacquainting himself with his children's handwriting sent Scott's spirits soaring. Yet one sentence was utterly confounding: 'Mummy says to tell you our horse won on the course where she had that lucky bet.'[22] Either this was a reference to a visit to the track in Sydney that had been recounted in previous letters that had gone undelivered, or Rosamond 'had fallen in with a gang of crooks and had taken up horse racing'.[23] Scott was talking over the puzzling passage with the others when it dawned on him. He remembered their epic voyage as newlyweds in the rusted old car: 'North Africa! And the time [Rosamond] accidentally backed a winner at Cairo.'[24] While in the old Egyptian capital, they had visited the racecourse. She had put a bet on the roughie in the steeplechase and the horse won. The feature of the steeplechase was the water jump. The passage was a cryptic reference to a major development in the war. 'Our horse' (Allied troops) who had surmounted the 'water jump' (the Mediterranean from North Africa) and won. In short, the Allies had landed in Sicily and were surging northwards through Italy. 'I was delighted,' wrote Scott, 'not so much with the news – which we had had already – as with [her] cleverness and my own stupidity.'[25]

The other letter and the parcel both came from Ann Paxton, a friend of the Scotts. She revealed that she had heard that he'd been interned in Singapore. Ann would doubtless have conveyed this information to Rosamond, which came as an immense relief to Scott: 'This was a great load off my mind, as the Japanese had kept my name off all lists for the first year.'[26] While interned in Changi, Scott had sent two postcards to Sydney and had a couple of others smuggled out under a false name. He rightly assumed that the letters would never make it to their destination.

Rosamond had been informed that her husband was missing and presumed dead. She drew from a widow's pension, but steadfastly believed he was alive. On learning that Scott was alive in June 1943, life for Rosamond 'had a new and wonderful meaning, the sun shines brighter and the otherwise raucous birds have attained a new and tuneful song'.[27] In one of her first letters to her husband, she offered delightful glimpses of their children growing up in their father's absence: '[Susan] is her own cheery self again and really getting very pretty. She is having extra drawing lessons as she is so keen on it and shows very definite talent [. . .] You would be very proud of your young son. He is doing very well and seems to be very much on the spot in his work, he is very sweet.'[28]

Ann's letter came with an American Red Cross parcel, 'for which she had wangled a permit from the American Provost Marshal'.[29] To Scott's astonishment, every item on the printed list of contents contained within the parcel was accounted for, 'down to a miniature chess board and a packet of safety pins'. All told, the items amounted to a luxurious smorgasbord of delicacies and delights: 'It contained a shirt, and four towels, and six hand-kerchiefs, and lots of soap; the biggest shaving brush I have ever seen, and the smallest piece of shaving soap; a couple of tooth-brushes; and small packets of raisins, prunes, Horlick's [malted milk powder], and cheese.'[30] Scott evenly divided the food among the men in the ward. The soap was shared until it was gone, and everyone used the towels.

How Ann Paxton's parcel made it to Scott is a mystery. Very few such parcels ever made it through to internees and practically none that were addressed to a prisoner of the *Kempei Tai*. It seems hard to believe that this was an administrative or clerical error, particularly given it was delivered by a non-commissioned officer of the *Kempei Tai*. Which leaves open the possibility that its delivery was approved on Sumida's instruction. If so – and there is no way to prove it – then why? It is conceivable that this was Sumida's way of recognising Scott's bravery, fortitude and resilience. But this was not Sumida's way. He was at pains to remind others of his links to Tokyo; a man who revelled in the status and rank of his position. Men of such vanity do not do anything anonymously. Which means that if Sumida was respon-sible for allowing the parcel to find its way to Scott, then he did it for the same reason he approved his main adversary's transfer to Miyako – he needed to keep him alive.

Sumida summed up the Number One Work in one word – 'unsatisfactory'.[31] His investigation was, in fact, an atrocity. Putting to one side the gross imposition of human suffering endured by the fifty-seven British internees and dozens of Chinese who were imprisoned as part of the case, there were – at that point – at least ten internees who had died as a direct consequence of the interrogations he had ordered. A further five men would die over the course of the next six months from a combination of illness and the injuries they suffered while interrogated. The total number of deaths among the townsfolk has never been tallied, but the deaths of at least five others have been linked to the investigation. Sumida would later state: 'I should like to take this opportunity to express my deepest regret for what happened.' He was quick to add, 'In spite of unavoidable circumstances.'[32] As apologies go, this was at once qualified and insincere. By every objective measure, the fate of all who died and suffered was avoidable.

There was a degree of cognitive dissonance to the manner in which Sumida conducted his probe that perhaps reflects the different aspects of his complex character. He was, at once, the blind zealot convinced of Hirohito's divine right to rule Asia who clung steadfastly to the belief that Japan would win the war, as well as the cunning schemer who surely knew that the Allies would emerge victorious. Like so many top commanders engaged in espionage and counter-espionage, he could hold two competing ideas in his head. In this way, he was able to relentlessly and brutally carry on his investigation to the bitter end in pursuit of what he deemed 'the truth' – that there was a fifth column operating under the command of Robert Heatlie Scott – while also making provisions for the probability that he had been wrong all along. Should his more reasoned mind prove correct, Sumida had a plan for the day he would be dragged before a court to answer for what he had done.

From the outset, Sumida built a defence that hinged on plausible deniability about the specifics of how interrogations were conducted: 'My instructions emphasized that no unduly harsh torture should be applied and that as little of it was to be used as possible.'[33] Having men and women die in his custody in one of his hellish prisons was naturally one of his defence's greatest vulnerabilities. For this reason, prisoners at the point of death would be transported to a hospital. Should they miraculously pull through – like Scott – he could claim that he'd had a hand in their survival. Should they die, which they often did, he could claim that he at least provided medical treatment when their condition deteriorated. He also made sure that the doctors and orderlies treating those men ascribed their deaths to disease or under-nourishment, factors that were ultimately beyond his control. He would later say:

> I believe the major cause [of death] was dysentery, which if not directly killing a person would cause emaciation and bring out some latent disease. The second reason for emaciation was the long period of detention with little scope for freedom. Thirdly, food had something to do with it, as it did not have nutritive ingredients.[34]

Sumida would also deploy the tactic of deflection. He laid much of the responsibility of the treatment of prisoners on one of his senior officers, Warrant Officer Ueno. None of the surviving internees or civilians who were interrogated would ever mention Ueno. The historical record is largely silent on his service and, conveniently for Sumida, he did not survive the war. Prior to the attack on Japanese shipping in Singapore Harbour, Ueno was responsible for the general affairs of the *Kempei Tai*, dealing with Japanese military personnel, maintenance and other tasks. After the attack, Ueno would essentially take responsibility for the health of the prisoners in the YMCA, Smith Street and Central Station. He was, nominally, Monai's direct superior. But as one Chinese interpreter observed: '[Ueno] was an old man and inexperienced M.P. [*Kempei Tai* officer who] left all things to his deputy [Sergeant] Monai.'[35] In addition to the torturing of prisoners, Sumida would have Ueno shoulder the blame for the food and outbreaks of disease.

There were, of course, other immediate concerns weighing on Sumida's mind than what might happen should Japan lose the war. He had to answer to his superiors. Sumida had received orders to gather reports concerning the blowing up of the ships in the harbour, to arrest suspects in Changi, to incarcerate spies in Syonan and to investigate and clean up enemy elements. His efforts turned up nothing that could substantiate any of his more absurd suspicions about well-organised spy rings, fifth columns, saboteurs, secret radio transmitters in Chinese tombs, evidence of collusion with communist Chinese insurgents and contact with the British in India. To be sure, radio receivers, vast sums of money, correspondence and other contraband had been discovered in Changi. Sumida's detective work also revealed links that existed between the Chinese community and the British internees. But none of what was revealed justified the six-month-long so-called *Ichigo Hosaku*, which expended huge resources and manpower, to say nothing of the misery and suffering imposed on so many. The party or parties responsible for the harbour attack remained a mystery and there was no longer anyone left to torture.

The Number One Work's aftermath, if not properly handled, could prove devastating to his reputation and therefore his career. He needed to save face. Sumida's superiors were expecting a report in December 1943 and it was now April 1944. Sumida probably pointed to the epidemic of disease that had swept through the prisoners as the reason for his delay; he surely made no reference to the fact he simply did not have the necessary information to bring the matter to a satisfactory close – with the guilty parties revealed and ready to face justice.

Sometime towards the end of April, he submitted his report to his commanding officer, Colonel Kojima Masanori. His report did not survive the war. It is highly unlikely that he admitted *Ichigo Hosaku* was a failure. His report instead recommended formal charges against several key individuals. The plan was to have them tried in a military court immediately. But they were all too sick. As Sumida pointed out, they 'would have been placed in the military prison right away, but through lack of accommodation they remained in the *Kempei* cell until May or a little after'.[36]

Scott was taken back to the YMCA with Long and several others. His previously bloated body was now a shrivelled, undernourished bag of skin and bones. The date was 8 May 1944. He had been given exactly four weeks of substandard care at Miyako. His condition had improved too, his swollen waistline contracting from 36 inches back to 26 inches in less than ten days. Scott attributed the improvement in his health to injections, but he does not name the drug with which he was injected. Beri-beri is caused by a prolonged thiamine deficiency that is easily treated with improved nutrition. The treats in the parcel from Ann Paxton very likely helped him, but Scott was the first to admit, 'I was far from fit.'[37]

By now, Sumida had cleared Scott of any serious wrongdoing. But until the matter was cleared up formally in military court, he would continue to be treated as the most dangerous man in the YMCA. That meant putting him back into cell number two, 'the worst of the lot, because it was opposite the sentry'.[38] That Long, Penseler, Bowyer and Hilary Cameron Russell Rendle, another senior administrator in the Malayan Civil Service, were all put in there with him was a relief. Not so much for their company – prisoners were still forbidden from communicating with each other, besides which he had nothing to say to Long – but because it meant there would be no more interrogations. Had the investigation been ongoing, the internees would be placed in separate cells to prevent them from getting their stories straight.

Life in the YMCA, however, was no less horrific. Nothing had changed: the open commode and its foul stench, the ceiling light constantly on, the food always meagre and pitiful. In addition to the same prisoners who had been wallowing in the cells for seven months, there were now a smattering of Japanese, 'in as usual for corruption and forgery and smuggling',[39] and over a dozen Chinese. There were some new arrivals, including an old Chinese peasant woman brought in to apply pressure to her husband in a repeat of the Choy saga. The husband was accused of fifth-column activity and she was periodically called out, presumably to witness his torture. She refused her food and cried for her husband until she was eventually taken to another cell.

One of the Chinese cellmates was a strongly built man of middle age. Scott never discovered the circumstances under which he was arrested, but it was likely on a charge of espionage, sabotage, communist leanings or some combination of all three. Towards the end of May, he came in for a frightful beating over a long day. He was dragged back into the cell and dumped among the other prisoners, barely conscious. He did not have time to recover before contracting dysentery: 'He could not crawl to the lavatory in the corner without help and he had to have his clothes washed, and the floor mopped up, continually.'[40]

The Chinese prisoner had contracted bacillary dysentery, a strain of the inflammatory bowel disease that in extreme cases results in the afflicted passing high volumes of faeces streaked with blood and mucous. Scott and the other prisoners did what they could to help, but his condition deteriorated quickly. With a dozen people crammed together, and small rivers of blood and faeces beginning to pool on the floor, these were prime conditions for an outbreak. Scott was the first to come down with a fever. He quickly lost his appetite and started suffering intense abdominal pain and nausea. In an attempt to stymie an epidemic, Scott and the Chinese prisoner were transferred to Miyako. They were loaded onto the tray of an open truck, barely conscious as the tropical rain poured down on them. They were driven to the prisoner ward and placed on beds next to each other. The Chinese man was in dreadful shape: 'He lay there, unable to do anything for himself, in a welter of blood and mucous, lacking the strength to reach out and take his dish of gruel.'[41] He called out for help. Scott could do little: 'I was almost helpless myself – 132 motions in four days, which is more than one an hour day and night – and I could do nothing.'[42] Three days later, the Chinese man died.

Once again, defying all expectations – perhaps even his own – Scott pulled through. He owed his life to a Chinese shopkeeper named Wee Aik Tek. Scott had heard Tek's name back in Changi.

He had been 'the channel by which thousands of dollars had come out to the Camp, and from the beginning of internment had done everything he possibly could to help the internees'.[43] Tek was known to be a man of influence in the Chinese business community and for this reason was approached by the Bishop of Singapore to help. Like the Choys, he acted as a conduit between the townsfolk – whom he managed to coax into giving vast sums of money – and internees who ventured outside the camp. The risks he took were immense. An informer eventually ratted out Tek and he was arrested sometime in October 1943, another victim of Sumida's Number One Work.

Though well into middle age, Tek was brutally tortured. He was transferred to Miyako after collapsing with beri-beri and heart trouble. Slowly, Tek's health recovered. In that first month in Miyako, Tek and Scott forged a firm friendship. They worked together to replace their filthy clothes, sourcing and repurposing wire, thread and stolen garments to make shorts and shirts. This was not the only way Tek deployed his resourcefulness. He used his seemingly inexhaustible influence to get a message to the Chinese community. Street hawkers started to appear outside the barred windows of the ward and would pass him food. The Japanese were fully aware that Tek was bringing food into the hospital, and they did not mind it one bit, since an external supplier of food slightly eased the ward's reliance on the meagre hospital rations. The practice also improved health outcomes because Tek divided the food among those who needed it most.

To help Scott build his strength, Tek would give him the largest portion of food that he smuggled into the ward. Despite Tek's help, it took Scott three and a half months to regain some semblance of his health. Gorsuch, in Miyako with beri-beri and dysentery, was the only other Changi internee. The ward was otherwise peopled by a diverse array of characters from all over Asia in whose company Scott was completely at ease. Speaking so many languages certainly helped him during those months, as did his skill in diplomacy and the easy way he endeared himself to all people. This was also important for his survival, because with a few exceptions, he was now in the company of a cast of reprobates, misfits and killers. The prisoner ward in Miyako was, in fact, a very dangerous place.

There was Joseph, an Indian railway clerk and part-time cock fighter who made no effort to conceal the vicious stab wound in his chest sustained, presumably, during the fight that led to his murder charge and incarceration. There was the traitor from Peshawar whom Scott christened Gaga Khan on account of his limited intellect and inability to speak any known language. (A giant of a man, Gaga was rumoured to have been imprisoned after inducing several comrades within his unit in the Indian National Army to mutiny. Nobody knew for sure, because Gaga was unable to answer questions.) There was the Chinese junk owner from Peking who had made a fortune smuggling goods into Japanese-controlled Singapore before being arrested for forging banana notes. And then there was Liu Yu-chen, the intelligent young man from Shanghai accused of being a communist, and a nameless Malayan thief who stole everyone's food.

But there was no greater miscreant than the ward's only Japanese prisoner, the interpreter Yamaguchi. Scott had first encountered Yamaguchi in cell number two during his most recent stint back at the YMCA. Like all Japanese prisoners incarcerated in the *Kempei* cells, he was given certain privileges, including the right to wear socks and the right to speak. Yamaguchi *loved* to talk. He was a swindler and a hypocrite, occasionally prone to high-minded rants – he once berated the other Chinese prisoners for not doing enough to help their fellow countryman who had been afflicted with dysentery, it never occurring to him or to the Japanese that 'they themselves ought to do anything about it'.[44]

Fluent in Malay, Yamaguchi had worked as an interpreter for the *Kempei Tai* in Batavia. He used his position to bribe *Kempei* suspects. As the only individual in the interrogation room fluent in Malay and Japanese, he could shape the outcome of an investigation by changing a suspect's answers in his translations. Yamaguchi's ask was simple: give me all the money you have and I will get you out of here and keep your family safe, or you and everyone you know will die a painful death. In this way, Yamaguchi embezzled huge sums of money before his scheme was discovered by members of his unit. He was sent directly to the YMCA to be reformed. He ended up in Miyako suffering an acute venereal disease. Sexually transmitted diseases were rife among the Japanese officers and enlisted men. But it is possible Yamaguchi, an inveterate liar without scruples, made the whole thing up or at least exaggerated his predicament to get out of his hellhole torture chamber.

At first, Yamaguchi and Scott bonded. They were both avid smokers and, along with the murderer Joseph, 'by one means or another, acquired some cigarettes, cheroot stubs, paper, and matches, with which [they] held smoking orgies in the bathroom when the coast was clear'.[45] A skilled exponent of extortion and blackmail, Yamaguchi made a sizeable contribution to the cigarette and cheroot supplies by threatening to expose the smuggling activities of the sentries.

He was unapologetically driven by self-interest. He nonetheless exhibited the zeal and fanatism in Hirohito's mission, notions if not inherited then certainly burnished while in the service of the *Kempei Tai*. The fervent belief in Japan winning the war and Hirohito supplanting the European powers and reigning over this region were, for Yamaguchi, accepted as articles of faith. Predictably, he grew increasingly frosty towards Scott as news of Japanese setbacks filtered into the ward. Eventually he stopped smoking with Joseph and Scott altogether, turning 'violently anti-European on account of the war development in the Pacific'.[46] Yamaguchi got his news from the Japanese sentries, whereas Scott got his news from a Chinese communist with a contact on the outside who somehow sourced and smuggled English and Chinese newspapers through the window of the ward: 'a risky business, but worth it.'[47] As Japan's defeat seemed increasingly more likely, Yamaguchi grew sullen and kept to himself. One day, he quite unexpectedly approached Scott.

'Where did you get that?' Yamaguchi barked, pointing at the enormous cheroot. 'The Indian orderly gave it to you?'[48]

Scott was aware that Yamaguchi was having a row with the Indian orderly, who was known to be 'the biggest crook of the lot'.[49] Scott's cheroot had, in fact, come from one of the Bengali policemen who patrolled Miyako. It was a gift, a show of appreciation after Scott had helped a sick Indian prisoner. Scott was damned if he was going to give the Bengali policeman away to Yamaguchi. He told him to leave off and continued smoking. Yamaguchi slunk away and snitched: 'The snake then went to the sentry, they took their boots off (ordinarily you could always hear a Japanese sentry coming) and tiptoed back and caught me red-handed.'[50]

The Japanese sentry was a newly enlisted *Kempei* man – 'a new, raw and inexperienced country bumpkin'[51] – no doubt eager to impress his superiors by exposing a smuggling ring run by the non-Japanese sentries. Scott needed to tread carefully. This child probably thought that catching a high-value prisoner breaking the law might secure him an early promotion. Little did he know that a sizeable portion of the *Kempei Tai* were on the take. The more likely outcome would be the handing out of some horrifically punitive measure to the guilty parties.

Scott noticed the Bengali policeman nervously saunter over to see what was going on. He was 'sweating with fear'[52] and for good reason. If Scott fingered the Bengali as the culprit, he may lose his head – the Japanese had executed others for much less. The *Kempei* sentry demanded to know who had given Scott the cheroot. Scott told him that he had found it: 'a very lame excuse, which might have passed if I had been smoking a butt, as the police smoke cheroots and sometimes threw their butts on the floor.'[53] The prisoners in the ward would scavenge for discarded butts, gleefully smoking the final dregs. But it was inconceivable that a sentry would discard such a fat cheroot. It was practically the size of cigar.

There was also the question of where Scott had found a light. Scott said it was handed to him by 'a passing lunatic'.[54] Mentally handicapped men were a constant presence outside the building. They would sweep the gutters around the ward, muttering to themselves, oblivious to the world around them. The idea that one of these men had a box of matches and could be coaxed into lighting the cheroot of a patient in the prisoner ward was absurd. 'But of course no one believed such obvious lies, they were indeed about the poorest I ever told the *Kempei*, and I was ashamed of them but couldn't think of anything better on the spur of the moment.'[55] For two years, Scott had dissembled, obfuscated, covered up and lied to save his life and the lives of others. In the end, he learned that 'some things can simply not be explained away'.[56]

The sentry duly reported to his superiors that Scott was found in possession of a cheroot. Had Scott given up the Bengali, there may have been graver consequences. But what could the *Kempei Tai* do to Scott that had not already been done? This man had been tortured on the false assumption that he was running a spy ring out of Changi and had orchestrated a major attack on the harbour. Smoking a cheroot on the hospital ward did not, in comparison, rise to the level of a punishable offence. All the same, Scott was livid with Yamaguchi: 'I never expected that [he] would go so far as to tell tales about my smoking.'[57] The ward bristled with tension. Everyone knew that Yamaguchi was a liar. It was the fact he was ratting on people that had everyone on edge. He was a very dangerous man to cross as he still had influence. Clearly he was prepared to use that influence to settle scores.

With not a small measure of satisfaction, Scott watched on as Yamaguchi became the author of his own demise. He duped the young and highly gullible *Kempei* sentry into letting him leave the ward under the pretence of teaching the Malayan kitchen staff how to cook Japanese delicacies. The kitchen staff were Malayan. It made sense. Yamaguchi was fluent in their language and seemed to know what he was talking about when it came to the culinary arts. Besides, a different menu would be a welcome change to the bland daily offerings that dribbled out of the kitchen. And so, whenever he was on duty, the sentry would look the other way as Yamaguchi slipped out. There was, of course, no change in either the style or quality of the food. Yamaguchi always had an excuse: the ingredients were substandard, the kitchen utensils were inadequate, the kitchen staff were too stupid to know how to follow his instructions. The sentry believed every word. Had he bothered to follow Yamaguchi, he would have observed that he never actually went to the kitchen. Instead, he walked directly to the canteen, where he bought up large quantities of cigarettes at the cheaper rates reserved for Japanese soldiers. How Yamaguchi convinced the canteen workers that he was a soldier is a mystery. He probab,ly told them he was a *Kempei Tai* interpreter, which – like the best lies – was partially true. Having bulk-purchased cigarettes at the cheaper rate, he then ambled around the hospital flogging them at an outrageous margin and gambling with the proceeds. Inevitably, he was caught: 'the Japanese Director [of Miyako] flew into a rage and made the *Kempei* take him back to the YMCA at once.'[58]

The prisoners in the prisoner ward breathed a sigh of relief when Yamaguchi was gone. But rather than use his selfishness as an edifying warning of the self-destructive perils of self-absorption, Scott observed, 'the ward relapsed into its usual placid existence of smuggling, bathroom smoking, petty theft, and starvation'.[59] Aside from isolated examples, there was no attitude of adopting a mutually beneficial system of sharing, much less of cooperating in a spirt of kindness, care and empathy. To be sure, Miyako was a physical relief from the hellish agony of the YMCA. But it was not a spiritually uplifting place. The selfish scheming and indifference to the suffering of others left Scott feeling hollow. What on earth had this war – all this suffering – been about? What hope was there for humanity?

To this point, Scott kept at bay the feelings of despondency that had threatened to overwhelm many other Changi internees. They felt as if their government had let them down, that their internment was unnecessary: 'that they had stayed [because] they had been told to stay and do their jobs.'[60] While sitting on the Governor's War Council in the final weeks before the capitulation, Scott had argued vehemently against the policy of keeping so many fit young men not only of fighting age but with useful knowledge of Singapore and Malaya when their capture and internment was inevitable. 'I had put it to the War Council in January 1942 that a few hundred able-bodied men of military age, who knew the country and could help us to recapture it, should be sent off – such as policemen, forest rangers, civil servants, survey and mines department men, planters and tin miners.'[61] Scott was sharply rebuked: 'the Council was horrified at the idea of letting able-bodied men go.'[62] It was yet another example of the misplaced belief in Singapore's invincibility.

The policy that forbade these men from leaving left many embittered. The internees were particularly venomous towards those who, prior to the capitulation, had set about 'wangling permits or without permission at all had gone [and] were now being hailed as sensible men, and would come back covered with medals and bag all the best jobs'.[63] Some harboured legitimate concerns that, while those who left would win the adulation and praise of their countrymen, those who did as instructed would be derided as idlers and cowards. Sure enough, there were disturbing reports from home about a memoir by Oswald Gilmour in which he dramatically recounted his escape from Singapore.[64] One internee recorded in his diary: 'Letters received mention a book about the attack on Singapore by one Gilmour in which he says anyone could have got away as he did, but people were cowering terror-stricken in their houses!'[65] One internee subsequently received a letter from his wife in Changi towards the very end of the war that began: 'I can't understand why you didn't escape. It seems to have been so easy!'[66]

Scott was sympathetic to their feelings of frustration and betrayal. He was even moved to write a bit of doggerel based on the army officer and poet Thomas Osbert Mordaunt's 'The Call'. The poem, written while Mordaunt was encamped in Prussia, is essentially a call to arms.

> Sound, sound the clarion, fill the fife,
> Throughout the sensual world proclaim,
> One crowded hour of glorious life
> Is worth an age without a name.

Scott's rendering mimics the poem's rhyme and metre, but transforms Mordaunt's grand statement of the inherent gallantry of a soldier's life into a satirical lament, dripping with irony:

> Sound, sound the clarion, beat the drum
> To all the listening world proclaim
> That he who stayed was but a bum
> And only idiots played the game
>
> Sound, sound the clarion, beat the drum
> See, See! The conquering heroes come!
> Hid in the cabins of our wives
> Rightly gloriously we saved our lives;
> We dodged the bomb, we dodged the sword:
> In Africa we reap award
>
> Having braved the ravening seas
> At last we loll in affluent ease.

But sometime at our evening drink
Of our deserted friends we think,
And though we know we are their betters,
Try to comfort them with letters.

And though doing what was ordered
Very near to madness bordered,
And though our splendid getaway
Was – Oh, by far – a better way
Yet, when the hurly burly's over
And we roll in cash and clover,

We won't forget our stupid friends –
We'll have the fags and they the ends.
Another bumper to remind us
Of the friend we left behind us!

Scott had experienced as harrowing an incarceration as can be imagined. Yet all this time, he had never indulged what he derided as a 'mood of bitterness – not unmixed with vainglorious self pity'.[67] But the longer he languished in Miyako, feelings of cynicism and despair chipped away.

On 1 October 1944, a detachment of *Kempei Tai* guards turned up, looking for Scott, Gorsuch and Wee Aik Tek. The Chinese shoemaker, whom Tek had nicknamed 'Black Heart' as a nod to his lack of gratitude to Gorsuch, who had nursed him back to health when he was half-dead, was also taken. They were bundled into a car and driven to the YMCA, where they were informed that they were going to be tried in a military court. A guard produced a length of thick rope and bound the four prisoners together. They were led outside and driven to Outram Road Gaol, where they would await their trial. Scott knew he was embarking on the final leg of his epic journey. It would surely not end well. How could it? And yet he seemed relieved that he was moving to the final act, however it may turn out, and above all thankful to put his stint in hospital behind him: 'I think that's enough about Miyako.'[68]

35
KANGAROO COURT

Twelve months after the attack

MORE THAN TWO YEARS had passed since Rob Scott was first incarcerated in Outram Road Gaol. Since then, the prison had been divided into a civilian section and a military section. Scott and the others were assigned to cells in the military section, and just as well; the civilian component held around 1500 criminals. The occupying force did not seem to know what to do with them – and nor did they care. They were kept in 'lonely cells, way down at the end of the block'.[1] A chalk circle would often appear on the lintel of these cells, marking the occupants within for execution. The Japanese assigned Malay and Indian guards who were greatly understaffed and who maintained order by administering savage beatings and viciously quashing any hint – real or imagined – of rebellion. The air was thick with the smell of faeces, from the 'hundreds of slop buckets'[2] that were left unattended inside the cells. The atmosphere of the civilian section was one of decay and disease; men 'were dying like flies of starvation or disease'.[3]

The military block was similarly overcrowded and unsanitary, but better resourced. This side of the gaol was run almost entirely by Japanese guards, with a smattering of Chinese who cooked and cleaned. Most of the prisoners were Japanese officers, troops and civilians, 'in for every crime under the sun: forgery of notes, smuggling, murder, desertion, disobedience, theft, corruption'.[4] Additionally, there were around seventy POWs who were being held for attempted escape, having somehow avoided summary execution. The rest were civilian political prisoners, who included – much to Scott's dismay – many internees swept up in the Double Tenth investigation. Scott had wrongly assumed that those who had been taken out of the YMCA had been sent back to Changi. They were instead left to rot in this place, all in a shocking state of health, some close to death.

On arrival, Scott, Tek, Gorsuch and Black Heart were taken to a room. They were stripsearched and had all their belongings confiscated, 'except one shirt and one pair of trousers – no socks, shoes, or even a handkerchief'.[5] They were then split up and assigned a cell. Scott recalled there having being more space in the Outram Road Gaol: 'In 1942, we had had a cell each, now it was two to a cell.'[6] Scott now shared his cell with a young Eurasian named Earl Ebert, a man with a rugged bearing whose build might have been solid had he been properly fed, and who pulsed with energy. He'd been arrested a year earlier for passing messages to internees in Changi. He was beaten but emerged high-spirited and in better shape than most. He was also 'extremely hot headed [. . .] constantly in hot water for talking and breaking rules and cheeking the sentries'. Scott thought him 'a splendid companion'.[7]

After making their introductions, Scott produced a bottle of vitamin tablets from the fob pocket of his flannel trousers. Astonished, Ebert asked how on earth Scott had managed to get the vitamins past the guards. The bottle had come from Ann Paxton's parcel, the remnants of which had been confiscated with some of Scott's other personal effects when he was returned to the YMCA after his initial stint in Miyako. On his stop-off at the YMCA prior to being transferred to Outram Road, Scott was handed back his kit. He knew that the Outram Road guards would confiscate the pills during the strip search, so he shoved the bottle into his fob pocket. From extensive experience – by now Scott had been searched 'dozens of times' – he registered one pocket the Japanese almost universally overlooked: '[I] had noticed that the Japanese don't usually look in a fob pocket because they never have one themselves in their trousers.'[8]

The vitamin tablets were a crucial supplement to the prisoners' inadequate diet, and were carefully rationed and closely guarded. During their daily exercise sessions, Scott and Ebert doled them out to the sickest men in the prison and strictly rationed them between themselves. The vitamins seemed to have magical medicinal properties that returned sick men to good health. Scott wondered if there was a placebo effect at play, particularly among the more gravely ill men: 'Whether the pills really did them good, or whether it was their imagination, I don't know, but [those who received the pills] certainly improved.'[9]

To prevent the Japanese from finding and confiscating the vitamins, the bottle was carefully concealed in the cell to avoid discovery during routine inspections. Weeks passed without a problem, until the inevitable crisis. On returning from an exercise session, Scott and Ebert were told that they were changing cells. This was a standard practice the guards used to prevent prisoners hoarding and hiding contraband. There were only twenty tablets left, but Ebert refused to write them off. He devised a scheme to retrieve them with the same wilful intent that characterised his approach to all things in life.

'At all costs,' he said to Scott, 'we must get them back.'

'But how?' Scott asked.[10]

Ebert, who spoke Japanese more proficiently than Scott, simply planned to ask the guards to get the bottle for them. If it were not for Ebert's skills in persuasion – he once talked a sentry into delivering a letter to his fiancée and his brother, who was also interned – Scott may have written the plan off as ludicrous. Instead, he went along with it. The two men agreed to a strategy that was bold, audacious and bound to fail.

The following day, Ebert called out for the sentry from their new cell, explaining that Scott had an important message. Ebert, acting as interpreter, told Scott to explain the problem.

'The *Kempei*,' Scott said to the sentry, '[gave] me a bottle of medicine and told me to take it into the prison and take it every day, as they knew how sick I was. Alas, the bottle [is] in our old cell.'[11]

Ebert translated in a most concerned tone. Scott then asked if the sentry would retrieve his medicine bottle. Scott could hardly believe it when he agreed: 'the sentry of course had merely to ask the office sergeant to discover that this was a lie from beginning to end; but he didn't.'[12] The sentry fetched the bottle. There was only one problem: 'He said he couldn't give me the bottle, because prisoners were not allowed to keep anything made of glass in the cells.'[13] Broken glass could be used as a weapon against the guards or to attempt suicide. Scott wanted that glass. He intended to break the bottle and use a glass splinter to cut his toenails. Otherwise, Scott would have to trim his toenails with his fingernails, 'which I have done, but it is not as neat a job as cutting them with a splinter of glass'.[14]

Scott protested that the pills would only retain their efficacy if they remained in the bottle, which was utter nonsense. The sentry would not bend. He emptied the pills into Scott's extended hand. In the end, Scott did not even have to lament the loss of the bottle. 'In a couple of days, we had scrounged some broken glass and a couple of nails (for hunting bugs) and smuggled them successfully back into the cell.'[15] Getting these objects into the cell was no mean feat. After the daily exercise, the prisoners were strip-searched, but 'there are always ways and means of getting a thing in [to the cell]. And of hiding them when you get them there.'[16]

While they waited for their trial to commence, Scott and Ebert enjoyed 'a very pleasant five weeks together – that is, as pleasant as it could be in such a place'.[17] They whiled away the hours discussing the war, sharing humorous yarns, teaching each other poetry. Ebert regaled Scott with his rugby and hockey exploits throughout Malaya, while Scott held Ebert in his thrall, recounting his tale of survival aboard the *Giang Bee*, his capture in Sumatra, return to Singapore, incarceration and torture. Through charm and persuasion, Ebert managed to prise information out of the Japanese guards, too. They learned that they were to face military court on 7 November. The night before the trial, both men had reconciled themselves to their fate. They knew that the trial would be a sham; the court would find them guilty of some false crime and they would doubtless be executed: 'We spent what we thought was to be our last evening together philosophising on the world and its ways.'[18]

The following day, Scott and Ebert were escorted out of the prison. They were driven down Bukit Timah Road, past the Singapore Botanic Gardens to Raffles College, a stately white building with broad arches that fringed its wide arcade. Japanese officers hurriedly made their way around, generally ignoring the prisoners. Scott and Ebert were ushered inside, where they met Ebert's brother and two other prisoners.

Guards escorted them inside. Much to Scott's surprise, 'the Court Martial was impressive and dignified, with all the outward semblance of justice'.[19] He was tried alongside a man named Walter Curtis, who had been charged with bringing a radio into Changi. The two men stood in the centre of the court facing a bench of five, one of whom was the prosecuting officer. It was all very formal, with all the trappings of a proper trial: 'The charges were read in Japanese and English; we were formally asked to confirm our identities and signatures.'[20] The prosecuting officer turned to the other judges and read the charges.

Once the prosecuting officer concluded his introductory comments, he turned to Walter Curtis. Curtis was an engineer. After his internment, the Japanese permitted him to live in the city for several months with a number of other British engineers to clean up the mess after the Fall of Singapore. During this time, Curtis acquired a short-wave radio. When his job was done, Curtis – who had grown attached to the radio – smuggled it back into the camp.

All of this information was known to the Japanese, since Curtis had admitted to it. The question the prosecuting officer wanted answered was 'whether he was wilfully breaking the law, or whether he had not realised that this was an offence'.[21] Scott observed that 'the accused's state of mind was always important to the Japanese – was he acting out of hatred and antagonism for the Japanese, or just being stupid and ignorant?'[22] During his cross-examination, Curtis did his best to skirt the issue. He repeatedly made the point that it was not a crime punishable by death to own a radio in the early days of the occupation: 'Walter made a great play with this point, but could not wriggle out of the fact that he had subsequently brought the radio into the camp concealed in a suitcase and had evaded a search.'[23] After summing up, the prosecutor turned to the presiding judge and asked for a sentence of four years' penal servitude.

Now it was Scott's turn. The charges against Scott were based on the information that he had freely admitted. Sumida had, in a way, been honest in what he told Scott in the first interrogation: the Japanese justice system required a confession before charges could be brought. For the first time, Scott began to wonder: did he actually have a chance of survival? That he never admitted under extreme torture to the serious – and utterly false – accusation that he had orchestrated the attack on the harbour meant that perhaps he stood a fighting chance. When the prosecutor referenced

Scott's position at the Ministry of Information, however, he began to lose hope. 'To operate short wave radios was an offence under the order of the Japanese Military Governor of Malaya,' the prosecutor stated.[24] But to conduct propaganda, he continued, was a far graver offence.

The prosecutor conceded that all countries found it necessary to control public opinion through the dissemination of carefully filtered and curated information. Japan was acutely aware of Britain's powerful and effective methods of propaganda in winning hearts and minds in World War I. 'It goes without saying,' he said, 'that Nippon must control public opinion in all territories administered by her.'[25] Every effort needed to be made to prevent the enemy-controlled information from seeping into the minds of the population: 'they must not be allowed access to any news except that which is issued to them by the Nipponese authorities.'[26] The prosecutor delivered these statements in a flat tone, the kind used when pronouncing hackneyed axioms.

For Scott, it was an interesting insight into the Japanese psyche. The Japanese regarded propaganda as a legitimate, useful and important weapon of war, while holding enemy propagandists in contempt; they were 'the lowest of the low'[27] – a tawdry, scheming, unseemly, unethical and undignified bunch, but incredibly dangerous. For the enemy to wield this weapon of war against populations that would ultimately come under Japanese control was viewed as an extreme offence: a threat that could undermine Japan's legitimacy and ability to control non-Japanese people now under the Emperor's control. It was, in a sense, more damaging than a major act of sabotage. Property could be repaired, loss of lives could be absorbed; an attack on the hearts and minds, however, had ongoing, wide-reaching, uncontrollable and potentially fatal consequences.

The prosecutor explicitly stated that Scott's case was more serious than Curtis's case. Scott's connection to the Ministry of Information meant he was a professional propagandist: 'It was on account of my presence in the camp and my activities and previous record that the whole case assumed a much greater importance than it would otherwise have had.'[28] To Scott, there was something familiar in the prosecutor's statements. He was parroting the accusations Sumida had levelled against him in his first interrogation at the YMCA. Sumida may not have been present at the trial, but Scott could hear Sumida's words intermingled with the prosecutor's bland legalese, which lent the whole affair the semblance of a properly considered legal argument. Everything – from the presentation of evidence and cross-examination to closing arguments and establishing guilt – was Sumida's work.

Having concluded his closing arguments, the prosecutor turned to Scott and asked if he had anything to say in his defence. What could he possibly say that would make a difference anyway? His fate was sealed. He had known people summarily executed for attempting to escape Japanese prison camps or savagely beaten for simply refusing to bow to a *Kempei Tai* officer, punishments wildly disproportionate to these so-called crimes. The central theme of the prosecutor's argument was that Scott was a very dangerous, wicked man who had inflicted great harm to the Japanese in Singapore and Malaya before and during the Occupation: 'I began to feel that he would ask for a very severe sentence.'[29]

After Scott declined the invitation to respond, the prosecutor turned to the presiding judge; he 'asked for a sentence of six years, under section 99 of the of the Japanese Penal Code – "spreading false rumours against Japan"'.[30] The prisoners would be taken away while the panel of judges considered the verdict. Before they went away, the presiding judge now asked Scott if he had anything to say. 'Emboldened by the knowledge that [the prosecutor] had already committed himself to a sentence of only six years,' Scott wrote, 'I made a little speech attacking Japanese methods of controlling public opinion in general.'[31] Scott savaged Sumida's investigation, the treatment of prisoners and the Japanese

justice system. He took close aim at the Japanese policy of censorship and their zealous approach to muzzling public opinion: 'In
Malaya and anywhere else in the British Empire anyone could
listen to any radio they liked at any time.'[32] He even referenced
a visit he made to a German internment camp in Hong Kong
before the outbreak of war in the Pacific. '[I] found the internees
listening to Berlin on a radio supplied to them by the British
authorities.' Scott knew that it was all an utterly pointless rant.
The sentence, in his mind, was already established. Nevertheless,
Scott would later say, 'I quite enjoyed myself.'[33] It was, in fact,
a huge gamble. Scott was assuming that the prosecutor always got
the sentence for which he asked. Although unlikely, who was to
say that the court might not award a sentence more severe than
that which the prosecutor had requested?*

As it happened, Scott was proven right. The judge confirmed
the prosecutor's recommended sentence for both Scott and Curtis.
As a former barrister, Scott was equal parts disgusted – 'the court
martial, though on the face of it dignified and fairer than one
would have expected, was actually a frame up'[34] – and ecstatic.
He would live.

On the drive back to Outram Road, the truck turned down
Lermit Road. Scott pointed out to the Japanese sentry – 'one of
the more intelligent sentries who saw which way the wind was
blowing'[35] – the house in which he had lived for a short while
with Rosamond and the children.

'Wouldn't you like to be living there again?' asked the sentry.

'Oh – it doesn't matter – I'll be back there in a couple of
months,' Scott said with a mischievous grin.

The sentry made no comment: 'he was as convinced as we
prisoners that Japan was going to lose the war.'[36]

The total number of individuals tried in connection to

---

*   In one case the prosecutor asked for a sentence of six and a half years and
      the court awarded a lesser sentence of six.

Sumida's investigation has never been properly accounted. Sumida would later say that 'after this long period of interrogation and detention, about [. . .] thirty were found guilty and sent over to the Military Courts'.[37] All received sentences, though of varying degrees of severity. Lionel Earl, one of the original members of the news committee, was given an identical sentence to Scott. Others, such as William Thorpe Cherry – who received four years' hard labour despite having done nothing – were sentenced for having confessed to crimes while being tortured. For his part in saving so many lives in Changi by arranging vast sums of money to be sent to the camp, Wee Aik Tek was sentenced to three years. He came down with dysentery while imprisoned and died a few months into his sentence. Scott – who credited Tek with saving his life in Miyako – was greatly affected by his death: 'He was one of the finest and most generous men I ever met.'[38]

Two weeks after the trial of Rob Scott, John Long was brought before the court and charged with secondary espionage. This charge included providing background information about the harbour, shipping movements and other useful intelligence that was communicated to the parties responsible for blowing up the ships. The prosecutor used as evidence Long's many 'confessions' and may also have produced his written statements, although this is unclear. Long was found guilty and sentenced to death.

Long, of course, had nothing to do with the attack. His trial, guilty verdict and sentencing were driven, at least in Scott's view, by other motivations: 'In Long's case, he was finally court martialled and executed, nominally for "secondary espionage", but actually for having wasted the time of the *Kempei Tai* by supplying false information.'[39] Sumida may well have been intent on punishing Long for having misled his interrogators, perhaps blaming him for drawing out the investigation. He may also have despised Long for what he perceived as the dishonourable act of doing everything to save himself, even implicating his friends and associates, 'ignoring the fact that the false evidence had been extracted by torturing men who were then scarcely responsible for what they said'.[40] But there is no way of knowing for sure.

What can be assumed is that Sumida needed to show something for an expensive year-long investigation that had in fact yielded nothing of real value. Someone – *anyone* – needed to die for the attack on the harbour, this despite his stunning admission that 'from the beginning I did not have the notion that there was any connection between the blowing up of the boats and the operation at Changi'.[41] Scott was the obvious choice. He was the number one suspect of the Number One Work. But he did not confess. As Sumida said to Scott during his first interrogation, 'Under our law, you cannot be tried until you confess.'[42] But Long *did* confess: many times to many different things and, importantly, he only partially recanted on some confessions. That gave Sumida the legal justification – at least in the Japanese system of justice – to sentence him to death. Sumida's investigation and sentencing recommendations satisfied his superiors. He had saved face. Sumida was promoted to lieutenant colonel and reassigned as the commanding officer of the North-East Burma *Kempei Tai*, headquartered in Lashio, a northern township not far from the Chinese border.

In the weeks after their sentences were handed down, John Long fell ill. Rob Scott spoke with him in what passed as Outram Road's medical ward. Long's continued refusal to apologise or even acknowledge that what he told his interrogators led to the suffering and death of many people clearly rankled. Perhaps Scott felt that Long at least deserved credit for the pivotal role he played in the smuggling of money, supplies, news and personal messages into Changi, which indisputably benefited the Changi internees. Besides, he was by no means the only internee to 'confess' under intimidation, flattery and torture. Whatever lingering discontent he felt for Long, Scott evidently felt compelled to offer him advice. He told him to act as if he was on the verge of dying. Scott had recognised the Japanese pattern of carting men off to hospital rather than have them die in custody so as to avoid future prosecution for war crimes. He wagered the same would be true of a man condemned to execution.

Long did not heed the advice. Six days after he was sentenced to death, several *Kempei Tai* guards, accompanied by an interpreter, approached Long's bed. Through the interpreter, a guard asked how Long was feeling and whether he could walk.

'Oh, I am alright,' Long replied.

'Well, we want you to come with us,' the soldier responded.

'Will I take anything with me?' asked Long.

'No, don't worry, you don't have to take anything with you.'[43]

Long walked out of Outram Road Gaol and was led into a waiting vehicle. He was driven to a rubber plantation, not far from Singapore Harbour, ordered to kneel and was then beheaded. Long's remains were buried in a shallow grave marked with a wooden cross.

Following Long's execution, two Chinese prisoners serving hefty sentences in Outram Road for espionage passed a message to Scott. They had been in the court awaiting their own trial while Long was being sentenced. After the guilty verdict was handed down, the Chinese prisoners heard Long mutter, 'I wish I had never said that.'[44] This statement, just like Long's complex character as a whole, would forever confound Scott, who 'never discovered what it was he wished he had not said'.[45]

36

THE DYSENTERY WARD

TO THEIR MUTUAL SURPRISE, Earl Ebert and Rob Scott were reunited back in their cell at Outram Road Gaol on the evening of their day-long trials. Ebert had been given fifteen years' hard labour. Townspeople like Ebert received considerably harsher sentences than the Changi internees because, in Scott's view, 'of the Japanese feeling that [. . .] Europeans could be expected to be anti-Japanese; townsfolk were Asiatics, who should support Japan, so it was more heinous of them than of us do anything against Japan'.[1] Ebert and Scott were in high spirits: 'after all, twenty years, fifteen years, six years, all meant the same thing – about another six months we reckoned.'[2] And then it would be over.

But there was still hardship to endure. Ebert was transferred to the civilian prison and Scott was reassigned to a new cell, which he shared at various points with Eurasians, Indians or British troops. He would spend most of his days outside among the POWs. Walter Curtis was the only other civilian in this section of Outram Road. Scott took his midday and evening rations at a long communal table in the main hall rather than in his cell. The food was bad but the company was exceptional. The seventy-five POWs comprised Australians, English, Welsh, Irish, Dutch and Indians. As the sole Scotsman in the group, Scott came to be known as 'Jock' – 'the only time in my life when I didn't find Scotsmen in a mixed group like that'.[3]

Scott kept busy, ever mindful of slipping into a state of deathly ennui that could occasion a lengthy spell in a cell. Thankfully, there was plenty of work to do: rope making, gardening but most of all polishing boots. The boots were taken from fallen soldiers and sent to the prison for polishing and repair. 'I became quite an expert on boots,' Scott wrote, 'we had thousands and thousands of pairs to grease and polish: British Army boots, British transport boots, British naval boots (a lovely job, light, leather lined, waterproof), Australian marching boots, American, Indian, South African and Japanese.[4] South African boots were adjudged the best for sturdiness. The Japanese boots, invariably in a state of ruin, were deemed the poorest, followed closely by the Indian boots: 'some contractor in India must have made a fortune out of providing the Indian army with dud boots.'[5]

The work was exacting and relentless and began to take its toll. 'Everyone had scabies,' noted Scott, 'some were going blind, and there were a couple of cases of malaria.'[6] The Japanese prisoners fared better than most, a fact Scott ascribed to diet: 'they got the flesh from fish, we got heads and tails and fins and bones, and ate every scrap.'[7] Scott had never fully regained his health since his incarceration and torture at the YMCA. When his legs began to swell and his body became bloated, the other prisoners suggested he consult the Japanese doctor. Scott did not think that a wise course of action; he did not want to signal to the Japanese that he was unwell. Rather than being relieved of work, sick prisoners were punished for being less efficient or ineffectual. Besides, it was obvious he had beri-beri and there was nothing a doctor could do anyway.

As his symptoms worsened, Scott had to contend with a new and more urgent health calamity – the near-constant urge to defecate. The only thing more dangerous than contracting dysentery was for a Japanese sentry to recognise that you had dysentery. Should that happen, the sick man's rations were cut: 'you got no solid food at all, only slops, and very little at that.'[8] While at work, even healthy prisoners avoided using the 'thunder box' (Australian slang for a portable wooden toilet) out of fear that they would be identified as being sick. Scott had to slink away and find a private patch of ground to relieve himself. On the occasions he was caught, he would receive a beating: 'I was constantly in hot water for this and for having beriberi [because I was] unable to carry heavy loads.'[9]

Scott's cellmates tried to help, recommending all sorts of remedies. Every culture seemed to have a salve. The Eurasian cure for dysentery was 'to eat masses of green chillies, which they stole from the garden'.[10] The chilli remedy worked for the Eurasians but did not help Scott one bit. Stealing lumps of charred wood from the kitchen fire and eating the charcoal was the preferred cure for the Indians; this treatment proved as ineffectual as the Eurasian method.

As December merged imperceptibly into January – Christmas passing unacknowledged – a dysentery epidemic whipped through Singapore's prisons and internment camps. Outram Road was hit harder than most. Every month since around September 1944, around five or six Outram Road prisoners afflicted with dysentery and reduced to skeletons had been carted off to a hospital ward at Sime Road. There were undoubtedly a greater number of prisoners in need of hospital treatment, but half a dozen seemed to be the limit the Japanese would transport at once. The sentries did not seem averse to sending the sick to hospital, as it effectively transported the problem elsewhere. The problem, at least in Scott's estimation, was the limitations on using automobiles by dint of a severe rationing of petroleum. 'Now, the Commandant of the Prison had a certain amount of petrol allotted to him every month for the transport of prisoners to and from hospital,' Scott wrote. The drive to Sime Road was around a 10-mile round trip. The sentries had to be judicious about who they selected. For the non-commissioned officers, there was a more pressing concern. Much of the petrol 'was used by Sergeants to take their girlfriends out on Saturday evenings, in one of the official prison cars', Scott wrote. 'But *someone* had to go to hospital – otherwise, how to explain away the disappearance of the petrol?'[11]

Whether the men who were transported to hospital lived or died was anyone's guess. The prisoners of Outram Road assumed some did not make it. In fact, the survival rate was poor; Scott was informed by an interpreter that of all the sick men sent to hospital since the previous October, only two were still alive. For Scott – whose condition was steadily deteriorating – survival therefore meant getting to hospital before he was at the very point of death. He needed to put on an act, and 'there was one small but very important factor in our favour: no prisoners had been sent to hospital that month'.[12] The Japanese sergeants would be anxious to take at least one man to hospital this month to explain how they spent all the fuel supplies after all their romantic drives.

But one had to be careful. The Japanese were ever mindful of malingerers. They had seen all the tricks to get out of work, from persistent complaints and exuberant moans to staging dramatic collapses complete with eyes rolling into the back of the head. Some men even went so far as chewing soap before they 'fainted' to properly demonstrate a 'fit', complete with foaming at the mouth. It was a risk. A suspected malingerer would receive a thrashing. The greater risk was being ratted out by a trustie – the 'good conduct Japanese prisoners who helped the guards to control us prisoners [. . .] and [who] were much more brutal than the guards themselves'.[13]

With Scott's health rapidly declining ('I had the strength of a kitten'[14]), he set about staging the fall with the help of the other prisoners. He decided to 'collapse' outside the carpenter's shop, where a large number of Japanese sentries and guards were working. He picked up a large bundle of planks from inside and, with enormous effort, hoisted them onto his shoulder and slowly trudged towards the door, making hard work of it. As arranged, he waited for a party of prisoners to arrive on the scene. Keeping their distance and watching Scott closely, the prisoners entered the shop. Scott deposited the planks on the ground, then 'reeled and fell "smack" on the pavement in front of the Japanese, our own party, our sentry and several other sentries'.[15]

The prisoners hurried over to Scott: 'The rest of my party (we were all very expert at this sort of incident) immediately set up a terrific hullaballoo: "He's dead!"; "No – not yet!"; "Get him to the cells!"; "Take his arm!"; "No, no, carry him like this!"'[16] The Japanese roared at them to stand back, utterly irate. This was precisely the reaction that Scott was after. It was all about face: the sentries 'would be the laughing stock of the prison, allowing these prisoners of war to create such a commotion'.[17] The prisoners ignored them. Scott lifted his head slightly to gauge the reaction of the Japanese.

'Lie still, you damn fool,' one of the prisoners hissed into his ear, 'you're unconscious, don't you understand?'[18] Scott shut his eyes and allowed the prisoners to bear him all the way back to the cell. A Japanese sentry, flustered and panicked, scurried in pursuit. He had given up attempting to control the situation. Better to look as if he was in command. This sentry, Scott wagered, was probably frightened that Scott might die: 'if I died whilst in his care there would be questions.'[19] Better to get the sick prisoner to the cell. If he died, another sentry guarding the cells would take over and have to field the questions.

Scott braced himself for the possibility of harsh interrogation. The manner of his collapse was suspicious. If he was tortured, he would die. The Japanese started by cutting his already meagre rations. Although dangerously underweight, dysentery had largely robbed him of his appetite. He did not need to fool the guards into thinking he was not interested in food. After a day and half of fasting, he was kicked and beaten intermittently for two days and told to get up and work. It was uncomfortable. But after what he had already endured, this was very manageable.

Finally, the sentries sent for a medical orderly: 'a moron who knew nothing at all about his job.'[20] The orderly asked several nonsensical questions and then left. He was sufficiently concerned to call for a doctor, who visited the prison towards the end of February. Scott was stretchered to the front office, where a doctor asked what was troubling him:

> Relying on the fixed Japanese disinclination to look at unpleasant things, and particularly on their fear of dysentery, I told the doctor I was passing blood, had been doing so for months (this was more or less true); that I hadn't eaten for days (also more or less true, because I hadn't been given anything to eat), that I couldn't eat (quite untrue – only try me with something worth eating!), and also – as he could see – I was horribly swollen.[21]

Three days later, Scott was loaded onto the back of a truck. As a convict, Scott had expected to be taken to the hospital at Changi. He was told he would instead be treated in the civilian camp hospital at Sime Road, an even better outcome. Sime Road held the great bulk of civilian internees. They had been relocated from Changi Jail, which was now part of the vast Changi POW complex, absorbing an enormous number of captured Allied servicemen who had been held in POW camps throughout South-East Asia and the islands of the former Dutch East Indies, now abandoned as Japan's area of control contracted.

The sentry who helped lift Scott to the truck offered him a cigarette. This was surely the last test. The Japanese probably knew of Scott's love of smoking. He fought an immense urge to accept the cigarette. 'No,' he said finally. 'I'm too ill to smoke.'[22]

The truck drove off: 'I was fairly chortling to myself as I was carried out, flat on the floor of the truck, eyes half-shut.'[23] The truck pulled up outside Sime Road Camp. When the sentry overseeing Scott's transfer was looking away, Scott took the chance to wink at a group of truck mechanics, 'so a few people at any rate knew I was not quite dead'.[24] He was carried on a stretcher to the dysentery ward. The civilian doctors and orderlies, some of whom Scott knew from his time in Changi, did a full examination. Worry lines were etched on the faces of the doctors looking down at him: 'I was so full of glee at having fooled the Japanese into thinking I was dying that it didn't occur to me that in fact I might be dying.'[25]

37

THE HEROINE OF SINGAPORE

BY THE TIME OF her release, Elizabeth Choy's father, Yong Than Yin, had been moved to a detention camp in Endau, a small town on the east coast of the Malay Peninsula. The relocation of a large number of Chinese to Endau served two purposes: removing potential undesirables, saboteurs and insurgents from the island while slightly easing the pressure on Singapore's severe food shortages. Endau – which is less than 130 miles from Singapore – was renamed New Syonan, a pitiful attempt to salve Chinese grievance at being removed from their home.

Elizabeth's elation at being reunited with her family was tempered by her father's absence. He was not the only member of her family missing. There was no word from her husband. The *Kempei Tai* had revealed nothing to Elizabeth about the fate of Choy Khun Heng. There seemed a high probability that he had been executed or had died of illness or injury. She could not afford to ruminate on her husband's fate. Her family – at once uplifted that she was alive and profoundly concerned at her rake-thin appearance – had clearly struggled without Elizabeth and Choy's income from the canteen at Miyako. That was evident in their gaunt faces and slight frames. Were it not for the meagre wages her sisters generated as nurses and the generosity of friends and extended family, Elizabeth's family would have starved. As for Elizabeth, there was no time to rest, recuperate and reflect on what she had just endured: 'I had to get some work.'[1]

Finding work was a challenge. The job market was tight in the late stages of the Japanese occupation. There were around 850,000 people in Singapore aged fifteen and over who were deemed by the Japanese able to work. Of that number, 514,000 were unemployed,[2] and teaching was hit particularly hard. The number of employed teachers in 1944 had halved since 1931. Not that it mattered; Elizabeth had already dismissed the idea of returning to the classroom while the Japanese were in charge of the curriculum. Her best option was picking up work as a coolie or unskilled labourer, which was the fastest-growing sector in Singapore – there were three times as many coolies in Singapore by the end of the war compared to before it.[3] Given her depleted physical state, Elizabeth simply could not work as a labourer without the risk of killing herself.

Elizabeth's sister Annie, who was still working as a nurse, made some enquiries and was told by the Director of Medical Services to ask if help was needed at the Sailors' Association, an old establishment repurposed by the Japanese for soldiers to socialise and rest. As it happened, they needed someone to run the canteen. The prospect of serving Japanese soldiers could not have been less appealing. The Sailors' Association was also located in the vicinity of the YMCA in Raffles Quay, requiring Elizabeth to walk past her former prison. But she had no choice. With great courage, she walked past the YMCA and entered the Sailors' Association and was given a job on the spot, receiving $80 a month – a reasonable wage before the war, a pittance by the end of it. By now, $80 would get you a tin of sardines.[4]

The work was manageable, but Elizabeth could not bring herself to go near the YMCA. She decided to take the long way to work, adding another thirty minutes to her walk each way. Her work was complicated by the fear of electricity she had developed while incarcerated. Monai's battery had left her traumatised, so she would avoid touching electronic appliances and even preferred not to flick on a light switch. She suffered other anxieties, coming to believe that the *Kempei Tai* had eyes on her: 'I had to be careful in everything [. . .] All the time I must think that I [am] being followed.'[5] She could not make sense of her release, which seemed an arbitrary, wholly inexplicable decision. A dark theory emerged in her mind: the *Kempei Tai* had set her free so she would lead them to others involved in their imagined conspiracy.

She soon discovered that old friends and acquaintances had arrived at the same conclusion. Outside of her immediate family, nobody wanted to go near her. The Double Tenth left a lasting impression on the entire Chinese community. The abrupt disappearance of so many people for no apparent reason had created a culture of mistrust and paranoia. Neighbours shunned each other, fearful that they had sold out to the Japanese for food. But the deepest suspicions were reserved for anyone released from *Kempei Tai* custody. This cruel and callous military police unit was not in the habit of releasing anyone held on suspicion of fifth-column activity. Even if Elizabeth had somehow proven her innocence, it was believed that they would sooner kill her than set her free. That Choy Khun Heng was still missing only deepened suspicions. Why was he still incarcerated – possibly dead – and she free? Had she struck a deal? Was she collaborating with the occupiers? Had the Japanese turned Elizabeth into an informant?[6]

Elizabeth did her best to become invisible. She did not want to unintentionally incriminate anyone. She was particularly careful about what she said to others, avoiding contentious topics and never daring to give voice to her hope that the British would return to reclaim Singapore. She was also wary of mentioning the war or speculating on when it might end, fearful that *Kempei Tai* ears would conclude she had access to a radio: 'Nobody dared to listen [to a radio] because we heard of so many cases where people tried to listen to radio and they were taken away and [nobody found out] what happened to them.'[7] Elizabeth entered a period of sullen isolation, avoiding eye contact with everyone outside her own family, barely speaking with her colleagues, keeping her distance from the Japanese where possible. All she could do was 'lie very low [and hope] for the end of the war to come'.[8]

Despite her best efforts to avoid the topic of the war, it was impossible to ignore the rumours. The Japanese were losing. There was talk of a devastating weapon – an Australian prisoner in Changi overheard the Korean guards describe it as a 'big bomb'[9] – that had been used on the Japanese; rumours of victory for the Allies in the Pacific; plausible tales of Lord Louis Mountbatten sweeping through South-East Asia on his way to liberate Singapore. In Elizabeth's estimation, these were perilous moments for the civilian population of Singapore. If Japan was facing imminent defeat, then what would Hirohito have his soldiers do next? The prospect of a Japanese killing spree seemed eminently possible. 'It was terrible,' remembered Elizabeth. 'Everybody [in my family] didn't dare to go out because it was so uncertain.'[10]

On 15 August 1945, Emperor Hirohito broadcast a public address ordering his military to surrender to Allied forces. Five days later, a report was carried in the *Syonan Times* that the war was over. Posters appeared over the city declaring the Allies victorious. Japanese soldiers were confined to barracks or POW camps on the orders of General Itagaki Seishiro, Commander of the Japanese 7th Area Army based in Singapore. Rather than seeing an outburst of unrestrained joy, Singapore's fragile social order collapsed. The city descended into a sudden and dangerous period of chaos and violence, quickly becoming hostage to justice seekers thirsting for revenge. They did not direct their enmity towards the Japanese; they turned on each other. This was a time of vigilantism, vengeance and a chance to settle old scores.

'It was surprising,' wrote one observer, 'that despite their maltreatment of civilians during the Occupation, Japanese soldiers were not widely targeted for revenge.'[11] In truth, it was not surprising in the least that the Japanese were avoided. The former occupiers may have been defeated, but they remained a large, well-trained and battle-tested force of military veterans and they were heavily armed. Vigilantes had others in their sights. 'Known collaborators,' wrote another observer, 'suffered a bloody fate. One Chinatown figure, Tan Boon Wu, who had gained wealth and status through his pro-Japanese efforts, had his corpse displayed on Banda Street. His body was tied to a tree, stab wounds visible on his chest and a placard written in Chinese that proclaimed the errors of his ways.'[12] Major Foong Fook Kay recalled seeing two hooded men tied to a tree, a sign above them identifying both as traitors while encouraging passers-by to stone them. 'In my heart,' Foong said nearly seventy years later, 'I curse the Japanese, but I cursed the hooded men more. [. . .] If I had known then [what they had done] I would have surely started stoning them too.'[13] No distinction was made between the collaborators who sought to benefit personally from the Japanese occupation and those forced into aiding the Japanese on pain of death. In some cases, mobs descended on the homes of suspected collaborators, killing entire families.

Racial tensions, having simmered away throughout the war, flared into bursts of shocking violence. Malays who worked as informants and detectives for the occupying force – known in some Chinese homes as the 'running dogs of the Japanese'[14] – were targeted by those whose own family members had disappeared. There were anecdotal reports of Malay families – wives, siblings and children – being murdered together. The Chinese went after individuals in the Indian community who had been conspicuously supportive of the Japanese. Among the top targets were the 'star men', prominent neighbourhood figures appointed by the Japanese as local leaders and informants who had received the star man honorific along with extra rations. Leaders and participants in Japanese-sponsored ethnic associations, essentially organisations tasked with keeping watch on their own people on behalf of the Japanese, and even with extorting money for the occupiers, were also targeted.*

Elizabeth spent many of these uncertain days indoors. She did not believe the surrender was real, at least not until old friends and acquaintances who had avoided her since her release started visiting the house. The Japanese had capitulated, her friends told her, and they wanted to explain themselves and apologise. Among the visitors were fellow prisoners who had shared a cell with Elizabeth, expressing their sincere gratitude to her for keeping their morale up. But the most cherished moment was the return of her father. The family had sent a cryptic message to him in Endau weeks earlier. Assuming the Japanese censors would be reading everything sent from the family of Elizabeth Choy, the message made obscure reference to Elizabeth without explicitly mentioning her name. Elizabeth's father knew exactly to whom they were referring. He arrived at the house and brought with him an infant, born only weeks earlier. Elizabeth's stepmother had become pregnant and given birth to a daughter. They named her Judith. Seeing her father and meeting her new sister made this one of Elizabeth's happiest days.

If there was a moment when Elizabeth received irrefutable proof that the war was over, then it was on the day journalists descended upon the house: 'The press people, the war

---

* The Overseas Chinese Association was set up in March 1942, ostensibly to secure the release of Chinese community leaders locked up in the early days of the occupation, and then co-opted by the Japanese. Some leaders and prominent figures were released on the condition that they mobilise support for the Japanese within the Chinese community and pay reparations to the occupiers to the tune of $50 million.

correspondents, foreign correspondents, all came to interview [me].'[15] Newspapermen practically elbowed their way inside, desperate to secure an exclusive interview with Singapore's war heroine. The press had heard her story from Elizabeth's cell-mates at the YMCA. In the interviews they had given about their imprisonment, Elizabeth's name kept coming up. 'These people were very appreciative. They talked [about how] Elizabeth Choy did this, [Elizabeth Choy] did that. [. . .] And they called me the heroine of Singapore.'[16]

Despite the euphoria of the moment, there was still no word of Choy Khun Heng. For the second time in her life, Elizabeth went searching for her missing husband. Enquiries were made and Choy was found in Outram Road Gaol. The facility was now under British guard, and a British soldier escorted her inside. Two years after the *Kempei Tai* hauled Choy away from the canteen at the Miyako hospital, he won his freedom. The Choys embraced. To Elizabeth it was clear that the brutality of those two years changed her husband in profound and permanent ways.

38

RUMOURS OF PEACE

ON THE FIRST MORNING after he was admitted to the medical ward at the Sime Road Camp back in February 1945, Robert Scott was asked by the camp medical officer how he'd slept. 'A splendid night,' he said in a hoarse whisper, 'not a wink of sleep.'[1] Scott was simply too comfortable to nod off: 'It was one of the most pleasant [nights] I ever spent, enjoying everything – the moonlight outside, the frogs croaking, a bed with a mattress and a pillow.'[2] In Outram Road, he had been sleeping on wooden planks, a billet of wood for a pillow and two thin, filthy sheets as blankets.

Despite the improvements in his living arrangements, Scott remained dangerously unwell. He had lost at least half his body weight and was about as sick as a man could be without dying. The medical staff were utterly perplexed as to how Scott was still alive. Scott believed it was the casual certainty with which he expected to live, and the fact that nobody ever told him how sick he had become: 'I honestly can't think of any other reason why I didn't die last February, excepting that it never occurred to me that it was expected of me.'[3] But he was not out of the woods. Through bitter experience, the medical staff had learnt that the critical period for serious cases of dysentery was the first few days. Scott's survival depended on around-the-clock nursing: 'the staff seemed to think I was made of eggshells and wouldn't let me reach out a finger to help myself.'[4]

Scott also benefited from the spiritual uplift of a mail delivery. The letters were from friends, family and colleagues and had accumulated since his arrest on the Double Tenth. It was a minor miracle the letters were not discarded. Amid the well wishes were more sobering letters sent from several families of passengers on the *Giang Bee*. Word had seeped through that Rob Scott had been aboard the ship and had somehow managed to survive. Perhaps, they wondered, their loved ones had managed to escape death too. The task of informing the families of those who'd perished of their relatives' demise would fall to Scott, assuming he survived the war.

Slowly, Scott's condition improved, but his recovery was probably hampered by the doctors' refusal to allow visitors, a policy enacted to curtail the spread of dysentery. The doctors were not willing to make an exception for anyone, notwithstanding the known healing properties of seeing friends. Scott insisted and eventually a compromise was reached; the medical staff permitted Scott to be taken out on a stretcher. 'These visits were kept up right to the end of the war, and developed (when I got into the main ward, where visitors were allowed) into very pleasant Monday afternoon coffee parties.'[5] It marked a turning point in his health: 'These months, like my month as an internee in 1943, were very pleasant. I had books to read, friends to talk to, music to listen to.'[6] And, of course, there was the mandatory secret radio to catch up on the war's progress.

It seems astonishing that a group of internees would risk being caught with a radio. The majority of those swept up in the Double

Tenth arrests were linked to smuggling, constructing, owning, operating or listening to radios. It was believed, moreover, that among the camp population of 1200 women and 4000 men at Sime Road there were informers. But a thirst for news outweighed the risk of being caught and punished. Precautions were nonetheless taken. Unlike in Changi before the Double Tenth, very few in Sime Road knew of the radio's existence – a dozen at most – and, by dint of his stature, Scott 'was added to the very select list of those who got the news straight from the BBC'.[7]

Grateful though he was to listen to the news, Scott was apprehensive about being taken back to the YMCA – not so much for his own sake, but for the sake of his friends: 'if I had been taken down town again, and if I had been tortured to get information about the camp, it was possible that owing to my weakened condition I might be forced to speak, and not be as lucky as in previous interrogations, when I had always managed to keep my mouth shut about anything that mattered.'[8]

In truth, the Japanese no longer deemed Scott a threat. Sumida was gone and the senior ranks of the *Kempei Tai* knew that he had no part in fifth-column activity in the town. But it was true that the Japanese wanted him back serving his sentence in Outram Road. 'Within half an hour of my arrival in the camp the Japanese were asking (a) would I live, and (b) if I lived, how soon could I go back.'[9] A week after arriving at Sime Road, a civilian dressed in a crisp white shirt and sharkskin suit entered the dysentery ward. He walked over to Scott, who was lying on his back in bed. His name, according to Scott, was Tominara, 'a gentleman attached to the camp office with wide powers but somewhat undefined status'.[10] Scott believed him to be *Kempei Tai*. He asked how Scott was feeling. With the fate of John Long still fresh in his mind, Scott put on a performance: 'I stared at him as if I were scarcely conscious and mumbled something.'[11] That was the last Scott ever saw of Tominara.

As his health improved, Scott's friends advised him to delay the progress of his recovery, to keep his weight down by eating a minimal amount and bringing the doctors in on it. Scott gave their suggestions careful consideration and decided on the opposite course: 'I argued if the [Japanese] wanted to take me back, they would come and do it, regardless of the state of my health: it would not be the first time they had arrested a man and taken him out on a stretcher.'[12] Besides, he thought, 'it wasn't fair to take [the European doctors] into my confidence and say outright that they had to certify me as "dangerously ill", for an indefinite period.'[13] Should a Japanese doctor appear and deem that Scott was fully recovered, the repercussions for the Sime Road medics could be disastrous.

Rather than keep himself sick, Scott committed to getting well. Obviously, he did not want the Japanese to know he was improving, nor did he want to telegraph his progress to the rest of the camp: 'I was widely known, by name if not in person, to almost everyone, and if it became common knowledge that I was fit again it was possible that someone would report it to the Japanese.'[14] Discretion was the order of the day.

Firstly, Scott had to attend to his physical weakness. He needed to eat better food and eat more of it. He knew where to find it. Just like in Changi, a black market was in full swing at Sime Road. The problem was he had no money. Singapore's economy was, moreover, in a state of total disarray. Food shortages and hyperinflation combined to drive the cost of basic commodities stratospherically high. To cover the costs of his food supplies, Bobby Burns, who had shown such kindness to the critically sick patients back at Miyako, and a couple of others offered to advance Scott whatever he needed. The debt would be deferred as long Scott needed. Scott gratefully accepted. 'With eggs at £1 each in March, and £2 and more each later on; bully beef at over £10 a tin; and so on, I must have spent about £1000.'[15] It was a substantial debt, equivalent today to around £55,000, racked up in the space of around seven months.

But that could be dealt with after the war. For now, Scott was focused on survival.

Sure enough, as Scott consumed more food, he grew stronger. He was now ready for exercise. This was more difficult: 'I could not hope to conceal progress from the doctors, but I had to try and hide it from the patients in the ward and from visitors.'[16] The only time to conduct a physical routine away from prying eyes was in the dead of night. Scott would slip out of bed after midnight and take strolls around the camp, lengthening the distance walked each day: 'by the end of May, you could have seen me striding round the camp half a mile away from the hospital, between 3 and 4 any morning.'[17]

It was not all smooth sailing. Around four o'clock one morning in June, Scott was walking past one of the camp kitchens when a dark figure emerged.

'Where are you off to, laddie?' he asked.[18]

Scott nearly leapt out of his skin. This man, unknown to Scott, was a member of the camp police – a group of internees who patrolled the camp to curtail the theft of food and supplies. It was a delicate situation. Scott did not want to be identified. This officious character would delight in reporting a suspected thief prowling outside the kitchen and, in so doing, blow his plan. Although it was dark, Scott was easy enough to identity. He did not have an internee's identity disc – 'a metal strip with a number stamped on it, issued by the Japanese to all internees, and ordered to be worn at all times by everyone.'[19] Scott was never issued a disc because he was no longer an internee (he was a convict). He managed to head off the camp policeman with 'a few pleasantries about being unable to sleep, and wasn't it a fine night, and so on, and I was past him before he had a chance to open his mouth again.'[20] He hurried off, the policeman's prying eyes boring a hole in the back of him: 'he was clearly in two minds, whether to follow me, or stay at the post of duty and guard the stores; he decided on the latter.'[21]

After that close call, Scott resolved to confine his strolls to the hospital ward. A bout of malaria and then pleurisy put paid to any temptation he may have felt to venture out on lengthy perambulations. Once again, he was a genuine patient. Scott was stricken by fever, chills, headache, chest pains and a vicious cough. His illness secured him a bed in the hospital for an indeterminate period.

Singapore's seasonless months of torpid humidity and tropical downpours rolled into May 1945. Germany surrendered. Japan would topple soon enough. Having endured so many years of hardship, the internees were now determined to live to see liberation. But tropical diseases became endemic: 'scratches, which in ordinary times would heal themselves in a day or two[,] developed into gaping sores and ulcers, lasting for weeks and often months. Universal malnutrition and under-nourishment caused or contributed to all sorts of diseases, from failing eyesight to dysentery, ulcers, and beriberi.'[22] The hospital ward at Sime Road was overwhelmed.

The biggest problem was the exorbitant rates to purchase medicine in the black market and a critical lack of healthy food – the internees were all dramatically underweight. The Japanese used food as an enticement to lure men into doing heavy work, offering extra portions in exchange for undertaking hard labour such as tunnelling. These men were deeply unpopular with the rest of the camp for carrying out work that was of a 'semi-military nature'[23]. At this juncture of the war, the only use the Japanese could possibly have for tunnels was to conduct a guerilla campaign should Singapore be retaken by force. These internees were regarded as borderline traitors who were aiding the enemy for one simple reason: 'the temptation of extra food was too strong.'[24]

This resentment was, in part, fuelled by an atmosphere of anxiety about what the Japanese would do with the internees should Singapore be taken back by force. The consensus was that 'the Japanese would kill us off to get us out of the way'.[25] Small numbers of internees quietly discussed plans to resist the Japanese if they should be rounded up one day, presumably to be herded off to the killing fields. These discussions were dangerous. If men were willing to debase themselves by digging tunnels for the Japanese for a few scraps of food, it was not hard to imagine that they would readily inform on these men should they overhear such talk. Accordingly, discussions were limited to internees who trusted each other with their lives.

As the weeks passed, the rumour mill spun out of control. Every comment – whether it was factual, speculative or sarcastic – was subject to the wildest distortions. A group of women were overheard idly discussing the true purpose of the tunnels. One joked that perhaps the Japanese were planning to dig a tunnel to Australia to allow a passage for the delivery of food parcels. 'In two days,' Scott noted, 'it was round the men's camp that Australian parcels had arrived in Singapore and were about to be delivered.'[26] Eyewitness accounts were equally unreliable. One internee swore he had seen trucks loaded to the hilt with food parcels draw up outside the camp office. Scott was sceptical and asked if he was certain. Indignant, the man bawled Scott out: 'Of course I am,' he bristled. 'I tell you, I saw it with my own eyes.'[27] The trucks were, in fact, unloading bales of cloth the Japanese intended the women to make into army uniforms.

But no subject generated as much wild speculation as the question of when the war would end. Discussed ever since the outbreak of the Pacific War, it soon became the only topic of conversation. Prior to Scott's transfer out of Miyako, POWs had been arguing among themselves for weeks as to whether Germany had been defeated. Everyone had some obscure source which they relied upon to stridently voice an opinion. Joseph the Indian clerk, 'in for murder and attempted suicide, stealer of and trainer of high-class fighting cocks in South India, authority on Indian cooking, and my smoking confederate', said Scott, heard from an Indian police inspector who had arrested the crews of four German ships in the harbour. Solely on the basis of this 'evidence', Joseph proclaimed that 'the white man's war is over'.[28]

An intellect and accused communist was adamant the war had ended a month earlier. His source – 'a friend of his who worked for the Japanese telegraph agency'[29] – was more credible than most. He claimed that the Japanese were sent a telegram confirming that Germany had surrendered on 10 September. The source and the specificity of the information was convincing, until it was countered by another source, who asserted that 'a British air borne force had been severely mauled in Holland'.[30] The communist would not be dissuaded from his conviction that the main German military had collapsed and that these reports of fighting merely indicated that some German units were holding out.

Initially suspicious about the veracity of all these claims, eventually Scott was swept up in the optimistic fervour that peace and freedom were near: 'The item about the arrest of the German crews seemed conclusive; we decided that Germany had collapsed.'[31] Finally, Germany surrendered. Most had expected Japan to fold soon after. The hold-up seemed to be Japan's resistance in Burma, the site of a series of brutal campaigns between the Southern Expeditionary Army and predominantly British forces under the command of Admiral Louis Mountbatten. The internees, who knew nothing of Japan's fierce resistance or the logistical difficulties of jungle fighting, nicknamed Mountbatten 'Lingering Louis'.

Yet even when the Burma campaign finally turned in favour of the British, the war dragged on. Scott had learnt that even in the face of certain defeat, surrender was an impossibility for the Japanese. To surrender ran counter to their most deeply held convictions. How would it all end, then? With only a few Allied soldiers left bloodied, bruised and still standing? With the streets of the occupied territories piled high with corpses? And what of the internees in Sime Road? 'Most of us – I amongst them – had expected that the Japanese would get tough when they knew they were beaten,' Scott wrote.[32] His fears were not misplaced.

There were 70,000 POWs and internees in Singapore at the end of the war. Their fate would ultimately be decided by General Seishiro Itagaki. Itagaki belonged to a sect of Nichiren Buddhism which promoted the idea of *mappō*, or the Final War. The Greater East Asia War, as the Japanese called the conflict that raged between 1937 and 1945, was for Itagaki more than a racial conquest or a struggle for regional dominance; it was a final cosmic battle of good versus evil. Itagaki had a Singaporean garrison of 70,000 troops in addition to nearly 30,000 soldiers in Malaya, standing ready to resist the Allies.

When Emperor Hirohito announced that Imperial Japan had surrendered, Itagaki was caught off guard. He bristled at the very notion of surrender. This could not be real. He flew to Saigon to consult with his superior, Field Marshal Count Terauchi, Commander of the Japanese Southern Army, who confirmed that Hirohito's broadcast was authentic. Disgusted, Itagaki returned to Singapore, stewing over the imperial command. A week after Hirohito's surrender broadcast, Itagaki met his generals and senior staff at his headquarters in Raffles College. He told them they were to surrender and keep the peace. That night, 300 Japanese officers and men gathered in a lounge at the Raffles Hotel to ply themselves with sake and bid each other farewell. They each removed their shirts, found a place to kneel and then disembowelled themselves with a short sword. Elsewhere, an entire Japanese platoon of fifty men blew themselves up with grenades.

Whether Itagaki ever entertained the notion of massacring all the POWs and internees in Singapore cannot be known. To Itagaki, who would ultimately be hanged for war crimes, it surely made sense militarily; the tens of thousands of liberated prisoners could aid the Allies' attempts to retake Singapore. There also exists evidence that such massacres had been planned elsewhere.

Documents found after the war revealed a *Kempei Tai* order sent to a POW camp commandant in Formosa relating to the disposal of POWs:

> Whether they are destroyed individually or in groups, or however it is done, with mass bombing, poisonous smoke, poisons, drowning, decapitation, or what, dispose of them as the situation dictates. In any case it is the aim not to allow the escape of a single one, to annihilate them all, and not to leave any traces.[33]

Fortunately, the demands of Itagaki's apocalyptic faith and his personal desire to fight on were subservient to the Emperor's command.

Contrary to Scott's expectation, the Japanese at Sime Road 'became sullen and sad, and slack in discipline'[34] as the war dragged on. And then, inexplicably and without warning, there was talk of peace. Those who professed to have heard the reports of Hirohito's surrender on their stashed radios were dismissed by many as fantasists. Then aircraft flew over the camp dropping leaflets stating that the Allies had won. Two days later, a unit of British paratroopers in red berets arrived. Mountbatten had ordered that paratroopers land in POW and internment camps across South-East Asia, previously identified by air reconnaissance, to guard those held captive, as he was fearful that the Japanese would embark on a murder spree. In contrast to the emaciated internees, the paratroopers were a picture of youthful health and exuberance. Scott observed them from afar: armed to the hilt, ready for anything, braced for action. They probably expected to be engaged in the horror of house-to-house fighting. Instead, 'they found the city calmly carrying on, light and water services in order, shops open, everything more or less normal. It was a complete anti-climax to the months of preparation for a battle in Malaya.'[35]

On 3 September, Lady Thomas visited Sime Road and hoisted the Union Jack. Two days later, Lady Thomas and Scott were driven to the Singapore Radio Station in the Cathay Building – Scott's old workplace – to deliver a message that would be broadcast across Malaya. Lady Thomas spoke first: 'Now that this miserable time is over, I am more than ever glad that I stayed here to share with you all whatever befell us,' she intoned.[36] She spoke of the importance for Singapore's diverse ethnic communities – Europeans, Eurasians, Malays, Chinese and Indians – to unite in 'rebuilding for the future'.[37] But her allusions to 'British forces [coming] across the seas and skies to relieve us'[38] was a nod to the past, not a glimpse into the future. Britain's capitulation – what Churchill deemed 'the worst disaster and largest capitulation in history' – was a breathtaking loss of prestige and a national disgrace. The Japanese may have lost the war but they nonetheless managed to loosen the British Empire's vice-like grip on Malaya; the days of the so-called Gibraltar of the East remaining a British possession were numbered. The British would return, but were they even wanted? Shortly before Lady Thomas delivered her message, the 5th Indian Infantry Division landed in Singapore. Trucks of Indian troops roared down the city's streets to seize important buildings and key infrastructure, to take back the island for the British. The delighted children who lined the streets were not waving the Union Jack; they were waving the flag of the Republic of China.

Scott was not oblivious to this shifting mood. There had been growing momentum for self-determination in Asia before his consular career had begun. He also recalled a critical moment before the Fall of Singapore when Duff Cooper – Resident Minister in Singapore and, at that point, chair of the War Council – ordered the evacuation of Europeans in Penang. Cooper, in Scott's view, 'failed to grasp the implications of a multi-racial society and he did not take into account British treaty relationships with the Malayan Sultans'.[39] This decision – 'a classic case of power without responsibility', where the British essentially demonstrated that they would cut and run at the slightest sign of trouble – 'did more than any other single event to shake public confidence in Britain'.[40]

But Scott would not share such sentiments publicly. He remained the Director of the Far Eastern Bureau's Ministry of Information and his job was to impart a message that advanced British interests. And so he delivered a nostalgic speech that riffed on a theme of freedom and appealed to the public's memory before the war when, as Scott said, 'I saw happy peoples of all ideals and of all creeds, going about their ordinary occupation without hindrance and without fear'.[41] The speech was replete with messages celebrating the imminent return of these virtues and liberties that would attend the British returning to the Far East: '[The] message I repeat now to you, the people of Malaya, because you now returned to the British Empire: Britain Stands for Freedom.'[42] These proclamations, broadcast to listeners who tolerated British colonial rule for more than a century only to be left for dead, were surely jarring to hear. '[But] propaganda,' as Scott wrote to his superiors before the outbreak of war in the Pacific, 'needs to be in terms of black and white.'[43]

Apart from promulgating British interests, Scott's speech, in the main, was deeply personal. He acknowledged the horrors the people of Singapore and Malaya had lived through and overcome, and the personal debt of gratitude he owed to so many for his survival. He worked into the speech aspects of his own suffering as a means of reminding all listeners of the horror over which all of them – Britons, Eurasians, Chinese, Indians, Malayans – had prevailed, the countless acts – big and small – of bravery and kindness, typified by the Choys.

> I found myself in the hands of the Japanese Gestapo, thrown into a filthy cell, starved, beaten, and tortured. Other people were cast into that hell to share it with me. Men and women

of all races; young women, old men, poor men, and men who had known wealth and comfort – the people of Malaya whom I had watched; whom I had spoken to over the radio; whom I had written to in the newspapers – now they were really near to me. We talked when we could; we shared our meals and we shared our dangers.

The old qualities were there: courage, hope, faith, and humour. But there was something different – a new strength appeared; faces showed signs of suffering – of weariness – and of fear. But there was strength there – something that could not be killed or beaten or tortured. Out of suffering had come strength and I shall never forget the kindness, the friendship and the bravery of these men and women, in particular such men as Wee Aik Tek, shopkeeper of Albert Street, Choy Khun Heng of the Hospital Canteen service, and such women as Elizabeth Choy, his wife. What they did for us European internees; what they suffered on our behalf; their courage, loyalty, and confidence, can never be forgotten.

Now the great hour has come and we turn to face the future with a new strength – a new strength born in those days of hatred and violence – those days of starvation and death. We know what freedom means! Men have fought for it in the past; they will fight for it in the future – and we understand why! Because we believed in freedom we had to suffer; many of our friends had to die; thousands upon thousands of our people were maimed fighting on battlefields all over the world.

Peace has come to Malaya again; happiness and prosperity will soon be here. Fear, violence and starvation have gone – gone for ever! But, of all the precious gifts that that victory has brought to us, the greatest and best is freedom, the value of which we now appreciate all the more because for a time we all, you and I, people of all races, did not have it.[44]

When Scott was finished, a party broke out in the station. They expected the Japanese to round them up and drive them back to Sime Road. If it came to that, Scott and the others resolved, they would refuse, holding the station by force until British forces arrived. But the Japanese made no attempt to end the proceedings or seize back control. The Cathay Building was theirs; the war was over.

39

RECKONING

A MILITARY COURT FOR the trial of Lieutenant Colonel Sumida Haruzo and twenty other officers and enlisted men of the *Kempei Tai* began on 18 March 1946. The so-called Double Tenth Trial was held in Singapore's Supreme Court and was closely covered by the international press. Newspapers carried detailed accounts of the callous treatment of victims of the Double Tenth and lurid descriptions of torture, stoking international outrage at a time when the world was learning the extent of Japanese atrocities. Sumida, described as the 'chief accused in the Double Tenth trial',[1] entered the witness box on the eighth day of proceedings. Reports of his demeanour in court – 'unperturbed and smiling'[2] – ensured that he became a lightning rod for public fury.

Sumida was arrested in October 1945 as a suspected war criminal in Tha Ton, Thailand, headquarters of the Japanese 33rd Army. He had retreated with the 33rd Army and the Rangoon *Kempei Tai* unit, which he commanded. He was eventually sent to Changi Prison, where he was interviewed by a US Army lieutenant attached to a war crimes unit. Sumida's record of statements made in the interview, which was submitted to the court as evidence and in which he admitted to leading the investigation that resulted in the imprisonment of fifty-seven civilian internees – fifteen of whom subsequently died – became his noose. He also acknowledged that prisoners were tortured with iron rods, bamboo sticks, the water treatment and electrocution. When asked if he took complete responsibility for the Double Tenth incident, his reply was unequivocal: 'I admit that these mistreatments were carried out with my knowledge and the fact that I did not forbid them makes me responsible.'[3]

He spent much of the trial attempting to wriggle out of that statement by reviving a defence strategy, first conceived during the weeks when his investigation began to unravel, that was characterised by blame shifting, mistaken identity and denial. He claimed that the Double Tenth prisoners were killed by disease, not ill-treatment ('I believe the major cause was dysentery'[4]); that witnesses were constantly misidentifying him for his (usefully) deceased subordinate ('I have never seen this undertaker and expect he has mistaken me for the warrant officer, Ueno'[5]); that obtaining information by limited force was necessary when material evidence continued to elude his investigations ('my instructions emphasised that no unduly harsh torture should be applied and that as little of it was to be used as possible'[6]).

During Sumida's cross-examination, the prosecution regularly reminded the court of his statements in his first interview in Changi. When asked if the statement was untrue, Sumida responded, 'When I made this statement I meant that I knew these things were done, but not severe torture. When I was asked whether different methods were used in torture I was shown the charge-sheet and the abstract of evidence and so took for granted that these things were done by my men even although I did not know about it.'[7] At times he tried to walk back the statement, blaming errors of translation and linguistic misunderstandings on either side.

When asked about the substandard food issued to the prisoners, Sumida attempted to establish some kind of moral equivalence with his present incarceration in Outram Road: 'I do not think the food for the inmates of the cells was any inferior to what we are receiving.'[8] Appearing to relish the intellectual joust with the prosecutor, Lieutenant Colonel Colin Sleeman, Sumida only ever made qualified admissions,[9] casting himself a victim of forces outside of his control, and with no choice but to stamp out a perceived enemy within, which unfortunately meant incarcerating dozens of British internees and Chinese, Indian and Malay civilians.

But nothing was more objectionable to the court than the manner in which Sumida comported himself while giving testimony. 'Sumida was in the box all yesterday,' *The Straits Times* reported, 'and continued assiduously in his calm and smiling ways [even] during his testimony on the death of Mr. Cornelius, when his irrepressible smile widened into a happy little grin.'[10] The press gleefully reported the 'battle of wits' between Sleeman – 'who was driving home the prosecution's allegations with skill and precision' – and Sumida – 'who was parrying them off with tales of temperance and moderation'.[11] At one point, Sumida's smile was too much for the prosecutor: 'Colonel Sumida, this is not funny.'[12] Sumida reportedly willed the smile to vanish, only for it to return before court adjourned for the day.

For all his high-minded deflections and smiling denials, Sumida's defence counted for little when weighed against the numerous and precise statements of the Chinese and British victims called to testify. Even Monai Tadamori, promoted to the rank of Warrant Officer shortly before the Japanese surrender, refuted Sumida's outrageous claim that he never heard screams and shouts from prisoners being tortured because most interrogations took place at night, when 'I was back at home'.[13] Monai even stated that Sumida 'gave the impression that the interrogation and torture went on at night [which] is not true'.[14] Monai also directly contradicted Sumida's claim that he specifically instructed his men to limit the kind of force they would be permitted to use against the prisoners: 'I do not remember that.'[15]

But it was the testimony of Robert Heatlie Scott CBE – lately awarded the honorific of Commander of the Order of the British Empire for contributions to civil service – that perhaps made the greatest impression on the court. That Scott was even in Singapore at the time of the trials was an astonishing coincidence. Until recently, he had been recuperating in England before being appointed political counsellor to the Special Envoy of the King and British Special Commissioner in South-East Asia, Lord Killearn – Scott's old boss Sir Miles Lampson, who had been raised to the peerage as Baron Killearn. As fate would have it, Killearn arrived with Scott in Singapore on the weekend before the trial began. In Scott's timely arrival the press saw the invisible hand of Lady Justice, treating the moment as a defining moment on which the case would turn. (One report claimed, erroneously, that, prior to Scott's arrival, 'the prosecution was largely depending on the sworn [written] testimonies of *Kempei Tai* victims who are now recovering in other lands from their experience in Japanese torture chambers'.[16] In fact, many victims testified in court.)

Billed as a victim courageously confronting his persecutors, Scott's dramatic appearance in court had press and public alike enraptured. In an article ironically titled 'Auld Lang Syne' – a Scots' phrase alluding to the practice of reflecting fondly on past experiences and relationships – the encounter between Scott and Sumida was deemed the high point in a riveting trial. The article captured a fascinating exchange between the two men:

Asked by Lieut. Col. S. C. Sleeman, prosecuting, whether he could point out Sumida, principal Jap accused, Mr. Scott

turned round, with a warm and friendly smile on his face
and a humorous twinkle in his eye, nodded in the direction
of the Japanese. Sumida's cherub-like face immediately lit up
in a happy smile, and he bowed in his most gracious manner
towards Mr. Scott.[17]

Rather than being fearful of Scott's testimony, Sumida seemed
honoured that his adversary was participating in his trial.

Scott answered the prosecutor and defence counsel's questions without embellishment or hyperbole. As one historian
observed, '[Scott's] testimony was given without rancour and
with such fairness that all were astonished – not least the
accused.'[18] Despite the restraint of his testimony, Scott made it
clear that there was no moral or legal justification for the arrests
and incarceration and subsequent death of so many people. He
also slipped in a few barbed comments: when asked if there was
any individual or organisation which had fooled the *Kempei
Tai*, Scott unhesitatingly responded, 'I think all the inhabitants
of Singapore.'[19]

The real evisceration of the accused was left to Sleeman. In
his closing remarks, the prosecutor linked the worst excesses of
the *Kempei Tai* – an organisation that 'stalked like a scourge
throughout Asia, carving its way with fire and sword'[20] – to
Sumida, who typified the callousness and cruelty of the military
police unit. Sumida was more than a cold and calculating zealot
doing the bidding of his emperor; he was a vicious tyrant who
delighted in the violent acts of his wicked henchmen:

> The Court will recall without much difficulty, I feel, the figure
> of Colonel Sumida in the witness-box: smiling seraphically
> at all around him – smiling upon the Court, laughing at me
> and beaming upon his fellow-assassins. But may I remind the
> Court of the immortal words put in the mouth of Hamlet:
> 'a man may smile and smile and be a villain'.[21]

The President of the second War Crimes Court, Lieutenant Colonel S.C. Silkin, would sentence eight men to death for the Double Tenth incident. Silkin described these men as 'the tools, the instruments of torture, in that deliberate and carefully planned campaign of torture which turned the prisons of the Singapore *Kempei Tai* into the Belsen of the East, and which brought into hatred and fear a term of high repute – the Double Tenth'.[22]

When Monai Tadamori heard his name read among those condemned to hang, he 'held his head up, his eyes glazed into a cold, hard look of indifference'.[23] Three Japanese were sentenced to life imprisonment, one to fifteen years and two to eight years. One prisoner was acquitted during the course of the trial on account of mistaken identity. But it was Sumida – among those sentenced to death – to whom Silkin devoted much of his sentencing remarks:

> You, Sumida, have shown by all that you did, ordered and willingly allowed, that to you there was nothing of higher consequence than domination by brute force and fear. You were prepared, for the glorification (as you thought) of your country, to reduce men and women below the level of beasts and to send them without pity or compunction to an agonising death [. . .] Accordingly it is in no spirit of vengeance upon a fallen foe, no desire to have an eye for an eye, a life for a life, that this Court has solemnly decided that you must die. Nor is it merely to rid the world – and your country now preparing for its moral rebirth – of one man who is a danger to all moral progress. Rather it is a stern example to all who would willingly support the powers of evil and brute force against the rule of law, justice and humanity.[24]

The final day of the trial, which had lasted four weeks, was conducted 'in an atmosphere of high tension'.[25] The gallery was packed. Those who could not find a seat had crowded the doors and the corridors outside. Inside the court were assembled 'people from many walks of life, from high-ranking officials like Major-Gen L.H. Cox, G.O.C Singapore district, and Major-Gen. H. Pyman, and members of the Services, to a professional boxer and an amah'.[26] There were representatives of the world's press, radiomen making recordings and local newspapermen. Once Silkin was finished, they all leaned forward, eager to catch a glimpse of the *Kempei Tai* chief's reaction after learning his fate: 'Sumida's lips were compressed into a hint of his notorious smile.'[27]

The sentencing was generally lauded by the Western press and the public. But some quietly expressed concern that the Double Tenth trial had the hallmarks of a show trial and was little more than victor's justice. In a review of the publication of a transcript of the trial – released only a year later – one commentator observed of the verdict: 'It was rough justice, with disquieting glimpses in court of a procedure alien to British traditions and offensive in the pre-trial stages to the Royal Warrant which established the special rules of war crimes courts. But it was justice.'[28] Though a minority of dissenting voices were heard, none was shedding tears for the condemned.

Seven of the eight men were hanged on 12 July 1946 in Changi Prison. The Singaporean-born Chinese interpreter Toh Swee Khun – described by the court president as 'something more than a bully – you were a traitor as well'[29] – successfully appealed his sentence, which was commuted to life in prison. On the morning of their execution, Sumida Haruzo led his men in patriotic song. They shook hands with each other before they were escorted outside into a tropical downpour, across the same courtyard where some of the Changi internees had assembled on the fateful Double Tenth and towards a wooden structure surmounted with a roof of corrugated iron and three gallows upon a scaffold.

Sumida and Monai were among the first three men hanged. They were taken up the stairs of the scaffold, then their hands and feet were bound. Before a white hood was placed over his head, Sumida saw Robert Heatlie Scott standing to one side of the scaffold. According to the ancient dictates of the *bushido* code, when a samurai was ordered to commit *seppuku* – ritual suicide to restore honour after defeat or disgrace – he was permitted to select someone to be a *kaishakunin*. After the samurai had disembowelled himself with a short blade, the *kaishakunin* would decapitate the samurai, swiftly ending the pain in an act of respect and compassion. The choice of *kaishakunin* was generally left to the samurai, who would usually select a loyal friend or relative, but he would sometimes choose a respected foe. Selecting an adversary as *kaishakunin* symbolised the restoration of balance, where the vanquished acknowledged his defeat to the enemy and the victor helped restore the vanquished's honour.

Sumida smiled at Scott before a guard pulled the hood over his head. A journalist who witnessed the moment wrote that Sumida 'might have been smiling still under that white hood that covered his face'.[30] Perhaps Sumida interpreted Scott's presence at this moment as echoing the ancient *bushido* code of *kaishakunin*. Scott's decision to witness the execution was, at least in Sumida's mind, a sign of respect. But this was not a ritual suicide, it was an execution. And Scott had no respect for Sumida. His reasons for attending the hanging can only be speculated. As Sumida's number-one suspect, Scott had become the public face of the victims of the atrocity, and may have felt a duty to bear witness to the executions on behalf of all those who had been incarcerated, tortured or killed.

Shuffling forward, aided by guards, the condemned men were each positioned in the middle of three circles drawn on a large trapdoor. After a noose was affixed and tightened around each of their necks, 'they shouted "Banzai" and hailed their emperor until the drop cut them short'.[31]

*

During the trial, both Sumida and Monai had expressed regret for the suffering resulting from *Ichigo Hosaku*; Monai went so far as to say, 'I am very sorry and it is my wish to pay for my sins.'[32] In truth, neither man believed they had done anything wrong. In his closing arguments, the counsel for the defence, Hori Masakaya, argued that Sumida was legally justified in authorising the arrest of British internees and Chinese suspected of fifth-column activity:

> In the Regulations governing the laws and customs of war, Article 44 states: 'A belligerent is forbidden to compel the inhabitants of a territory occupied by it to furnish information about the army of the other belligerent, or about its means of defence' [. . .] When such activities are suspected it is only natural that the suspects are rounded up, questioned and detained.[33]

Hori went on to say:

> It was suspected that in Changi Internment Camp there was a spy organisation, hidden wireless receiving and transmitting sets, and that funds were collected for anti-Japanese activities. It was not only natural, therefore, for the Japanese Army to institute a search, but there was justification for the detention and questioning of suspects.[34]

That Sumida's investigation unearthed radio receivers, a smuggling operation, evidence of regular interactions between the Chinese in Syonan and the British internees in Changi, and a huge cache of money, when taken as a whole, proved – at least to Sumida – that there was an anti-Japanese conspiracy and that a raid was justified. He remained steadfast in his belief that the charges for which Scott and the other internees were found guilty in the Japanese military court were fair and their sentences were just. In fact, he believed that those internees who were imprisoned and survived the Number One Work were treated reasonably well and that Scott – in not ever making a confession – had bested him. During his cross-examination, Sumida was repeatedly asked if he had found evidence that proved beyond doubt that Scott was running an espionage ring from Changi. 'No definitive evidence as yet,' he said, as if the matter was yet to be resolved.

Undermining his entire premise, however, was his investigation's link to the very event that set *Ichigo Hosaku* in motion and gave rise to the Double Tenth atrocity – Operation Jaywick. The theory that the British internees had conceived and ordered the attack on Japanese shipping in the harbour no longer stacked up. While in the witness box, Sumida was at pains to disassociate his investigation from Jaywick: 'From the beginning I did not have the notion that there was any connection between the blowing up of the boats and the operation in Changi.'[35]

Although a lie, Sumida's revisionist history poses an interesting question: would there have ever been a raid on Changi if not for Jaywick? That Sumida not only contrived a meeting with his number-one suspect, Rob Scott, in the Changi Commandant's office three months before Jaywick but also sent undercover *Kempei Tai* auxiliaries to investigate evidence of a conspiracy suggests the Changi raid was very likely. Sumida stated in the trial that the raid would likely have taken place in December. But his actions before the attack merely demonstrate a desire to arrest British internees; he did not have the authority to execute a raid. Jaywick was the inciting incident that led to the raid. As such, whether so many people would have been arrested, tortured and killed, or whether it would have happened at all but for Jaywick, is unknowable.

The exploits of Captain Ivan Lyon and the commandoes of Operation Jaywick were reported in the Singaporean press three weeks into the Double Tenth trial. Articles depicted the Japanese as a flailing occupying force who, in the attack's immediate aftermath, underwent 'brainstorms [. . .] to explain the phenomenon of six ships in safe anchorage, ringed round by thousands of miles of seas they commanded, suddenly blowing up in the night'.[36] While acknowledging that 'in the months that followed those six explosions, Singapore was to go through the worst period of terror it endured throughout the occupation',[37] journalists lauded the bravery of the commandoes while apportioning all the blame for the subsequent reign of terror to the Japanese. No reporting of Jaywick would ascribe any culpability for the atrocity to the Australian military's decision to not take responsibility for the attack, thus leading to another question: would the Double Tenth incident have happened if the Allies had claimed responsibility for Jaywick?

At the time of the attack, Sumida was in the grip of so-called fifth-column fever; he saw conspirators, saboteurs and insurgents everywhere. Having made up his mind about an enemy operating from within, he just as likely would have argued that the commandoes had received intelligence from inside Syonan. Such a claim would have snugly fit his preposterous narrative around transmitters in Chinese tombs being used to contact the British in India. Whether Field Marshal Count Terauchi, commander of the Japanese Southern Army, whose authority Sumida required to raid Changi, would have believed such a theory is, once again, unknowable. Similar attacks on the Japanese in occupied territories were deemed an affront to Japanese prestige and a threat to their control, and they often led to reprisals. There is every chance Jaywick would have given rise to a similar period of outrageous and severe reprisals.

But accepting that Jaywick was, if not the cause, then at the very least the catalyst for the Double Tenth atrocity, was the attack worth it? Measuring the military worth of commando operations against the tragic cost in lives and livelihoods is a calculus that has always bedevilled military strategists. The history of

World War II is replete with such examples. In Japanese-occupied Timor during this time, an Australian Independent Company carried out guerrilla operations behind enemy lines for more than a year. In a significant win for the Allies, the Japanese were forced to redirect resources and manpower away from the front lines to consolidate control of Timor. After the Australian unit was evacuated, the Japanese killed somewhere between 30,000 and 70,000 Timorese men, women and children in reprisal.[38]

In the case of Operation Jaywick, the cost emphatically outweighed the military gains. Whatever strategic benefits may have resulted from the attack on the Japanese ships in Singapore Harbour – a morale boost and the possible (although improbable) redistribution of forces to shore up the defence of significant Japanese naval bases – were never realised because the Australian military never took responsibility. As such, the military worth of Jaywick must be judged solely on the destruction of two freighters and the damaging of several other ships, all of which were put back into service. Sinking and damaging those ships with limpet mines deep in enemy waters was an incredibly bold, tactically brilliant, sublimely executed operation that had negligible impact on Japan's capacity to wage war. Beyond the subsequent deaths of fifteen internees and an unaccounted number of Chinese and Malayan civilians murdered and the lifelong trauma of scores of others who were tortured, the entire population suffered as Sumida turned Syonan into a police state. That the Australian military knew, through intercepted signals, that the Japanese were questioning locals and internees makes the decision to approve a second raid all the more astonishing.

Operation Rimau sought to replicate Jaywick's achievement of destroying Japanese shipping in Singapore Harbour. The operational party consisted of twenty-three men, up from thirteen, and involved Jaywick veterans including Donald Davidson, Robert Page and Ivan Lyon, who once more led the mission. Following Jaywick's success, Lyon had been promoted to the rank of lieutenant colonel and was the recipient of the Distinguished Service Order. The commandoes were delivered to Bintan Island by a British submarine, whereupon a Chinese junk was captured and used to take the commandoes to an island in the vicinity of Singapore. The plan was to use 'sleeping beauties' (SBs) – motorised one-man semi-submersible canoes – to infiltrate the harbour and limpet-mine enemy ships. On the one-year anniversary of the Double Tenth raid on Changi and shortly before the attack was to begin, the junk engaged an enemy patrol boat. After successfully fighting it off in a skirmish where several Japanese were killed, Lyon aborted the operation. The junk was scuttled along with the top-secret SBs.

Lyon then ordered the party to split up into four groups and head back to the rendezvous point with the submarine. Having been alerted to the presence of enemy soldiers, the Japanese sent a force to hunt down the commandoes. The entire Rimau party was either captured or killed. The captured commandoes were imprisoned in Outram Road and executed shortly before the end of the war. Ivan Lyon made it to Soreh Island before the enemy caught up with him. With two comrades, he fought off a unit of at least eighty Japanese soldiers over nine hours, inflicting heavy losses. Lyon climbed a tree, shooting down on the Japanese, until he was eventually killed by grenades.

Before he embarked on the doomed operation, Lyon at least discovered that his wife and child were alive. Gabrielle Lyon and little Clive would survive the war and resettle in England, only learning of Ivan's fate after they were released.

40

FORGIVING

FROM THE BEGINNING, Sir Robert Heatlie Scott had treated his incarceration as a game where the aim was to survive without disclosing any useful information. He did this by gaining moral and intellectual ascendancy over his interrogators with the power of his words. 'Words are the tools of our trade,' Scott would later say of diplomats, 'we must know how to use our tools if we are to be any good in our job.'[1] And few wielded words with such power and efficacy as Scott.

When the game was won and done, Scott bore no ill will towards his Japanese captors. He swiftly moved on: '[A]lready,' he wrote a month after the war, 'the *Kempeitai* and their brutalities are receding into the background.'[2] To all who knew him well, Scott emerged from his ordeal without trouble or trauma. Although deeply empathetic for those victims whose mental and physical scars would not heal, Scott did not believe it was sensible to dwell on the past. Those accused of committing atrocities had received justice in the various war crimes trials and tribunals, and the nation had been punished by the International Military Tribunal for the Far East, to say nothing of the devastation wrought across the Japanese islands by the United States Air Force.

A demilitarised but recovering Japan, for its part, had a crucial role to play in the rapidly changing dynamics of East and South-East Asia. Furthermore, Scott was adamant that Britain should play an active role in Japan's postwar recovery rather than leave everything to the Americans. But the memory of the Pacific War was casting a long shadow over Anglo-Japanese relations and proving an obstacle to diplomatic efforts. On a visit to Japan several years after the war, Scott – the former propagandist who knew the impact of grand gestures – invited former *Kempei Tai* officers and enlisted men who served under Sumida Haruzo in Singapore to dinner at the British Embassy in Tokyo. These men, who had tortured many of Scott's friends and cellmates, had recently been released from prison and 'after a slow start the gathering proved a great success'.[3] It was an act of astonishing magnanimity and a symbol of postwar civility that would live long in the memory of the British consular service and Japanese foreign affairs officials.

By the early 1950s, Scott's star was on the rise. Appointed CMG, the Order of St Michael and St George, for conspicuous and extraordinary non-military service in a foreign country, Scott was made Assistant Undersecretary of State of the Foreign Office. After a successful three-year stint in this position – where he had responsibility for Far Eastern Affairs during the complex, rapidly changing and extremely dangerous Korean War – Scott was appointed KCMG. Sir Robert, as he was now styled, then served as minister at the British embassy in Washington, DC. In mid-August 1955, returning by aircraft from a diplomatic duty, Sir Robert and Lady Rosamond were met by an embassy official who brought shocking news from home; Douglas, their eighteen-year-old son, had been killed in a training accident while on national service with the Royal Marines. No measure of physical or psychological torture inflicted on Scott during the war came even close to the depth of pain he experienced on learning of Douglas's death. In their shared grief, Robert and Rosamond leant on each other and somehow carried on, summoning the resilience and fortitude that had always been their hallmark. But no parent ever truly comes to terms with the loss of a child.

Two months after Douglas was killed, Sir Robert took up his appointment as Commissioner-General for South East Asia in Singapore, a regional post with civil and military responsibilities. Whether through contrivance or extraordinary coincidence, the Scotts were scheduled to land in Singapore on the Double Tenth, but engine trouble delayed their flight by one day. Scott pointed out to reporters who greeted him at the airport that he was 'glad to be back in Singapore',[4] particularly on such a momentous day: his twenty-second wedding anniversary. Sir Robert's appointment was widely celebrated in the press; he was feted almost like a returning son of Singapore, particularly among the Chinese reporters, who were delighted when he answered their questions in Mandarin.

As ever, Sir Robert assumed an important post at a time of immense political and social upheaval. Although not explicitly stated, the CG's role was to promote decolonisation and contain communism, this during the time when the Malayan Emergency – the communist insurgency that had raged since 1948 – was becoming increasingly vicious. After serving four challenging years in this post, Scott was promoted to GCMG, the highest rank of the Order of St Michael and St George, for his distinguished service in foreign affairs.

By dint of his unique experience in both civilian life and public service, in addition to his war record, Sir Robert was appointed as the first civilian commandant of the Imperial Defence College, and later the permanent secretary of the Ministry of Defence, before retiring in 1963. The Scotts went to live near Peebles, on the banks of the Tweed, where Sir Robert bought a disused railway station and built a new house across one of the platforms. He received an Honorary Doctor of Laws degree from Dundee in 1972. He would live out his days as a keen salmon fisherman and the doting grandfather of Susan's three children, while devoting much time to counselling young offenders and to local matters as Lord Lieutenant of Tweeddale. He died of cancer at his home in 1982, aged seventy-six. Among his most cherished activities towards the end of his life was staying abreast of world affairs and maintaining correspondence with old friends and colleagues with whom he had served in the foreign office. But few letters brought the Scotts more cheer than those sent by the heroine of Singapore, Elizabeth Choy.

An Asian woman travelling by train from London to Scotland was not a common sight in the immediate aftermath of World War II. Nevertheless, none of the passengers who shared the same carriage with Elizabeth Choy on her journey north paid her any attention. It was never the British custom to stare at others; one minded one's own business. Had they known anything about her astonishing story and the further extraordinary turns her life was to take, they may have behaved differently. Elizabeth sat with her back straight, hands resting in her lap, lost in thought as she gazed at the unfolding landscape – stark and beautiful – through the window. Her pilgrimage was nearing its end.

At the cessation of hostilities, Elizabeth received a personal invitation from Lady Mountbatten – who had read about Mrs Choy's ordeal and been told of her work in the Medical Auxiliary Services during the Battle of Singapore – to attend the official signing of the instrument of surrender. Lord Mountbatten presided over the surrender ceremony, which took place in the Municipal Building on 12 September 1945.* Under an overcast

---

* The Japanese had, in fact, agreed to terms of the reoccupation of Singapore by the British on 4 September aboard HMS *Sussex*. After resolving to abide by Field Marshal Terauchi's order and Hirohito's instructions, Itagaki signalled Lord Mountbatten. Mountbatten sent his representative – Lieutenant General Alexander Christison – to accept Itagaki's surrender, at which point plans for a grand ceremony would be made.

sky, huge crowds lined the streets and filled the Padang – the open field before the Municipal Building – hissing at General Seishiro Itagaki, commander of the Japanese 7th Area Army, as he made his way up the steps with other high-ranking Japanese officers. They had been driven in cars bearing a white flag. The crowd was kept in check by Royal Marines and a double file of men from the Chinese Resistance Army who stood just inside the building.

A great roar emerged from Stamford Road as Lord Mountbatten's motorcade made its way towards the Padang. Lord Louis' car pulled up before the grand old building and he stepped out to inspect the parade – '[H]e did it leisurely,' one reporter noted, 'stopping here and there to talk to a British marine, a Dogra, a Punjabi, a Commando, a British soldier, a French sailor, and so on until the long line of British sailors.'[5] As he made his way inside, a squadron of Mosquito bombers flew over in salute.

Elizabeth was already inside the building with Lady Mountbatten in the gallery of the council chamber, looking down as Itagaki and the other generals stood in wait for Mountbatten. The recently shaved heads of the Japanese officers caught the soft glow of the chamber's two bronze chandeliers. Elizabeth recognised the Reverend John Leonard Wilson, the Bishop of Singapore, sat behind the representatives of the Allied nations, who were arranged along a table, facing the Japanese delegation.

As Mountbatten entered the room, a rapt silence fell. He took up his position at the table opposite the Japanese and said, in a stern voice:

> I have come here today to receive the formal surrender of all the Japanese forces within the South East Asia Command . . .
> I wish to make this plain: the surrender today is no negotiated surrender. The Japanese are submitting to superior force, now massed here in this port of Singapore.[6]

After calling on Itagaki to produce his credentials, Mountbatten read the Instrument of Surrender. Once finished, eleven copies of the instrument were placed before Itagaki. With precise, measured movements, Itagaki retrieved his spectacles, dipped a pen in an inkwell and signed each copy. When he was finished, Itagaki produced from his pocket a large seal of vermilion-coloured wax. This was the square seal of the Japanese Army, which he placed on the table. He then took out his own personal seal. He then 'chopped' each copy of the instrument with both seals. Once he was finished, all eleven copies were brought to Mountbatten to sign: 'the signing [had] taken nine minutes.'[7]

Following the surrender, Lady Mountbatten escorted Elizabeth to a garden party at Government House. She was introduced to Lord Mountbatten, who spent much of the afternoon at her side, 'keenly interested in Mrs Choy's personal account of life as a prisoner of the Japanese'.[8] In quick time, Elizabeth's story would become intertwined with the plight of thousands of internees and prisoners of war. She accepted an invitation to board a ship bound for Java, to visit the recently liberated internment camps in Jakarta: 'I remember so well the exotic flowers, and the vegetation was so green and nice. People there were very polite, dignified and graceful.'[9] But the city was gripped by violence as the Dutch sought to seize back control of their lost colony following Indonesia's declaration of independence. Despite the dangers, Elizabeth remained in Jakarta for a month, accepting an invitation to visit the presidential palace, where she met Indonesia's first president, Sukarno, who kindly obliged her request for an autograph.

She returned to Singapore to find the city pulsing with energy, as ruined families started to rebuild their lives and shopkeepers unshuttered their stores: a people tentatively taking their first steps towards an uncertain destiny. She was ready to reforge her life in Singapore with Choy Khun Heng and return to the classroom to guide a new generation of youth into adulthood. But fate weaved a different path. Probably at the instigation of Lady Thomas, the Red Cross invited the Choys to travel to England to recuperate for six months. Shortly after she was released from internment, Lady Thomas visited Elizabeth. The messages and parcels Elizabeth had especially arranged to be delivered to Changi had been a godsend. She gave Elizabeth a necklace in the shape of snake, the head made of ruby. Choy Khun Heng immediately declined the offer to travel to England, as the prospect of a long trip did not appeal whatsoever. Besides, the house remained badly damaged. He nonetheless encouraged Elizabeth to go.

Beyond the obvious allure of living in Britain for half a year, the trip would absolve her of any obligation to appear in court to testify against the Japanese war criminals. Elizabeth was not ready to look into the faces of her torturers; she was even less inclined to participate in a trial that would likely result in their execution. At the end of the war, British servicemen attached to the unit investigating war crimes had approached Elizabeth. 'Who are the people you want executed?' some would ask. Elizabeth remembered the Book of Luke in the New Testament: 'Do not judge, and you will not be judged. Do not condemn, and you will not be condemned. Forgive, and you will be forgiven.'

'Please,' she said, shaking her head, 'now everything is finished [. . .] Forgive. I cannot forget, but forgive.'[10] The investigators persisted. Elizabeth was adamant: 'I don't want to mention anyone for execution. Because war is war. It's not the people who are wicked. War is a wicked thing. If you're an officer you have to do your duty for the country. You have to be brutal and be as ruthless as you can. They're just doing their duty. These people, though they are so brutal, they've got their own families. They've got their own children.'[11] She nevertheless relented and provided a sworn statement, a one-page document that provided the merest glimpse of her suffering. When he submitted her statement to the court, the clearly perturbed prosecutor, Lieutenant Colonel Sleeman, said: 'It is rather unfortunate that Mrs. Choy is not available to give evidence. She is at present recuperating in England from the treatment she received.'[12]

On a sunny January day in 1946, Elizabeth farewelled her family and boarded an aircraft for the first time in her life. When the plane stopped over in a bitterly cold Cairo, Elizabeth realised she was shockingly unprepared for the trip. Her clothes were suitable for Singapore's tropical humidity and not much else. Members of the Red Cross accompanying her on the journey scrounged warm clothes for her to wear. Elizabeth arrived in London dressed like a man. She was not the least bit concerned: '[The clothes] kept me warm and I was grateful for them.'[13] Walking London's streets was beyond her wildest imaginings. Where Londoners perceived that the war had reduced their city to something drab, decrepit and bomb-damaged, Elizabeth saw a vast place of immense grandeur. This indeed was the beating heart of the great empire whose history she had learnt as a child and within whose enormous boundaries she had grown up.

She found the English 'friendly, warm, and ever ready to help'; above all, she found them to be resilient: 'when I saw all the war damage in the city, and heard people talking about what they had gone through in such a cheerful way, I did realise why the British had been great for so long – because of their sturdy power of endurance and the qualities necessary to become a great people.'[14] Whenever she felt homesick, she would visit a Chinese restaurant where she would talk to the staff in Mandarin, 'and sure enough I felt better'.[15] Time slowly cured her yearnings for home, as did a rigorous social schedule. She met former internees she had helped, including the Scotts, shortly before Sir Robert travelled to Singapore to give testimony in court. At the victory garden party at Buckingham Palace, she would once more be charmed by Lord Mountbatten, who insisted on introducing Elizabeth to his two daughters. She had dinner with the family of Justice Arthur Newnham Worley, Judge of the Straits Settlements, who had shared a cell with Choy Khun Heng and would subsequently forge a lifelong friendship with his wife. She would also meet with Bishop Wilson and his wife. At the Girl Guides' headquarters in Queen's Gate, South Kensington, she was honoured by Lady Baden-Powell, the Chief Guide, who awarded Elizabeth the Bronze Cross – the highest award in the Girl Guide movement.

And then came the invitation from Queen Elizabeth, the Queen Consort. Elizabeth could not sleep the night before. She was escorted to the palace by Sir Shenton and Lady Thomas. While they waited outside the White Drawing Room, Elizabeth whispered to Sir Shenton, 'Do people ever ask the Queen for her autograph?'[16] Bemused, Sir Shenton advised against it.

On being presented to the Queen, Elizabeth curtsied before Her Majesty as she had been instructed. 'Imagine – there was I, almost a wild woman from Borneo, walking into Buckingham Palace and meeting such a great Queen.'[17] Her Majesty proceeded to ask Elizabeth about her husband, her family and how Singapore had fared through the occupation. Elizabeth could not find her voice. Perhaps her mind strayed to all that she had suffered – her miscarriage, her torture, her husband's ongoing trauma, the murder of her brother Chau Vui, the deaths by violence or disease of many tens of thousands during those dark years. For the first time since the war had begun, Elizabeth lost her poise; she broke down and cried. The Queen soothed her with kind words. When Elizabeth regained her composure, they spoke for half an hour. A week after her audience with the Queen Consort, Elizabeth received a parcel from Buckingham Palace. Inside was a signed portrait of the Queen.

One day, not long after her private audience with the Queen, Elizabeth received a call from a man named E.N.T. Cummings. A former Changi internee, Cummings explained that he was to accompany Elizabeth to Buckingham Palace to meet Princess Elizabeth. Elizabeth could barely comprehend what she was being told – she would be returning to the palace to meet the heir to the throne. She asked if Cummings was drunk. He was most decidedly not. He told her that the princess was inspired by the courage of nurses who served in the Medical Auxiliary Services during the Battle of Singapore. Elizabeth was being invited back to represent the nursing corps.

She wore a *qipao* – a traditional Chinese dress with a high collar, tight fit, distinctive side slits made from silk and embroidered with intricate designs: 'the floral design was in vibrant shades of pink and tangerine on a background of midnight blue; the piping was of satin, in pink.'[18] The *qipao* was from her wedding trousseau, which was left untouched by looting Japanese in the Mackenzie Road house. In her hair she wore a pink carnation. Cummings and Elizabeth presented the princess with a Malayan silver casket of Kelantanese craftmanship that an internee had buried in the grounds of Changi. Inside the casket was an honour roll of the nurses who served in the Medical Auxiliary Services. The princess was not yet a grown woman, but Elizabeth noted her regal qualities: 'I remember the graciousness and beauty of the Princess, and her soft voice.'[19] This would not be the last time she would meet the eldest daughter of George VI.

Seven years later, while serving as a member of parliament in Singapore, Elizabeth would attend the Queen's Coronation. The other twenty-four members of Singapore's Legislative Council – all male – unanimously voted that Elizabeth should be sent as representative of Singapore's Parliament. It was an echo of her appointment as the leader of her cell in the YMCA; just like the prisoners of the *Kempei Tai*, the men of the Legislative Council all recognised a true leader. In what had become her preferred formal dress, Elizabeth wore a satin *qipao* with elegant floral prints (it is now displayed at the National Museum of Singapore) and a flower in her hair. 'The *qipao*,' wrote her biographer, 'underscored her Chinese ethnicity; the flower reflected a life-long love of nature, of the ways of Kadazans of the Land Below the Wind.'[20] To the Coronation Banquet she wore on her left wrist dozens of hand-braided Kadazan bracelets made of bracken fern, and her *qipao* featured a hand-embroidered dragon motif and an eight-word couplet in Chinese characters that read: 'Long live the Queen; may there be universal peace.' 'Who could help but admire the grace, dignity and youthfulness of the Queen,' Elizabeth would say of the coronation in a radio interview, 'the loveliness of the music, the charm of the Queen Mother, the brilliance of the coronets, the radiant loveliness of the princesses and the maids-of-honour, and the charming innocence of the page boys?'[21]

Elizabeth decided to extend her stay in the United Kingdom. She was not ready to return to Singapore, to return to the place where she had endured so much suffering. She studied domestic science at London's Northern Polytechnic and attended the London School of Oriental Languages, where she studied art, funding her studies by modelling nude, including for Dora Gordine, the revered Latvian-born artist, whose subsequent two statuettes modelled on Elizabeth – *Serene Jade* and *Flawless Crystal* – were celebrated as modernist explorations of idealised female beauty. Elizabeth taught at a local primary school, and was thoroughly adored by staff, students and parents. And, of course, she travelled: fruit picking in East Anglia, trout fishing in the Yorkshire Dales and sightseeing in France, Switzerland and the Netherlands. Her six-month period of recuperation in Great Britain would become a life-changing adventure of freedom, wonder and self-discovery that would last four years.

But Elizabeth would not leave before completing her pilgrimage. Through the farmlands and towns of northern England, the train passed through undulating green hills, the land divided by stone walls and hedgerow. She caught glimpses of estuaries and ancient forests as the train rattled into southern Scotland. On arrival at Glasgow's Queen Street Station, Elizabeth boarded a connecting train headed for Fort William and into the Highlands. Beyond Glasgow's outer-urban areas, remote glens were framed by woodlands and glassy lochs shimmered in the soft winter light. She was getting close.

Elizabeth recalled her conversation with John Dunlop, the bald clairvoyant who had taught her sign language in the YMCA cell and claimed – on reading her palm – that one day she would travel the world. Perhaps she had been too dismissive of his purported skills as a palmist. But she would never be able to accept his prediction that she would one day become famous. The life that Elizabeth would create was scarcely imaginable to her then.

Eventually, when she returned to Singapore, she found an altogether different city to the broken place she had left four years earlier: 'To my great surprise, I found the city full of activities, very bright and cheerful, not like the war-torn city I left.'[22] She would, at the persuasion of others, stand as an independent candidate in the municipal election, campaigning on issues relating to social welfare, the rights of the poor, family planning, education and youth, eventually winning a seat in the Legislative Council. And then there came numerous accolades: the OBE, the Order of the Star of Sarawak, a Centenary Medal from St Andrew's School, the Fulbright Scholarship, the Singaporean Pingat Bakti Setia or Long Service Medal. There would be her world speaking tour, where she would once more be feted by an adoring press and fawned over by significant personalities of the twentieth century. There would be more private audiences with Queen Elizabeth II, and meetings with the Duke of Edinburgh, Vice President Richard Nixon, Governor Thomas Dewey of New York, and Singapore's first prime minister, Lee Kuan Yew, among many others. On her speaking tour of North America, she would quite unexpectedly see Dunlop in the audience at an event in Ottawa. He had travelled 300 miles to listen to her speak: 'There, I told you,' he said to her afterwards, '[that] everybody would read about you [and that you would] become famous one day.'[23]

But she kept the adulation in perspective, eschewing all the trappings of fame: she opted to sleep on the plainest bed, wear the simplest clothes and remain moderate in all things. She rededicated herself to helping others: 'I think the fundamental law for happiness is to forget yourself and help others, and then happiness automatically comes to you.'[24] Her guiding principle was always service: service to her family as a mother, sister, cousin and wife; service to her students as a teacher; service to her constituents through politics; service to her nation as a second lieutenant in the women's auxiliary arm of the Singapore Volunteer Corps, where she was known as Gunner Choy; and finally, and always, service to the destitute, the downtrodden and the forgotten through the Church.

All life's vicissitudes attended her remarkable story: moments of great personal joy, such as when she and Choy Khun Heng adopted three girls, and moments of immense sadness, such as when she lost Marie, her youngest sister, whom she raised as her own and who died aged thirty-one of cancer. When her political career was over, Elizabeth would re-enter education, serving as inaugural principal for Singapore's School for the Blind, before returning as a teacher to her beloved St Andrew's School, the place where she first heard the former principal Canon Sorby Adams' favourite song, whose soothing melody and vivid lyrics had helped her survive the hell of her imprisonment.

Elizabeth died of pancreatic cancer aged ninety-five in 2006. Her funeral was an intimate gathering of family and close friends, in keeping with her very modest wishes. Hundreds would attend a memorial at St Andrew's Cathedral, including former students and colleagues, members of Parliament, military representatives and the President of Singapore, S.R. Nathan.

That was all ahead. As her train journey neared its end, this day was not about the future; it was about the past. Her future would have seemed as fantastical and unimaginable to her as the place at which she was soon to arrive. Towards the end of her life, in one of the many letters she sent to Lady Rosamond – whose firm friendship was rekindled following Sir Robert's appointment as Commissioner-General of Singapore – Elizabeth included the notes of a speech she delivered at the opening of an exhibition at the National Museum of Singapore that celebrated her life. Titled *Elizabeth Choy: A Woman Ahead of Her Time*, the exhibition included one of Dora Gordine's sculptures, the *qipao* she wore to the Queen's coronation, the black frock she wore through her imprisonment in the YMCA, the necklace from Lady Thomas, as well as hundreds of newspaper clippings, photographs and other artefacts.

'Perhaps the exhibition is of some help to our school children who now have two new subjects to learn, namely "National Education" and "Singapore History",' she wrote. 'It's good for our young to learn more about Singapore – both its past as well as its present, because [there is a] Chinese saying: "To see the present, one should learn from the past; without the past, there can be no present."'[25] But Elizabeth did not believe in endless rumination. She had long since forgiven her captors. To truly be free of her incarceration, she had to unshackle herself from the memories of those past horrors. Only then could she return home.

As Elizabeth disembarked the train at Arrochar & Tarbet railway station, the final stop on her pilgrimage, she approached the station master for directions to her destination. It was not a long walk, he told her, but the day was cold. Elizabeth waved away his concerns. She was warmly dressed. Besides, she had known much greater discomforts. She found a path that wended its way through a wood of pristine silence that presently gave way to an open glen. Elizabeth could scarcely believe the beauty unfolding before her. The surface of Loch Lomond mirrored the snow-dusted peaks of the Arrochar Alps. The mighty Ben Lomond dominated the eastern sky, tendrils of ice and snow streaking down the mountain's craggy slopes.

Elizabeth walked on, at last reaching the bonnie banks, a breeze raising ripples across the loch's otherwise glassy surface.

'I knelt by the bank and I took three sips of water.'[26] The water was as ice. She stood up, shoulders back, back straight. She was renewed; ready to face her future. She said a prayer of thanks to God, a silent 'thank you'[27] to the loch, and then turned for the path that would take her home to Singapore.

ENDNOTES

Introduction: The YMCA

1 Choy, Elizabeth (Mrs) @Yong Su Moi, 'Japanese Occupation of Singapore, Accession Number 00597' – interview transcript, reel 2, pp. 12–13.
2 Ibid.
3 Choy, Elizabeth, as told to Shirley Gordon, 'The Autobiography of Elizabeth Choy Su-Mei', *INTISARI: The Research Journal of Wider Malaysia*, vol. IV, no. 1, 1974 (reprinted as *My Autobiography as Told to Shirley Gordon*, Kuala Lumpur, 1974).
4 Ibid., p. 37.
5 Choy, Elizabeth (Mrs) @Yong Su Moi, 'Japanese Occupation of Singapore, Accession Number 00597' – interview transcript, reel 2, pp. 22–3.

1: HMS *Giang Bee*

1 Papers of Sir Robert H. Scott and Lady Scott, National Library of Scotland, Edinburgh, ACCC. 8181, Robert Heatlie Scott (formerly Far Eastern Representative, MOI), 'Sinking of HMS *Giang Bee* on February 13, 1942', 19 September 1945, p. 4.
2 Ibid., p. 2.
3 Ibid., p. 3.
4 Ibid., p. 4.
5 Ibid.
6 Ibid., p. 5.
7 Brooke, Geoffrey, *Singapore's Dunkirk: The Aftermath of the Fall*, Pen & Sword, Barnsley, 1989, p. 160.
8 Scott, 'Sinking of HMS *Giang Bee*', p. 5.
9 Ibid.
10 Diary of Mr M.J.V. Miller, Imperial War Museum 88/62/1.
11 McDougall Jr., William H., *By Eastern Windows: A Battle of Souls and Minds in the Prison Camps of Sumatra*, Uncommon Valor Press, New York, 1949, p. 157.

12 Ibid.
13 Scott, 'Sinking of HMS *Giang Bee*', p. 5.
14 Ibid.
15 Ibid.
16 Ibid.
17 Ibid.
18 Ibid.
19 Ibid., p. 7.
20 Ibid.
21 Ibid.
22 Ibid.
23 Ibid.

2: The Bloated Man

1 Sleeman, Colin, and S.C. Silkin (eds), *Trial of Sumida Haruzo and Twenty Others (The 'Double Tenth' Trial)*, Hodge, London, 2007, p. 70.
2 Ibid.
3 Choy, Elizabeth (Mrs) @Yong Su Moi, 'Japanese Occupation of Singapore, Accession Number 00597' – interview transcript, reel 2, p. 19.
4 Sleeman and Silkin (eds), p. 71.
5 Zhou, Mei, *Elizabeth Choy: More than a War Heroine*, Landmark Books, Singapore, 1995, p. 70.
6 Choy, Elizabeth (Mrs) @Yong Su Moi, 'Japanese Occupation of Singapore, Accession Number 00597' – interview transcript, reel 3, p. 30.

3: Castaways

1 Scott, 'Sinking of HMS *Giang Bee*', p. 7.
2 Ibid.
3 Papers of Sir Robert H. Scott and Lady Scott, National Library of Scotland, Edinburgh, ACCC. 8181, Robert Heatlie Scott (formerly Far Eastern Representative, MOI), 'First Instalment: The Dinghy – February 13th to March 2nd 1942', p. 1.
4 Ibid.
5 Ibid.
6 Ibid.
7 Ibid.
8 Ibid., p. 2.
9 Ibid.
10 Ibid.
11 Ibid.
12 Quoted exchange in Scott, 'First Instalment', p. 2.
13 Ibid., pp. 2–3.
14 Ibid., p. 3.

15 Ibid.
16 Ibid.
17 Ibid.
18 Ibid.
19 Ibid.
20 Ibid.
21 Ibid.

4: *Sook Ching*

 1 Choy, Elizabeth, as told to Shirley Gordon, 'The Autobiography of Elizabeth Choy Su-Mei', pp. 27–8.
 2 Ibid., p. 27.
 3 Barber, Noel, *Sinister Twilight: The Fall of Singapore*, Arrow Books, London, 1968, p. 159.
 4 Lee, Geok Boi, *The Syonan Years: Singapore Under Japanese Rule 1942–1945*, National Archives of Singapore, Singapore, 2005, p. 105.
 5 Heng Chiang Ki, oral history, quoted in Lee, p. 106.
 6 Choy, Elizabeth, as told to Shirley Gordon, 'The Autobiography of Elizabeth Choy Su-Mei', p. 33.
 7 Ibid.
 8 Choy, Elizabeth (Mrs) @Yong Su Moi, 'Japanese Occupation of Singapore, Accession Number 00597' – interview transcript, reel 3, p. 8.
 9 Ibid.
10 Ibid., p. 7.
11 Choy, Elizabeth, as told to Shirley Gordon, 'The Autobiography of Elizabeth Choy Su-Mei', p. 33.
12 Arthur Thompson, oral history, quoted in Lee, p. 111.
13 *Syonan Times*, 24 February 1942, quoted in Lee, p. 111.

5: Sumatra

 1 Scott, 'First Instalment', p. 3.
 2 Ibid.
 3 Ibid., pp. 3–4.
 4 Ibid.
 5 Ibid.
 6 Ibid.
 7 Ibid.
 8 Ibid., p. 4.
 9 Ibid.
10 Ibid., p. 6
11 Scott, 'Sinking of HMS *Giang Bee*', p. 5.
12 Scott, 'First Instalment', p. 4.
13 Ibid.

14 Ibid.
15 Ibid., p. 5.
16 Ibid., p. 4.
17 Ibid., p. 5.
18 Ibid.
19 Ibid.
20 Ibid.
21 Ibid., pp. 5–6.
22 Ibid., p. 6.
23 Ibid.
24 Ibid.

6: Mackenzie Road

1 Curiously, British films were not banned until September 1943; see Lee, p. 192.
2 Ibid., p. 190.
3 Huff, Gregg, and Shinobu Majima (translated and edited), *World War II Singapore: The Chosabu Reports*, NUS Press, Singapore, 2018, p. 137.
4 Choy, Elizabeth (Mrs) @Yong Su Moi, 'Japanese Occupation of Singapore, Accession Number 00597' – interview transcript, reel 2, p. 13.
5 Zhou, p. 45.
6 Ibid., pp. 44–5.
7 Choy, Elizabeth (Mrs) @Yong Su Moi, 'Japanese Occupation of Singapore, Accession Number 00597' – interview transcript, reel 2, p. 13.
8 Ibid.

7: The Survivor of Radji Beach

1 Scott, 'First Instalment', p. 6.
2 Papers of Sir Robert H. Scott and Lady Scott, National Library of Scotland, Edinburgh, ACCC. 8181, Robert Heatlie Scott, Correspondence and Papers: 'Second Instalment: March 2nd 1942 to May 30th 1942', p. 1.
3 Ibid.
4 In Papers of Sir Robert H. Scott and Lady Scott, National Library of Scotland, Edinburgh, ACCC. 8181, Robert Heatlie Scott, Correspondence and Papers: 'Third Instalment: The Gymnasium: May 30 – June 7th 1942', p. 1.
5 Ibid.
6 Scott, 'Second Instalment', p. 1.
7 Vivian Bullwinkel, from Sir William Webb at the Australian Board of Inquiry into War Crimes in October 1945, AWM54 1010/4/24B.
8 Burgess, Colin, *Sisters in Captivity: Sister Betty Jeffrey OAM and the Courageous Story of Australian Army Nurses in Sumatra, 1942–1945*, Simon & Schuster, Sydney, 2023, p. 98.

 9 Sir William Webb at the Australian Board of Inquiry into War Crimes in October 1945, AWM54 1010/4/24B.
10 Ibid.
11 Ibid.
12 Ibid.
13 Quoted in Burgess, p. 99.
14 Ibid., p. 106.
15 Ibid., p. 103.
16 Scott, 'Second Instalment', p. 2.
17 Ibid.
18 Ibid., p. 3.
19 Ibid.
20 Ibid.
21 Ibid.
22 Ibid.
23 Ibid.
24 Ibid.
25 Ibid.
26 Ibid., p. 4.
27 Ibid.
28 Ibid.

8: The Bishop

 1 Choy, Elizabeth, as told to Shirley Gordon, 'The Autobiography of Elizabeth Choy Su-Mei', p. 37.
 2 Ibid.
 3 Zhou, pp. 71–2.
 4 Choy, Elizabeth (Mrs) @Yong Su Moi, 'Japanese Occupation of Singapore, Accession Number 00597' – interview transcript, reel 2, p. 13.
 5 Zhou, p. 45.
 6 Ibid., p. 74.
 7 Hayter, John, *Priest in Prison: Four Years of Life in Japanese-occupied Singapore*, Churchman Publishing, Worthing, 1989, p. 60.
 8 Ibid.
 9 Letter of appointment from Bishop John Leonard Wilson, quoted in Thambiah, Joseph, *The History of Anglicanism in Singapore 1819–2019*, Armour Publishing, Singapore, 2020, p. 170.
10 Leong, Keith, 'John Leonard Wilson: Bishop of Singapore (1941–1949)', St Andrew's Cathedral information booklet.
11 Hayter, pp. 83–4.
12 Thambiah, p. 192.
13 Ibid., p. 85.
14 Peet, George L., *Within Changi's Walls: A Record of Civilian Internment in World War II*, Marshall Cavendish, Singapore, 2011, p. 72.

15 Thambiah, p. 155.
16 Papers of Sir Robert H. Scott and Lady Scott, National Library of Scotland, Edinburgh, ACCC. 8181, Robert Heatlie Scott, Correspondence and Papers: 'Fifth Instalment: Solitary: July 15, 1942 – February 19, 1942', p. 1.
17 Hayter, p. 156.
18 Scott, 'Fifth Instalment', p. 2.
19 Letter to Father John Hayter from Hans Schweizer-Iten, quoted in Hayter, p. 312.
20 Choy, Elizabeth (Mrs) @Yong Su Moi, 'Japanese Occupation of Singapore, Accession Number 00597' – interview transcript, reel 2, p. 14.
21 Sleeman and Silkin (eds), pp. 21–2.
22 This exchange is recounted in a BBC interview Bishop Wilson gave in October 1946 and is quoted here from Hayter, p. 163.
23 Ibid.
24 Ibid.
25 Ibid., p. 164.
26 Ibid.
27 Choy, Elizabeth, as told to Shirley Gordon, 'The Autobiography of Elizabeth Choy Su-Mei', p. 36.

9: The Diplomat

1 Morrison, Ian, Malayan Postscript, Faber and Faber, United Kingdom, 1942, p. 161.
2 'Mainly about Malayans', The Straits Times, 24 November 1940, p. 7.
3 Lowe, Peter, 'Sir Robert Heatlie Scott (1905–82) and Japan', in Britain and Japan: Biographical Portraits, vol. VII, pp. 148–49, Taylor and Francis, Abingdon, 2010.
4 Telegram from Robert Heatlie Scott to Secretary of the Colonies: Far East – Propaganda, National Archives, Kew: PWD/42/1026/7.A.
5 Bix, Herbert P., Hirohito and the Making of Modern Japan, Perennial, New York, 2000, p. 274.
6 'Japan in the National Emergency', reel/segment 9, quoted in Bix, p. 276.
7 Morrison, p. 161.
8 Ibid., p. 162.
9 'Mainly about Malayans', p. 7.
10 The Singapore Free Press, Monday April 28, 1941, 'Japan's "New Order" Slogan Analysed and Answered: How the Nation Has Deluded Itself', Robert H. Scott broadcasts, Scott Family Papers, pp. 1–4.
11 Scott, Robert H., '30 Years Ago Singapore Fell', The Straits Times, 16 February 1972, p. 8
12 Ibid.
13 Robert Heatlie Scott, 'Answering Co-Prosperity', Far East Propaganda, National Archives Kew, PWD/42/1028/7.A.

14 Ibid.
15 Scott, '30 Years Ago Singapore Fell', p. 8.
16 Morrison, p. 161.
17 Papers of Sir Robert H. Scott and Lady Scott, National Library of Scotland, Edinburgh, ACCC. 8181, Robert Heatlie Scott, Correspondence and Papers: 'Tenth (And Last) Instalment Sime Road Civilian Internment Camp Hospital, Singapore: February 28th – September 9th 1945', p. 6.
18 Scott, 'Second Instalment', p. 1.
19 Ibid.
20 Ibid.
21 Ibid.
22 Ibid.
23 Ibid.
24 Ibid., p. 2.
25 Ibid.
26 Dialogue exchange taken from Scott, 'Second Instalment', p. 2.
27 Ibid.
28 Ibid., p. 4.
29 Ibid.
30 Ibid.
31 Ibid., p. 5.
32 Ibid.
33 Ibid.
34 Ibid.
35 Ibid.
36 Ibid.
37 Ibid.
38 Ibid.
39 Ibid.
40 Ibid.
41 Ibid.
42 Ibid.
43 Ibid.
44 Ibid.
45 Ibid., p. 6.
46 Ibid.
47 Ibid., p. 7.

10: Cell Leader
1 Zhou, p. 74.
2 Ibid., pp. 72–3.
3 Choy, Elizabeth, as told to Shirley Gordon, 'The Autobiography of Elizabeth Choy Su-Mei', p. 31.

4 Ibid., p. 25.
5 Ibid.
6 Ibid.
7 Ibid., pp. 25–6.
8 Ibid.
9 Zhou, p. 43.
10 Choy, Elizabeth, as told to Shirley Gordon, 'The Autobiography of Elizabeth Choy Su-Mei', p. 65.
11 Ibid.
12 Ibid.
13 Ibid.
14 Choy, Elizabeth (Mrs) @Yong Su Moi, 'Japanese Occupation of Singapore, Accession Number 00597', interview transcript, reel 4, p. 47.
15 Choy, Elizabeth, as told to Shirley Gordon, 'The Autobiography of Elizabeth Choy Su-Mei', p. 63.
16 Choy, Elizabeth (Mrs) @Yong Su Moi, 'Japanese Occupation of Singapore, Accession Number 00597' – interview transcript, reel 3, pp. 37–8.
17 Choy, Elizabeth, as told to Shirley Gordon, 'The Autobiography of Elizabeth Choy Su-Mei', p. 65.

11: Mistaken Identity

1 Scott, 'Third Instalment', p. 1.
2 Ibid.
3 'William Probyn Allen', from muntokpeacemuseum.org
4 Scott, 'Third Instalment', p. 1.
5 Ibid., p. 2.
6 Ibid.
7 Ibid.
8 Ibid.
9 Ibid.
10 Ibid., p. 1.
11 Ibid., p. 2.
12 Ibid.
13 Ibid.
14 Ibid.
15 Ibid., p. 1.
16 Ibid.
17 Ibid.
18 Ibid., p. 3.
19 Ibid.
20 Ibid.
21 Ibid.
22 Ibid.

23 Ibid., p. 4.
24 Ibid.
25 Ibid.
26 Ibid.
27 Ibid.
28 Ibid., p. 1.
29 Ibid., p. 4.
30 Ibid.
31 Ibid.
32 Ibid.
33 Ibid., p. 5.
34 Ibid.
35 Ibid.
36 Ibid., p. 6.
37 Ibid.
38 Ibid.
39 Ibid.
40 Ibid.
41 Ibid.
42 Ibid.
43 Ibid.
44 Ibid.
45 Ibid.
46 Ibid.
47 Ibid.
48 Young, Bill, *Return to a Dark Age*, B. Young, Allawah, 1992, pp. 135–7.
49 Ibid.
50 Ibid.
51 Ibid.

12: Sam the Sergeant Major

 1 Papers of Sir Robert H. Scott and Lady Scott, National Library of Scotland, Edinburgh, ACCC. 8181, Robert Heatlie Scott, Correspondence and Papers: 'Fourth Instalment: Cross Examination June 8 – July 15, 1942', p. 1.
 2 Morrison, p. 168.
 3 'Everyday Life of the People of Singapore', *The Sunday Times*, 9 February 1942, transcript of Robert Heatlie Scott's broadcast on the Malayan Broadcasting Corporation, Singapore Station.
 4 Morrison, p. 169.
 5 Ibid.
 6 Scott, 'Fourth Instalment', p. 3.
 7 Ibid., p. 1.

8 Scott, 'Third Instalment', p. 5.
9 Ibid.
10 Scott, 'Fourth Instalment', p. 2.
11 Ibid.
12 Ibid.
13 Ibid.
14 Ibid.
15 Ibid.
16 Ibid.
17 Ibid., p. 3.
18 Ibid.
19 Ibid.
20 Ibid.
21 Ibid.
22 Ibid.
23 Ibid., pp. 2–3.
24 Ibid.
25 Ibid., p. 3.
26 Ibid., p. 4.
27 Ibid.
28 Ibid.
29 Ibid.
30 Ibid.
31 Ibid.
32 Ibid.
33 Dialogue exchange taken from quotes in: Scott, 'Fourth Instalment', pp. 3–5.
34 Ibid., p. 4.
35 Ibid.
36 Ibid.
37 Ibid.
38 Ibid., p. 5.
39 Ibid., p. 4.
40 Ibid.
41 Ibid.
42 Ibid., p. 5.
43 Ibid.
44 Ibid.
45 Ibid.
46 Ibid.
47 Ibid.
48 Ibid.
49 Ibid.

13: The Shakespeare Adventure
1 Scott, 'Fourth Instalment', p. 5.
2 Ibid., p. 6.
3 Ibid.
4 Ibid.
5 Ibid.
6 Ibid.
7 Ibid.
8 Ibid., p. 7.
9 Scott, 'Second Instalment', p. 5.
10 Ibid.
11 Scott, 'Fourth Instalment', p. 7.
12 Ibid.
13 Ibid.
14 Ibid.
15 Ibid.
16 Ibid.
17 Ibid.
18 Ibid.
19 Ibid.
20 Ibid.
21 Ibid.
22 Ibid.
23 Ibid., p. 8.
24 Ibid.
25 Ibid.
26 Ibid., p. 7.
27 Ibid.
28 Ibid.
29 Morgan's report, quoted in Scott, 'Fourth Instalment', p. 8.

14: To Cast Good Seed
1 Choy, Elizabeth, as told to Shirley Gordon, 'The Autobiography of Elizabeth Choy Su-Mei', pp. 27–8.
2 Ibid., p. 32.
3 Ibid.
4 Ibid.
5 Choy, Elizabeth (Mrs) @Yong Su Moi, 'Japanese Occupation of Singapore, Accession Number 00597' – interview transcript, reel 2, p. 14.
6 Ibid., p. 23.
7 Choy, Elizabeth, as told to Shirley Gordon, 'The Autobiography of Elizabeth Choy Su-Mei', p. 59.
8 Zhou, p. 86.

9   Kitching, Thomas, *Life and Death in Changi: The War and Internment Diary of Thomas Kitching (1942–1944)*, Landmark Books, Singapore, 1998, p. 187.

10 Chee, Yam Cheng, '7th Tan Tock Seng oration: Surgical Excellence at TTSH – 100 Years on and onward', transcript available at http://annals. edu.sg/pdf/41VolNo8Aug2012/V41N8p368.pdf

11 Choy, Elizabeth (Mrs) @Yong Su Moi, 'Japanese Occupation of Singapore, Accession Number 00597' – interview transcript, reel 2, p. 14.

12 Ibid.

13 Ibid., p. 16.

14 Zhou, p. 68.

15: The Man in the Tower

1   Peet, p. 18.

2   Ibid., p. 21.

3   Scott, 'Fifth Instalment: Solitary', p. 1.

4   Ibid.

5   Ibid.

6   Ibid.

7   Ibid.

8   Ibid., p. 2.

9   Ibid., p. 1.

10 Ibid., p. 4.

11 Ibid.

12 Ibid., p. 2.

13 Ibid.

14 Ibid., p. 3.

15 Ibid., pp. 2–3.

16 Ibid., p. 3.

17 Ibid.

18 Ibid.

19 Ibid.

20 Ibid.

21 Ibid.

22 Ibid., p. 4.

23 Ibid.

24 Ibid.

25 Ibid.

26 Dialogue exchange quoted in Scott, 'Fifth Instalment', p. 5.

27 Ibid., p. 4.

28 Ibid., p. 5.

29 Ibid.

16: The Black Market

1 Peet, p. 20.
2 Ibid., p. 18.
3 Ibid., p. 111.
4 Ibid., pp. 18–19.
5 Ibid., pp. 18–19.
6 Ibid., p. 18.
7 Papers of Sir Robert H. Scott and Lady Scott, National Library of Scotland, Edinburgh, ACCC. 8181, Robert Heatlie Scott, Correspondence and Papers: 'Sixth Instalment: Changi: February 19 – October 10, 1943', p. 1.
8 See Jones, E.H., *The Road to Endor*, Bodley Head, London, 1920.
9 Scott, 'Sixth Instalment', p. 1.
10 Kitching, p. 182.
11 Peet, p. 114.
12 Scott, 'Sixth Instalment', p. 1.
13 Ibid.
14 Ibid., p. 2.
15 Ibid.
16 Peet, p. 115.
17 Scott, 'Sixth Instalment', p. 2.
18 Ibid.
19 Ibid.
20 Ibid.
21 Ibid.
22 Peet, p. 74.
23 Scott, 'Fifth Instalment', p. 1.
24 Ibid., p. 2.
25 Ibid.
26 Peet, p. 76.
27 Ibid.

17: The Suspected Insurgent

1 Dialogue extrapolated from various quotes in Choy, Elizabeth (Mrs) @Yong Su Moi, 'Japanese Occupation of Singapore, Accession Number 00597' – interview transcript, reels 2–4.
2 Ibid.

18: The News Bulletin

1 Scott, 'Sixth Instalment', p. 2.
2 Ibid., p. 3.
3 Ibid.

4 Ibid.
5 Ibid., p. 4.
6 Ibid.
7 Ibid., p. 3.
8 Ibid.
9 Ibid.
10 Ibid.
11 Ibid.
12 Ibid.
13 Ibid.
14 Ibid., p. 4.
15 Ibid.
16 Ibid.
17 Ibid.
18 Ibid., p. 4.
19 Ibid.
20 Ibid., p. 1.

19: The Smiling Torturer

1 Mallal, Bashir A. (ed.), *The Double Tenth Trial, War Crimes Court: In Re Lt.-Col Sumida Haruzo and 20 Others*, The Malayan Law Journal Office, Singapore, 1947, p. 566.
2 Lamont-Brown, Raymond, 'Kempeitai: Ruthless Policemen of the Rising Sun' in *The Police Journal*, vol. 67, issue 2, April–June 1994, pp. 163–67, doi.org/10.1177/0032258X9406700213, p. 18.
3 Ibid., p. 33.
4 Sleeman and Silkin (eds), p. 261.
5 Ibid., p. 41.
6 Papers of Sir Robert H. Scott and Lady Scott, National Library of Scotland, Edinburgh, ACCC. 8181, Robert Heatlie Scott, Correspondence and Papers: 'Seventh Instalment: The "Y": October 10th, 1943 – April 10, 1944', p. 4.
7 Sleeman and Silkin (eds), p. 238.
8 Kratoska, Paul H., *The Japanese Occupation of Malaya and Singapore, 1941–45*, NUS Press, Singapore, 2018, p. 250.
9 Scott, 'Fourth Instalment', p. 2.
10 Kratoska, p. 269.
11 Ibid., p. 250.
12 Mallal, p. 595.
13 Sleeman and Silkin (eds), p. 237.
14 Ibid., p. xviii.
15 Ibid., p. xx.

20: The Sadist

1 Dialogue extrapolated from various quotes in Choy, Elizabeth (Mrs) @Yong Su Moi, 'Japanese Occupation of Singapore, Accession Number 00597', interview transcript, reel 2, pp. 23–4 and 'World War 2 Survivors: Elizabeth Choy', Interview with Elizabeth Choy, Accession Number 2023014477, available at www.nas.gov.sg/archivesonline/audiovisual_records/record-details/32b65ce8-4717-11ee-9776-0050569c7836

2 Quoted in Zhou, p. 76.

3 Choy, Elizabeth (Mrs) @Yong Su Moi, 'Japanese Occupation of Singapore, Accession Number 00597', interview transcript, Reel 3, p. 31.

4 Dialogue extrapolated from various quotes in Choy, Elizabeth (Mrs) @Yong Su Moi, 'Japanese Occupation of Singapore, Accession Number 00597', interview transcript, Reel 2, pp. 13–26, and "World War 2 Survivors: Elizabeth Choy", Interview with Elizabeth Choy, Accession Number 2023014477, available at www.nas.gov.sg/archivesonline/audiovisual_records/record-details/32b65ce8-4717-11ee-9776-0050569c7836

5 Dialogue extrapolated from various quotes in Choy, Elizabeth (Mrs) @Yong Su Moi, 'Japanese Occupation of Singapore, Accession Number 00597', interview transcript, reel 2, pp. 24–5.

21: The Attack

1 Silver, Lynette, Deadly Secrets: The Singapore Raids 1942–45, Sally Milner Publishing, Binda, 2010, p. 87.

2 Clive Lyon, the son of Ivan Lyon, quoted in Thompson, Peter, and Robert Macklin, Operation Rimau: Australia's Heroic and Daring Commando Raid on Singapore, Hachette, Sydney, 2015, p. 23.

3 Ibid., p. 27.

4 Silver, Deadly Secrets, p. 96.

5 Ibid., p. 112.

6 Thompson and Macklin, p. 50.

7 Ibid., p. 123.

8 Ibid., p. 129.

9 'Report of Operation "Jaywick" Carried Out by MV Krait Sept–Oct 1943, Part II', National Archives of Australia (NAA), Canberra, MP1185/8, 1932/2/85, p. 1.

10 Ibid.

11 Ibid.

12 Ibid., p. 4.

13 Ibid., p. 5.

14 Ibid., p. 6.

15 Ibid.

16 Ibid., p. 1.

17 Ibid., p. 6.

18 Ibid., p. 7.

19 Ibid.

20 Ibid.

21 Ibid.

22 'Report of Operation "Jaywick" Carried Out by MV *Krait* Sept–Oct 1943', Appendix B: 'The Attack by Canoe No. 3 (Lieut. Page and AB Jones)', National Archives of Australia (NAA), Canberra, MP1185/8, 1932/2/85.

23 Ibid.

22: The Number One Work

1 Sleeman and Silkin (eds), p. 239.

2 Ibid.

3 'Operation "Jaywick" September 1943. Proposed Awards to Personnel. Report submitted in a letter to the Prime Minister John Curtin sent by the Minister of the Army, 21/7/44', National Archives of Australia (NAA), Canberra, A816, 66/301/532, p. 5.

4 Sleeman and Silkin (eds), p. 239.

5 Ibid., p. 241.

6 Ibid., p. 239.

7 Ibid., p. 238.

8 Sleeman and Silkin (eds), p. 127.

9 Ibid., p. 265.

10 'Intercepted signal Staff Telegram No. 1647', quoted in 'Operation "Jaywick" September 1943. Proposed Awards to Personnel. Report submitted in a letter to the Prime Minister John Curtin sent by the Minister of the Army, 21/7/44'. National Archives of Australia (NAA), Canberra, A816, 66/301/532, p. 5.

11 Sleeman and Silkin (eds), pp. 106–7.

12 Ibid., p. 240.

13 Ibid., p. 42.

14 Ibid., p. 41.

15 Boi, pp. 225–6.

16 Sleeman and Silkin (eds), p. 226.

17 'Operation Jaywick, Part 1 – General Summary', National Archives of Australia (NAA), Canberra, A3269, E2/1.

18 'Report of Operation "Jaywick" Carried Out by MV *Krait* Sept–Oct 1943, Part II', National Archives of Australia (NAA), Canberra, MP1185/8, 1932/2/85, p. 8.

19 Ibid.

20 Ibid.

21 Ibid.

22 'Report of Operation "Jaywick" Carried Out by MV *Krait* Sept–Oct 1943, Appendix A – The Attack by Canoe 2 and the Return to Pompong', National Archives of Australia (NAA), Canberra, MP1185/8, 1932/2/85.
23 'Report of Operation "Jaywick" Carried Out by MV *Krait* Sept–Oct 1943, Part II', National Archives of Australia (NAA), Canberra, MP1185/8, 1932/2/85, p. 7.
24 'Graphic Story of Raid on Singapore', *Melbourne Herald*, 2 August 1946.
25 Ted Carse logbook, quoted in Thompson and Macklin, p. 101.

23: The Double Tenth Incident
1 Curiously, Robert H. Scott alludes to the real culprits – a 'small party of Javanese thugs were caught, and went to their execution definitely and cheerfully' – being responsible for the attack on Japanese shipping. It is unknown to which Javanese guerrillas he is referring but they may have been involved in other acts of sabotage. See 'Seventh Instalment', p. 7.
2 Scott, 'Sixth Instalment', p. 5.
3 Ibid., p. 5.
4 Interview and correspondence with Sarah Peterson, Helena Steedman and Scott Steedman, grandchildren of Sir Robert Heatlie Scott and Lady Rosamond Scott, 28 August 2024.
5 'Pretty Peiping Wedding', 12 October 1933, unknown newspaper, Scott Steedman family papers.
6 Scott, 'Sixth Instalment', p. 3.
7 Kitching, p. 291.
8 Ibid.
9 Ibid.
10 Scott, 'Sixth Instalment', p. 5.
11 Ibid.
12 Kitching, p. 291.
13 Peet, p. 160.
14 Kitching, p. 292.

24: Confessions
1 Sleeman and Silkin (eds), p. 42.
2 Ibid., p. 161.
3 Ibid., p. 87.
4 Ibid., p. ix.

25: Cell One
1 Scott, 'Seventh Instalment', p. 1.
2 Ibid.
3 Ibid., p. 2.
4 Ibid.

5   Ibid.
6   Ibid.
7   Ibid., pp. 2–3.
8   Ibid., p. 2.
9   Ibid., p. 1.
10 Ibid.
11 Sleeman and Silkin (eds), pp. 12–13.
12 Ibid., p. 13.
13 Ibid., p. 2.
14 Papers of Sir Robert H. Scott and Lady Scott, National Library of Scotland, Edinburgh, ACCC. 8181, Robert Heatlie Scott, Correspondence and Papers: 'Eighth Instalment: Miyako: April 10 – October 1, 1944', p. 5.
15 Ibid.
16 Ibid., p. 6.
17 Ibid.
18 Sleeman and Silkin (eds), p. 62.
19 Scott, 'Seventh Instalment', p. 3.
20 Papers of Sir Robert H. Scott and Lady Scott, National Library of Scotland, Edinburgh, ACCC. 8181; R.H. Scott, 'Internment in Singapore: 1942/45', p. 4.
21 Sleeman and Silkin (eds), pp. 67–8.
22 Scott, 'Internment in Singapore', p. 3.

26: The Torment of Dr Stanley
1   Sleeman and Silkin (eds), p. 263.
2   Ibid., p. 131.
3   Scott, 'Internment in Singapore', p. 7.
4   Sleeman and Silkin (eds), p. 129.
5   'Beatings in "Double Tenth" Case Admitted', *The Straits Times*, 6 April 1946.
6   Scott, 'Seventh Instalment', p. 3.
7   Ibid.
8   Sleeman and Silkin (eds), p. 32.
9   Ibid.
10 Ibid.
11 Ibid., p. 22.
12 Ibid., p. 32.
13 Ibid., pp. 136–7.
14 Ibid., p. 32.
15 Ibid.
16 Ibid., p. 33.
17 Ibid., p. 99.
18 Ibid., p. 94.

19 Ibid.
20 Ibid.
21 Ibid.
22 Ibid.

27: An Unravelling Investigation
1 Sleeman and Silkin (eds), p. 85.
2 Ibid., p. 87.
3 Ibid.
4 Ibid.
5 Ibid., p. 313.
6 Ibid.
7 Ibid., p. 315.
8 Ibid., p. xxv.
9 Ibid., p. 314.
10 Ibid., p. 158.
11 Lamont-Brown, p. 10.

28: The Battery
1 Choy, Elizabeth, as told to Shirley Gordon, 'The Autobiography of Elizabeth Choy Su-Mei', p. 38.
2 Exchange quoted in Choy, Elizabeth (Mrs) @Yong Su Moi, 'Japanese Occupation of Singapore, Accession Number 00597', interview transcript, reel 4, pp. 12–13.
3 Sleeman and Silkin (eds), p. 141.
4 Ibid., p. 62.

29: A Deadly Game
1 Scott, 'Seventh Instalment', pp. 3–4.
2 Ibid., p. 4.
3 Scott, 'Third Instalment', p. 5.
4 Scott, 'Seventh Instalment', p. 4.
5 Ibid.
6 Ibid.
7 Ibid.
8 Ibid., p. 5.
9 Ibid.
10 Sleeman and Silkin (eds), p. 59.
11 Scott, 'Seventh Instalment', p. 4.
12 Ibid., p. 5.
13 Ibid.
14 Ibid.
15 Ibid.

16 Ibid.
17 Ibid.
18 Ibid.
19 Ibid.
20 Ibid.
21 Scott, '30 Years Ago Singapore Fell', p. 8.
22 Ibid.
23 Ibid.
24 Ibid.
25 Ibid.
26 Ibid., p. 6.
27 Sleeman and Silkin (eds), p. 129.
28 Ibid., p. 116.
29 Ibid., p. 308.
30 Ibid.
31 Ibid., p. 309.

30: Lying and Surviving
1 Sleeman and Silkin (eds), p. 81.
2 Ibid., p. 140.
3 Ibid., p. 79.
4 Scott, 'Internment in Singapore', p. 7.
5 Choy, Elizabeth (Mrs) @Yong Su Moi, 'Japanese Occupation of Singapore, Accession Number 00597', interview transcript, reel 2, p. 26.
6 Sleeman and Silkin (eds), p. 78.
7 Scott, 'Internment in Singapore', p. 7.
8 Sleeman and Silkin (eds), p. 79.
9 Hayter, p. 162.
10 Ibid.
11 Sleeman and Silkin (eds), p. 140.

31: A Broken Man
1 Mallal, p. 608.
2 Ibid.
3 Ibid., p. 609.
4 Ibid.
5 Ibid.
6 Ibid., p. 610.
7 Ibid.
8 Ibid., p. 611.
9 Ibid.
10 Ibid.
11 Ibid.

12 Ibid.
13 Ibid.
14 Ibid.
15 Ibid.
16 Ibid., p. 612.
17 Ibid.
18 Ibid.
19 Ibid., pp. 612–13.
20 Ibid., p. 613.
21 Ibid.
22 Ibid., p. 611.
23 Ibid.
24 Ibid.
25 Sleeman and Silkin (eds), p. 134.
26 Ibid., p. 135.
27 Ibid.
28 Ibid., pp. 134–5.
29 Mallal, p. 613.
30 Scott, 'Internment in Singapore', p. 7.

32: Unending Horror
 1 Scott, 'Seventh Instalment', p. 6.
 2 Scott, 'Internment in Singapore', p. 5.
 3 Ibid.
 4 Ibid.
 5 Ibid.
 6 Ibid.
 7 Ibid.
 8 Ibid.
 9 Ibid., p. 6.
10 Ibid., p. 5.
11 Ibid.
12 Scott, 'Seventh Instalment', p. 5.
13 Ibid., p. 6.
14 Ibid., p. 7.
15 Ibid., p. 6.
16 Papers of Sir Robert H. Scott and Lady Scott, National Library of Scotland, Edinburgh, ACCC. 8181, Robert Heatlie Scott, Correspondence and Papers: 'Ninth Instalment: Outram Road Gaol: Oct 1, 1944 – Feb 28, 1945', p. 4.
17 Ibid.
18 Ibid.
19 Scott, 'Fourth Instalment', p. 6.
20 Sleeman and Silkin (eds), p. 35.

21 Ibid., p. 60.
22 Scott, 'Eighth Instalment', p. 5.
23 Scott, 'Internment in Singapore', pp. 8–9.
24 Ibid., p. 9.
25 Ibid.
26 Ibid.
27 Ibid.
28 Ibid., p. 6.
29 Ibid.
30 Ibid.
31 Ibid.
32 Ibid.
33 Ibid.
34 Ibid.
35 Ibid.
36 Ibid., p. 8.
37 Ibid.
38 Ibid.
39 Ibid.

33: The Death Houses of Sago Lane

1 Choy, Elizabeth, as told to Shirley Gordon, 'The Autobiography of Elizabeth Choy Su-Mei', p. 50.
2 Zhou, p. 132.
3 Choy, Elizabeth, as told to Shirley Gordon, 'The Autobiography of Elizabeth Choy Su-Mei', p. 52.
4 Yuen Sin, 'Theresa Chan, Singapore's Helen Keller, Dies after Battle with Lung Cancer', The Straits Times, 14 September 2016.
5 Choy, Elizabeth, as told to Shirley Gordon, 'The Autobiography of Elizabeth Choy Su-Mei', p. 50.
6 Ibid., p. 17.
7 Ibid.
8 Ibid.
9 Ibid., p. 26.
10 Ibid.
11 Ibid.
12 Choy, Elizabeth (Mrs) @Yong Su Moi, 'Japanese Occupation of Singapore, Accession Number 00597' – interview transcript, reel 5, p. 55.
13 Ibid.
14 Sleeman and Silkin (eds), pp. 71–86.
15 Choy, Elizabeth (Mrs) @Yong Su Moi, 'Japanese Occupation of Singapore, Accession Number 00597' – interview transcript, reel 4, p. 49.
16 Ibid.

17 Choy, Elizabeth, as told to Shirley Gordon, 'The Autobiography of Elizabeth Choy Su-Mei', p. 26.
18 Choy, Elizabeth (Mrs) @Yong Su Moi, 'Japanese Occupation of Singapore, Accession Number 00597' – interview transcript, reel 3, p. 33.
19 Ibid.
20 Ibid.
21 Choy, Elizabeth, as told to Shirley Gordon, 'The Autobiography of Elizabeth Choy Su-Mei', p. 38.

34: Swindlers, Thieves, Liars and Murderers

 1 Scott, 'Eighth Instalment', p. 1.
 2 Ibid.
 3 Ibid.
 4 Ibid.
 5 Ibid.
 6 Ibid., p. 2.
 7 Ibid.
 8 Ibid., p. 3.
 9 Ibid.
10 Ibid.
11 Ibid.
12 Ibid., p. 6.
13 Ibid.
14 Sleeman and Silkin (eds), p. 98.
15 Ibid.
16 Scott, 'Eighth Instalment', p. 3.
17 Ibid.
18 Ibid.
19 Scott, 'Internment in Singapore', p. 7.
20 Ibid.
21 Scott, 'Eighth Instalment', p. 3.
22 Ibid.
23 Ibid.
24 Ibid., pp. 3–4.
25 Ibid., p. 4.
26 Ibid., p. 4.
27 Papers of Sir Robert H. Scott and Lady Scott, National Library of Scotland, Edinburgh, ACCC. 8181, letter from Mrs R.H. Scott to Robert Heatlie Scott, 23 June 1943.
28 Ibid.
29 Scott, 'Eighth Instalment', p. 4.
30 Ibid.
31 Sleeman and Silkin (eds), p. 117.

32 Ibid., p. 116.
33 Ibid., pp. 115–16.
34 Ibid.
35 Ibid., p. 42.
36 Ibid., p. 111.
37 Scott, 'Eighth Instalment', p. 4.
38 Ibid.
39 Ibid.
40 Ibid., p. 2.
41 Ibid.
42 Ibid., p. 3.
43 Ibid.
44 Ibid., p. 2.
45 Ibid., p. 6.
46 Ibid.
47 Ibid.
48 Ibid.
49 Ibid.
50 Ibid.
51 Ibid.
52 Ibid.
53 Ibid.
54 Ibid.
55 Ibid.
56 Ibid.
57 Ibid.
58 Ibid., p. 7.
59 Ibid.
60 Scott, 'Ninth Instalment', p. 4.
61 Ibid.
62 Ibid.
63 Ibid., p. 5.
64 Gilmour, Oswald Wellington, *Singapore to Freedom*, E.J. Burrow, London, 1943.
65 Kitching, p. 289.
66 Scott, 'Ninth Instalment', p. 4.
67 Scott, 'Tenth (And Last) Instalment', p. 5.
68 Scott, 'Eighth Instalment', p. 7.

35: Kangaroo Court

1 Young, Bill, *Return to a Dark Age*, B. Young, Allawah, 1992, p. 137.
2 Ibid.
3 Scott, 'Ninth Instalment', p. 3.

4 Ibid.

5 Ibid., p. 2.

6 Ibid.

7 Ibid.

8 Ibid.

9 Ibid.

10 Ibid.

11 Ibid.

12 Ibid.

13 Ibid.

14 Ibid., p. 3.

15 Ibid.

16 Ibid.

17 Ibid.

18 Ibid.

19 Ibid.

20 Ibid., pp. 3–4.

21 Ibid., p. 5.

22 Ibid.

23 Ibid.

24 Ibid.

25 Ibid., p. 4.

26 Ibid.

27 Ibid., p. 5.

28 Ibid.

29 Ibid.

30 Ibid.

31 Ibid.

32 Ibid.

33 Ibid.

34 Ibid.

35 Ibid., p. 6.

36 Ibid.

37 Sleeman and Silkin (eds), p. 117.

38 Scott, 'Eighth Instalment', p. 3.

39 Scott, 'Internment in Singapore', pp. 7–8.

40 Ibid., p. 7.

41 Sleeman and Silkin (eds), p. 117.

42 Scott, 'Seventh Instalment', p. 4.

43 Interview with J.D Erskine, Electrical Engineer Malaya 1928–64, conducted by Susan Scott (daughter of Sir Robert Scott), 20 June 1993, private papers of Scott family.

44 Scott, 'Internment in Singapore', p. 8.
45 Ibid.

36: The Dysentery Ward

1 Scott, 'Ninth Instalment', p. 5.
2 Ibid.
3 Ibid., p. 6.
4 Ibid.
5 Ibid.
6 Ibid.
7 Ibid.
8 Ibid., p. 7.
9 Ibid. .
10 Ibid.
11 Ibid.
12 Ibid.
13 Ibid.
14 Ibid.
15 Ibid.
16 Ibid.
17 Ibid.
18 Ibid.
19 Ibid., p. 8.
20 Ibid.
21 Ibid.
22 Ibid.
23 Ibid.
24 Scott, 'Tenth (And Last) Instalment', p. 1.
25 Scott, 'Ninth Instalment', p. 8.

37: The Heroine of Singapore

1 Choy, Elizabeth (Mrs) @Yong Su Moi, 'Japanese Occupation of Singapore, Accession Number 00597', interview transcript, reel 4, p. 49.
2 Huff and Majima, *World War II Singapore: The Chosabu Reports*, p. 157.
3 Ibid., p. 143.
4 Zhou, p. 82.
5 Choy, Elizabeth (Mrs) @Yong Su Moi, 'Japanese Occupation of Singapore, Accession Number 00597', interview transcript, reel 5, p. 52.
6 Boi, pp. 244–9.
7 Choy, Elizabeth (Mrs) @Yong Su Moi, 'Japanese Occupation of Singapore, Accession Number 00597', interview transcript, reel 5, p. 52.
8 Ibid.

9   Thompson, Peter, *The Battle for Singapore: The True Story of the Greatest Catastrophe of World War II*, Piatkus, London, 2006, p. 597.
10 Choy, Elizabeth (Mrs) @Yong Su Moi, 'Japanese Occupation of Singapore, Accession Number 00597', interview transcript, reel 5, p. 52.
11 Lim, Jason, 'Revenge Killings in Singapore', in Christina Twomey and Ernest Koh (eds), *The Pacific War: Aftermaths, Remembrance and Culture*, Routledge, Abingdon, 2014, pp. 152–65.
12 Ibid.
13 Ibid.
14 Ibid.
15 Choy, Elizabeth (Mrs) @Yong Su Moi, 'Japanese Occupation of Singapore, Accession Number 00597', interview transcript, reel 5, p. 53.
16 Ibid.

38: Rumours of Peace

1   Scott, 'Tenth (And Last) Instalment', p. 1.
2   Ibid.
3   Scott, 'Ninth Instalment', p. 8.
4   Scott, 'Tenth Instalment', p. 1.
5   Ibid.
6   Ibid.
7   Ibid.
8   Ibid., p. 2.
9   Ibid.
10 Ibid.
11 Ibid.
12 Ibid.
13 Ibid.
14 Ibid.
15 Ibid.
16 Ibid.
17 Ibid.
18 Ibid.
19 Ibid.
20 Ibid.
21 Ibid., pp. 2–3.
22 Ibid., p. 3.
23 Ibid.
24 Ibid.
25 Ibid., p. 6.
26 Ibid., p. 5.
27 Ibid.
28 Scott, 'Ninth Instalment', p. 1.

29 Ibid.
30 Ibid.
31 Ibid.
32 Scott, 'Tenth Instalment', p. 6.
33 Quoted in Thompson, p. 597.
34 Scott, 'Tenth Instalment', p. 6.
35 Ibid., p. 7.
36 'Lady Thomas Looks Back on Captivity', *The Straits Times*, 7 September 1945, p. 2.
37 Ibid.
38 Ibid.
39 Scott, '30 Years Ago Singapore Fell', p. 8.
40 Ibid.
41 Transcript of R.H. Scott's broadcast, Singapore Station, Malayan Broadcasting Corporation; transmission 9 September 1945.
42 'Lady Thomas Looks Back on Captivity', *The Straits Times*, 7 September 1945, p. 2.
43 Robert Heatlie Scott, 'Answering Co-Prosperity': Far East Propaganda: National Archives Kew, PWD/42/1028/7.A.
44 'Lady Thomas Looks Back on Captivity', *The Straits Times*, 7 September 1945, p. 2.

39: Reckoning

 1 'The "Double Tenth" Trial', *The Straits Times*, 29 March 1946, p. 3.
 2 Ibid.
 3 Sleeman and Silkin (eds), p. 41.
 4 Ibid., p. 115.
 5 Ibid., p. 114.
 6 Ibid., p. 116.
 7 Ibid., p. 122.
 8 Ibid., p. 120.
 9 Ibid., p. 116.
10 '"Impossible Not to Use Force", Says Kempei Chief', *The Straits Times*, 30 March 1946, p. 4.
11 Ibid.
12 Ibid.
13 Sleeman and Silkin (eds), p. 130.
14 Ibid., p. 143.
15 Ibid., p. 148.
16 'Former M.O.I. Chief Testifies Against Japs', *The Straits Times*, 21 March 1946, p. 3.
17 'Auld Lang Syne', *The Straits Times*, 21 March 1946, p. 3.

18 'Scott, Sir Robert Heatlie (1905–1982), Diplomatist and Civil Servant', *Oxford Dictionary of National Biography*, published online September 2004, doi.org/10.1093/ref:odnb/31666
19 Sleeman and Silkin (eds), p. 64.
20 'Kempeitai "Stalked like Scourge Throughout Asia"', *The Straits Times*, 14 April 1946, p. 4.
21 Sleeman and Silkin (eds), p. 260.
22 Ibid., p. 281.
23 'Eight Japs to Hang for "Double Tenth" Atrocities', *The Straits Times*, 16 April 1946, p. 3.
24 Sleeman and Silkin (eds), p. 281.
25 'Eight Japs to Hang for "Double Tenth" Atrocities', *The Straits Times*, 16 April 1946, p. 3.
26 Ibid.
27 Ibid.
28 'Double Tenth Trial', *The Singapore Free Press*, 26 July 1947, p. 4.
29 Sleeman and Silkin (eds), p. 281.
30 '"Double Tenth" Men Hanged at Changi', *The Straits Times*, 12 July 1946, p. 5.
31 Ibid.
32 Ibid.
33 Sleeman and Silkin (eds), p. 226.
34 Ibid.
35 Ibid., p. 117.
36 'A Mystery of Jap-Occupied Singapore Solved!', *The Straits Times*, 7 April 1946, p. 3.
37 Ibid.
38 See Cleary, Paul, *The Men Who Came Out of the Ground*, Hachette, Sydney, 2010.

40: Forgiving

1 Papers of Sir Robert H. Scott and Lady Scott, National Library of Scotland, Edinburgh, ACCC. 8181, transcript of R.H. Scott speech delivered to the Singapore Union of Journalists, Phoenix Park, Singapore, 20 February 1956.
2 'Victim of the Kempeitai – Survivor's Account of Japanese Brutalities', *The Times*, 15 September 1945.
3 'Scott, Sir Robert Heatlie', *Oxford Dictionary of National Biography*.
4 'Scott "Glad to Be Back" – on Wedding Anniversary', *The Straits Times*, 12 October 1955.
5 'Japanese in Malaysia Surrender at Singapore', *The Straits Times*, 13 September 1945, p. 1.

6   Ibid.

7   Ibid.

8   Zhou, p. 87.

9   Choy, Elizabeth, as told tc Shirley Gordon, 'The Autobiography of Elizabeth Choy Su-Mei', p. 40.

10 Choy, Elizabeth (Mrs) @Yong Su Moi, 'Japanese Occupation of Singapore, Accession Number 00597', interview transcript, reel 3, p. 31.

11 Ibid.

12 Sleeman and Silkin (eds), p. 77.

13 Choy, Elizabeth, as told to Shirley Gordon, 'The Autobiography of Elizabeth Choy Su-Mei', p. 40.

14 Ibid., pp. 40–1.

15 Ibid., p. 42.

16 Ibid.

17 Ibid.

18 Zhou, p. 90.

19 Choy, Elizabeth, as told to Shirley Gordon, 'The Autobiography of Elizabeth Choy Su-Mei', p. 40.

20 Zhou, p. 94.

21 Elizabeth Choy, radic interview in Singapore 1953, quoted in Zhou, p. 96.

22 Choy, Elizabeth (Mrs) @Yong Su Moi, 'Japanese Occupation of Singapore, Accession Number 00597', interview transcript, reel 1, p. 2.

23 Ibid., p. 29.

24 Choy, Elizabeth, as told to Shirley Gordon, 'The Autobiography of Elizabeth Choy Su-Mei', p. 59.

25 Personal note from Elizabeth Choy to Lady Rosamond Scott, private papers of Sir Robert Heatlie Scott.

26 Choy, Elizabeth (Mrs) @Yong Su Moi, "Japanese Occupation of Singapore, Accession Number 00597" National Archives of Singapore – reel 3, p. 37

27 Zhou, p. 91.

BIBLIOGRAPHY

Published Works
Books
Allen, Louis, *Singapore 1941–1942*, Routledge, London, 1977.
Allen, Louis, *War, Conflict and Security in Japan and Asia Pacific, 1941–1952*, Brille, London, 2011.
Barber, Noel, *Sinister Twilight: The Fall of Singapore*, Arrow Books, London, 1968.
Bass, Gary J., *Judgement at Tokyo: World War II on Trial and the Making of Modern Asia*, Alfred A. Knopf, New York, 2023.
Bix, Herbert P., *Hirohito and the Making of Modern Japan*, Perennial, New York, 2000.
Borch, Fred L., *Military Trials of War Criminals in the Netherlands East Indies 1946–1949*, Oxford University Press, Oxford, 2017.
Brooke, Geoffrey, *Singapore's Dunkirk: The Aftermath of the Fall*, Pen & Sword, Barnsley, 1989.
Browne, Courtney, *Tojo: The Last Banzai*, Holt, Rinehart and Winston, New York, 1967.
Burgess, Colin, *Sisters in Captivity: Sister Betty Jeffrey OAM and the Courageous Story of Australian Army Nurses in Sumatra, 1942–1945*, Simon & Schuster, Sydney, 2023.
Cleary, Paul, *The Men Who Came Out of the Ground*, Hachette, Sydney, 2010.
Connell, Brian, *Return of the Tiger*, Evans Brothers, London, 1960.
Dunlop, E.E., *The War Diaries of Weary Dunlop: Java and the Burma–Thailand Railway 1942–1945*, Penguin, Sydney, 1987.
Felton, Mark, *Japan's Gestapo: Murder, Mayhem and Torture in Wartime Asia*, Pen & Sword, Barnsley, 2009.
Gilmour, Oswald Wellington, *Singapore to Freedom*, E.J. Burrow, London, 1943.
Gough, Richard, *SOE Singapore, 1941–42*, Kimber, London, 1985.

Baron Greenhill of Harrow, revised by Alex May, 'Scott, Sir Robert Heatlie (1905–1982), Diplomatist and Civil Servant', in *Oxford Dictionary of National Biography*, Oxford, 2004.

Hall, Timothy, *Fall of Singapore*, Methuen Australia, Sydney, 1983.

Hastings, Max, *Retribution: The Battle for Japan, 1944–45*, Knopf, London, 2007.

Hastings, Max, *The Secret War: Spies, Codes and Guerrillas 1939–1945*, HarperCollins, London, 2015.

Hayter, John, *Priest in Prison: Four Years of Life in Japanese-occupied Singapore*, Churchman Publishing, Worthing, 1989.

Huff, Gregg, and Shinobu Majima (translated and edited), *World War II Singapore: The Chosabu Reports*, NUS Press, Singapore, 2018.

Jones, E.H., *The Road to Endor*, Bodley Head, London, 1920.

Kitching, Thomas, *Life and Death in Changi: The War and Internment Diary of Thomas Kitching (1942–1944)*, Landmark Books, Singapore, 1998.

Kratoska, Paul H., *The Japanese Occupation of Malaya and Singapore, 1941–45*, NUS Press, Singapore, 2018.

Lamont-Brown, Raymond, *Kempeitai: Japan's Dreaded Military Police*, Sutton Publishing, Cheltenham, 1998.

Lee, Geok Boi, *The Syonan Years: Singapore Under Japanese Rule 1942–1945*, National Archives of Singapore, Singapore, 2005.

Lim, Jason, 'Revenge Killings in Singapore', in Christina Twomey and Ernest Koh (eds), *The Pacific War: Aftermaths, Remembrance and Culture*, Routledge, Abingdon, 2014.

Low, N.I., *When Singapore Was Syonan-To*, Eastern Universities Press, Singapore, 1973.

Lowe, Peter, 'Sir Robert Heatlie Scott (1905–82) and Japan', in *Britain and Japan: Biographical Portraits*, vol. VII, Taylor and Francis, Abingdon, 2010, pp. 148–9.

Ma, Sally, Mei Mei Chun-Moy and Mark Witzke, *Fall of Singapore: The Undefeatable British Fortress Conquered*, Pacific Atrocities Education, San Francisco, 2017.

Mallal, Bashir A. (ed.), *The Double Tenth Trial, War Crimes Court: In Re Lt.-Col Sumida Haruzo and 20 Others*, The Malayan Law Journal Office, Singapore, 1947.

McDougall Jr, William H., *By Eastern Windows: A Battle of Souls and Minds in the Prison Camps of Sumatra*, Uncommon Valor Press, New York, 1949.

McKie, Ronald, *The Heroes: The True Story of the Krait: Australian WW2 Raids on Singapore*, Angus & Robertson, Sydney, 1961.

McPhedran, Ian, *The Mighty Krait: The Little Boat That Pulled off Australia's Most Daring Commando Raid of WWII*, HarperCollins, Sydney, 2018.

Montgomery, Brian, *Shenton of Singapore: Governor and Prisoner of War*, Pen & Sword Books, Barnsley, 1984.

Morrison, Ian, *Malayan Postscript*, Faber and Faber, United Kingdom, 1942.

Peet, George L., *Within Changi's Walls: A Record of Civilian Internment in World War II*, Marshall Cavendish, Singapore, 2011.

Lord Russell of Liverpool, *The Knights of Bushido: A History of Japanese War Crimes During World War II*, Cassell & Company, London, 1953.

Silver, Lynette, *Deadly Secrets: The Singapore Raids 1942–45*, Sally Milner Publishing, Binda, 2010.

Silver, Lynette, *The Heroes of Rimau: Unravelling the Mystery of One of World War II's Most Daring Raids*, Leo Cooper, Sydney, 1990.

Sleeman, Colin and S.C. Silkin (eds), *Trial of Sumida Haruzo and Twenty Others (The 'Double Tenth' Trial)*, Hodge, London, 2007.

Stevenson, William, *A Man Called Intrepid*, Lyons Press, London, 1976.

Sutherland, Jackie, *Doctor Behind the Wire: The Diaries of POW Captain Jack Ennis, Singapore 1942–1945*, Pen & Sword, Barnsley, 2021.

Thambiah, Joseph, *The History of Anglicanism in Singapore 1819–2019*, Armour Publishing, Singapore, 2020.

Thompson, Peter, *The Battle for Singapore: The True Story of the Greatest Catastrophe of World War II*, Piatkus, London, 2006.

Thompson, Peter and Robert Macklin, *Operation Rimau: Australia's Heroic and Daring Commando Raid on Singapore*, Hachette, Sydney, 2015.

Toland, John, *The Rising Sun: The Decline and Fall of the Japanese Empire, 1936–1945*, Random House, New York, 1970.

Ward, Ian, *The Killer They Called a God*, Media Masters, Singapore, 1992.

Wigmore, Lionel, *Australia in the War of 1939–1945: The Japanese Thrust*, Naval and Military Press, Canberra, 1957

Yeo, Stephanie, *Changi Chapel and Museum: Remembering the Internees and Legacies of Changi*, National Museum of Singapore, Singapore, 2021.

Yeo, Stephanie, *Witness to War: Remembering 1942*, National Museum of Singapore, Singapore, 2018.

Young, Bill, *Return to a Dark Age*, B. Young, Allawah, 1992.

Zhou, Mei, *Elizabeth Choy: More than a War Heroine*, Landmark Books, Singapore, 1995.

Magazines, Journals, Booklets, Articles

Balasingamchow, Yu-Mei, 'My Grandmother's Story', National Library of Singapore, url.au.m.mimecastprotect.com/s/e2OVCnxy1gFXk5XrUvHr UJOgv7?domain=biblioasia.nlb.gov.sg"http://biblioasia.nlb.gov.sg/vol-12/issue-2/jul-sep-2016/my-grandmother-story/

Choy, Elizabeth, as told to Shirley Gordon, 'The Autobiography of Elizabeth Choy Su-Mei', *INTISARI: The Research Journal of Wider Malaysia*, vol. IV, no. 1, 1974 (reprinted as *My Autobiography as Told to Shirley Gordon*, Malaya Publishing House, Kuala Lumpur, 1974).

Goh, Sin Tub, 'The Sook Ching', National Library of Singapore, https://
biblioasia.nlb.gov.sg/vol-12/issue-4/jan-mar-2017/the-sook-ching,
9 January 2017.

Lamont-Brown, Raymond, 'Kempeitai: Ruthless Policemen of the Rising
Sun', *The Police Journal*, vol. 67, issue 2, April–June 1994, pp. 163–67,
doi.org/10.1177/0032258X9406700213

Leong, Keith, 'John Leonard Wilson: Bishop of Singapore (1941–1949)',
St Andrew's Cathedral information booklet.

Tan, Fiona, 'Surviving the Japanese Occupation: War and its Legacies', National
Library of Singapore, https://biblioasia.nlb.gov.sg/vol-12/issue-4/jan-mar-
2017/surviving-jpnese-occu, 10 January 2017.

Newspapers

'A Mystery of Jap-Occupied Singapore Solved!', *The Straits Times*, 7 April 1946.

'Auld Lang Syne', *The Straits Times*, 21 March 1946.

'Beatings in "Double Tenth" Case Admitted', *The Straits Times*, 6 April 1946.

'"Double Tenth" Men Hanged at Changi', *The Straits Times*, 12 July 1946.

'Double Tenth Trial', *The Singapore Free Press*, 26 July 1947.

'Eight Japs to Hang for "Double Tenth" Atrocities', *The Straits Times*, 16 April
1946.

'Everyday Life of the People of Singapore', *The Sunday Times*, 9 February
1942, transcript of Robert Heatlie Scott's broadcast on the Malayan
Broadcasting Corporation, Singapore Station.

'Former M.O.I. Chief Testifies Against Japs', *The Straits Times*, 21 March 1946.

'Graphic Story of Raid on Singapore', *Melbourne Herald*, 2 August 1946.

'"Impossible Not to Use Force", Says Kempei Chief', *The Straits Times*,
30 March 1946.

'Japanese in Malaysia Surrender at Singapore', *The Straits Times*, 13 September
1945.

'Kempeitai "Stalked like Scourge Throughout Asia"', *The Straits Times*,
14 April 1946.

'Lady Thomas Looks Back on Captivity', *The Straits Times*, 7 September 1945.

'Mainly about Malayans', *The Straits Times*, 24 November 1940.

'Pretty Peiping Wedding', unknown newspaper, 12 October 1933, Sir Robert
Heatlie Scott papers.

'Scott "Glad to Be Back" – on Wedding Anniversary', *The Straits Times*,
12 October 1955.

'The "Double Tenth" Trial', *The Straits Times*, 29 March 1946.

'Theresa Chan, Singapore's Helen Keller, Dies after Battle with Lung Cancer',
The Straits Times, 14 September 2016.

'30 Years Ago Singapore Fell', *The Straits Times*, 16 February 1972.

'Victim of the Kempeitai – Survivor's Account of Japanese Brutalities', *The
Times*, 15 September 1945.

Archival Sources
Australian War Memorial, Canberra (AWM)
AWM54 (Written records, 1939–45 War)

> 1010/4/24B, War Crimes and Trials – Affidavits and Sworn Statements (Vivian Bullwinkel, from Sir William Webb at the Australian Board of Inquiry into War Crimes in October 1945).
>
> 553/6/2, Campaign in Malaya and Singapore – Escape before and after capitulation and evacuation of civilians.
>
> 553/2/3, Top Secret Messages from Australian Force Malaya, to AHQ Melbourne, Jan–Feb 1942.
>
> 627/5/1 PART 13, [Services Reconnaissance Department – Malaya and Singapore:] SRC – Reports – XV-14 Singapore (Habour and Naval Base) Collation of all available intelligence on the Rimau Area from interrogation of ex-British POW and Jaywick Operations.

AWM69 (Official History, 1939–45 War, Series 2 (Navy): Records of G. Hermon Gill)

> 98, [Official History, 1939–45 War: Records of G Hermon Gill:] Two copies of a typescript entitled 'Operation Jaywick' (September 1943).
>
> 99/1, a photographed copy of the logbook of HMAS *Krait*.

AWM113 [Records of the Military History Section (Army)]

> 5/8/12, [Records of the Military History Section (Army)] 'The Heroes'. Z Force Operations. Jaywick Rimau, 1959–1960. Includes news clippings re McKie book.

National Archives of Australia, Canberra (NAA)
MP1185/8 (Secret and confidential correspondence files, multiple number series)

> 1932/2/85, 'Report of Operation "Jaywick" Carried out by MV Krait Sept–Oct 1943, Part II'.

A816 (Correspondence files, multiple number series)

> 66/301/532, Operation 'Jaywick' September 1943. Proposed Awards to Personnel. Report submitted in a letter to the Prime Minister John Curtin sent by the Minister of the Army, 21/7/44.

A3269 (Collection of Special Operations Australia [also known as Inter-Allied Services Department and Services Reconnaissance Department] records, incorporating records of the Far Eastern Liaison Office, alphanumeric series).

> E2/A, Lower South China Sea, Singapore –] JAYWICK, copy I [Singapore] [Contents different from 'copy II'].
>
> E2/C, [Lower South China Sea, Singapore –] Diary/ Log Book relating to Operation JAYWICK, [Singapore] Compiled by Lieutenant D M N DAVIDSON, RNVR [?Royal Navy Volunteer Reserve].
>
> E2/D, [Lower South Chine Sea, Singapore] JAYWICK Report [Singapore].
>
> E2/E, [Lower South China Sea, Singapore -] JAYWICK Operation [Narrative] [Singapore].
>
> E2/1, 'Operation Jaywick, Part 1 – General Summary.'

National Archives of Singapore (NAS)

Choy, Elizabeth (Mrs) @Yong Su Moi, 'Japanese Occupation of Singapore, Accession Number 00597' – interview transcript, reels 1–5.

Choy Elizabeth (Mrs) @ Yong Su Moi, 'Political History of Singapore 1945–1965', Accession Number 00.862 – interview transcript, reels 1–4.

National Library of Singapore

Tonight in Person: Glen Goei and Mrs Elizabeth Choy, Elizabeth Choy, audio-visual, 1 September 2001,10.15 p.m., www.nas.gov.sg/archivesonline/audiovisual_records/record-details/2aca3ac4-4717-11ee-9776-0050569c7836

Living in Fear: Memories of the Japanese Occupation (interview with Elizabeth Choy, May 2001), Elizabeth Choy, audiovisual, 1 May 2001, programme from the Central National Education Office, www.nas.gov.sg/archivesonline/audiovisual_records/record-details/2dc5724a-4717-11ee-9776-0050569c7836

World War 2 Survivors: Elizabeth Choy, Elizabeth Choy, audiovisual, www.nas.gov.sg/archivesonline/audiovisual_records/record-details/32b65ce8-4717-11ee-9776-0050569c7836

National Library of Scotland

8181, Papers of Sir Robert H. Scott and Lady Scott

Letters from Mrs R.H. Scott to Robert Heatlie Scott, 23 June 1943 – Robert Heatlie Scott, Correspondence and Papers.

R.H. Scott speech delivered to the Singapore Union of Journalists, Phoenix Park, Singapore, 20 February 1956.

R.H. Scott, 'Internment in Singapore: 1942/45'.

Robert Heatlie Scott (formerly Far Eastern Representative, MOI), 'Sinking of HMS *Giang Bee* on February 13, 1942', 19 September 1945.

Robert Heatlie Scott, Correspondence and Papers: 'First Instalment: The Dinghy – February 13th to March 2nd 1942'.

Robert Heatlie Scott, Correspondence and Papers: 'Second Instalment: March 2nd 1942 to May 30th 1942'.

Robert Heatlie Scott, Correspondence and Papers: 'Third Instalment: The Gymnasium: May 30th – June 7th 1942'.

Robert Heatlie Scott, Correspondence and Papers: 'Fourth Instalment: Cross Examination June 8th – July 15th, 1942'.

Robert Heatlie Scott, Correspondence and Papers: 'Fifth Instalment: Solitary: July 15th, 1942 – February 19th, 1942'.

Robert Heatlie Scott, Correspondence and Papers: 'Sixth Instalment: Changi: February 19th – October 10th, 1943'.

Robert Heatlie Scott, Correspondence and Papers: 'Seventh Instalment: The "Y": October 10th, 1943 – April 10th, 1944'.

Robert Heatlie Scott, Correspondence and Papers: 'Eighth Instalment: Miyako: April 10th – October 1st, 1944'.

Robert Heatlie Scott, Correspondence and Papers: 'Ninth Instalment: Outram Road Gaol: Oct 1st, 1944 – Feb 28th, 1945'.

Robert Heatlie Scott, Correspondence and Papers: 'Tenth (And Last) Instalment Sime Road Civilian Internment Camp Hospital, Singapore: February 28th – September 9th 1945'.

National Archives, Kew (NAUK)

WO 235/891, Judge Advocate General's Office: War Crimes Case Files, Second World War. War Crimes in the Far East. Defendant: Sumida Haruzo. Defendant: Monai Tadamori. Defendant: Umeda Hisao. Defendant: Sakamoto Shigeru. Defendant: Makisono [sic] Masuo. Defendant: Terada Takao. Defendant: Nozawa Toichiro. Defendant: Tsujio Shigeo. Defendant: Takeuchi Noboru. Defendant: Mori.

CO 825/38/8, Colonial Office: Eastern Original Correspondence. WAR PROPAGANDA IN THE FAR EAST. Bureau of Ministry of Information.

CO 967/75, Personal papers of Sir Shenton Thomas, Governor, relating to the Malay campaign and the fall of Singapore.

CO 323/1663/13, Colonies, General: Original Correspondence, MINISTRY OF INFORMATION. Dissemination of propaganda. FAR EAST.

CAB 106/13, War Cabinet and Cabinet Office: Pamphlet: The Economy of Japan (Q 3130) (Ministry of Information, 1943).

FO 898/268, Political Warfare Executive and Foreign Office, Political Intelligence Department: Papers: Anglo-American liaison: Ministry of Information Propaganda Committee reports.

FCO 141/15563, Singapore: correspondence concerning recommendations for honours by Sir Shenton Thomas, Governor and High Commissioner; report on work of Air Raid Precautions (ARP), Singapore.

INF 1/901, Ministry of Information: Files of Correspondence: Political Warfare Executive activities in the Far East, 1942 Mar–1945 May.

PWD/42/1026/7.A., Telegram Robert Heatlie Scott to Secretary of the Colonies: Far East – Propaganda, National Archives, Kew.

Imperial War Museum, London (IWM)

88/62/1, Diary of Mr M.J.V. Miller.

90/2/1, Private Papers of H. Schweizer-Iten, 'Experiences of a Delegate (Unrecognised) of the International Committee of the Red Cross during the Occupation of the Japanese of Singapore and Malaya'.

Private papers

Papers of Sir Robert Heatlie Scott (London).

PICTURE CREDITS

ACKNOWLEDGEMENTS

I VIVIDLY RECALL, as an impressionable nine-year-old boy in the late 1980s, watching over two consecutive Sunday nights a mini-series called *The Heroes*, a highly entertaining, albeit historically inaccurate, dramatisation of Operation Jaywick. In some ways, it was that mini-series that established in me an ongoing fascination with the Pacific War and, more broadly, the Australian experience in World War II. On a recent viewing, I would contend the show still stands up as a piece of entertaining television drama, but the factual errors are as problematic as what is ignored in the show.

It is, I suppose, hardly surprising that the show left the viewer with the strong impression that Operation Jaywick not only dramatically hampered Japan's capacity to wage war but bore no consequences for the civilian population in Singapore or, for that matter, the British internees in Changi Prison. After all, Jaywick's link to the Double Tenth atrocity did not fit into the Boys' Own narrative of *The Heroes*.

That this omission occurs in most published histories of Operation Jaywick is a little harder to comprehend. With the exception of Lynette Silver's *Deadly Secrets*, which devotes a chapter to the Double Tenth incident, most of the works of non-fiction dealing with Jaywick devote less than a paragraph – if anything at all – to the consequent events of 10 October 1943. Were there a rich history of the Double Tenth to balance the very full shelf of books devoted to Jaywick, then perhaps these scant mentions would be easier to understand. Alas, there is not, and my decision to write this book – at least initially – was motivated by a fiery determination to correct this imbalance; to fill, as it were, the historical gap.

My initial research led me to Elizabeth Choy, the deeply inspiring and compassionate leader, and quite rightly feted as a great hero in Singapore, who is synonymous with the Double Tenth incident. Mrs Choy's life is well documented in Singapore. In addition to two authorised biographies, numerous recorded interviews and documentaries, permanent exhibitions at the National Museum of Singapore and the Changi Museum, there is no shortage of easily accessible, high-quality information about her. Thanks to the team at the National Archives of Singapore, in particular Miss Clara Poh, I was able to access more obscure, but no less crucial, primary source material.

Finding an individual who could relate experience of those British internees who were sucked into the miserable vortex of the *Kempei Tai*'s investigation was a considerably harder assignment. The introduction to *The Double Tenth Trial* – the published transcript of the war crimes trial that dealt with the perpetrators of the atrocity and that served as a crucial resource – alludes intriguingly to a man the Japanese suspected of being a master spy and ringleader of a fifth column. In that book, the man's name was repeatedly given as 'Robert Heeley Scott'. In histories and works of non-fiction, there are often falsehoods and mistakes that have a single point of origin – in this case the official transcript of a trial – that are repeated so often that they became accepted as fact. The misspelling of Robert Heatlie Scott's name is one such example. In histories and articles that deal with the Double Tenth, Scott's name is consistently misspelled – footnotes always pointing to the same culprit – and, as such, he has been overlooked as an obscure, mid-level government bureaucrat about whom no other information exists.

My initial research attempting to find out more about 'Robert Heeley Scott' turned up nothing, despite weeks spent scouring online resources and archives. In a last-ditch effort, I deployed the extremely unsophisticated technique of searching for him on Google by using his first two initials and last name alongside his job title referred to in *The Double Tenth Trial*. Sure enough, I found a chapter devoted to one Sir Robert Heatlie Scott in a book with the less than scintillating title *Britain and Japan: Biographical Portraits*, vol. VII. In that chapter there were references to Sir Robert's brutal torture by the *Kempei Tai* in Singapore. Surely this was the same man.

If there was a single breakthrough moment in the research of this book – the kind of moment that historians and writers of non-fiction live for – then it was learning that Sir Robert's family had donated his personal papers to the National Library of Scotland (NLS). Included within that significant collection was Sir Robert's superbly written ten-part report of his escape from Singapore aboard the doomed HMS *Giang Bee*, his capture in Sumatra and internment in Singapore, his imprisonment and torture in the YMCA and much else besides. On reading this document I came to realise that Sir Robert was not only a man of great stature in British foreign affairs before and after the war, who possessed a fierce intellect and an astonishing memory, but also a writer of searing insight, humanity and, at times, sparkling humour.

It is true to say that had it not been for the decision made by Sir Robert and Lady Rosamond's three surviving grandchildren – Robert 'Scott' Steedman, Sarah Peterson and Helena Steedman – to donate their grandfather's private papers to the NLS, then this book likely would not have been written. Not only have I had the great pleasure of discussing the project with Scott, Sarah and Helena on Zoom on several occasions, I was hosted by Scott and Sarah at the Reform Club on Pall Mall for a memorable dinner on a hot London night in the summer of 2024. I am particularly grateful to all three for giving me so much assistance in the research of this book including personal insights, access to personal correspondence and material, and the right to reproduce private photographs.

As ever, I owe much to the team at Penguin Random House, in particular my publisher, Alison Urquhart. I pitched this project to Ali back in the Australian spring of 2021 and set myself a wildly ambitious deadline, which I succeeded in pushing out on three subsequent occasions. Throughout the process, Ali showed incredible patience with me and remained steadfast in her belief in the book. For evaluations of pace, grammar and structure, I relied on my excellent editor, Clive Hebard. Clive did a heroic job in tidying up a manuscript that was complex and, at times, overwritten, proving himself expert at the editor's art of offering praise while gently guiding me towards changes that were inevitably always right. Clive also assumed the role of fact checker, although I must assert that if errors persist in this book, then the responsibility is mine.

As ever, a big thank you to my darling partner, Gabrielle Munzer, who provided unwavering support and exceptional feedback throughout the entirety of the project, at the same time as holding down a senior position in the world of high finance and entrepreneurship, being the beautiful mother to our two sons, William and Ted, and all the while coping with the dreadful disease and death of her own mother, Irena Valdor – a loving grandmother and a wonderful mother-in-law to me, whose loss, which occurred during the writing of this book, we continue to feel keenly. To Will and Ted, who found every possible way to pull me away from completing this book and who continue to make my life infinitely richer and more fun each day, I say thank you . . . and tidy up your room! A particular thanks to my old friend Professor Michael Fabinyi, who unhesitatingly gave exceptional (and free) research assistance whenever I made a request.

Also, cheers to my parents, Mary Ann and Simon, who continue to be my great inspiration.

Finally, I dedicate this book to my late uncle and godfather, Angus Trumble. Angus was – among many things – aide-de-camp to the Governor of Victoria, a Fulbright Scholar, a world-renowned art curator, an award-winning and bestselling author, the Director of the National Portrait Gallery and, towards the end of his life, a senior research fellow at the National Library of Australia and fellow of the Australian Academy of the Humanities. With his incandescent intellect, wit, wisdom and charm, Angus had many senior appointments ahead of him that have been left unfulfilled, and important works of history, non-fiction and satirical literature that have been left unwritten. His untimely death, aged fifty-eight from a heart attack, is a significant loss for the world of art, history and literature and utterly devastating for our family. To me, Angus was an inspiring writing mentor, occasional confidant and hilariously fun godfather. I mourn his loss greatly.

INDEX

Note: Page locators in italics denote footnotes